85 0022721 6

KU-745-489

**Author** GARTENBERG

**Title** Mahler

WITHDRAWN

2 2 JUL 2024

**Stock no.** 8532

This item should be returned or brought in for renewal
by the last date stamped below

-3. JUN. 1979
-7. DEC. 1979
14. SEP. 1981

22 APR 1985

-7. DEC. 1990
23. MAY 1991
20. MAR. 1992
25. NOV. 1992
-9. JUN. 1993

-3. DEC. 1993
19. SEP. 1994

24. MAR. 1995
-9. DEC. 996
24. FEB. 7
25.
27. JAN. 1998
25. FEB. 1998

23. MAR. 1998
J. FEB. 2001
22. FEB. 200

13. MAR. 2001
26. MAR. 2001
24. APR. 200
-6. MAY 2002
31. JAN. 2005
24. FEB. 2005
16.

24. APR. 2007

Welsh College of Music and Drama, Castle Grounds,
Cathays Park, Cardiff, CF1 3ER

12/77 GP10392PSC PPP

Mahler

# MAHLER

The Man

and

His Music

Egon Gartenberg

CASSELL
LONDON

N
MAH
G

*To*
*Valerie, Vicki, and Andy*
*with love*

CASSELL & CO. LTD.
35 Red Lion Square, London WC1R 4SG
and at Sydney, Auckland, Toronto, Johannesburg,
an affiliate of
Macmillan Publishing Co., Inc.,
New York.

Copyright ©    Schirmer Books 1978
           A Division of Macmillan Publishing Co., Inc.

All rights reserved. No part of this publication may be reproduced, stored in
a retrieval system, or transmitted, in any form or by any means, electronic,
mechanical, photocopying, recording or otherwise, without the prior permission
of Cassell & Co. Ltd.

First published in Great Britain 1978

ISBN 0 304 30058 6


Printed in the United States of America

We wish to thank the various publishers for permission to use the following material:

Selections from *The Musician's World* by Hans Gal. Copyright © 1965 by Hans Gal. Published by Arco Publishing Company, Inc. Reprinted by permission of the publisher.

*The Song of Lament,* translated by Jack Deither. Used by permission of the translator and Caramoor Center for Music and The Arts, Katonah, New York.

Excerpts from *Gustav Mahler* by Bruno Walter, translated by Lotte Walter Lindt. Copyright © 1941 and 1957 by Alfred A. Knopf, Inc. Used by permission of the publisher.

Excerpts from *Gustav Mahler: Memories and Letters* by Alma Mahler, edited by Donald Mitchell. Copyright © 1946 by Alma Mahler Werfel. Reprinted by permission of Viking Press and John Murray (Publishers) Ltd.

Excerpts from *Gustav Mahler* by Kurt Blaukopf, translated by Inge Goodwin, pages 161, 51, 53, 56, 59–60, 116, 133, 148, 168, 172, 151, 152, 157, 158, 200, 212, 47, 46, 21. Published by Allen Lane. Copyright © 1973 by Allen Lane. Reprinted by permission of Penguin Books, Ltd.

Excerpts from *Legend of a Musical City: The Story of Vienna* by Max Graf. Published in 1945 by Philosophical Library Inc. Used by permission of the publisher.

Letter from Lotte Lehman, *Time,* August 17, 1953. Reprinted by permission of *Time,* The Weekly Newsmagazine; Copyright Time Inc. 1953.

# Contents

# Preface

"Why another Mahler book?" Because the author feels that a volume on Mahler is needed to satisfy a broad base of listeners from the music lover and concertgoer to the student and scholar.

To avoid constant interweaving of biographical and musical fact, a tripartite form was decided on, opening with a Mahler biography, "The Man." In the course of the biography his musical achievements are alluded to with respect to time and place; they are discussed at length in the third section of the book, "The Creator." Here the author aims at compactness, so that the reader interested in a specific Mahler composition will not be obliged to consult innumerable references to a specific work strewn throughout the book, but instead can find within a single chapter a discussion of any Mahler composition he wishes to investigate.

Important personalities, musical and otherwise, who tangentially entered into Mahler's personal or musical life (indicated in bold type within the text) are discussed in condensed biographical sketches in the appendix. Between "The Man" and "The Creator" we have inserted a compact pictorial biography.

The third section of this book, "The Creator," begins with the inauguration of the romantic era by Beethoven, Schubert, and Weber. From there the text leads the reader through the "romantic" nineteenth century to Mahler's door, with discussions of the development of virtuosity by Paganini, Liszt, and Berlioz; the romantic idealism of Mendelssohn, Schumann, and Chopin; the romantic realism of Berlioz and Liszt; the neo-Germanic school of Wagner and Liszt; the neo-classicism of Brahms; and the burgeoning Slavic nationalism.

The harmonic development and the consequent enlargement of the orchestra, brought about by the need to express emotion, and the resurrection of polyphony, due to the rediscovery of Bach, are discussed along with the blossoming of the purest form of homophony, the single human voice, in the purest of the romantic creations, the Lied. Of both the delicate expression of the art song and the vast symphonic edifice, Mahler was the master.

Our examination of Mahler's music is nontechnical. His music is viewed in the context of musical history and of Mahler's musical and personal development. His works are discussed in the order of their creation, beginning with *Das Klagende Lied* and his two early song cycles, so that the reader entering into the early symphonic period of Mahler may already be familiar with the spirit of the songs which Mahler was to incorporate into his early symphonies.

The author's sincere thanks go to musicologists and Mahler scholars Kurt Blaukopf, Karl Heinz Füssl, and Rudolf Klein in Vienna and Deryck Cooke and Donald Mitchell in London, for sharing their vast fund of knowledge and research on the subject; to Professor Rudolf Jettel for material on the Vienna Philharmonic; and to Professor Harry Zohn of Brandeis University for rare material on Vienna and Jewish life in Vienna. The author is especially deeply indebted to Deryck Cooke, whose personal detailed discussion of Mahler's Tenth Symphony greatly enriched the author's knowledge of the work and of the background of Cooke's performing version. Further thanks are due to Dr. Günther Brosche of the Music Collection of the Austrian National Library and Dr. Rudolph Kittel of the Picture Archives and Portrait Collection of the Austrian National Library, for bibliographical research and pictorial continuity, respectively. The author also acknowledges the able assistance of Wolfgang Kraus of the Wiener Verkehrsverband, the Pressedienst of the Austrian Chancellory, the archives of the Stadtbibliothek in Vienna, the Presse und Informations-amt der Bundesregierung in Bonn, the Concertgebouw Orchestra in Amsterdam, and the Istituto Italiano di Cultura in Rome. The author gratefully acknowledges the untiring efforts of Elizabeth Thomas, librarian of Pennsylvania State University, and her staff in securing rare and out-of-print publications on the subject. Lastly, my thanks to my wife who not only endured the writing of this book but also faithfully proofread it.

January 1977

# The Man

# Pre-Vienna (1860–97)

## THE EARLY YEARS

THE COMPLEXITY THAT WAS TO BE Mahler's heritage and his destiny began with his birth. The specific fact which pinpoints his place of birth as the village of Kališt in Bohemia is of little consequence. The date, 7 July 1860, and the general location bear considerably greater importance. The former places Mahler's main productive period within the time span that represented the eventide of romanticism, when one century relinquished its artistic treasure to the next. The general location was in a part of the Austro-Hungarian monarchy, Bohemia and Moravia, that reflected the multinational and multilingual character of much of the Austrian empire. Kališt was a Bohemian town, while the nearby city of Iglau (Jihlava), to which the Mahlers eventually moved, reflected a more German background. Czech was, of course, universally spoken, but with 50 percent of its population German-speaking, those with intellectual or social ambitions, many of the Jewish population among them, tended towards the German idiom and towards such German-speaking islands within the Czech milieu.

Gustav Mahler's father, Bernhard Mahler, was originally a peddler who, with cart and horse, carried on his trade of cloth and ribbons among the Moravian and Bohemian small merchants and peasants. He was welcomed among them because the possession of a means of transportation made it possible for him to do favors, to carry messages and news as well as merchandise. It also enabled him to carry books—the Jewish prayer book, German and French tomes—to read and study, and to widen his horizons. He was persistent, shrewd, and tough, and he advanced to the point where he could acquire a modest home in Kališt and marry Marie Hermann, from a nearby town, in 1857.

In conversation Bernhard Mahler gave a surprisingly strong impression, yet he was outwardly a retiring man who did not mix well, who was

3

well read but vaguely dissatisfied. Biographers attach the adjectives "harsh, brutal, coarse, overbearing, tyrannical" to Bernhard Mahler, the family man, but these words must be read with caution, because they view a nineteenth-century husband and father through twentieth-century eyes, and thus out of context. And Bernhard Mahler *was* a nineteenth-century husband and father. His word was law, his will supreme, his opinion paramount. Yet, despite these characteristics, Bernhard Mahler had not inherited the vigor and exuberance of his mother. Possessed by an irrepressible drive to achieve her goals, modest as they may have been, she somehow passed over her son Bernhard and endowed her grandson, Gustav, with the near-fanatic drive that was to be one of his hallmarks.

Bernhard Mahler eventually arrived at a measure of modest well-being which allowed him to abandon the peddling trade and open a distillery in Kalist. Marie Mahler, however, did not love her husband. The girl with the slight limp, barely twenty years old, had loved someone else. As Gustav, her son, was to tell later, "her parents and my father broke her will and had their way." Her marriage was one of loveless resignation, her plight aggravated by a heart ailment brought on by household drudgery and childbearing. Her meek and gentle mien only underlined her husband's harsh and dictatorial regimen. Young Gustav knew his father, even understood him, but never loved him. His love was reserved for that gentle, suffering, childbearing woman, his mother. The son detested many of his father's traits, such as his treatment of his wife. Others he respected, such as the father's decisive action when he found out that his young son was being maltreated; still others he observed and absorbed subconsciously, such as his father's stance as a Freethinker in curious accommodation with his Jewish studies. The father's pursuit of intellect and learning, of culture (German culture, to be precise) in a Bohemian environment, was to leave a lasting impression in Gustav's young mind.

Such pursuit, however, was not an easy task. Trade could easily be maintained with the Bohemian and Moravian populace, but social barriers from higher social strata were not only erected but closely—and anti-Semitically—guarded. On the other hand, owing to a liberalism forced on Emperor Franz Joseph as a result of circumstances of time and empire, Jews in the eastern provinces saw a new light, the light being Vienna, the cultural, financial, and trade *Knotenpunkt*—crossroads—of that part of Europe. There they streamed in pursuit of intellect, of freedom, of trade, and, perhaps, of wealth. Still fearfully remembering the anti-Semitic spirit of the places they had just left, Jews settled in Vienna in large numbers, most densely near the railroad station where they had arrived, feeling a measure of safety among their own.

In the Austrian provinces and eastern parts of the empire, the Jew, by serving his overlord—the gentile aristocrat who found it beneath his dignity or beyond his ken to engage in commerce—had received excellent training and, owing to his usefulness to the aristocrat, a measure of protection. Once the Jew removed himself to Vienna, the mantle of protection was removed, but the acquired knowledge was ready to be applied again in the new milieu. And it was applied, skillfully and successfully. The Jew, safe in the liberalism officially espoused and in the strength of his success, was driven to further successes, now in the professions newly opened to him after the 1848 revolution—the arts, jurisprudence, journalism, medicine, music—as well as in commerce and industry. Concomitantly, the Jewish presence in Vienna became a subject of envy and hatred—fueled in those cases where the Jew was insensitive to local lifestyle or did not care to assimilate, at least in dress and language, to Viennese custom. While the emperor officially disdained anti-Semitism, the old, unwritten law concerning major court positions (i.e., they were unavailable to non-Catholics) prevailed. Anti-Semitism (the term was coined by Wilhelm Mass in 1879), ever smoldering, abetted by dapper, popular mayor Dr. Karl Lueger (who boasted of Jewish friends) and the rabid Georg von Schönerer, the Austro-German nationalist,[1] became so ingrained as to become a part of the Viennese psyche. It deplored and despised, in the person of the Jew, ambition and success, drive and cunning, yet lusted after these in the deplorers themselves. The unceasing tension was between the outwardly successful, inwardly displaced, subconsciously insecure Jew on the one hand, and his frustrated, exasperated, and envious gentile counterpart. The paradox was that while disdaining the Jew and hating him for his success in many fields, the aristocrat as well as the gentile entrepreneur wished to *become* Jews in the sense of emulating their financial expertise and speculative prowess, as well as their drive for achievement and betterment. The Jews, in turn, desired to acquire the outward, official manifestations of their success and of their contribution to their newly adopted society (baronial titles and such) and sought a dedicated involvement in the arts of the city among whose best citizens they desired to be. All those avenues to achievement had been opened to the Jew only a few decades earlier when they were relieved from ghetto existence, that straightjacket from which even the most illustrious Jewish names had not been able to extricate themselves.

If Mahler also harbored a Viennese dream, its realization would have to wait. In 1860 came the first significant move of the Mahlers, from the confining village of Kališt to the town of Iglau, a more suitable settlement and a center of German-speaking population. Bernhard's sense of independence was further enhanced by his again opening a small brandy distillery. It offered an enlarged base of income, which was needed because

---

[1] So rabid was Schönerer's German national sentiment that he seriously suggested that Germany abandon the Christian calendar and rearrange its calendar timetable to start with the year 9 A.D., when the Teuton Hermann (Arminius) routed the Roman legions of Quintilius Varus.

the second child, Gustav, had been born. Twelve more were to follow.[2] In observing the names the father gave his children we find a reflection of his thinking. Only the first-born's name reflects his Jewish ancestry. The names of all the others reflect the German culture to which the father aspired. With Isidor dead in infancy, the role of first-born—a role he never cherished nor adopted—fell on Gustav. Indeed, the loveless household (except for Gustav's feelings for his mother) held out little for him to cherish. The father was domineering, the mother constantly overburdened by pregnancy and the cares of the household, brothers and sisters either sickly or dying. The cheerless, tense atmosphere, replete with morbidity, had a profound effect on all the children. Justine would "play at dying," six would die young, Otto was to commit suicide, and throughout life thoughts of death would never be far from Gustav's mind.

The earliest and darkest shadow in Gustav's life was cast by the death of his brother Ernst. Only one year had separated the two brothers. Thus they spent much of their early lives together, and Ernst's death at age thirteen deprived Gustav of his closest playmate and only confidant. So deeply engraved became the early image of the brother that years later, while writing his first opera, *Herzog Ernst von Schwaben* (Duke Ernst of Swabia), at age nineteen, Mahler admitted that the image of the duke and the brother, both named Ernst, merged.

> Among the discordant strains I hear the voice of Ernst von Schwaben and he himself steps forth, opening his arms to me, and when I look closely it is my poor brother.
>
> Mahler to Josef Steiner
> (who wrote the opera libretto), June 1879

Under such circumstances, the retreat into a dream world of his own began early with Gustav. As his younger brothers and sisters passed away in infancy, Gustav's dream world sheltered him. He was not oblivious of his mother's daily sufferings nor of his father's household tyranny; he simply endured them. Only the death of Ernst, of a heart ailment, pierced his dream world with pain. Nor did his eventual departure to Prague to

| [2] Isidor | born 1858 | died in infancy |
|---|---|---|
| Gustav | born 1860 | |
| Ernst | born 1861 | died in 1875 |
| Leopoldine | born 1863 | died in 1889 |
| Karl | born 1864 | died 1865 |
| Rudolf | born 1865 | died 1866 |
| Alois (Hans) | born 1867 | |
| Justine | born 1868 | |
| Arnold | born 1869 | died in infancy |
| Friedrich | born 1871 | died in infancy |
| Alfred | born 1872 | died in infancy |
| Otto | born 1873 | committed suicide in 1895 |
| Emma | born 1875 | |
| Konrad | born 1879 | died in infancy |

study music basically change his dream cocoon; he simply transported his shell from one locality to another. People in his new domicile might mistreat him; he would barely notice and take it as a matter of course. A poor student, he seemed to wait in dreamy quiet, just as he had endured suffering with stubborn tenacity. Yet he was not dumbly enduring, even in his youth. He constantly observed the world about him, be it human meanness or kindness, his mother's humiliation, his father's wrath.

Yet it was the father who divined his son's destiny. Noting that Gustav could never resist the lure of a piano, the father decided on the career of a virtuoso for his son—one of his typical, peremptory decisions of the kind that often spell disaster for a child but that, in Gustav's case, happily coincided with the child's dreams and instincts: Gustav drank in with avidity the Czech folk tunes, the Saturday night dance tunes, and the military sounds emanating from the Iglau barracks. The decision made, the father purchased a piano and arranged for music lessons for Gustav. A long line of anonymous instructors began to teach him. While the reality of school lessons was often neglected, the dream world of Gustav intensified and enlarged at the piano, which now served as retreat, safety valve, and magic carpet. Luckily, the father's decision had been an inspired one. Already at age four, music pervaded Mahler's life, and he later admitted to having composed before he had mastered the scales on the keyboard. But composition was not in the father's plans. Like Mozart's and Franck's fathers, he wanted to exhibit the boy as a virtuoso. Such a display would surely reflect favorably upon the father. A first concert was arranged in due course at age ten, and the "future piano virtuoso" was adjudged a success.

Iglau became too small for Gustav. Prague, with its larger musical possibilities, beckoned. Gustav was boarded with the Grünfeld family, which was destined to produce in later years **Alfred Grünfeld**, one of the most famous pianists of his day and Johann Strauss, Jr.'s favorite interpreter of his music. Surprisingly Prague saw no musical progress. The conservatory provided no stimulus, and in regular schooling Gustav slumped to the bottom of his class. We may assume that the substandard living conditions provided by the Grünfelds, borne by the eleven-year-old Gustav in stoic silence, had much to do with his low spirits and lack of achievement. When the father was apprised of the poor treatment his son was receiving, he furiously whisked the boy home. During his presence in the Grünfeld household the boy was also witness to a rape scene, which filled him with a horror that was to remain with him for decades and which for much of his younger years made sexual passion synonymous with horror, struggle, and pain.[3]

---

[3] La Grange, however, says that Mahler merely witnessed sexual intercourse, which, misunderstanding the woman's reactions, he mistook for rape.

Entry into college life proved no different. "Learned nothing" was Mahler's succinct comment on those days. The friendships he made at that time, however, were to influence his thinking deeply. Otherwise, Mahler pursued the bent that he was to follow to the end of his days—books and music. Both allowed him to dwell in the dream world of his own. Yet, when dreams took on a reality of their own, such as the operas he composed in early years, he destroyed them.

If the son had failed in many early attempts, the father had succeeded socially in the reflection of Gustav's pianistic prowess. A casual acquaintance, meanwhile, was to have a vast influence on Mahler's future. In roaming the countryside with his friend Joseph Steiner, Gustav had made the acquaintance of Gustav Schwarz, the estate supervisor of a nearby farm and a music lover of perception. Schwarz had somehow received into his possession the piano manuscripts of Sigismund Thalberg, considered by many as too difficult to be played by anyone but virtuosi. When young Gustav played them by sight, Schwarz became convinced that the boy's future was in music and set out to convince Bernhard Mahler (who, after initial reservations, gave his consent) to give the boy more extensive musical training than was provided in virtuoso study. The shrewd father, who had watched his oldest son closely, had witnessed in him a trait which had impressed him as much as Schwarz's persuasive arguments—namely, a determination, not noticed in other fields, where matters of artistic weight were concerned. Realizing his son's gift, Bernhard Mahler went into action. Just as Haydn's father and Liszt's father had grasped the significance of their sons' musical destiny and, despite hardships, had prevailed to bring their sons to study in the capital of music, Vienna, so Gustav's father also saw to it that his son took up domicile in Vienna and studied at its famed *Konservatorium der Gesellschaft der Musikfreunde,* concomitantly with study at the Vienna *Gymnasium.* Surprisingly, it was not the father but Schwarz who acccompanied Gustav to Vienna and the conservatory, where he was accepted as a student in 1875. Vienna was about to cast its spell.

At the conservatory, Mahler was to study piano with the formidable Julius Epstein, renowned pianist and a teacher and close friend of Brahms; harmony with Robert Fuchs; and composition with Franz Krenn. This was supplemented with university lectures by Anton Bruckner and other studies in art, history, and music at the Vienna university, which he was allowed to attend at age seventeen and where he remained for two years. The conservatory became a haven for Mahler. There he also met those who were to become some of his closest friends: Guido Adler, Hugo Wolf, and the gifted and sensitive Hans Rott. Rott was to be rudely rebuked by Brahms, to whom he had submitted some of his compositions for an opinion. When Brahms brusquely advised him to leave music altogether, the sensitive Rott went insane. A tragic figure, he continued to compose even after confinement.

Most importantly, in 1878 Mahler joined the **Pernerstorfer Circle**. The Circle, founded in 1867, consisted of a group of high school and university students who were deeply concerned with and involved in the significant political developments of their time as well as with the thoughts and writings of the great thinkers of their day, specifically those of Schopenhauer, Nietzsche, and Wagner. The Circle had adopted the name of one of its founders, the youthful **Engelbert Pernerstorfer**, who was destined to later play a major political role in the early years of the Austrian republic. Mahler had been introduced to the Circle through one of its members, the poet **Siegfried Lipiner**. He subsequently became acquainted with Viktor Adler, the future founding father of the republic, because many of the meetings of the Circle were held in the home of Adler's parents. That acquaintance soon grew into such a close friendship that Viktor Adler made a concerted effort to find piano pupils for the struggling Mahler during his conservatory days.

It is not difficult to understand Mahler's attraction to the Circle, whose thoughts ranged about three of his idols: Nietzsche, and his mentors Wagner and Schopenhauer. The adulation of the members for these three prompted them, individually as well as collectively, to make veritable pilgrimages to Bayreuth to "drink at the source." The interest was not one-sided, because Wagner as well as Nietzsche considered Lipiner a youthful genius, holding him in an esteem which he, in later years, was not able to justify.

Philosophically the group was particularly attracted to Wagner's dictum that the killing and eating of animals was akin to cannibalism and that the world should therefore unite in vegetarianism so as to find regeneration and purification. Mahler was so taken with the idea that he not only became a vegetarian but also strongly advanced the idea to anyone who would listen:

> I have been a complete vegetarian for a month. The moral effect of this way of life resulting from the voluntary servitude of my body and the resulting freedom from want is immense. You can imagine how convinced of it I am when I expect regeneration of the human race from it.
>
> Mahler to Dr. Emil Freund, a Viennese
> lawyer and a friend of Mahler's since youth

For a brief period, Guido Adler also came under the vegetarian spell. In 1879 Hugo Wolf was also introduced to the Pernerstorfer Circle, presumably through his roommates Mahler and **Rudolf Krzyzanowski**. If all the members of the Circle were Wagner adherents, Wolf was a Wagner fanatic. One day, during Wagner's presence in Vienna, the composer left his hotel to be driven to the opera house. Wolf, having hung around the hotel in the hope of getting a glimpse of his idol, rushed over to open the door to Wagner's coach. After having closed the door behind Wagner, he ran the several blocks to the opera, preceding Wagner there, in order to be able to open the coach door again when Wagner arrived. Eventually Wagner granted Wolf an interview. Although he charmed his disciple with kindness, he declined to listen to his compositions, which, of course, did not dampen Wolf's adulation.

The spiritual involvement of the Pernerstorfer Circle became even more concentrated in a more tightly knit group known as the *Sagengesell-schaft* (Saga Society), whose aim was nothing less than the regeneration of the German people and the unification of all German-speaking people. It was a goal fully congruent with Mahler's aspirations as a Jew, specifically his desire to become fully a part of the German-speaking community into which liberalism had admitted Jews. Thus it is in no way surprising that a number of the Pernerstorfer members were Jewish, because they saw in the society the way to the fulfillment of their aspirations, both for participation in the noblest German thoughts and for regeneration of the world, even if through revolution. Adler in particular, in the course of his political career, was to see that dream come to fruition in the socialist awakening in Germany and the birth of the Republic of Austria. Wrote Richard Kralik, a member of the Circle, in his book *Tage* (Days):

> A new world view should come into being, . . . one opposed to the modern scientific one. Life should become nature; nature should become life and spirit. Inspiration and will may temporarily compensate for lack of clarity and logic. Thus we want to found an entire [culture], a new magnificent culture.

It was in the Saga Society that Mahler's musicianship and his German cultural background and aspirations first made themselves heard. There he played the *Meistersinger* Prelude so magnificently on the piano that, wrote Kralik, "an entire orchestra seemed to sound forth from his hands." It was there that the seed of Mahler's future philosophical attitude towards Apollonian and Dionysian myths (and their consequent appearance in his music) found its fertile soil. These two attitudes and philosophies are to be considered in their extended senses, the Apollonian spirit expressing the serene, calm, balanced, poised, disciplined; the Dionysian reflecting the uninhibited, undisciplined, frenzied, orgiastic. Both Nietzsche and Schopenhauer use the term "Dionysian" in the extended sense of "individualistically uninhibited" and thus destructive, as compared to the uplifting principles of the serene, balanced Apollonian myth and philosophy. Bertrand Russell, in his *History of Western Philosophy,* substitutes the terms "prudence" and "Bacchus" (passion):

Prudence may . . . involve the loss of some of the best things in life. The worship of Bacchus reacts against prudence. In intoxication, physical and spiritual, the [passionate man] recovers an intensity of feelings which prudence had destroyed. . . . The Bacchic ritual produced what was called "enthusiasm," which means, etymologically, having the god enter into the worshipper, who believed that he became one with the god. Much of what is greatest in human achievement involves some element of intoxication, some sweeping away of prudence by passion. Without the Bacchic element life would be uninteresting, with it, it is dangerous.

In contrast to Mahler, who was to give himself freely to the spirit of Dionysus, Russell hedges in his conclusion:

Prudence versus passion is a conflict that runs through history. It is not a conflict in which we ought to side wholly with either party.

The results of the Circle's aesthetic, philosophical, and cultural labors were not always meritorious. Lipiner, for example, concocted the libretto to Karl Goldmark's opera *Merlin,* of which Wolf opined: "From this fantastic and symbolically moving saga Lipiner has drained off a banal libretto" (*Salonblatt,* 21 November 1886). Mahler, however, was at least for a while captivated by Lipiner's philosophical concepts, particularly those expressed in his play *Adam.*

It is a truly Dionysian work! . . . The wine intoxicated the drinker— music wafts from your poetry! . . . It does not speak of wine and describe its effect—it *is* the wine, it *is* Dionysus.

Mahler to Lipener

Mahler was to be deeply influenced by the myth of Dionysus, by the cult of wine and its deleterious effects, physically and spiritually, on man, as expressed by both Schopenhauer and Nietzsche. In 1896 Mahler was to write: "In speaking of nature [people] only think of flowers, birds, the forest, etc. No one seems to know anything of Dionysus, the great god Pan." That opinion is also borne out in a second letter to Lipiner after the completion of Mahler's Third Symphony. "I have made myself completely at home in your *Adam.* . . . I have known that region for a long time." Actually, in examining the music of Mahler, specifically his Third Symphony, one learns that Mahler's creation and its profundity reach above and beyond Lipiner's philosophizing, which emerges as shallow.

Thus the initially superficial judgment "Mahler writes philosophical music"—misquoted, debated, questioned, and rejected in Mahler's day —retains its validity. Another human factor emerges with greater clarity. The deeper reason for the eventual rejection of Lipiner by Alma Mahler may have been Gustav's near-captive affinity to Lipiner's philosophy and thus his (Lipiner's) influence on Gustav, rather than Lipiner's rejection of Alma as an intruder into the circle of close friends. Regardless of

Lipiner's temporary influence, there can be no question as to the importance of the Pernerstorfer Circle's lasting aesthetic and metaphysical influence on Mahler's thinking and work. Mahler biographers often bypass the Pernerstorfer Circle in general and Lipiner in particular and go directly to the source, Nietzsche. Nietzsche, as evidenced in the Third Symphony, was an influence which Mahler, at the time (1894) described as "epoch-making." His influence was paralleled in significance only by Wagner's writings, particularly his treatise on Beethoven, in itself an extension and adaptation of Schopenhauer's. In it Wagner pedestaled Beethoven as the true symbol of Germanic musical spirit uninfected by foreign (French, Italian) influences. Surprisingly, we find Mahler influenced much more deeply by Wagner's writings (at least at that time; he was to strongly deprecate his writings later) than by his music, which he interpreted superbly but whose stage realm he never entered compositinally. However, as far as the relationship between words and music was concerned, Mahler fully entered into Wagner's reasoning:

> Have you noticed that with me the melody always proceeds from the word, which, so to speak, creates for itself, never in reverse? It is that case with Beethoven and Wagner.[4] . . . only in this way is there created . . . the identity of word and tone. The reverse, where . . . words must accommodate themselves to a melody, is a conventional association but not an organic fusion of the two.
>
> Mahler to Natalie Bauer-Lechner

This statement should not be construed as reflecting a predominance of the word—of a text or program—in Mahler's thinking. Mahler achieved a perfect, supportive balance between the words and the music, the poet and the composer. Indeed, Mahler permitted the inclusion of a program in only a general sense; though he did not object to one, because he saw the composer as a multilevel creator:

> There is indeed nothing to object to concerning a "program" (even if it is not the highest rung of the ladder) [5] —but the composer must express himself in it and not a writer, philosopher, or painter (all of which are contained in a composer).
>
> Mahler to Bruno Walter

[4] A comparison to Wagner and Schubert would have been more apt. It was with Schubert that the word was immediately sublimated into music while Beethoven was constantly hampered by the spoken word.

[5] Mahler made a distinct differentiation between a "program" and "program notes." A "program" constituted an overall meaning, be it metaphysical, cosmic, or philosophical, while Mahler was to disdainfully refer to "program notes" as "a crutch for a cripple."

It would, then, be a grave fallacy to dismiss his experience with the Pernerstorfer Circle as an episode of overwrought romanticism in young Mahler's life and of short duration. On the contrary, it was there that the total spiritual world of Mahler was formed. Its influence, on the other hand, was totally lost on Hugo Wolf, who followed his own unbridled urges. While Mahler reluctantly submitted to the rigid discipline of the conservatory, Wolf could not abide by it. He was critical of what he considered an arid atmosphere, intensified by petrified teaching methods. Wolf as well as Mahler went so far as to openly criticize the institution. Mahler retracted his statement by writing a letter of apology; Wolf intensified his by threatening to assassinate the director, Josef Hellmesberger. Wolf was expelled; Mahler remained and succeeded brilliantly —most of the time.

In a sense Mahler felt freed, in the congenial atmosphere of Vienna, from the dreary surroundings of his home, where things were going poorly. Sister Leopoldine shared her mother's fate of an unloved husband; only in her case a brain tumor ended her young, dreary life. Sister Justine suffered deeply from her father's harshness and had hallucinations of death. Brother Otto, also a talented musician, was now the one to whom Gustav felt closest. He tutored Otto through years of schooling and found him positions later in life. But Otto was consumed by envy, considering himself unfairly maligned and deprived because he felt he was the better of the two. Death by his own hand ended his life. Brother Alois, although sickly, used his imagination and boastfulness in ways that reflected poorly upon the family. He often misrepresented himself as a cavalry officer and changed his first name to Hans because he felt that it sounded more Austrian or German than Alois. He dressed elegantly, lived beyond his means, and eventually began to forge checks. Only flight to America kept him from being arrested. All these events left scars on the sensitive Gustav, who could not help but be subconsciously receptive to the influences of the unhappy familial household.

For a number of years, mutual ties were to bind the stoic Mahler and the paroxysmal Wolf. Lack of funds, the search for students, feuds with landladies, amateur singers, and crying babies prompted them to move or be forcibly moved from lodging to lodging. What bound them most strongly during those youthful years was their devotion to musical ideals. But while Wolf roamed the streets of Vienna, where every house seemed to exude music for him, Mahler continued in his methodical ways. At the conservatory he had ingested the thorough training which that world-famous institution provided: piano, theory, harmony, counterpoint, composition, and an exhaustive acquaintance with the instruments of the orchestra. His desire for active participation in the orchestra, however, was stymied by a double dilemma. For one, orchestral conducting had not yet become a discipline to be taught as a regular curriculum course. Conducting depended to a great extent on the ingenuity of the individual if he wished to convey more than simple beating of time. Furthermore, his chosen instrument, the piano, had no regular place in the orchestral ensemble. Determined to participate at all costs, Mahler joined the orchestra —as a timpanist.

All this was to be of immense benefit to Mahler in years to come. In his day, at a time when specialization was unknown and worse, frowned upon, all-around knowledge of every aspect of music was considered a necessity for any aspiring musician. Not until the Conservatory became the Austrian State Academy of Music and Dramatic Arts was a specialized course in conducting added to the curriculum. Until then, the composer and conductor were often united in the same person.

Compulsively, Mahler began to compose. Composition was, of course, part of the curriculum, and students vied with each other for compositional honors and prizes. Being too poor to have the orchestral parts of his compositions copied by professionals, Gustav undertook the task himself, with the result that innumerable errors crept into individual copies. The resulting dissonance during performance once so infuriated the conductor that he flung the score in question at the luckless student. Mahler took the humiliating setback in his customary stoic stride, just as he had endured ill-treatment before and was to endure critical vicissitudes later. He was successful, however, in winning a contest when his Piano Quintet (later destroyed by the composer) was acclaimed in Vienna on 11 July 1878, with Gustav at the piano.

Surprisingly, there is no record of Mahler having conducted the conservatory orchestra, but the intimate knowledge he acquired in Vienna prepared him for the individualistic style that was to make him famous as a giant of conductorial prowess, a stature which he shared only with a chosen few who had risen to prominence in a similar way. Felix Mottl, the great Wagnerian conductor, had begun in Vienna by studying composition. Hans Richter had started as a horn player in the *Kärnthnerthor Theater,* Vienna's first opera house. Arthur Nikisch followed a similar path by graduating from a violinist's chair at the Vienna Court Theater, ascending from there to a brilliant career.[6]

Conducting initially had been a simple, artless affair. As early as the fifteenth century it had been the habit in the *Schola Cantorum* in Rome to beat time with a rolled-up piece of paper, a custom that was recalled in England in 1827 by Samuel Wesley:

I remember that in the time of Dr. Boyce it was customary to mark the measure to the orchestra with a roll of parchment or paper, in hand, and

[6] Later the composer Franz Schmidt was to rise to his calling from a cello desk of the Vienna Philharmonic Orchestra.

this usage is yet continued at St. Paul's Cathedral at the musical performances for the Sons of the Clergy.

This manner of conducting had been preceded by the "time beater," who, with the score at his elbow, would beat the time with a stick on a table, its noise on occasion overshadowing the music. The method of "beating time" had actually caused the death of one composer. Lully, while celebrating Louis XIV's recovery from illness, beat the time, by stamping a staff on the floor, so vigorously that he rammed the staff through the soft leather of his shoe. An ensuing infection, worsened by the quackery of his doctors, caused his death. The decline of polyphonic music all but eliminated the "time beater." He was replaced by the composer–conductor, directing the ensemble from the harpsichord. This method extended roughly from the time of Bach to the Viennese Classical period. Both Weber and Mendelssohn are credited with having used a baton for the first time in conducting an orchestra, but it is Wagner who is generally credited with having inaugurated the modern technique of conducting. In his wake rose the prominent conductors mentioned above. Most of them became "virtuoso" conductors, giants in their field without benefit of a single lesson in conducting or interpretation. Their calling had rather been thrust upon them. The increasing size of audiences in the nineteenth century had demanded larger halls and, subsequently, larger orchestras to perform in them. These new circumstances had demanded a specialist, a *Dirigent,* a conductor of superior coordinating and interpretive powers. Mahler was to reach such an apex in conductorial interpretation.

Once he started composing, Gustav never stopped. Only the fact of his having composed at that early age is known, because later judgment did not permit him to have those compositions published and they were destroyed or lost. The early parental and Iglau German influence as well as the later Pernerstorfer Circle influence made themselves felt in an early *Nordic* Symphony (also destroyed). Yet it would be a mistake to categorize Mahler along nationalistic lines. Like the empire that harbored him, he was neither narrowly German, narrowly Bohemian, nor narrowly Jewish. He was Austrian, an indefinable mixture which had attracted so many before Mahler (and was to attract many after) because of its intellectual climate, relaxed mode of living, and artistic history. This did not keep him from feeling dispossessed at times. "I am thrice homeless," he used to say. "As a Bohemian in Austria, as an Austrian among Germans, as a Jew throughout the world, everywhere an intruder, never welcomed." This was, of course, an exaggeration, a kind of romanticism in reverse, but it reflected an inner insecurity which he never lost and from which he forever fled.

Had the *Nordic* Symphony been preserved, it would not have been surprising if it had revealed that the impressionable young composer had been inspired by the mightiest musical influence of the time, Richard

Wagner, whose indelible stamp few composers then could escape. His influence could only have been reinforced by Mahler's acquaintance at the University of Vienna with Bruckner, himself a devoted Wagner disciple. In conservative Vienna, Wagner's name had been anathema, and the doors of the Imperial Court Opera had been closed to him for a long time. Even when Wagner was performed in the concert hall, the customary royalty payments were denied the composer for many years. The formation of a nucleus of Wagner admirers in Vienna was, of course, inevitable. Wolf, Mottl, Bruckner, Richter, and Mahler belonged to it. Impresario Albert Gutmann, who was to play a decisive role in Mahler's later life, cooperated financially with this group and was instrumental in arranging the first Wagner concert in Vienna, to be conducted by Richter. Thus, excerpts from *Tristan und Isolde* and *Die Walküre* were heard in Vienna for the first time early in 1875. A few months later, Wagner personally led three concerts in Vienna amid ovations and catcalls. Surprising support for Bruckner and Wagner came from a different musical quarter, as tangential to Wagner as he was important in Vienna—Johann Strauss. He included Wagner selections in his concerts long before the opera house opened its doors to the composer.

Wagner became the hero of the hour with the young conservatory students, who either espoused or emulated him. Mahler was among the latter, working at times on several operas simultaneously. Again the previously touched-on German trend is observed. *Herzog Ernst von Schwaben* is presumably based on the drama by the poet Uhland, while *Die Argonauten* employs the middle drama of Grillparzer's trilogy *Das goldene Vlies,* and *Rübezahl* is grounded in the collection of German fairy tales by the brothers Grimm. While Wagner's dramatic prominence and presence may have been the artistic impetus behind such feverish operatic activity by Mahler, the music may be assumed to have followed the example of an earlier German period of romanticism, that represented by Weber—which was then more nearly consonant with Mahler's outlook. Actually some of these perished works may be assumed to have stemmed from Mahlers earliest post-conservatory period (approximately 1880), while he held a demeaning summer conducting position at Bad Hall.

While Wolf, explosively, and Mahler, studiously, became Wagner admirers, the proliferation of Wagner's genius and music in Vienna remained in the capable hands of Richter, whom Wagner entrusted with correcting his scores and conducting actual performances in Bayreuth, the Wagner sanctum. Despite his early operatic creations opera seems to have remained a relatively unstudied field for Mahler, according to his lifelong friend Guido Adler who goes so far as to state that many operas remained unknown to Mahler until, as an opera conductor, he actually had to produce them. Mahler having destroyed all of his early opera attempts, his reconstruction of *Die drei Pintos* from Weber's sketches remains his only tangible product in that field. Thus he joined the older symphonist and Wagner disciple Bruckner, who also remained aloof from opera.

Kurt Blaukopf proposes that such abstention from operatic creation indicates Mahler's and Bruckner's adherence to symphonic tradition as opposed to the German concept of *Gesamtkunstwerk* (total work of art). Such a premise, however, does not explain the operatic production of such arch-Austrians as Mozart and Schubert nor the symphonic achievements of such German transplants to Vienna as Beethoven and Brahms.

After Wolf's departure from the conservatory, he and Mahler drifted apart and their friendship dimmed. By then Mahler had made other friends who were to become meaningful, among them the Rosé brothers. Eduard, a future prominent cellist, was to marry Mahler's youngest sister, Emma, and Arnold, the brilliant violinist, was to marry Mahler's sister Justine. A number of factors led to the cooling between Mahler and Wolf. One, as Alma Mahler relates, was coincidental. The two men had discussed the fairy tale of the German sprite *Rübezahl* as a possible subject for an opera. Both began work on it without telling the other, and when Mahler completed his libretto before Wolf, the surprised Hugo was so infuriated at his friend's parallel attempt and earlier achievement that he stopped work on the libretto and never returned to it. After that incident, they no longer sought each other out. A less obvious but logical factor in their estrangement must have been their character differences. Intuitively, subconsciously, the contrast between Mahler's controlled mien and emotions and Wolf's unrestrained temperament and thoughtless visits to brothels must have contributed to their estrangement even while a continued superficial friendship was maintained For reasons already mentioned, Mahler also abandoned work on *Rübezahl*. His mind was more attracted to a more romantic fairy tale, a story of fratricide and vengeance that he had found in Grimm's and Bechstein's *Märchenbücher*. The title alone—*Das klagende Lied* [The Song of Lament]—was far more intriguing.

Thus, at age nineteen, Mahler followed the artistic trend and emotions of his day, characterized by a rousing intellectual vitality romantically tinged and entwined with thoughts of death and physical passion. At that time he had become a private tutor in Tétény in Hungary. It would be difficult to imagine that Mahler's intellectual aspirations and physical longings had been assuaged there. We may assume that in the heart of Hungary he had little opportunity to gratify either need. Wolf had been less circumspect and had already contracted the disease that was to eventually mortally ravish his body and mind. By then Mahler's emotions were fully in tune with the out-of-tune emotionalism of the time. Sexual promiscuity was both a need and a dread: a need because it was the only available outlet to satisfy youthful urges, a dread because of the ever-present fear of infection (with its cure then only in its infancy), which might mark its victim physically and socially for life and often drove him to insanity or suicide. Of course, death was not a new experience to Mahler. Yet we also realize that once early "self-abuse" and restraint gave way to sexual enjoyment with a number of young partners, Mahler was to find, time after time, that his temperament had involved him, beyond mere erotic gratification, in emotional entanglements from which he found it difficult to extricate himself. Most of these intimate involvements had, of course, to be dealt with in utter secrecy (which gave rise to the rumor of Mahler's chastity), and could be related only to the closest of friends. Only as Mahler gained prominence and power did he break out of his wall of secrecy, heedless of public opinion and a growing reputation as a roué.

Mahler's comparatively sheltered world at the conservatory had been rudely rent when the brilliant student was faced with the task of proving himself as a professional musician. Tutoring in Hungary had only brought to mind the lowered horizons of Schubert, who had also engaged in the demeaning task of giving piano lessons at the home of a minor Hungarian aristocrat. The next phase, conducting operettas in a spa, was hardly a step upwards. The disillusioning discrepancy between the romantic wrestling with musical giants at the conservatory and the demeaning tasks of reality prompted some of Mahler's overwrought romantic outbursts in his letters from that time. It is therefore not at all surprising that Mahler's earliest preserved composition from that period bears the title *Das klagende Lied*. He had considered *Das klagende Lied* worthy of being entered in a competition for the coveted Beethoven Prize, which, he also hoped, would provide a measure of sustenance. But news of his admiration for Wagner and friendship with Bruckner had preceded him to the jury, which consisted, among others, of two of the most literate and outspoken critics of Wagner—Brahms and the critic Eduard Hanslick. Fate and conservatism conspired against Mahler; he failed to win. Mahler's artistic path might yet have led him into operatic effort had not fate intervened in 1880 in the person of Gustav Levy, who contracted with Mahler to act as his agent for a commission of 5 percent of his earnings. It was Gustav Levy who was responsible for that first demeaning position to be held by Mahler, conducting third-rate operettas in the Austrian spa of Bad Hall. There he was also to provide music for *Lustspiele* (farces), check the orchestral parts before performance, and set up chairs and music stands. Although he gained grass-roots experience there, he considered his activities totally devoid of artistically redeeming features and went so far as to offer his agent an additional fee should he be able to provide him with a better position. Nothing came of it and Mahler resumed work on a revision of *Das klagende Lied* instead, dreaming of a performance. The full realization of such aspirations, however, was to await the music of the future. At present, the key word in Vienna was struggle. The fire of Mahler's spirit was not enough to keep him warm in winter, and the hunt for piano pupils went on unabated.

Undaunted, Mahler persisted and in 1881 and 1882 found solace in a slight elevation in the level of his artistic activity. It is a blessing bequeathed by the nineteenth century, still enjoyed in the twentieth, that every city in western and central Europe worth its artistic weight aspired to an opera house. It thus became a part of the life of the burgher to betake himself and his family to the local opera house for an evening's entertainment of opera, operetta, or dance. Many an American artist of our time still enjoys the fruits of this phenomenon. Having only limited operatic establishments at their disposal in the United States, these young aspiring artists turn to the innumerable small opera houses in Europe for employment, active stage experience, and artistic growth, often returning to their native country with an excellent reputation acquired abroad. This is already an amelioration of the conditions that prevailed for American singers in the nineteenth century. So low was the opinion of the American public of the singers and instrumentalists graduating from American conservatories that the acquisition of European experience or at least a European name, preferably Italian, Russian, or French, was an absolute requirement for artistic recognition in this country.

It was to two of these small provincial opera houses with questionable artistic standards that Mahler escaped from his early menial musical tasks. They were the opera house in Laibach (Ljubljana) and that in Olmütz (Olomouc), both in eastern Europe (today in Yugoslavia and Czechoslovakia, respectively), then within the confines of the Austrian empire. It is not surprising that it was mostly the German element in both cities that supported operatic ventures, although both locations were non-German.

Another Mahler trait appeared at this time. Despite his increasing association with opera houses, he no longer felt the impulse to enter the operatic field, but soon began the pursuit of the symphonic style, with the occasional infusion of a text or song previously created, but always one of his own choosing, never foisted upon him in the confining totality of a libretto. It is the adherence to the symphonic style rather than the abstention from opera creation which marks Mahler as an Austrian composer. Remarks Ernst Krenek: "It is certainly more than a mere coincidence that this symphonic style was first developed in Vienna and remained at home there as long as the Empire lasted."

## LAIBACH, OLMÜTZ, KASSEL

Although Laibach was a settlement known since Roman times and in 1821 had enjoyed the brief distinction of hosting a conference of European powers (the "Congress of Laibach," which comprised Austria, Prussia, France, Great Britain, and Russia), no lasting importance had fastened itself to the provincial capital. Located in Slovenia, its main cultural fare consisted of German and Austrian plays and Italian opera at the *Landestheater*. In his position as conductor, Mahler widened his horizons. The small group of local singers and instrumentalists at the *Landestheater* were called upon to perform in anything from operas to operettas to plays, sometimes under the most ludicrous conditions. When Mahler arrived he had to perform Gounod's *Faust* with but one male singer in the chorus.

As was to be expected from Mahler, he took his duties seriously and, despite the limited artistic personnel at his disposal, presented a wide variety of programming, ranging from the *Magic Flute* to *Il Trovatore* to the *Merry Wives of Windsor* and, a year later, Johann Strauss's *Der lustige Krieg*, only months after its Vienna premiere. The 1881–82 season opened with a play by the Austrian poet **Eduard von Bauernfeld** and *Egmont* by Goethe, for which Mahler provided Beethoven's incidental music. In retrospect it comes as no surprise that the artistic level of production at the *Landestheater* soon rose to a height never attained before. Praise from the press prompted Mahler to expand his artistic activities and appear as pianist with the Laibach Philharmonic Society, a venerable institution of no mean repute. If the press had spoken before of "great verve" and "unsuspected powers," the new reviews of his pianism referred to his "bravura renditions" and "brilliant technique."

His first "benefit night," a European custom designed to secure additional income for a composer, conductor, actor, or singer as well as to recognize his accomplishments, was destined to be one of the great moments of his young life. As he entered the orchestra pit he was greeted by a *Tusch,* a fanfare played by the orchestra. The director presented him with his first laurel wreath, amid the applause of the audience. After the performance (of Flotow's *Alessandro Stradella*), the *Laibacher Zeitung* joined the general acclaim, calling the honor "well deserved" and referring to

> this highly trained musician, who takes his difficult task most seriously and has given much hard work and care to it throughout the season.

It was heady praise indeed for a twenty-one-year-old musician and budding composer who, as the sole conductor of the entire musical repertoire, truly labored at a difficult but also educational task of musical training.

It is surprising, and no actual reason for it was ever given or determined, but Mahler's contract in Laibach was not renewed nor did Mahler seek to have it renewed. Instead he returned to Vienna in 1882, a much more experienced musician who could point to a positive achievement. Upon arrival he promptly contacted his agent, asking him to find him a new position. Nearly a year passed without result, until in January 1883 word was received that the theater in Olmütz in Moravia was in dire need of a conductor. Actually the place was in need of everything: stage settings, artists, money. Why Mahler would wish to exchange the musically conducive, although small-scale, atmosphere of Laibach for the miserable artistic conditions of a city best known for its *Quargel,* a cheese of offensive pungency, will remain an enigma. Whether or not Mahler knew about Olmütz, the town, in turn, had been apprised of Mahler. A staff member of the theater, the baritone Jacques Manheit, relates that the director described Mahler beforehand to the staff as an eccentric genius and asked for indulgence and tolerance.

Mahler, now surefooted in the handling of opera and opera personnel, did not disappoint them. He asked for, or rather demanded, prompt compliance with his terse directives. The results were not long in coming. The premiere of Verdi's *Un Ballo in Maschera* in February 1883 proved to be his first success in his new position. Again we thank Manheit (as quoted in Blaukopf's *Mahler*) for a report.

> Gradually the little town got used to the peculiarities of the young conductor, whom the musical fraternity had learned, if not to love, at any rate, to fear. He had such a decisive way of making demands and giving orders that nobody dared oppose him, particularly since under his direction performances improved tremendously. Strange to say, Mahler hardly knew any of the operas; he learned them as he went along.[7] He did not seem to care that he was not popular; he merely insisted that everyone do his task.

Artistically Olmütz proved to be sheer hell for Mahler, however.

> I have to make a tremendous effort to pull myself together and write to you. I am quite paralyzed, as though I had fallen from heaven. From the moment I crossed the threshold of the theatre in Olmütz, I have felt like a man awaiting the judgment of God.
>
> If a thoroughbred is harnessed to a cart with oxen, the best he can do is to sweat and haul with them. I can hardly bear to write to you, I feel so defiled. . . . Up to now, thank heaven, I have had practically nothing but Meyerbeer and Verdi to conduct. I have craftily and perserveringly shouldered Wagner and Mozart out of the repertory—for I could never bear to drag *Lohengrin* and *Don Giovanni,* for instance, down to this.
>
> > Mahler to Dr. Friedrich Löhr,[8]
> > 20 January 1883

Thus Mahler limited himself to Bizet, Mehul, Meyerbeer, and Verdi. But he considered himself the composer's representative, and even with such

---

[7] A fact borne out by Mahler's close friend Guido Adler.
[8] See p. 36.

a limited repertoire, more than once he may have apologetically raised his eyes to heaven in the face of incompetence.

Another benefit performance was, in time, to have a decisive influence on his career. Karl Überhorst, director of the Dresden Court Opera, heard him rehearse and conduct Mehul's *Joseph et ses frères* [Joseph and his brothers]. He was surprised and impressed by the disheveled young man's tireless imagination, versatility, and inventiveness. "One can only marvel at the man who created such a performance," he raved. Despite such an enthusiastic endorsement, Überhorst did not yet consider Mahler's countenance and bearing dignified enough for a position at his own theater in Dresden, however. In the spring of the year to follow, 1883, money at Olmütz predictably ran out and thereby abruptly ended the season and the young conductor's position. Mahler left Olmütz hurriedly and without regret.[9] What troubled him to a much greater extent was the news of Wagner's death, which had reached him in Olmütz. Only the fiercest discipline enabled him to continue work there after receiving the news of that loss.

Vienna was like a breath of fresh air after Olmütz. Mahler spent the time between engagements rehearsing the chorus of an Italian opera troupe at the *Carltheater* for two months while Gustav Levy again looked for a position for his young, peripatetic genius. He eventually received an inquiry from the Royal Theater in Kassel, Germany, regarding the position of second conductor. Überhorst, remembering the Olmütz performance, wholeheartedly recommended the young man:

> Not only did he produce the operas with fine discrimination and great precision despite the limited talent at his disposal, but as a conductor he succeeded, by dint of hard work, and tact, in welding the rather feeble resources at his disposal into a harmonious whole.

After some correspondence Mahler was offered and accepted the position in Kassel, with Levy drawing up the contract. That document contains a significant clause. For reasons unknown, Levy reduced his agent's fee but insisted that the Kassel management deduct his fee at the source and remit it directly into his hands. This may have been an indirect slap at Mahler, whose finances were always in a constant state of neglect and confusion. The contract was signed in May 1883, but Mahler's duties did not commence until autumn of that year, which gave him time to visit his family in Iglau. It was a depressing experience, because both parents were now ailing.

In October Mahler presented himself to the impresario of the opera house in Kassel.

---

[9] In 1934 a tablet was placed at the house in the Michaelergasse where Mahler had lived in Olmütz. It was removed during the German invasion in 1939. In 1962 the town named a street after Mahler.

"Can you conduct *Martha* tonight without rehearsal?"

"Of course."

"Excellent."

Mahler had never seen the score nor heard the music to Flotow's opera.

"May I look at the score to refresh my memory?"

"Certainly."

During that afternoon Mahler committed the entire score to memory, and to the acclaim of all he conducted the opera without a score, in a brilliant tour de force.

Kassel, the humming industrial provincial capital, was, without question, a step upward as far as artistic achievement was concerned, but it proved a disappointment in other ways. Mahler was soon to learn that the artistic freedom he had enjoyed in Olmütz and Laibach did not apply in Kassel. Despite his resounding title, "royal musical and choral director," he had to report all cuts and changes to be made in a performance, and these were subject to the approval of the principal conductor, *Hofkapellmeister* Wilhelm Treiber. Over and above his regular duties, Mahler was also obliged to compose music "for special occasions" and to make reports on all rehearsals. He was also instructed that rehearsals with members of the opposite sex could be held only in the presence of a third party. Artistic friction was not long in coming. Mahler's activities were restricted to the French and Italian repertoire (Adam, Delibes, Donizetti, Rossini), with only minor German composers (Flotow and Lortzing) included and with all major works reserved for the premier conductor. The restriction was doubly painful because it was carried out in the manner of a Prussian military boys school, with "misdemeanors" such as lateness for a rehearsal or impatient stamping of one's feet during rehearsal marked in a black book. Such demeaning restrictions as well as the absence of his idols from his delimited repertoire, had a depressing effect on Mahler and prompted him to look for an avenue of escape.

Such an avenue seemed to open in January 1884, when **Hans von Bülow**, the court conductor of the famed Meiningen Orchestra, conducted a concert in Kassel. Bülow was as famous as he was controversial. He had been a Wagner apostle who had been accorded the signal honor of conducting the premieres of *Tristan und Isolde* and *Die Meistersinger*. But after Wagner lured away Bülow's wife, Cosima (*née* Cosima Liszt, the daughter of Franz Liszt), to become first his mistress and later his wife, Bülow's loyalties visibly shifted to Brahms, whose famous interpreter he became. (Brahms entrusted him in 1885 with the complete orchestral rehearsals for the premiere of his Fourth Symphony.) Bülow's musicianship and personality made such a strong impression on the young Mahler that he, in an ill-conceived move, decided to call on Bülow for help. The next day *Freiherr* von Bülow received a letter.

I am a musician who is wandering without a guiding star through the desolate night of contemporary music, exposed to all the dangers of doubt and confusion. When at yesterday's concert I saw my highest hopes and dreams realized, it dawned on me. . . . this is your master—now or never your journeying shall cease. And now I come to ask you; take me with you. In whatever capacity—let me be your pupil, even if I have to pay for it with my own blood. I am twenty-three years old, studied at the University of Vienna, learned composition and the piano at the conservatory, and after the most ill-starred wandering find myself employed as second conductor at the local theatre. Whether this futile clatter can satisfy a man who with all the love and longing in him believes in art, yet sees it maltreated everywhere in the most abominable manner, you yourself will best be able to judge. I put myself completely in your hands, and if you will accept this present, there is nothing that would make me happier. . . . Please, do at least give me an answer.

In expectation,

Gustav Mahler

How Mahler expected to succeed with such a letter must remain an enigma. To begin with, he was bound to the theater by contract and therefore was not at liberty to move about as he pleased. Furthermore, young Mahler was a total unknown to the great conductor, who therefore would presumably be reluctant to assume artistic responsibility for someone whose musical capabilities he had not had an opportunity to assess. Finally, the near-hysterical tone of the letter could not possibly have disposed Bülow in favor of the young Mahler. Instead of being answered, the letter found its way into the hands of First Conductor Treiber, and through him to the director, *Herr von und zu* Gilsa. Mahler had made his position in Kassel untenable and was so given to understand, although the director, hard-pressed for a second conductor and realizing the potential of Mahler, did not dismiss him on the spot. Instead, Mahler lingered and languished in Kassel until 1885.[10]

It was at this time that Mahler heard Wagner at the peak of his perfection—*Parsifal*—in Bayreuth. The importance and solemnity of the occasion were heightened by the fact that it was an in memoriam performance, the first after Wagner's death. The impression of the splendor of the performance was to be a lasting one, firing Mahler on to greater efforts. "I knew that I had undergone the greatest tragic experience of all and that I would carry it unprofaned through life."

Even if artistic circumstances had not been as demanding and depressing as they were, Kassel could have been no more than a way station in Mahler's ambitious plans. To further his career he no longer relied on

---

[10] But Bülow did eventually recognize Mahler's talent. When he was asked two years later to recommend conductors for the Berlin Opera House he gave Mahler's name.

letters, remembering his ill-fated missive to Bülow, but instead traveled to Dresden for a conference with Überhorst, who had described him as a conductor "of quite exceptional distinction" in his Kassel recommendation. But again, Mahler, with typical intensity, moved for the "overkill." Although the Dresden director saw fit to give Mahler a contract for Leipzig, the young conductor composer also began contract negotiations with the German opera house in Prague, bringing about a situation which was bound to present problems in the near future for the intense, driving young conductor. Friedrich Eckstein describes Mahler during his Kassel tenure as "of small stature. Already in the curiously wagging manner of his gait [induced by an affliction of St. Vitus's dance suffered in early years] his unusual irritability manifested itself. His tense and intellectual face, thin and extremely mobile, was framed by a full-grown beard, changed to a moustache in 1886. He was clean shaven in 1887. His speech was pointed with a strongly Austrian intonation. He invariably carried a parcel of books or music under his arm."

If Mahler found any comfort or reward from prevailing activities and conditions, it did not come from the opera but rather from a historic music festival which he conducted there. Kassel had planned the music festival for 29 June to 1 July 1885. The main works to be performed were Mendelssohn's *St. Paul* oratorio and Beethoven's Ninth Symphony. Four choral societies, including the one Mahler conducted, were to take part. Mahler was also to be overall music director of the event, which would employ his opera orchestra. This did not sit well with principal conductor Treiber. He was the first conductor; he considered himself the foremost musician in Kassel. He was to be in charge and he stated so, loudly and clearly, to the director. The director approached Mahler, who refused outright to yield to Treiber. With his musical future secure, Mahler could afford to be stiff-necked. Besides, here was the ensemble of his fondest dreams (a dream he was to realize later in his compositions): a giant choral group of four hundred voices, a large orchestra, and such outstanding soloists as Heinrich Gudehus from Bayreuth and Rosa Papier from Vienna. Finally a compromise was reached: Treiber would be in charge of rehearsals and Mahler in charge of performance. At that point Germany's latent anti-Semitism reared its head. The Jew Mahler had arrogated unto himself the spot in the limelight; Germans would do all the work and the Jew would take the bows. The theater orchestra, under pressure, refused to participate in the festival. Mahler was undismayed. Kassel's was not the only orchestra in Germany. He scoured the nearby cities and, with musicians from Braunschweig, Meiningen, and Weimar, formed an orchestra to which he added the band of an infantry regiment. To find no ready chorus available in Kassel must have struck Mahler as surprising, because the Germans excelled in choral singing. Mahler again began to search, combining a number of local choruses into a homogenous musical body in endless rehearsals. Then and there, for the first time, the world received a glimpse of things to come. The various choruses and organizations, who had questioningly succumbed to Mahler's visions and grudgingly submitted to his unyielding, demanding zeal in rigorous rehearsals, suddenly found themselves singing at a level which obliterated the mediocre standards in which they had unknowingly wallowed. Finally the day arrived, and the miracle of Mahler's tenacious genius unfolded in splendid performances leading to jubilant ovations for the conductor. His superhuman efforts bore fruit to such an extent that the Kassel populace were to discuss the festival in tones of awe for decades to come.

Mahler had become "too big" for Kassel. Treiber realized this and so did the director. But Mahler could not simply be dismissed, because this was a court theater and permission to terminate a contract before it had run its course had to be obtained from the appropriate department in Berlin. Upon Kassel's urging, the intendant saw to it that the requisite permission was promptly granted.


## PRAGUE, LEIPZIG

Upon receipt of the news of the early termination of his Kassel contract, Mahler was not only undismayed; he was elated. He had gained prominence; he was the man of the hour, feted at receptions with honors and ovations in addition to more tangible material gifts. Neither these honors and presents, however, nor the achievement of his song cycle *Lieder eines fahrenden Gesellen* [Songs of a wayfarer], which had had its inception in Kassel in 1884, could ease his present precarious financial situation. Securing the musicians needed for the festival orchestra had been costly; besides, he was again in forced hiatus owing to the one-year span between his prematurely terminated contract in Kassel and the projected start of his position in Leipzig. It was for that (possibly foreseen) time span that he had accepted the Prague appointment in 1885 in addition to the Leipzig contract. But if Mahler was in something of a dilemma because of the looming Leipzig commitment, Prague was in a dilemma of its own, one bordering on despair.

The numerous nationalities within the Austrian empire exhibited a constant tendency to strain away from Vienna's and Habsburg's hegemony, protesting the neglect of their particular language, heritage, and customs and championing their particular nationalistic artistic expression. Most successful among them were the Magyars, who, with the help of Empress Elisabeth, eventually succeeded in their aspirations. But the Czechs were no exception. Their nationalistic surges had finally found a foothold in the Czech capital and burned brightly in the *Národni Divadlo* (National Theatre). This development threatened the long-standing supremacy of German culture as the major artistic medium in Prague. The German Theatre in Prague was in dire straights. A frantic search succeeded in bringing to Prague Angelo Neumann, a former singer and successful director and a man of considerable artistic and commercial know-how.

Kassel, like Olmütz and Laibach before it, had been provincial theater; thus the name of Mahler was not yet a familiar one to Neumann. Nonetheless, the latter was so impressed with Mahler's letter of inquiry that he interviewed him. Suffice it to say that Neumann felt the spark and engaged Mahler. He actually did not care for the young conductor's "exaggerated fidgety gestures" while conducting but the quality of Mahler's execution of his first assignment, a Cherubini opera, proved an overriding consideration, and a pleasant working relationship developed between the two men. Mahler actually was the second in command; **Anton Seidl** occupied the position of first conductor. Seidl was much on tour with his truncated versions of Wagner operas, but he had also conducted the Prague premiere of *Lohengrin* during the 1885–86 season; therefore Wagner remained within his domain. When Seidl's fame reached America and he assumed his post at the Metropolitan Opera Company in New York, Mahler took command of the entire repertoire. Ludwig Slansky, the other chief conductor, still occupied a position nominally above Mahler's but was satisfied to let the younger man do the work. Mahler approached his monumental task with his customary zeal. Already in December 1885 he produced *Das Rheingold* and *Die Walküre,* a tremendous feat. Neumann, in order not to slight Slansky, assigned the production of *Don Giovanni* to him, but Slansky refused the offer with the comment that Prague had never appreciated the opera.[11] Neumann then turned *Don Giovanni* over to Mahler, who was delirious with joy. When he was informed that he was also to conduct a performance of Beethoven's Ninth Symphony, his elation was complete. Public and press felt the joyful surge in the twenty-five-year-old bearded musician and Prague acclaimed his achievement, which had lent renewed distinction to the fading reputation of the German Theatre and, incidentally, left Mahler in full command.

Despite the pronounced Germanism of his Beethoven–Mozart–Wagner performances, Mahler, steeped in Bohemian lore and music since the Iglau days of his youth, did not neglect to inform himself of the Czech music of his day. Nationalism in music, however, was not confined to the efforts of the Bohemians Bedřich Smetana and his son-in-law Antonin Dvořák.

11 That comment sheds light on Slansky's ignorance of musical history. For the people of Prague, more than those of any other city on earth, had adored Mozart and his music. *Don Giovanni* was especially written for Prague, as was Symphony No. 38 in D Major (K. 504). "*Die Prager verstehen mich*" ("The people of Prague understand me") had been Mozart's appreciative comment.

A vigorous musical nationalism had begun to blossom in all corners of Europe, within and without the Austrian empire, and it was to bear rich fruit. It had actually begun in a most unlikely corner of the continent, when Glinka and Dargomijsky spawned an entire generation of nationalists in Balakirev, Borodin, Cui, Mussorgsky, and Rimsky-Korsakov. They were actually as much interested in oriental music as they were in the music of their own country—Russia. Pointedly, their friend Tchaikovsky was excluded from their nationalistic circle, known as "The Magnificent Five," because he as well as the brothers Rubinstein were considered too tainted by Western European music to be considered Russian nationalistic composers. The nationalistic surge had spread to Bohemia, Norway, France, Italy, Finland, and Spain, and had opened a new field for the romantic movement of the nineteenth century.

Mahler was strongly receptive to these new musical expressions; he frequently attended performances at the *Národni Divadlo* to hear Smetana, Dvořák, and Glinka. Remembering the sounds of his childhood, he found a particularly pleasant echo in Smetana's opera *The Bartered Bride,* which became Mahler's favorite non-German opera. Prague began to appeal to Mahler; it was like a green oasis between the desert of Kassel and the yet to be explored territory of Leipzig. There was another reason why Prague's appeal intensified. Kassel and Leipzig were German; Prague was part of Austria. There were, of course, consistent wranglings and nationalistic upheavals within the empire, but in times of danger from without there could be no question as to loyalty (as was to be seen later in World War I). In Prague Mahler felt himself to be an Austrian; in Leipzig he would be a German-speaking stranger. Worse, whereas in Prague, Mahler was first conductor in all but name and was actually in charge, in Leipzig, as in Kassel, he would clearly be a second conductor again. But in contrast to Kassel and Prague, the "other" conductor was no mediocre nonentity but one of the most illustrious conductorial geniuses alive, **Arthur Nikisch.** Belated doubts assailed Mahler, who now would have preferred to stay in Prague. But Überhorst insisted that the contract be honored—particularly now that Mahler was an unknown no longer.

Thus Mahler approached his Leipzig task with apprehension. At first his requests were granted, and the Wagner operas *Tannhäuser* and *Rienzi* became part of his repertoire, as did Weber's *Freischütz* and Halévy's *La Juive.* Matters became stagnant at that point, however. When Mahler expressed his resentment of the fact that only early Wagner operas were assigned to him, he was informed that it was deemed wise that such productions as the *Ring* remain in the hands of the more experienced and more mature (by five years) Nikisch. Mahler threatened to leave; the director calmed him into staying, but Mahler was determined. After inquiries by himself and by friends, he soon heard favorably from Hamburg, then from

Karlsruhe—which was most flattering because none other than Felix Mottl had reigned there—and then from Prague, where Neumann would receive him with open arms. Again, fate and time were Mahler's allies. Nikisch became ill and was forced to take a long leave. All of his repertoire now fell on Mahler's willing shoulders. Although his title still designated him as second conductor, he was actually in charge of the entire repertoire. His confidence grew as he produced in brief succession *Die Walküre* and *Siegfried,* and he soon considered himself the artistic equal of his more famous colleague. Only a man with Mahler's white-heat energy, enthusiasm, and ambition would have been able to conduct over two hundred performances during the 1887–88 season, presenting fifty-four operas.

> As you probably know, for about the last 3 months my nose has been kept to the grindstone in a way which is without precedent; my colleague Nikisch has been sick and I have had to do two men's work. I conduct grand operas nearly every day and am literally scarcely ever away from the theater. You can imagine how exhausting this is when one takes art seriously, and what strenous efforts are needed to acquaint oneself worthily of such a tremendous task with practically no preparations.
>
> Mahler to Dr. Fritz Löhr, May 1887

It was Leipzig which witnessed Mahler's only foray—of sorts—into opera composition. There lived in Leipzig Carl Maria von Weber's grandson, Carl von Weber, who approached Mahler and offered to supply him with his grandfather's sketches to the opera *Die drei Pintos* if Mahler would undertake the task of completing the opera. Mahler agreed, and his version was performed to great applause on 20 January 1888 at the Leipzig *Stadttheater.* What made work on *Die drei Pintos* particularly pleasant was the constant presence of Frau Weber, who, although Mahler's senior by seven years, had mellowed to the charms of the impetuous conductor. The ensuing affair became so torrid that the two lovers, in order to avoid public scandal, saw no other way out but to elope. Mahler was not too taken with the idea, because in so doing he would automatically forfeit his Leipzig position; at a time when he was the sole support of his brothers and sisters, he would have to provide also for his newly acquired mistress, to whom only passion—but no love—bound him. But a misguided code of honor seemingly left no avenue of escape open for Mahler, and a secret midnight departure was arranged. Relief outweighed a sense of loss when at the appointed hour his paramour failed to appear.

What also eased Mahler's Leipzig woes was work on his First (*Titan*) Symphony. This first of nine formidable symphonic creations consumed his energies to such an extent that, for the first and only time in his entire career, he was accused of being remiss in the execution of his duties. Whether there was actually neglect on the part of Mahler, dissatisfaction on the part of Nikisch, or intrigue by the director to make Mahler's life and position miserable, the end result was that Mahler's position in Leipzig became untenable. If there was actually neglect of duty (and knowing Mahler's drive and vitality, it is to be doubted), it was to be the only instance in his career of a conflict between Mahler the conductor and Mahler the composer. Later we will observe Mahler's simultaneous and successful efforts in both fields.

Mahler and the director were now thinking and proceeding at cross purposes. With Nikisch ill or convalescent, the director needed more than ever that tense, inspired second conductor, who would shoulder a full season's operatic load successfully. Mahler, on the other hand, had decided that he did not care for Leipzig any longer. The reasons for such a realization were both musical and materialistic. The load was crushing; and furthermore, Nikisch's negotiations with the Budapest Opera had apparently come to naught and he therefore had no intention of leaving Leipzig. This made advancement for Mahler impossible there. Meanwhile, both his parents were ill, and sister Justine, somewhat of a spendthrift, was running the household inefficiently. The education and future of younger brothers and sisters had to be planned. Financial assistance to all became imperative. Besides, Mahler was solely a conductor no longer; he was now a full-fledged composer, with a "titanic" symphony to his credit. His Leipzig stint was ended as far as he was concerned. The director seems to have eventually come to feel the same way. Mahler thought of Budapest and corresponded with Bernhard Pollini in Hamburg. He left Leipzig. As before, Bayreuth became balm, inspiration, and refuge as Mahler drank in *Parsifal* and *Die Meistersinger*.

## BUDAPEST, HAMBURG

The list of positions held by Mahler had swelled to five, (Olmütz, Laibach, Kassel, Prague, Leipzig), and Mahler's reputation, too, had grown. In light of this growing reputation, it was not surprising that in the autumn of the same year (1888) Mahler was "working" again. Having traversed Europe, from Leipzig's north-central location to the east, Mahler welcomed being again in complete charge of an entire opera house, this time a young yet in many senses major house—Budapest. What especially pleased Mahler was the elevation in position, which made him the equal of the director in Leipzig.

Of course there were difficulties and complications. First of all, the Budapest Opera was in financial straits. Compared with Prague, Leipzig, or Vienna, opera in Budapest was a relatively new venture, the opera house having opened only a few years previously with high hopes and poor management.[12] In addition, the Hungarian language, a tongue steeped in its Asiatic history, was unlike any other Mahler had ever spoken or heard. Finally, nationalistic feelings ran high in Hungary, and Mahler had been made aware that he might be buffeted by the gusts of political winds. The ceaseless agitation of the Hungarian faction within the monarchy had finally led, in 1867, to the granting of certain nationalistic rights and prerogatives.

Since the opera house in Budapest, like most of those in Europe, was state-subsidized, a government functionary, Ferenc von Beniczky, was appointed in 1888 to look after the financial as well as artistic well-being of the enterprise. Beniczky realized that the artistic house had to be put in order by a competent director and chief conductor. He had heard about Mahler, but sought advice from knowing sources rather than undertaking unilateral action. He approached the famed cellist David Popper, who, in turn, contacted Guido Adler, then professor at the German University in Prague, a friend of Mahler and well acquainted with his work. Adler replied most favorably. Another authority, Odön von Mihalovich, director of the Budapest Academy of Music and Drama, also expressed himself in favor of Mahler. Last but not least there was Mahler's adaptation of Weber's *Die drei Pintos,* which had received a favorable reception at the nearby Imperial Court Opera in Vienna, one of the foremost music centers in the world.

Beniczky engaged Mahler by means of a carefully worded contract. The only clause which Mahler was never to fulfill required him to acquire a knowledge of the Hungarian language. But in every other respect he surpassed the results expected of him, including those relating to nationalistic emphasis.

Mahler had accepted with alacrity even though the contract, drawn up for ten years, stipulated that his tenure could be terminated at any time, since it was subject to the highly volatile political climate of Hungary. Mahler did not give that clause another thought. The prospect of being his own master in an opera house, even a run-down, deficit-ridden, and presently second-rate one, fired his imagination and quickened his pulse. Less than three years later, changing politics did end Mahler's Budapest tenure. But what happened in that span of time catapulted the Budapest house into the front ranks among European opera houses and made the name Mahler a byword in European operatic circles. For upon Mahler's departure Budapest could proudly point to an opera company

[12] Opera had been performed previously, but it was not until 27 September 1884 that a house specifically devoted to opera was opened by Emperior Franz Joseph, to be known as *Magyar Királyi Operaház* (Royal Hungarian Opera House).

without debt or deficit and possessed of an outstanding ensemble and repertoire. Oddly enough, Mahler's epochal innovations drew as much criticism as had the haphazard management before him. First of all, and we assume that it was mainly because of budgetary limitations, Mahler did away with the star system and instituted an arrangement which brought into the opera house young, enthusiastic, and talented singers of promise. Impatient with old-time stars who disdained acting in favor of a wooden stance, relying solely on pear-shaped tones to reap applause, Mahler became involved in every phase of a production, even those aspects not directly related to the music (direction, design, lighting) as he sought to integrate all the components of opera art into unified entities meeting high standards.

As if this were not sufficient for an enterprising young opera director-conductor, Mahler then took his most applauded and eventually most critical step: he decided to have operas performed in Hungarian. While the public cheered and again filled the opera house, which had yawned emptily for years, the purists sneered. Verdi and Mozart in Hungarian? Mahler disregarded the pained outcries of the elite, who had stayed away for so long; his aim was to bring the Hungarian music lover back to opera and to make opera, for the first time, a vital part of Hungarian artistic life. If he was to achieve such a goal, the paying customer tentatively approaching a new medium, had to understand in order that he could enjoy. How revolutionary Mahler's step was can be appreciated if one realizes that the controversy of original text versus native language remains unresolved to this day.

Mahler's nationalistic gesture won him much popular sympathy but also added fuel to the long-standing controversy. There are valid arguments on either side. The music will sound best when sung in the original language because it has, in a sense, been fitted to it; on the other hand, the contention that the opera goer will enjoy the opera more when the language familiarizes him with the action and continuity cannot be rejected out of hand, particularly when the opera goer is called upon to support an opera house financially.

The Mahler breeze which began to blow through the Budapest opera house soon became a whirlwind. With his proverbial abruptness, Mahler ended the laissez-faire custom of using more than one language in an opera. This "traditional" privilege on the part of guest artists of singing in their native tongue—sometimes Italian, sometimes French or German—while the opera was sung in a different language had invaded even the Vienna Opera, where the belief prevailed that the voice was the thing and the text of secondary importance. Mahler further expressed his pro-Hungarian musical intent (an assumption of which had been implicitly written into the text of his contract) by promising to foster Hungarian musical nationalism, then represented by Ferenz Erkel, the leader of the Hungarian national school of opera, and the one-armed composer **Count Geza von Zichy.**[13]

True to contract, conviction, and character, Mahler not only followed through but went to extremes. It was one thing to do *Carmen, Cavalleria Rusticana,* or even *Don Giovanni* in Hungarian, but quite another. to produce the *Ring* cycle in that language, particularly since Wagner's libretti first had to be translated from Wagnerese into German. But Mahler persisted and prevailed. The difficult task was compounded by Mahler's lack of knowledge of Hungarian. He could be guided only by his total knowledge of the original, after which the Hungarian version had to be patterned. Zealously he built a Wagner ensemble, and he had the distinction of training a splendid singer, Arabella Szilágyi, until then an undistinguished member of the ensemble, as the first Hungarian Brünhilde, thus producing *Das Rheingold* and *Die Walküre* in 1889, as well as the opera *Brankovics György* by Erkel. Another of Mahler's "gods" followed in quick succession, as Mozart was presented to Budapest in a completely revamped *Le Nozze di Figaro* [The marriage of Figaro] and *Don Giovanni.* The press was ecstatic and so was Johannes Brahms, who was quoted as saying that to hear a true *Don Giovanni* one should hear it in Budapest. This statement is remarkable because it illuminates Brahms's one-sided appreciation of Mahler. While from then on he was always to highly praise Mahler's interpretations, he was to dismiss Mahler's compositions as *Kapellmeistermusik* ("conductor's music"—a pejorative term denoting music that is formally correct but lacks imagination and originality).

To Mahler's dismayed surprise, his musical fortunes then took an unexpected turn. When, during the second year, he prepared the remaining *Ring* dramas for performance, plus some minor masters such as Nicolai and Marschner, he was suddenly attacked in the press and accused of fostering the German repertoire, despite the performance of those operas in Hungarian. Mahler's surprise was profound, because he had taken the declarations of the Hungarians concerning a national opera house at face value and in the widest possible sense. He had not realized that a gesture, an occasional opera in Hungarian, would have sufficed. Wagner was difficult to comprehend, even in Hungarian, and the public began to clamor again for *bel canto* fare. Mahler felt doubly depressed: first, because his honest efforts had been misinterpreted, and also because he himself yearned for German opera—in German.

His strenuous efforts left little time for composing, but Mahler took advantage of his position to make himself heard as a composer. In November 1889, three of his songs were performed by the soprano Bianca Bianchi, with Mahler at the piano. It was a mere *succèss d'éstime.* But

[13] In 1896 Emperor Franz Joseph acceded to an invitation of Zichy to attend the performance of his latest opera. Reported Franz Joseph to Katharina Schratt: "I was duly at Count Zichy's opera. . . . A lively ballet kept me from falling asleep."

Mahler had greater ambitions, and only days later, with Mahler at the helm of its Philharmonic orchestra, Budapest heard his First Symphony. The effect was devastating. Critics found it "infuriating," "endless," and "confused." But Mahler had powerful friends in musical as well as political circles. Besides, and most telling with the powers that be, receipts at the opera had increased to a point where the previously financially ailing opera house was ailing no longer. A subsequent concert in 1890 devoted solely to Hungarian music, including Liszt and Edmund von Mihalovich (and in which Mahler introduced a stunning novelty— conducting without a score), was heartily applauded again.

But Mahler had become apprehensive of conditions in Budapest and had begun to look around again. His earlier correspondence with Bernhard Pollini, director of the Hamburg Opera, had been cordial and promising, and he now resumed correspondence with him. Pollini responded decisively with a contract offer, which Mahler promptly accepted. This favorable turn of events had not come one moment too soon, because the artistic atmosphere in Budapest began to turn bitter. Mahler's musical friends and superiors were themselves being hard pressed, in a political move instigated by Count Zichy. To reinforce his position and reputation, Zichy always emphasized that he had been a pupil of Liszt's, thus attempting to reflect a measure of Liszt's fame on his own meager musical accomplishments. An attempted coup by Zichy failed, but Mahler was not oblivious of such interference and its inherent dangers. With the foreseeable future secure and the signed contract in his pocket, his musical forays became more daring.

A new trend in Italian opera, verismo (crudely labeled "blood and guts"), had risen in favor, with Leoncavallo and Mascagni as its main representatives, and with the blessing of Verdi. Shortly after its premiere in Rome, Mahler acquired one such opera for Budapest, and in December 1890 Mascagni's Parasztbecsület (Cavalleria Rusticana) was heard, with the versatile Arabella Szilágyi singing Santuzza. It was a musical event of worldwide importance, perfectly tailored to Mahler's efforts and ambitions, and it received proper attention from the news media and opera directors in attendance. Thus the paradox of an Italian opera in Hungarian becoming a world success in Budapest (and not in Rome) became one more major accomplishment to be added to Mahler's lengthening list.

A second attempt, in 1891, to topple the reigning musical powers in Budapest succeeded, and through it Count Zichy rose to prominence, determined to minimize Mahler's influence and powers. Harsh exchanges between the two men ended in threats against Mahler, who one day actually found himself locked out of his office. Zichy, using his newly acquired political and artistic leverage, went even further and, although Mahler's official position had in no way been severed, proceeded to offer the position to Felix Mottl. The correct German not only refused but forwarded the letter of invitation to his colleague in Budapest (shades of Bülow in reverse), forewarning him of the impending threat. Mahler, however, was not to be hurried or pressured into any premature move; Hamburg would welcome him. Shrewdly he approached Count Zichy with a compromise plan. He, Mahler, would relinquish some of his rights and powers (sought by Zichy) in exchange for a new two-year contract (there were eight years remaining under his original contract) and compensation in the amount of 25,000 gulden. Zichy, sensing a weakness in Mahler's stance and proposal, seized the opportunity. With the connivance of his superiors and political friends he offered Mahler the stipulated sum of 25,000 gulden, to be paid promptly at the end of the contract—which was to be terminated upon payment of the above sum, the payment to be made immediately! Mahler's plan had worked; he accepted promptly. Zichy surveyed the scene in triumph. Little did he know that Mahler was to leave Budapest anyway to fulfill his Hamburg commitment, which stipulated that Mahler's arrival be no later than 1 April 1891. Thus Zichy, had he waited, could have saved his superiors the sum paid out as severance pay. The scheme also backfired in another way. The public now saw Mahler as a martyr driven from his post by Hungarian politics. The public response was balm to Mahler's soul. In addition to the considerable sum he had received, his admirers betokened him with a gold baton and a laurel wreath in Hungary's national colors, and the archnationalist Jenö Rakosi stated: "This German Jew [was] the only man capable of transforming the hitherto polyglot Hungarian opera into a unified national institution." High praise indeed from a Hungarian chauvinist.

As spring 1891 approached, Mahler found himself again temporarily "between opera houses." Owing to the favorable settlement, however, he was in an unworried financial position. He had nearly three months to relax between engagements, but even temporary freedom did not agree with him, idleness being an intolerable state for Mahler. Besides, his personal situation, while financially improved, had otherwise taken dismal turns. During 1889 both his parents had passed on, and the title and responsibilities of "head of the family" had fallen on Gustav's shoulders, he being the oldest and most successful. Gustav's burden was increased through near-tragedy, and tragedy. Brother Alois, the next male in line, had to remove himself to America to escape prosecution for some shady deals, and sister Leopoldine passed away. This left three—Justine, Emma, and Otto—to care for. But Justine, now the next oldest in line, was seemingly incapable of coping with finances and caring for her younger brother and sister after having nursed her sinking parents; Gustav found her on the verge of a nervous breakdown. Thus in addition to directing and conducting duties Mahler found himself forced to make repeated round trips between Budapest and Iglau to settle family affairs, place the two younger children in Vienna, and have Justine medically attended to.

With the two younger ones safely settled, Gustav decided to have Justine move in with him in Budapest. With his beloved mother dead, the mother image apparently persisted in Mahler, now transferred to Justine in his subconscious. To restore her health and spirit he had also taken her on a journey to Italy, which touched Bologna, Florence, Genoa, and Milan. Considering the art treasures to be found in those cities, it strikes one as curious that Mahler should never have mentioned attending an art gallery, museum, cathedral, or palace. Such lack of artistic appreciation or interest would seem odd, particularly in so sensitive an artist as Mahler. But Mahler had eyes only for the beauty of Italy's landscape and thoughts only for the music of his Second Symphony, now seething within him.

At that time the influence of a friend of his youth, the archeologist Dr. Friedrich (Fritz) Löhr (with whom Mahler had also lodged his younger brother and sister) was decisive. In the course of a vast volume of correspondence he opened new vistas to Mahler such as medieval art, the culture and thoughts of the Middle Ages, and German romanticism and its views, specifically as expressed by Goethe and Brentano. There can be no doubt that the correspondence with Löhr, spanning years, was at least as influential in shaping Mahler's views and insights as his correspondence with the erratic literary genius Siegfried Lipiner, whose enthusiastic opinions and thoughts quickly inflamed Mahler but subsided equally quickly. (In a similar fashion, the early influence exerted on Mahler by the writings of Wagner and Nietzsche eventually paled, while the writings of Kant and Goethe were to have a lasting impact.)

Mahler's sights were actually beginning to fasten themselves on vistas beyond Hamburg, although he had not even started his position there. His yearning was for Vienna. As fate would have it, all his family had arrived in Vienna years before Gustav. Mahler had found it impossible to impose on his friend Löhr any longer and he established a new home for his family, with Justine in charge of upbringing and himself in charge of support. Justine seems to have been wholly inadequate to the task, and letters crisscrossed Europe between Hamburg and Vienna expressing Gustav's anger because money was being squandered without even minimal results. Otto's death by suicide proved to Gustav the impossibility of the Vienna abode; he subsequently brought his sisters to Hamburg.

In a sense, and as was to be expected, Hamburg proved an artistic regression for Mahler. Whereas in Budapest he had been his own master, in full charge and command, in Hamburg he again became a *Kapellmeister* (a first *Kapellmeister*, to be sure), with limited assignments. There were some counterbalancing considerations, however. For one thing, Hamburg was an opera house of considerable importance and influence. Furthermore, not being bogged down with administrative duties and problems allowed Mahler in Hamburg to address his energies wholly to the artistic task at hand. Perhaps the greatest satisfaction for him at that time was the turnabout of Bülow, then conductor of the Hamburg Symphony Orchestra, who acknowledged Mahler's talents as an interpreter. (Mahler was to succeed Bülow as conductor of the Hamburg orchestra after his death.) Even Brahms, who had lost no love on Mahler, the Wagner admirer, now endorsed him as a master interpreter.

Mahler opened in Hamburg on 29 March 1891 with *Tannhäuser*. But his first great success came with the German premiere of Tchaikovsky's *Eugène Onegin*. Pollini had been successful in getting Tchaikovsky to agree to conduct the premiere early in 1892. But the German adaptation presented complications and language difficulties to which the Russian composer was not equal. Neurotic and emotionally frail, Tchaikovsky announced that he would not be able to conduct the premiere. Mahler could, and on 19 January 1892 he conducted a splendid performance which prompted the composer to write to his nephew: "The conductor here is not of the usual ilk but a man of genius who would give his life to conduct the premiere."

Mahler's efforts were thus artistically rewarding and financially successful. Pollini was pleased, and Mahler's star shone brighter in the increasing acknowledgment of his genius. In 1892 Mahler also paid his musical respects to his old friend and mentor Anton Bruckner by performing his *Te Deum* to great acclaim. Yet it was still only Mahler the conductor who had come to the fore, not Mahler the composer. Wrote Bülow, who had harsh words for Mahler's music:

> Hamburg has now acquired a simply first-rate conductor in Herrn Gustav Mahler (serious, energetic Jew from Budapest), who, in my opinion, equals the very best conductors (Mottl, Richter, etc.). Recently I heard *Siegfried* under his direction. . . . sincere admiration for him filled me when without an orchestral rehearsal he compelled the musical rabble to whistle according to his dance.

Brahms also continued to dispose of Mahler's music, as opposed to his interpretations, with a mental wave of the hand—this in the face of performances of Mahler's First Symphony in Budapest as well as Hamburg. Brahms and Bülow were not alone in their appraisal. The romantic air which pervades the Mahler First left critics and public alike groping for meaning and explanation. Somehow the romanticism of Mahler's song cycle *Des Knaben Wunderhorn,* which provided so much material for the symphony, did nothing to enlighten listeners or critics. Undismayed, Mahler, determined to give Hamburg his best, carried on. And Hamburg, the old and respected Hanseatic city whose opera commanded respect and whose premieres were covered by Berlin's leading critics, demanded no less. Times had changed from the days when Brahms had aspired to the position of conductor of the Hamburg orchestra only to be rebuffed. If Hamburg now constituted an important musical center, it was primarily due to the efforts of Pollini, *né* Bernhard Pohl, of Cologne. Before arriving in Hamburg he had managed Italian opera in Moscow and St. Petersburg; he was thus well qualified when in 1873 he invested his Russian savings in the Hamburg *Stadttheater*. He soon branched out into other theaters as well as beyond the Italian repertoire. After presenting *Aida* in 1876 he ventured into the German repertoire with Wagner's *Ring* in 1878 and into French opera with *Carmen* in 1880, before returning to the Italians with a German "first," Verdi's *Othello*. These artistic efforts during his eighteen-year tenure had raised Hamburg's artistic importance to a position of respect in musical Germany; and the artistic and ensuing financial accamplishment engendered local satisfaction as well. What was particularly appreciated was Pollini's constant striving for modernization in the theater—including the introduction of electricity! It thus provided a measure of satisfaction for Mahler to become associated with a highly respected German operatic institution, replete with first-rate singers and a first-rate orchestra.

He was, nonetheless, to be disappointed. Upon his arrival in 1891 he was to find out that the revolutionary spirit of Wagner and Bayreuth no longer found an echo on the Hamburg stage. Conditions were nearly a carbon copy of Budapest; vocal virtuosity was what the public came to hear, and since it made the house profitable, it was featured. Mahler also soon realized that little cooperation could be expected from Pollini in finding a way out of the prevailing artistic morass.

Surprisingly, and almost against his better judgment, Pollini did not impede Mahler's attempts at emotional realism, vocally as well as instrumentally, although he did not cease to look upon Mahler as an eccentric talent. But if it made money, it was all right with Pollini. (Mahler meanwhile found solace in the creation of his Second [*Resurrection*] Symphony.) Equally surprising was that Pollini proved unselfish with respect to the use of Mahler's services. He proudly recommended his chief conductor to Sir Augustus Harris, impresario of Covent Garden, praising him unstintingly as the most important conductor of his day. Sir Augustus quickly responded by engaging Mahler for an entire season of German opera in London. In order to ensure success, Mahler brought with him to London a number of the finest voices available as well as a number of Hamburg players, again with the blessing of Pollini. The London papers were unanimous in their praise of Mahler's mastery of the Wagner repertoire. But they had yet underestimated Mahler's sense of excellence, which he was to bring to bear on *Fidelio*. Inconceivable as it may seem today, the Beethoven opera had been heard in London only with Italian text. Mahler restored the original German, supplanted the Italian *recitativo* with the German dialogue, and included the *Leonore No. 3* overture between the first and second acts.[14] London critics were at first apprehensive and later annoyed by Mahler's changes and innovations and minced no words, finding his tempo changes particularly disturbing. The London public, however, fully appreciated the innovations. While critics listened with wrinkled brow and jaundiced eye, the public responded with rhythmic shouts of "Mahler, Mahler" until the conductor appeared before the footlights, sometimes even between the acts.

Mahler's trail was blazing. News of the London applause preceded him back to Hamburg, where during the 1893–94 season he ventured again into the music of his time with Puccini's *Manon Lescaut* and Verdi's *Falstaff*, daring to bring the Verdi opus to Hamburg after its premiere at La Scala in Milan. "My position here is unchallenged, thanks to the out-and-out championship of Brahms and Bülow," wrote Mahler to Fritz Löhr late in 1894.

Although the two men were only superficially acquainted, there now developed an artistic kinship between Mahler and Bülow, with the latter obviously intent on publicly showing his regard for Mahler. On different occasions during concerts, Bülow, seeing Mahler in the audience, would descend from the podium and extend his baton to Mahler, inviting him to conduct. Mahler had the habit of sitting in the front row during concerts; Mahler reports: "From the rostrum he hands down the scores of unknown works to me to follow during the performance. The moment he catches sight of me, he honors me ostentatiously with a deep bow. Sometimes he talks to me from the podium." But the perverse situation remained. After leafing through a Mahler score he still pontificated: "If this is still music, then I know nothing of music." Thus the person as well as the opinion of the mighty Bülow was at once a stimulant and a deterrent to Mahler's creative instincts until Bülow's death in Cairo in 1894.[15]

It was in Hamburg that Mahler began a life-long friendship with Bruno Walter, although a difference of sixteen years in age separated the two. When Walter presented his letter of introduction to Pollini he saw Mahler for the first time; "lean, fidgety; a short man with an unusually high forehead, long dark hair, [and] deeply penetrating bespectacled eyes." Mahler, in turn, eyed the eighteen-year-old new man piercingly, questioningly.

"So you are the new coach? Do you play the piano well?"
"Excellently."
"Can you read well at sight?"

[14] Only later, in his Vienna production, was Mahler to change the position of the overture to its logical place before the last scene of the second act.

[15] Blaukopf propounds an intriguing theorem concerning the effect of Bülow's death on Mahler's psyche: "Bülow's death removed at one stroke all the obstacles that had blocked the completion of the Second Symphony."

"Oh yes, everything."
"Do you know the regular repertoire operas?"
"I know them all quite well."
(Mahler laughed and patted young Walter on the back.)
"Well, that sounds promising."

Walter, *Theme and Variations*

Walter was to prove himself soon. Mahler was then rehearsing Humperdinck's opera *Hänsel und Gretel,* which was very much in vogue. Mahler was not fully convinced of its merits but was impressed enough to stage it. (It was "fashioned in a masterly manner but not really in the manner of a fairytale," he wrote.) Mahler was being kind. Hanslick, after the opera performance in Vienna on 18 December 1894, expressed himself in *Music Criticisms,* in stronger terms:

> The aesthetically acute are made uncomfortable when an overartificial, pompous orchestra illustrates the scolding of the mother, or when music directly descended from the *Ring* accompanies the children while they pick strawberries. . . . Humperdinck's personality is completely submerged in Wagner. . . . He not only composes after Wagner's method; his score swarms with reminiscences from *The Ring* and *Die Meistersinger.* . . . What he offers from his own means as an inventor of melodies is insignificant and cheaply sentimental.

During a routine rehearsal of *Hänsel und Gretel,* Mahler was greatly annoyed by the inadequacy of the piano accompanist. Suddenly he saw Walter. "Would you trust yourself to play an opera you don't know?" he asked him. When Walter said he would, Mahler dismissed the luckless accompanist with a wave of the hand and motioned Walter to the piano. Another episode illuminates Walter's early ability. Mahler put him in charge of chorus rehearsals without knowing that Walter had no experience in chorus work. Nonetheless Walter rehearsed the chorus in *Lohengrin.* When Pollini later inquired as to Walter's ability, a chorus member opined: "He's got a lot of experience."

At piano rehearsals Mahler impressed with his imaginative, deeply penetrating insight. At orchestra rehearsals he was, writes Walter, "stimulating, intimidating, fascinating, tyrannical, demanding utmost effort from all, soloists, chorus, orchestras, himself." The roster of singers which Mahler had inherited included such outstanding voices as Ernestine Schumann-Heinck, Bertha Förster-Lauterer, tenor Max Alvary, and bass Wilhelm Hesch; all, already excellent, became outstanding under Mahler's direction. Bülow's sentiments when watching Mahler turned to admiration. His tribute to Mahler, ever preserved by him, was inscribed on the ribbon of a wreath Bülow had sent him: "To the Pygmalion of the Hamburg Opera."

The relationship between Mahler and Walter soon blossomed into a much more personal one, although Mahler, at that time, was almost twice as old as Walter. Mahler sensed a kindred spirit in Walter and was not afraid to discuss Schopenhauer and Nietzsche as well as his own plans and compositions with the much younger man, or to play Schubert with him, four-handed on the piano. Walter, in turn became Mahler's disciple and apostle.

> I felt as if a higher realm had opened up to me—Mahler, in looks and behaviour, struck me as a genius, a demon; life itself had suddenly become romantic. I cannot better describe the elemental power of Mahler's personality than by saying that its irresistible effect on a young musician was to produce in him . . . an entirely new attitude to life.

By then several matters had begun to annoy Mahler and try his patience (a virtue which he had never, in any case, possessed in abundant measure): viz., signs of antagonistic treatment by Pollini, and the inability to have his own music performed. In order to overcome the second obstacle, Mahler now began to gravitate towards one of Germany's focal points—Berlin. Friends as well as professionals helped to make this possible. Money was made available to him, and the same concert impresario who managed the artistic affairs of Bülow and Richard Strauss made himself available to Mahler. Mahler was determined to gamble his future as a composer on a Berlin concert. The Berlin Philharmonic was engaged along with the Berlin *Singakademie* for a performance of his Second Symphony, with Mahler conducting. It turned out to be a decisive event, perhaps the decisive event—the breakthrough—for Mahler the composer. Although subsequent critics expressed themselves disapprovingly, the audience sat breathlessly mesmerized, particularly upon hearing the emotional, touching mystery of the final movement.

At that time Mahler was much more affected by adverse criticism than he would be in later years; extreme tension would also have deleterious effects. The anticipation of that Berlin performance created such tension, which could be alleviated only by total seclusion. Despite extensive rest during the afternoon before the concert, it was only through sheer exertion of total will power that he was able to conduct and provide a masterly reading of the work. Next to Mahler it was Walter who was most deeply affected. More than any other event that performance made him a Mahler disciple.

The dam had burst: Mahler, the composer, had arrived. The Berlin concert was followed by another in March 1896, again devoted entirely to his music, and including the first movement of his Second Symphony, *Lieder eines fahrenden Gesellen,* and his entire First Symphony. Dresden and Leipzig clamored for performances, and one of the foremost young conductors, Felix Weingartner, requested Mahler's scores for performance.

Help also came from another source. If the first performance of his

First Symphony in Budapest and the succeeding one in Hamburg had met with antagonism or raised eyebrows, the next performance drew world attention because the conductor was Richard Strauss. Strauss also offered Mahler's Second Symphony, with qualifications: he wanted to do only the first three, orchestral movements, not the two final, vocal parts. Mahler, eager for performance, compromised but was beset by doubts. To ensure that all of the pertinent dynamic instructions were indicated to enable Strauss to perform the three movements in the spirit he intended, Mahler prepared a two-piano arrangement and later conducted a rehearsal performance by his Hamburg orchestra. While he was conducting an assistant stood behind him, marking into a score every comment Mahler made while playing the work.

It was a far cry from the scores of baroque composers, which sometimes did not even indicate what instruments were to play a specific part, let alone the simplest dynamics information. Mahler at no time left anything to chance where instrumentation or dynamics were concerned. If he wished for continued strength without ebbing he would exhort the players, in the score, with the words *"Immer wuchtig"* [always powerful]; to ensure a brilliant trumpet sound in a finale or in a march melody, he would admonish there *"Schalltrichter in the Höhe"* [bells raised]. When the opposite effect was to be achieved he would note *"Beinahe unhörbar eintreten"* [enter almost inaudibly]. On other occasions he would admonish: "[The soloist] must be accompanied so discreetly that the singer may be heard without effort" (Fourth Symphony) or "Under no circumstances may a particular [extremely low] bass passage be played an octave higher than written." Surprisingly, it was Mahler who conducted three movements in the actual performance. He apparently was satisfied and grateful to have found "such a friend and comrade-in-arms" in Richard Strauss.

Although he was four years Mahler's junior, Richard Strauss, at age thirty, had already attained a status in the musical world above that of Mahler. Strauss at that time could already point to such achievements as his symphonic poems *Don Juan, Macbeth,* and *Tod und Verklärung,* the symphony *Aus Italien,* and his first opera, *Guntram.* Mahler appreciated Strauss's interest, and over the years a love–hate relationship developed between the more realistic, materialistic Strauss and the philosopher–idealist Mahler. Strauss, at that time, was still interested in contemporary music and gave Mahler's First Symphony a rousing performance. The title of *Titan,* which Mahler had originally given the work and later abandoned, was reinstated, presumably by Strauss, thus giving the work a quasi-programmatic aspect which Mahler no longer wished it to have.

It was a peculiar bond which attracted the two men to each other. Strauss, an orchestral colorist of incredible invention who was nonetheless superficial in thought and materialistic in spirit, may have approached Mahler's creations with a certain condescension. Yet Mahler's preoccupation with matters of philosophy, cosmos, and conscience was forever beyond Strauss's comprehension. Mahler was often repulsed by the narrowness of Strauss's mind and means, but he never failed to acknowledge the incredibly luminous palette of the younger master; the difference between them was that Strauss's immense apparatus for sound was devoted to theatricality, whereas Mahler's massed sounds were an expression of innately felt drama.[16] The comparatively early death of Mahler robs us of a definite means of comparison, but all signs pointed to the two men going in diametrically opposite directions musically. Strauss, whose musical spirit had always progressed with a backward glance at the nineteenth century, was destined to find himself no longer an expression of his own time but an echo of times past, a mere monument to the man who, fifty years earlier, had been considered exciting and avant-garde. Mahler, on the other hand, never ceased to grow and grope and strive for new means to express in music the complex web of his mind and thus became the monumental crossroads figure which the world now acknowledges. It was not long before Mahler rivaled Strauss in importance, and he soon became the more controversial and discussed composer. If the symphonic poems of Strauss's younger days had aroused discussion, their importance in the musical world yielded in the face of heated discussions on the merits of Mahler's creations.

In 1895 Mahler's family affairs had become settled to the point where he could be joined in Hamburg by his sister Justine, who took over the running of her brother's household. With his life again more ordered, his mind was turning to intensified composition when things suddenly began to go awry in Hamburg. The other conductor, Otto Lohse, left abruptly for America, lured by a more lucrative contract than Hamburg could afford. He took with him his wife, Katharina Klafski, who happened to be one of the foremost Wagner interpreters in Hamburg. With the ubiquitous Mahler around, Pollini was concerned only about a voice replacement for his Wagnerian singer. Without even the courtesy of a consultation he shouldered Mahler with the additional conducting chores, and Mahler found himself conducting literally every night.

In his search for a replacement for his departed Wagnerian soprano, Pollini turned to a once famous contralto who was now an equally famous voice teacher in Vienna—Rosa Papier, the same woman who had been the star singer ten years earlier when Mahler had performed the miracle of the music festival in Kassel. Frau Papier again came to the rescue and recommended to Pollini a then somewhat insignificant looking twenty-

---

[16] Strauss once scraped a fork across a dinner plate, making the familiar screeching sound, then looked at Pfitzner and challenged: "Can you duplicate this sound in music?" Pfitzner looked stupefied and Strauss laughed. "I can!" When Strauss, as a child, attended his first concert, he replied to the question "What did you like best at the concert?" with "The tuning before the concert began."

two-year-old girl, Anna von Mildenburg, who was then under contract with the Leipzig opera but was persuaded by her mentor to audition for Pollini. He, in turn, was so impressed that he made a deal by telephone with Leipzig and engaged Anna on the spot. His only objection was to her figure. Realizing that Wagnerian singers need energy, power, and weight, he asked Rosa Papier to relate this message: "She must put on weight." But Anna von Mildenburg (who was to marry the famed Viennese writer Hermann Bahr in 1909) was not concerned with Pollini; her fears were of Mahler—or, at least, of the implacable tyrant that some had described to her. But the first rehearsal with the chief conductor was destined to be a comfort as well as a revelation to the young, apprehensive singer. "Mahler's manner," she wrote,

> gave me a confidence that freed me from all my doubts and anxieties. A boundless sense of security came over me in that first hour of being with him. . . . There was this man speaking to me with true kindness—the very man I had most cause to fear, the chief conductor.

As Anna von Mildenburg grew artistically under Mahler's guidance and tutelage, so her relationship with him grew, artistically as well as personally. On the one hand, Gustav and Anna were lovers; they became an "item" and there were rumors that they were engaged. Yet such aspects pale into insignificance beside the artistic relationship between Anna and Gustav. Mahler's trust and confidence in her were without bounds. And if in the beginning he had encouraged her on her operatic path, she now seemed to have instilled in him a new confidence and a desire for composition, performance, and recognition.

Having attained a measure of financial security, mainly owing to the Budapest settlement, Mahler had begun to spend his summers in attractive Austrian vacation resorts. For a while the spa of Ischl in the Salzkammergut had attracted him. The emperor had a villa there, as did Johann Strauss and Brahms, and, to quote Brahms, "In the summer all of Vienna was there." Mahler visited Brahms repeatedly and was shaken by the sick old master's somber mood, which, Mahler felt, was deeply expressed in his *Vier Ernste Gesänge*. Those songs had been prompted by the death of Clara Schumann, whom Brahms had once loved and who had always remained his closest friend and confidante. One day, after taking leave of the old master, Mahler turned around at the door and saw him take some sausage and bread from an iron stove. The chilling contrast between Brahms's fame and the frugality of his life made an indelible impression upon Mahler.

Later it was either the magnificent Carynthian lakes and mountain vistas or the Salzkammergut's overwhelming alpine scenery which invigorated Mahler physically and inspired him musically. His reflections on beauty, death, and immortality were stimulated in such majestically imposing surroundings as the Alps, which had such an aura of starkness that the local population dubbed some of its peaks *Totengebirge* ("mountains of death") and *Höllengebirge* ("mountains of hell"). Mahler, aside from being mentally stimulated by these sights, also felt physically inspired while walking and climbing among the peaks. This was the physical and artistic context in which Mahler created his Third Symphony. In its strange statements Mahler reflects on nature, immortality, and man's final station, in what amounts to one of his strongest, most positive symphonic creations.

How strongly the alpine summer surroundings influenced Mahler's musical vision can be gleaned from Mahler's welcoming words to Bruno Walter, whom he had asked to join him at his summer domicile. As Walter let his eyes wander over the forbidding alpine peaks, Mahler remarked, smiling: "You needn't bother to look at that—I've composed it all away." Wherever Mahler spent the summer he satisfied his need for creative isolation in one of two ways: either by retiring early in the morning to the "composer's cottage" which he usually had built or by taking brisk walks alone for hours through the alpine landscape which he loved. Upon his return to the cottage, isolation again became imperative and its observance was demanded of all, unless otherwise invited. (Later, Mahler's wife, Alma, like Walter a "sounding board" whose opinion he respected, would be invited to join him to hear a new work.) During such periods of creation, even Anna von Mildenburg's presence, despite Mahler's deep feelings for her, was undesirable. His reply to an apparent letter of complaint from her is indicative of the man and his relationship to his work:

I have already told you that I am at work on a great composition [the Third Symphony]. Can't you understand how that takes up all of a man?

Sister Justine was likewise completely excluded from Mahler's world of creation. There was a peculiar bond with his sister, however, a bond of protectiveness which made the relationship seem like a kind of spiritual marriage. Whatever Justine's attributes may have been, there can be no doubt that Gustav intuitively received understanding from her, although mentally and spiritually she never was or was considered by Mahler to be his equal; Alma was the only woman whom he was to consider on the same intellectual level as himself.

In the "composer's cottage," Mahler now opened to Walter that world which he had closed to Anna. If in the early months of their acquaintanceship Mahler had introduced Walter to Nietzsche and Schopenhauer, he now introduced him to Mahler.

I was overwhelmed by the sense his playing conveyed, of the fire and rapture in which the work was conceived. Only now, through his music, did I really understand him; his entire being seemed to breathe a mysterious rapport with nature. I had faintly sensed the elemental intensity of this before, while now I experienced it directly through the sound language of his symphonic world dream.

Walter, *Theme and Variations*

Mahler was still speaking then in terms of the symphony, but how many worlds apart was he from Haydn's world of symphonic creation—from the bewigged, liveried servant of Prince Esterhazy, whose graceful entertainment in four contrasting movements lasted about twenty minutes. Here again we glean the gigantic accomplishment of Beethoven and the *Eroica*. The symphonic world changed with him and it. Just as his work, and that of Berlioz, Bruckner, and Brahms after him, expanded the length as well as the vistas of symphonic vision, so Mahler again vastly expanded the world of symphonic creation.

By then Mahler was subconsciously at a crossroads. While maturing away from the medieval romanticism of his younger years, so dear to him then that it filled not only his music but his very life, he still clutched to it in an almost desperate attempt to prevent its slippage from his grasp. But death and doom began to assert their importance in his thinking, and in his musical thoughts romantic excitement gave way to a feverish discourse which some commentators ascribe to Mahler's Semitic background. Torah and Talmud study and discourse were part of the life of the European Orthodox Jew, who took delight in them and derived consolation from them. To ascribe Mahler's philosophical changes to such a background would be a dubious oversimplification in his case, however. Mahler's intricate personality was then in transition. While clinging to a medieval romanticism, it searched for a more individualistic, personal expression, and that search and the expression that came out of it were in no way anchored in or related to his Jewish background. It was in that phase of development that Mahler, despite his unwavering admiration for Wagner, began to develop into a third force, disengaged from and uninfluenced by Wagner's course—veering away from established tonality on the one hand as well as from Brahms's neoclassic anti-Wagnerian tendencies and Bruckner's baroque visions. It was that subconscious, unplanned, but irrevocable development as a third force, leading into the twentieth century, which made Mahler the most influential musical innovator of his time.

Conductorially he was to arrive at a crossroads at the same time. The direction was clear: home. Vienna.

# Vienna (*Fin de Siècle*, 1897–1900)

## THE JEWISH PRESENCE

MAHLER HAD GIVEN HIS FAREWELL PERFORMANCE in Hamburg of *Fidelio* on 24 April 1897 and had taken two momentous steps. He had accepted a position at the Imperial Opera in Vienna, and he had left the faith of his fathers and converted to Catholicism.

The problem of Mahler's Jewish origin followed him most everywhere, in part because certain basics could not be wished or converted away. Although he had embraced Catholicism, his Semitic characteristics, especially his emotional speech and motions (he repeatedly asked his wife, Alma, to stop him when he emphasized his speech with too much gesticulation), were obvious and unmistakable.

Conversion gave rise to misunderstanding and misinterpretation. Some, like Gabriel Engel, accused Mahler of opportunism; Ernst Křenek, on the other hand, convincingly argues that Mahler's conversion was an outgrowth of his philosophical outlook. In fact, both philosophical and artistic factors may account for Mahler's conversion. Mahler was a Jew by background and birth but not by conviction. He found religious practice and observance—"organized" religion—meaningless and unfulfilling; but Catholic mysticism (a Bruckner influence) had always intrigued him and appealed to his artistic nature. The mysterious silence of Europe's cathedrals, of their dark naves and candled altars, broken only by the gentle rise and fall of Gregorian chant or the splendor of a Bach Chorale, exuded a magic from which Mahler did not wish to extricate himself.

Despite his European eminence, Mahler had been aware of the unwritten law of the Habsburg Court, which forbade that any non-Catholic hold an official position of importance. There can be no doubt that at that stage in Mahler's life and career, his gaining a position in the ranking opera house in Europe represented an artistic apex. Such an achievement

—and the opportunities for artistic fulfillment it represented—meant everything to Mahler; whereas a formal change in religion meant nothing.

Had Mahler not been driven by artistic ambition, had he retained a spark of ancestral feeling for Judaism, he could have felt comfortable in Vienna, since the Jewish presence there was prominent in many aspects. By simply looking about him in the Vienna to which he had returned, Mahler would have discovered a galaxy of Jewish brilliance. Vienna's foremost newspapers, *Die Neue Freie Presse* and *Das Wiener Tagblatt,* were then espousing astoundingly liberal views under the leadership, respectively, of Moritz Benedikt and Moriz Szeps. Eduard Hanslick, the eminent music critic, was Jewish (though he was reared as, and remained, a Catholic), as was the man to follow him as music critic of the *Neue Freie Presse,* Julius Korngold (father of composer Erich Wolfgang Korngold). So was the foremost music historian of the time, Max Graf, and the concertmaster of the Vienna Philharmonic, Arnold Rosé, Mahler's future brother-in-law. Mahler's close friend, the musicologist Guido Adler, belonged to the same faith, as did Arnold Schönberg. Also of Jewish parentage was the builder of Austria's Social Democratic Party, Dr. Victor Adler. Adler, however, had turned to Protestantism and even went so far as to make anti-Semitic statements. Schönberg also turned away from Judaism and became a Catholic; but in the hour of mortal danger to the Jews under Hitler, he returned to the Jewish faith.

The Jewish literary/philosophical presence in Vienna was no less illustrious. Hugo von Hofmannsthal mixed blue blood with Jewish blood. Peter Altenberg wedded Viennese charm with poetic genius in gently erotic poetry. Arthur Schnitzler, the most magnificently eloquent writer on the negative aspects of Mahler's Vienna, was Jewish, as was the brilliant psychological biographer, Stefan Zweig. Karl Kraus, the formidable satirist, illumined, through the lashing review *Die Fackel* [The torch], all that was deplorable and corrupt in that era of Austria's "Merry Apocalypse." With his superb command of language, Kraus approached in his writings the philosophical depth of yet another brilliant Jewish Viennese, Ludwig Wittgenstein.

In a related literary field, the actor and director Adolph Sonnenthal was instrumental in making the *Burgtheater* (Court Theater) the foremost stage in the German-speaking world. Karl Goldmark and Ignatz Brüll, both close friends of Brahms, wrote operas which were successfully performed throughout Europe. Alfred Grünfeld, the pianist, played up a storm of Viennese charm. Of him Johann Strauss said: "He plays my waltzes more beautifully than I write them."

Aside from these variegated manifestations of the Jewish presence in the city, had Mahler's Jewish instincts not become numbed by indifference and near disdain, he would surely have been stirred by the art and accomplishment of a man who had died only seven years before his arrival in Vienna and whose memory and work were still fresh—Salomon Sulzer (1804–90). Sulzer's life had spanned the century. Possessed of a splendid tenor voice while still in young manhood, he had sung Schubert songs to Schubert, had later been made an honorary citizen of Vienna (a rare distinction for a Jew in his day), had been given medals by the emperor of Austria, the tsar of Russia, and the sultan of Turkey, and had become professor at the famed Vienna Conservatory and an honorary member of the Academy of Arts in Rome.

Young Sulzer had been a *chazzan* (cantor) at the main synagogue of Vienna, where the eminent Rabbi Noah Mannheimer, a leader in Reform Judaism, then officiated. When the rabbi and his cantor attempted to superimpose the service and liturgy of Reform Judaism on the Vienna Jewish community, steeped in the melodic orthodoxy of eastern Europe, they encountered vociferous resistance. Thereupon Rabbi Mannheimer ceremonially, and Cantor Sulzer melodically, decided to seek a middle ground between Orthodoxy and Reform by adopting what they considered to be the noblest features of the two Jewish worlds. German was introduced into the service side by side with Hebrew, the sermon was incorporated, and the ministerial robe made its appearance. The major achievement, however, was wrought by the inspired precentor, Salomon Sulzer. In the excitement which had accompanied the attempted change in liturgy, Sulzer promulgated a theory which was to have far-reaching implications:

> It behooves us to resist a total break with the past and the abolishing of all traditional and inherited liturgy. . . . the [present] confusion of the synagogue service needs only a reform on historical ground. . . . Jewish liturgy must satisfy the musical demand while remaining Jewish, and it should not be necessary to sacrifice Jewish characteristics to artistic forms. . . . The old melodies and singing modes which became national [heritage] should be improved . . . and adjusted to the rules of art.
>
> Sulzer's *Shir Zion* [Song of Zion] (1838)

It soon became apparent that Sulzer's inspired "improvements" were much more than that. Since he was also a tenor of renown and deeply steeped in Jewish traditional chant, he proceeded to fashion an entirely new Jewish synagogue chant and liturgy. The achievements of Sulzer were so monumental that their religious and melodic reverberations were eventually felt even in Reform Judaism, and their inspiration traveled from Vienna across the Old World and the New. Aided by his musical knowledge, his reverence for Jewish tradition, and the inescapable influence of the Catholic liturgy in Vienna, Sulzer fashioned liturgical gems reflecting an inspired blending of Jewish musical heritage and the music of the nineteenth century. "Thus," as I have written elsewhere,[1] "the unique art of Sulzer created in Vienna a synagogue chant which, although innately Jewish, remained inscrutably oriental to the gentile while carrying distinctly modern overtones to the Jew." Liszt was profoundly stirred upon listening to Sulzer:

> In Vienna we knew the famous tenor Sulzer, who served in the capacity of cantor in the synagogue, and whose reputation was so outstanding. . . . We went to the synagogue to hear him. . . . Occasionally we could penetrate into the real soul and recognize the secret doctrines of the fathers. Seldom were we so deeply stirred by emotion as on that evening, so shaken that our soul was entirely given to meditation and to participation in the service.
>
> Liszt, *Gesammelte Schriften* [Collected writings], vol. VI:
> *Die Zigeuner* [The gypsies] (1859)

Mahler, so sensitive to emotion, was either unaware of or uninterested in Sulzer's achievement, a deplorable blind spot due to Mahler's lack of interest in matters Jewish. That failing was doubly regrettable since both Mahler and Sulzer had been strongly influenced by Catholic liturgy and mysticism as they could be experienced in the innumerable churches of Vienna, most of which boasted excellent choirs and organists.

It was in Mahler's Vienna that the Utopian dream, destined to become reality, of Theodor Herzl's *Der Judenstaat* [The Jewish state] first took shape, and that Sigmund Freud began his probings into the unconscious. This account of the Jewish presence in Mahler's Vienna (at the end of the nineteenth century and the beginning of the twentieth) leaves untouched the most obvious and potent aspect of the Jewish community's presence, the world of finance and industry, which is beyond the province of this discussion.

Yet the Vienna which Mahler entered with a sense of anticipation was one in which the covert anti-Semitism of Mayor Dr. Karl Lueger and the overt anti-Semitism of Georg von Schönerer had made anti-Jewish feelings a part of the Viennese psyche. It was a city whose conservative, cynical sentiments and instincts, verging on the reactionary, were exemplified by Johann Nestroy, who said in one of his comedies: "I believe the worst in everyone . . . and I have seldom been wrong." (Half a century after Nestroy, Schnitzler describes its citizens in these words: "Here with us, indignation is as little genuine as enthusiasm; only pleasure at the misfortunes of others and hatred of talent are genuinely felt here.") It was a city proud of its baroque palaces and Gothic churches, which dreamed fearfully and fitfully of its glorious past in order to escape a present which threatened to become dreary; and it was a city

---

[1] Egon Gartenberg, *Vienna: Its Musical Heritage* (Pennsylvania State University Press, 1968).

which nightly danced with abandon to Johann Strauss's music while it allowed a planless, aimless, political, administrative, and diplomatic bureaucracy to muddle along in day-to-day indecision and stopgap policies.

But Vienna changed abruptly where artistic matters were involved. Then rigidly high standards were observed, because such had been the history and tradition of Vienna. By adherence to that tradition, Vienna had joined the great cities of the Renaissance—Venice, Florence, Rome—not only in attracting artists to its courts and institutions, but in conferring importance on them and raising them to greatness. Thus, Gluck, Mozart, Beethoven, Brahms, Bruckner, Goldmark, and Mahler were destined to create their finest works in Vienna. The upholding of such standards was taken to be the responsibility of the entire city. Not only the artists and the professional critics but an artistically aware citizenry exacted them. A poor performance, slovenly acting, a missed cue, or a spectacularly high note or long trill became food not only for professional comment but also for avid conversation, discussion, and debate in the coffeehouses and salons of Vienna. Nothing was overlooked; no deviation tolerated. Those were the standards to which all, actors, singers, players, and conductors, were forced to adhere or else vanish from the Vienna scene.

The collective perpetuation of these standards reflected a total change in the artistic history of the city over the previous century, a change that had brought the Jewish presence in Vienna to the fore.

> The nobility (as well as the emperor) . . . had relinquished its erstwhile protector's role; gone were the glorious days when the Esterhazys harbored a Haydn, the Lobkowitzes and the Kinskeys and Waldsteins competed to have a premiere of Beethoven in their palaces. . . . Now Wagner, Brahms, or Hugo Wolf had not received the slightest support from them. To maintain the Philharmonic on its accustomed level, to enable the painters and sculptors to make a living, it was necessary for the people to jump into the breach, and it was the pride and ambition of the Jewish people to cooperate in the front ranks to carry on the former glory of the fame of Viennese culture. They had always loved this city and had entered into its life wholeheartedly, but it was first of all by their love for Viennese art that they felt entitled to full citizenship, and that they had actually become true Viennese.
>
> Stefan Zweig, *The World of Yesterday* (1943)

With their liberation from ghetto bondage, both Austrian and German Jews had become deeply and enthusiastically imbued with the national spirit of their respective countries, in part to prove their patriotism. (The arch-German first name of "Siegfried" was given to so many German and Austrian Jewish youths that it eventually became a "Jewish" first name.) Jewish admiration for German achievements, especially German literature and music, knew no bounds. Mahler, too, had been swept up in that tide. He had been raised in such a milieu. The city of Iglau had been a German island within Moravian territory. Thus Bach, Beethoven, Goethe, and Wagner became his life-long heroes. While his illustrious contemporary, Richard Strauss, fully recognized the literary brilliance of the Jewish presence in Vienna and chose both Hofmannsthal and Zweig as his librettists, Mahler was oblivious of that presence. The dislike, or at least lack of interest, apparently was mutual, for on 26 July 1928 Hofmannsthal wrote to Richard Strauss:

> I am open to all that is creative and have always, even amid the clamor of enthusiasts and sycophants, refused to countenance what is heterogeneous, hybrid, and vague aspiration rather than solid achievement, as in Gustav Mahler's music, for instance.

But let it be said to Mahler's credit that of three Austrian Jews who, each in his own way, changed the world—Freud, Herzl, and Schönberg—Mahler knew Freud from correspondence and conversation and counted Schönberg among his close friends. In viewing these friendships and others, such as that of Guido Adler, we should not lose sight of the fact that with Mahler the friend's Jewishness had no bearing on acquaintanceship or friendship. Faith was incidental and of no consequence. It was solely the brilliant intellect of these men which attracted Mahler to them.

## THE VIENNA OPERA

The Vienna Court Opera was ailing and so was its director, the able Wilhelm Jahn; trouble was brewing. Troubles and crises in an opera house—from scenery to scenario, from prima donna to superintendent—are, of course, commonplace, and the Vienna Opera was no exception.

Opera had deeply embedded roots in Vienna. Baroque opera had found its first proud home outside Italy in that city, and Vienna had witnessed splendid performances; that of Cesti's *Il Pomo d'Oro* outshone anything produced in opera anywhere at that time.

Already during the period of Viennese classicism, the *Theater an der Wien* had made operatic history. Mozart's *Zauberflöte,* in 1791, and Beethoven's *Fidelio,* in 1805, were given their first performances there. Another theater, the *Kärnthnerthor Theater,* could point to an even older history, having produced the comic opera *Der krumme Teufel* [The crooked devil], by a twenty-year-old unknown by the name of Joseph Haydn, in 1752, and the opera *Die Zwillingsbrüder* [The twin brothers], by an equally unknown twenty-three-year-old, Franz Schubert, in 1820. The artistic encouragement of the Habsburgs, whether in the time of medieval Maximilian I or during the reign of Emperor Franz Joseph in the nineteenth century, rarely flagged. It brought to Vienna poets and librettists—Metastasio, Calzabigi, and Lorenzo da Ponte, all from Italy—and composers—Cesti, Draghi, and Porpora from Italy; Beethoven and Brahms from Germany; Gluck and Mahler from Bohemia; Goldmark from Hungary.

The artistic heritage of the emperors of the Vienna Baroque, when every member of the Habsburg household, from page to emperor, was obliged to either sing, play an instrument, dance, compose, or act, bore proud fruit by the beginning of the nineteenth century. The historic *Kärnthnerthor Theater* had essentially established itself as the imperial theater devoted exclusively to opera, and it remained in that capacity for five decades. The name of the house, "Theater by the Kärnthner Portal," precisely reflected its location close to the massive walls of the medieval city, which had withstood the Turkish sieges and thus kept Europe Christian.[2] Although Napoleon's guns proved the walls useless (Beethoven fled to the cellar of a friend, covering his sensitive ears with a pillow during the bombardment), the walls remained, serving mainly as a vantage point from which the promenading Viennese could view their bustling city on one side, and beyond the greening countryside, extending on the horizon onto the vineyards dotting the last alpine foothills descending to the Danube, on the other. Internal political reasons also protected the no-longer-protecting walls from destruction, but empirical, financial, and commercial interests continued to press for their removal. On 20 December 1857, by order of the "Christmas Decree" of Emperor Franz Joseph, the still towering, moss-grown bastions were assigned to the wrecker's axe as the maudlin Viennese watched in tearful sentimentality, while Johann Strauss composed his *Demolition Polka* to commemorate the occasion.[3]

In the newly acquired space created by the leveled walls—the former moat and the vast space beyond it known as the *glacis*—there arose, in a horseshoe curve three and one-half miles long whose ends rested on the Danube Canal, one of the most magnificent boulevards in the world, the *Ringstrasse,* one of Emperor Franz Joseph's most cherished projects. In a profusion of styles, there arose on the *Ringstrasse* the neo-Grecian Parliament building, the neo-Gothic *Rathaus* (city hall), the Renaissance *Burgtheater* (court theater), the museums flanking the monument of Empress Maria Theresia, the university, the Academy of Fine Arts, the *Börse*

---

[2] Its location was the same as that now occupied by the Hotel Sacher, exactly behind the present opera house.

[3] Remnants of the walls can still be seen. There is the towering *Mölkerbastei* (Mölker bastion), crowned by a Beethoven house, across the *Ringstrasse* (see below) from the main university building, and also the *Burgthor* (now a hero's monument), which, until 1857, was the main entrance, through the walls, to the *Hofburg,* the imperial palace.

(stock exchange), the Ministry of Education, the *Musikvereinssaal*—and the new Imperial Opera House.

Despite its location in the center of the mighty horseshoe, the site selected for the opera house was not the most favorable. Unlike the Parliament, the City Hall, and *Burgtheater,* which were placed within or near vast park spaces, the opera house was promptly hemmed in by commercial and apartment buildings which made it impossible to do full justice to its graceful French Romanesque features. Difficulties with the building and the building site promoted unrelenting criticism (a Viennese specialty) of the two architects, August von Siccardsburg and Eduard Van der Nüll. Despite all such handicaps, the architects labored valiantly on the creation of what was to be one of the loveliest and acoustically finest opera houses in the world.

But the constant critical barrage to which they were subjected—the critics went so far as to discredit their work as "the Waterloo of architecture"—so robbed them of their artistic vitality and physical strength that Van der Nüll committed suicide in April 1868. Siccardsburg, bereft of his artistic partner, in ill health, and broken in spirit, survived him by only two months. Neither of them was privileged to see the magnificent fruits of their artistic collaboration vindicated when the opera house on the *Ringstrasse* was opened on 25 May 1869, twelve years after the razing of the walls. This did not mean the immediate end of the *Kärnthnerthor Theater,* which continued for a number of years to present opera. But although many criticized the new house, fewer and fewer people frequented the old one.

The opening of the new opera house was a musical event of European importance. The emperor occupied the royal box opposite the stage, along with his guest, the King of Hanover, and their two entourages—their ladies in glittering array, their officers in full-dress uniform complete with medals. Empress Elisabeth was not present, although the inauguration date had been set to suit her; she decided to attend a week later. She was accompanied by the emperor and their guest, the viceroy of Egypt; the opera was *La Muette de Portici* by Auber.

As the curtain rose for the first time, the stage resembled the old *Kärnthnerthor Theater,* with Charlotte Wolter, the great tragedienne of the *Burgtheater,* at the footlights. In a prologue written by Franz von Dingelstedt, she extolled Vienna and the new edifice "resplendent with marble and gold," invoked the memory of Siccardsburg and Van der Nüll, and spoke of the unity of Austria's nationalities. The prologue ended, Haydn's *Kaiserlied* (the national anthem) rang out, and to the tumultuous applause of those present the nationalities of Austria entered the stage, carrying their flags and banners and rallying around the allegorical figure of *Vindobona* (Vienna) holding the Austrian banner. The house rose in homage, and the beaming young emperor acknowledged it with bows and waves of the hand in all directions.

Although the opening opera to follow, Mozart's *Don Juan* (Vienna uses the Spanish title instead of the Italian *Don Giovanni*), seemed almost an anticlimax after the jubilation which had preceded it, the artistic success of the opening totally depended on it. Franz von Dingelstedt, the director who had written the prologue, was also in charge of the entire production; he had been named director of the new house just as he had been director of the old one. Surprisingly, Dingelstedt was not a professional musician but rather an unusually successful man of the theater: brilliant, with wide-ranging interests. A somewhat cynical man of the world, he commanded respect in the artistic world and administered his operatic duties with even-handed discipline. In the opening performance he proved his worth. With Johann Nepomuk Beck and **Luise Dustmann** in the roles of Don Juan and Donna Anna, the opera was performed on a high artistic level, with every department, including orchestra and chorus, approaching a star level. Attention to ensemble rather than to individual stars was to become the open secret of the Vienna Opera. Other houses had equally famous or even superior voices at their disposal, but attention to the overall artistic entity, the carefully nurtured balance between soloists, chorus, and orchestra, gave Vienna a surpassing artistic edge.

Of Dingelstedt's three main conductors who had moved with him into the new edifice, Heinrich Proch was the most reliable and experienced, Heinrich Esser the most ceremonial, and **Otto Dessoff** the most energetic and inspiring. But the first two were on the verge of retirement, and competent replacements became a necessity. Dingelstedt's search secured for the Vienna Opera the city's most beloved and most enthusiastic conductor, Johann Herbeck. He had reached a pinnacle of sorts, having conducted practially all of the instrumental and choral ensembles in Vienna; he had been called the "fiery spirit of Viennese music" by the critic Eduard Hanslick. His quest for new music had led him to the old, frustrated composer **Anselm Hüttenbrenner** in Graz. In Hüttenbrenner's dusty coffers he had found the yellowed original manuscript of Schubert's Eighth Symphony in B Minor, the "Unfinished," which received its first performance under Herbeck's baton on 17 December 1865, after having been "lost" for forty-two years.

Herbeck initially came to the Vienna Opera, in the autumn of 1869, as a temporary adviser. But luck was, or appeared to be, with him. A year later Dingelstedt was called upon to change the direction of his artistic endeavors. He moved from the opera to the Court Theater, a logical sphere for him, and Herbeck, practically overnight, became his successor as director of the opera. It was, in the end, to prove an ambiguous triumph.

Herbeck's credentials were impeccable: choral director of the *"Männergesangsverein* (male choral society), choral conductor of the *Gesellschaft der Musikfreunde* (Society of Friends of Music), and conductor of its famed orchestra. His enthusiasm and idealism were unbounded; his zeal and popularity unexcelled. His flowing mane and beard completed the picture of the musical romantic. What could bring about the failure of so excellent a musician? The answer was politics. The little men in high places who had installed him soon began to undermine his position and finally dethroned him. And Herbeck, who could hold musicians, singers, and audiences in thrall, had neither the personality nor the cunning to effectively deal with officials. They, in turn, having perceived his weakness, rallied against him. The more he wished to please them, the more they bent him to their will until they broke him. Richard Wagner, who knew how to deal imperiously with everybody, immediately detected Herbeck's tragic flaw. From then on nothing that that devoted Wagner apostle would do could please the composer. Herbeck prepared *Die Meistersinger* with fervor for its Vienna premiere; Wagner only heaped long-distance insults upon him. Disappointed but undismayed, Herbeck prepared *Rienzi,* one of the gala productions of Vienna and the favorite of the emperor. Wagner attended, summoned Herbeck to his box, and showered devastating criticism on him. Subsequently Wagner administered his crushing blow: when Herbeck expressed the desire to conduct *Tannhäuser, Tristan,* and *Die Walküre* in Vienna he was curtly refused.

On 17 April 1870 the *Kärnthnerthor Theater* finally closed its doors, but not without a final show of deep affection for the house which for fifty years had meant "opera" to Vienna. On a balmy summer night, magically illuminated by a bright moon, Joseph Erl, once the leader of the opera chorus, led a crowd of affectionate opera enthusiasts into the half-demolished house, clambered up onto the still intact stage, and bade Vienna's and his own farewell to the once hallowed walls with a resounding rendition of "Ah Mathilde" from Rossini's *William Tell.*

Despite setbacks and critical wounds, Herbeck still felt that all would work out well, and events seemed to bear him out. The International Exhibition was to be one of the wonders of the time; commerce boomed, the stock market soared, and expectations were great. Herbeck's production of the opera *Hamlet* by Ambroise Thomas was praised, and Weber's *Oberon* was acclaimed as the supreme production of the season. Then financial disaster struck Austria. Herbeck was not to be the only artistic victim of the financial collapse; Vienna's operettic pearl, *Die Fledermaus* by Johann Strauss, although thunderously acclaimed, closed after sixteen performances. People who suddenly had barely enough money for tomorrow's meal had no money for the theater. Herbeck, ever the impractical enthusiast and romantic, could not cope with the deteriorating situation. Officialdom, ignoring Austria's financial dilemma, blamed him for the diminishing attendance. Herbeck still remained artistically undismayed. Robert Schumann's *Genoveva* and Gluck's two *Iphigenia* operas appeared under his aegis, but the dam would not hold and a thunderous torrent of criticism descended upon him. Herbeck, still clinging to his ideals, ignored reality. Suddenly he thought he had a trump card in Vienna's traditional love for Italian music. What could be more impressive than that new opera by none other than Verdi. Thus on 29 April 1874, Vienna witnessed *Aida*. Despite the precarious financial situation, the sum of 60,000 gulden had been lavished on it, and Vienna's finest singers were cast under the baton of the redoubtable Otto Dessoff. But Vienna masochistically rejected it and, through it, Herbeck. Nothing he undertook could please any longer. *Der Widerspensigen Zähmung* [The taming of the shrew] by Hermann Götz, delightful but too advanced, did not please. *Die Königin von Saba* [The queen of Sheba] by Karl Goldmark, destined to become one of the most successful operas in the Vienna repertoire, was acclaimed, but by then Herbeck's reputation had sunk so low that it occurred to nobody to credit him with the success. He had overstayed his welcome. Too late, he decided to leave. Broken in spirit, he lingered on for two and a half years before his untimely death at the age of forty-six.

The pendulum now swung to the opposite extreme. The poet, the idealist, was replaced by the realist; the visionary musician by the hard-eyed businessman. Franz Jauner was no novice to the theater. When he assumed the position of operatic director in May 1875, he could point with satisfaction to a brilliant financial success at the *Carltheater,* a house that had mainly featured operetta. Jauner proved from the outset that he possessed in abundance the faculties which Herbeck had so sadly lacked: shrewdness, good business sense, and a no-nonsense attitude in his negotiations with officialdom, composers, and singers alike. To begin with, he had accepted the post only after having insisted on several conditions. Miraculously, the authorities who had all but hounded Herbeck out of office granted Jauner privileges unheard-of before him: a considerably larger salary, a free hand in directing his office, and, incredible as it may have seemed, the abolition of bureaucratic channels, which allowed him direct access to the Lord Steward's office without interference from the Office of General Management. Next, with a businessman's eye, Jauner looked around for a lucrative "mission." In the *Carltheater* it had been Offenbach who had brought ever-flowing financial rewards as well as acclaim. Now, with unfailing instinct, Jauner turned to Wagner, whose time in Vienna, he felt, had arrived.

Wagner, at that time, was hardly favorably disposed towards Vienna, although fourteen years earlier he had listened to *Lohengrin* for the first time with tears in his eyes and bestowed an accolade upon the Vienna Opera. After the furious encounters with Herbeck, Wagner's bilious gaze had turned away from Vienna. Jauner, an astounding judge of character, knew how to turn Wagner's gaze around. He convinced his superiors that tradition should be changed and that royalties should be paid the composer. Now *that* was a gesture Wagner understood. Jauner went one step further to fully regain Wagner's confidence and cooperation. He knew one of the foremost Wagner disciples, the conductor Hans Richter, to be then in Budapest. He succeeded in luring Richter away, and on 1 May 1875 Jauner and Richter simultaneously assumed the positions of director and chief conductor, respectively. Now there could be no question as to Jauner's artistic intentions. Wagner looked benignly at the Jauner–Richter combination. In consequence, all that had been denied the devoted disciple fell into the lap of the shrewd businessman. The consequences for the Vienna Imperial Opera were both historic and ironic. It was the astute commercialist showman and not the innate musician before him who made the five years of his tenure a Wagner era in Vienna.

The fruits of the Wagner–Jauner "friendship" promptly became apparent. Not only did *Tannhäuser* immediately enter the repertoire, but the composer proved his "love" for Vienna by personally directing the entire production, with Amalie Materna singing Venus. Next *Lohengrin* was produced anew, again with Wagner taking a personal interest in the production. Vienna was his, and when he left Vienna after conducting a benefit performance in March 1876, the chorus serenaded him at the railroad platform. It was to be the last time Vienna was to get a glimpse of Wagner. In the meantime Wagner and Jauner had developed a realistically close relationship in which Jauner did not shrink from artistic blackmail if it suited his purposes. This prompted Wagner, on occasion, to jocularly refer to Jauner as *Gauner* (sharper, swindler). Jauner knew exactly how to play his artistic aces. He had developed a roster of Wagnerian singers of unsurpassed caliber at the Vienna Opera, and they became pawns in his "game" with Wagner. Wagner wished for Materna to sing in *Die Walküre* in Bayreuth? Of course—*if* Wagner gave Vienna the performance rights to the opera.[4] Wagner wished for Richter to conduct the *Ring* cycle? Of course—*if* Vienna received the performance rights for the entire cycle. Thus Vienna heard *Die Walküre* in March 1877, *Das Rheingold* in January 1878, *Siegfried* in November 1878, and *Götterdämmerung* in February 1879.[5]

[4] During that era singers were often bound to a specific opera house or manager by firm contracts, and it was at the option of the director to allow their performance in other houses. This condition changed drastically after World War I, when singers and conductors became artistic nomads, at home nowhere but heard everywhere.

[5] There was, however, one important difference between the performances in Bayreuth and those in Vienna. While Vienna, thanks to Jauner's business sense and Hanslick's scathing critiques, played to packed houses, Bayreuth amassed a huge deficit.

Having skimmed the top of the Wagner wave, Jauner turned to France and Bizet's *Carmen*. Here again Vienna was more understanding than Paris, which had rejected the work. Although there can be no doubt that the Wagnerian *Leitmotif* conception had influenced the French work, anti-Wagnerian forces saw fit to pit the Gallic work against Wagner's ponderous nordic pathos. Having properly ignited a Bizet–Wagner controversy, the sort of pastime in which Vienna excelled, Jauner turned to Italy, from where he lured Verdi to Vienna to personally conduct his *Requiem* and *Aida*. By then Jauner was so firmly in control of the Vienna operatic scene that aesthetic considerations could be disregarded with impunity. Consequently Delibes's ballet *Sylvia* vied with *Die Walküre*. Jauner threw one more sop to the Viennese. All the performances of all of the great composers of the day—Wagner, Verdi, Saint-Saëns, Bizet— were buttressed with great singers, Adelina Patti and Pauline Lucca among them, to ensure commercial success and, incidentally, artistic success, and keep his watchful superiors content.

Nobody, except Jauner, could expect to stay at the pinnacle indefinitely. Repeat performances inevitably began to be criticized as inferior, and praise turned seemingly overnight into ominous silence and then to talk of reorganization. Jauner would have none of it and abruptly took his leave in 1880. Little did he know that from the pinnacle of success he was to slide into oblivion and suicide. The brief period thereafter, in which Dingelstedt took the helm again, was inconsequential. What was important was the continued presence of Hans Richter, who had become the artistic conscience of the Vienna Opera, the symbol of artistic integrity and, beyond that, an interpreter of stature. Thus a cultural continuity was ensured regardless of whether the intellectual (Dingelstedt) was followed by an idealist (Herbeck) or a businessman/showman (Jauner). Richter's growth and maturity extended into all phases of musical life. He became conductor of the Vienna Philharmonic and director–conductor of the prestigious *Gesellschaft der Musikfreunde*. Over a period of twenty-five years (a miracle in Vienna!) the teutonic-looking, bearded, blue-eyed giant was the symbol not only of musical stability but of the highest standards of musical performance in Vienna.

As luck would have it, at that unfortunate junction in the fortunes of the Vienna Opera there stepped into the void left by Jauner's abrupt departure a man of fine musical instincts, an accomplished musician and conductor of renown, Wilhelm Jahn. This could have been a cause of immediate friction between the two conductors, but Richter's tact and diplomacy made for a smooth transition and adjustment. For one thing, he had had a taste of directorship in his one year in Budapest and desired no more of it. "I shall never be director again," he wrote. "I know that for certain. For as such, one must be able to put up with a great deal. And even if all goes well, one makes no progress as an artist with all the worries of management." As it happened, Richter and Jahn found the field of musical activity in Vienna to be so vast and diversified that instead of competing with each other they complemented each other with perfect artistic understanding. Only once, at the opening of their Vienna collaboration, was there the possibility of friction, not in the opera house but on the concert podium. A group within the Philharmonic Orchestra decided to favor Jahn over Richter as their conductor. Fanned by the press, the conflict promised to be grist for the Vienna gossip mills, but Richter was not going to let the Viennese indulge in their favorite pastime. Tactfully he stepped aside, only to have the satisfaction of witnessing the sorry sight of an inept Jahn at the orchestral podium. The brilliant man of the theater found himself completely out of his depth in the concert hall. Again the character of the two men resolved the embarrassing situation. Realizing his shortcomings, Jahn turned the baton back to Richter and stepped down from the Philharmonic podium into his own domain, the opera.

There Jahn's talent and vision were unsurpassed, and as a director he laid the foundation for the future glory of the Vienna Opera. So superlative an ensemble did he build and maintain that he could point out with pride that all the leading parts of the 1882 Bayreuth premiere of *Parsifal* were sung by Viennese. They were joined in Vienna in 1883 by baritone Theodor Reichmann and later by the brilliant coloratura Bianca Bianchi.[6] In the contralto register it was Rosa Papier whose versatility had enabled her to master most of the parts in the Vienna repertoire, although Wagner parts appealed to her most.

The two artists who were closest to Jahn were mezzo-soprano Marie Renard (born Marie Pölzl, from the province of Styria) and tenor Ernest van Dyck. Marie Renard started in operetta, but, guided and trained by Jahn, she developed a voice described in turn as "soft and graceful," "vibrant," and "voluptuous." At the height of her career she wisely decided, before her vocal powers faded, to leave the stage and marry Count Kinsky. Her final performance turned into a farewell of tumultuous proportions, as the audience demanded encore after encore for half the night. Ernest van Dyck started out as a journalist on the Paris newspaper *La Patrie.* He was touted as a promising Wagnerian tenor, but language difficulties prompted him to turn to the Franco-Italian repertoire of Gounod, Massenet, Leoncavallo, and Mascagni. He sang a splendid and elegant Faust, but it was together with Marie Renard that he created the immortal pairs of Massenet lovers, Manon and des Grieux and Lotte and Werther. Guided by Jahn, Renard and van Dyck brought to those roles a vocal splendor and wealth of feeling which brought the French

6 It was Bianca Bianchi who premiered Johann Strauss's famous waltz *Voices of Spring* as a coloratura composition.

composer a greater triumph in Vienna than in Paris. *Manon* premiered
in Vienna in November 1890 and *Werther* in February 1892; these two
superb performances and stagings must be considered the acme of the
Jahn era.

But the popular high point of the Vienna Opera in March 1891 was
not an opera from the French repertoire but an opera by a young promising Italian—*Cavalleria rusticana* [Rustic chivalry] by Pietro Mascagni.
If the Vienna of Beethoven had gladly surrendered itself to "Rossini
fever," so Vienna now indulged in a "Mascagni orgy," which prompted
sixty repetitions of the opera in 1891 alone.

Ballet in Vienna, despite the glorious memory of Fanny Elssler's
dancing, had never attained the level which, for instance, it enjoyed in
Paris, simply because in Vienna ballet always remained entertainment
while in Paris it was art. But there were exceptions. Even in Johann
Strauss's less successful operettas the ballets were acclaimed to the point
where Hanslick remarked that Strauss's *Ritter Pazmann* was an opera built
around a ballet. It comes, therefore, as no surprise that the most popular
dance production of the day, with a total of seven hundred performances,
was a homegrown ballet, *Die Puppenfee* [The doll fairy], by Joseph Bayer.
Although it did not attain the artistic level of Johann Strauss, its charm
ensured its success in a Viennese world in which music in general and
the opera in particular were part of the city's life and in which a mediocre
ballet was a welcome addition to a thoughtlessly happy way of life.

Eighteen ninety-two brought musical excitement of another sort to
Vienna, in the form of the Musical and Dramatic Exhibition. For that
momentous event, all of artistic Europe streamed into Vienna to hear and
be heard. Ruggiero Leoncavallo brought *I Pagliacci* and, predictably,
registered the same success that his compatriot Mascagni had achieved
a year earlier. The two operas, from then on, were destined to be performed together—and they also remain splendid examples of two composers who were never again able to live up to their early promise. A
Polish opera company brought Stanislaw Moniuszko's fifty-year-old opera
*Halka,* but it kindled no sparks. The exact opposite was the case with the
twenty-six-year-old *Bartered Bride* by Bedřich Smetana, the Bohemian. It
was the first opportunity for the Viennese to hear the work, and it was
clearly a case of love at first hearing. Outside its homeland it was in
Vienna that *Die verkaufte Braut,* to use its German translation, enjoyed
the greatest number of performances, and it all but became a Viennese
opera by popular acclaim.

These were by no means all of Jahn's innovations. We have already
mentioned his efforts on behalf of Massenet. He was equally enthused
about Mascagni's *L'Amico Fritz,* but the charming work could never rival
*Cavalleria rusticana, Der Barbier von Bagdad* by Cornelius, or *Hänsel und
Gretel* by Humperdinck.

Almost imperceptibly, however, discord entered into Vienna's artistic life. A new generation had arisen, with disturbing new ideas. The young and the nationalists undertook new evaluations of their age's superficial superabundance, glossed over like a mantle of gold by the music of Johann Strauss, and found a surprising response from the provinces of the realm and, more surprisingly, from within, from the very heart of the monarchy, in the person of Crown Prince Rudolf, the emperor's son. Shortly before his death by his own hand in 1889, he was to openly describe the monarchy as a "mighty ruin . . . which will ultimately disappear altogether (through) . . . a great powerful upheaval . . . a social revolution."

The splendor of Vienna's prideful institution, the Imperial Opera, continued with all the outward signs of continued success under Jahn. Wilhelm Kienzl's *Der Evangelimann,* the opera of an Austrian, was premiered with all the trappings the Imperial Court Opera could muster. It proved a lasting success, and was followed by the seasonal success of Goldmark's *Das Heimchen am Herd* [The cricket on the hearth]. But those on the inside and those who followed events closely sensed a creeping paralysis approaching, aggravated by a pernicious eye disorder which plagued Jahn. It was time for a change. Quietly the word went out; find a successor for Jahn.

## MAHLER AND THE VIENNA OPERA

Only this boundless innocence of a man completely blind to the world, led only by his holy vision, could have succeeded for years on end in conducting the Imperial Royal Opera in Vienna as if we were in Athens at the time of the great tragedies.

Hermann Bahr, *Mahler und das deutsche Theater* (1910)

[Mahler] was a master of scenic form. From the dreary day of gray reality he assembled a band of beings for intoxicating festivals of music. Every performance was a rebirth from the spirit of the creator. The singers became servants of the work, the stage a sanctuary.

Eduard Castle, *Geschichte der deutschen Literatur in Österreich-Ungarn im Zeitalter Franz Josef I*

The secretive manner in which those in charge went about choosing a man for the most prestigious musical post in Vienna was almost unique in the annals of the city and its opera. The atmosphere of stealth in which the negotiations were conducted over a period of nearly two years was tantamount to treason in a city in which such an event was considered to belong to the public domain—a proper subject for discussion everywhere and a most welcome occasion for intrigue and counterintrigue, editorials, animated salon and coffeehouse *Klatsch* (gossip) and second-guessing. Actually the second-guessing went on anyhow, and the names of Felix Mottl of Munich and Ernst von Schuch of Dresden were bandied about. Aside from the powers behind the Court Opera and Mahler, apparently only one man in Vienna, the journalist Ludwig Karpath, knew the actual details, and he had been sworn to secrecy by Mahler, because Mahler was actually torn by conflicting emotions. On the one hand he expressed the hope to Bruno Walter that he would receive a call from "the God of the Southern Zones"—Vienna. On the other hand, he expressed grave doubts.

> Suppose I did come to Vienna. With my attitude to things, what would happen to me there? The first time I tried to impose my interpretation of a Beethoven symphony upon the celebrated Philharmonic Orchestra, trained by the doughty Hans [Richter], the most hateful battle would ensue. . . . I should bring a storm around my head whenever I departed from routine to make some contribution of my own.
>
> Mahler to Dr. Friedrich Löhr, 1894

> With regard to Vienna and the conductor's crisis there, nothing definite can be said as yet. Between ourselves, the crisis cannot be solved until the autumn, and the choice now seems to be between Mottl and my humble self.
>
> To be frank, I don't know whether I ought to welcome the idea of the post, for it might turn me aside from my original aims. However, I am completely fatalistic about it.
>
> Mahler to Dr. Arthur Seidl, 12 Feb 1897 [7]

But Mahler apparently modeled his fatalism on Beethoven's—"*Mensch, hilf Dir selbst*" [Man, help thyself]—because, whether or not he admitted it, Mahler longed for the artistic fulfillment of the position in Vienna, and once the news of an opening there reached him he began to make his move.

Vienna moved equally circumspectly, because the man in charge, Josef von Beseczny, did not want anybody to know of his plans—viz.,

---

[7] Even after the decision had been made, Mahler was full of doubts.

> For the time being, the summons to Vienna has brought me only unprecedented disturbance and the anticipation of battles to come. Whether it is the right place for me time alone can tell. In any case I must steel myself for a year's violent hostility on the part of all those who either will not or can not cooperate. (The two things usually go together.)
>
> Hans Richter, in particular, is reported to be doing his level best to raise hell against me. . . . But I am going back to my own country, and I shall do all I can to put an end to my wandering in this life.
>
> Mahler to Dr. Arnold Berliner (a young acquaintance in Hamburg who taught Mahler English), 22 April 1897

Richter apparently was only one of those who did everything in their power to prevent Mahler's appointment. His efforts were paralleled by Jahn himself and by Nepomuk Fuchs, the second conductor.

that the second conductor to be engaged was to be chosen also as the presumed successor of Jahn and, therefore, in order to be able to assume so prestigious and responsible a post, had to be of exceptional caliber in all aspects of opera-house work. Beseczny appointed Eduard Wlassack, the head of the Chancellory, and the opera singer Rosa Papier to make the necessary diplomatic artistic moves carefully and stealthily. Mahler, seeing the opportunity, used the summer months which he usually spent in Carynthia to marshal a number of influential personalities to act or at least speak on his behalf when the time was ripe. His sponsors: Brahms, whom he visited several times during the summer to discuss the matter; Anna von Mildenburg, an ideal link to her former teacher Rosa Papier, now the delegate from "the other side"; and Count Albert Apponyi, who still remembered Mahler's magnificent work at the Budapest Opera.

Finally, the groundwork having been properly prepared, Mahler, on 21 December 1896, mailed his letter of application for the position of conductor of the Vienna Court Opera, and events were set in motion. Already at that point, positions pro and con Mahler began to emerge. Brahms's admiration for his interpretations was known. The Court had been advised that Mahler had converted to Catholicism; that potentially huge barrier to his employment was therefore removed. With Rosa Papier, a friend of Mahler from Kassel days, and her husband, the Vienna music critic Hans Paumgartner, on Mahler's side, the artistic momentum in his favor was well under way. It only remained to secure some political recommendations. In that regard, Count Apponyi's letter of 10 January 1897 [8] presumably addressed to Prince Montenuovo or Prince Liechtenstein, turned the tide.

> I am informed by a reliable source that the Imperial and Royal Vienna Court Opera is on the verge of a crisis concerning its conductor and director, and that among others Herr Gustav Mahler is considering the post. Since the work of this outstanding artist at the Budapest Opera is vivid in my memory and since in my fairly comprehensive acquaintance with this distinguished conductor I have not found his like, I take the liberty of saying a few words by way of recommending him.

But before speaking of Mahler in detail, Count Apponyi could not pass up the opportunity to take a swipe at a man he heartily disliked.

> Through the incompetence and misplaced ambition of Count Géza von Zichy during the latter's unhappy directorship of our opera house . . . this institution has to its detriment lost a leader who, within two years, succeeded in training a completely discredited company to achieve considerable artistic results; built up a rich and varied repertoire; and, while preserving the highest artistic ideals, ended his second season with a not inconsiderable financial surplus.

[8] Quoted in Blaukopf, *Mahler.*

The shrewd politician in Apponyi fully realized the impact that the words "financial surplus" would carry. He continued:

> Mahler is not merely . . . an orchestra musician, but with all the works he produces he dominates the stage, the action, the expressions and motions of actors and chorus, with supreme control, so that a performance prepared and conducted by him attains artistic perfection in every dimension. . . . I have never met such a well-balanced all-around artistic personality. I would beg your Excellency by way of confirming this opinion to ask Brahms what he thought of the *Don Giovanni* performance conducted by Mahler, which he watched in Budapest; please ask Goldmark how *Lohengrin* under Mahler's direction struck him. Both will remember their impressions, for they were of the kind one remembers for a lifetime.
>
> When I add that Mahler as a person, too, is a highly estimable, eminently respectable character, I shall have completed a portrait which, I trust, suggests that the Opera would be fortunate indeed to gain his service.

One formidable obstacle to Mahler's appointment arose in the person of Cosima Wagner, who set in motion all the influence she could muster from far-away Bayreuth. Cosima Wagner used her prestige against Mahler mainly because the presence of a Jew, even a baptized one, at the helm of an institution of such magnitude was anathema to her. This was totally incongruous, because she must have been aware of the fact that Mahler had become one of the foremost Wagner interpreters of his day. Her initial opposition to Mahler's appointment in Vienna did not prevent Cosima Wagner from approaching Mahler later, at the zenith of his opera activities, and reminding him of a previous tentative promise to consider performing her son Siegfried Wagner's mediocre operas. Once Mahler had attained worldwide fame, Cosima could bring herself to turn aside her former intransigent hostility and, with a brilliant mixture of wile, fawning affability, cajolery, and logic, attempt to sway Mahler in favor of her son.

Bayreuth, 8 June 1905

My dear Director,

May I trespass on your kindness to ask you two questions? The first relates to Fräulein von Mildenburg, whom you were once so good as to recommend to me for the part of Kundry. I hear very different, in fact contradictory, opinions expressed about the achievement of this gifted singer. Some praise her unreservedly, others say she is very inconsistent and explain it by her poor health. I should like to take your verdict as final, and if you will be so kind as to give it to me you may rely on our silence as implicitly as I rely on you to regard this letter as confidential.

My second question is likewise of a confidential nature. It concerns my son's new opera *Bruder Lustig*. . . . My son told me that it might be troubling you to no purpose to send you his opera after the rejection of *Kobold,* but at the same time it might seem discourteous not to ask whether the director of the Royal Opera would like to consider his work. . . .

I undertook to put this question before you and told him that there was nothing importune in submitting his opera; for you had given sufficient proof of your good opinion of his work by the fine production of his [opera] *Bärenhäuter,*[9] and although the season's program or other reasons had prevented you from accepting *Kobold,* you were certainly acquainted with the score and had presumably taken note of the performance, as you were well aware of his merits as a playwright and composer. Therefore you would certainly tell me, without previous acquaintance with the score, whether you wished to see *Bruder Lustig* or not. May I request a reply by telegram? This will spare you the need to give your reasons. . . .

With my best thanks in advance for your replies to both my questions, I am,

Yours most sincerely,
C. Wagner

Bayreuth, 13 June 1905
My dear Director,

My best thanks for your sympathetic and early reply to my questions. . . . Your opinion, dear Herr Mahler, has decisive weight with me. . . . I thank you also very cordially for your reply to my second question, for which I am perhaps even more indebted.

I did certainly assume that the achievements of my son as conductor, as dramatist and composer, and as stage manager of the Bayreuth Festivals [through the indulgence of his mother] . . . should be given to the public, which then was at liberty to give its verdict.

Your answer to this assumption of mine shows me, Herr Mahler, that you take no account of such circumstances in the case of a composer; you wish in the first place to gain a thorough knowledge of each work, so that if you accept it you can take its part, even against opposition, if necessary. I find this not merely understandable but greatly to your credit. But the present case has an aspect of its own, and I beg your indulgence while I explain it to you.

After the performance of *Bärenhäuter* in Vienna, and in consequence of it, you expressed to my son a wish to have his next opera (without having any knowledge of it). Unfortunately Siegfried was already committed to Munich; but in the consideration of the honor you did him in the case of *Herzog Wildfang* he sent *Kobold* to you in the first place. You kept it, dear Herr Mahler, for a considerable length of time, owing no

[9] *Bärenhäuter* [Bear skinner] was performed in Vienna in 1899, shortly after its Munich premiere. It was well received but soon disappeared from the repertoire. It is forgotten today.

doubt to the innumerable demands made on you, and when you were asked for a decision you declined the work without giving any reasons for doing so. Thus a new situation arose. It is difficult, I might say impossible, for my son to subject you and himself to the risk of another refusal, and you would not be the artist you are if you did not understand and esteem pride and sensibility in another artist. Now, however, we are gladdened by the good news that you look forward to his new work with great interest.

Will you not give rein to this feeling of yours and decide on the production without more ado, as you did for *Wildfang?* Even though *Kobold*. . . did not appeal to you. . . you cannot have thought it unworthy of performance, for in that case you would not have been able to feel any interest in its successor. It is to this interest I appeal. I ask it to stir up the warm-hearted, trustful [!] artist and to conquer the cautious and critical director. . . . Whether I have the happiness to persuade you, dear Herr Mahler, or whether you hold to your previous opinion, you may be sure that my son and I will accept your decision with sympathy, and that I remain with renewed warmth of esteem

Yours, etc.,
C. Wagner

In any case, her opposition was an insufficient deterent, and Court Steward Prince Rudolf Liechtenstein was able to advise his sovereign that Gustav Mahler was acceptable for the position of conductor at the Opera.[10] Little did the public know that plans were afoot to promote any conductor accepted under such stringent scrutiny to director in the shortest possible time without hurt or embarrassment to Wilhelm Jahn. Thus after Mahler had rid himself of his Hamburg ties (Pollini being equally relieved to rid himself of his difficult conductor) and the contract was signed by both parties on 15 April 1897, it was, incredibly, ratified the same day. It was an ironic twist that it was Jahn's signature that formally engaged Mahler for one year.

Mahler was immediately put to the test. On 11 May 1897 he conducted *Lohengrin* in a new house, with a new orchestra and new singers, after one (!) rehearsal. Reported he to Anna von Mildenburg: "The whole of Vienna greeted me with real enthusiasm. Next week there will be *Walküre, Siegfried, Figaro,* and *Zauberflöte.* There can be no doubt that I shall be director soon." But he did not take all the credit, because he appreciated and acknowledged Viennese musicianship—its élan and

---

[10] Dika Newlin considers his appointment an indication of unexpected racial tolerance on the part of the Austrian court. We beg to differ. It is to be highly doubted that as a Jew Mahler could have attained a position at the Austrian Court, where it was tacit law that no non-Catholic should hold a Court position of consequence. Had Mahler not converted, another "name" conductor and director would have been found and engaged, even if he presented less impressive credentials.

warmth and the great natural talent which everyone brought to bear on the production. Vienna responded fully.

> Last night, on which Wagner's *Lohengrin* was given . . . evoked special interest through the presence of the newly acquired conductor Gustav Mahler in his first conducting appearance. Herr Mahler is of small, slender, energetic figure, with sharp, intelligent features. . . . As the looks so the conductor, full of energy and fine understanding. He belongs to the younger school of conducting, which, in contrast to the statuesque presence of the older conductors, has developed a livelier mimicry. Those younger ones speak with arms and hands, with twists of the entire body. . . . The dry wood of the baton beats between their fingers and becomes green. Through such exterior means, which fully attained spiritual character, Herr Mahler conducted *Lohengrin*. With great understanding did he enter the dream world of the prelude; only at the high point of the composition, when the brass enters with all its weight, did he grip the entire orchestra with quick energetic transformation, his baton, swordlike, attacking the trombones. The result was magic. In the richly dramatic first act . . . Mahler exercised his conductor's art fully. His presence was everywhere. He stood in living relationship to orchestra, choir, individuals. Nobody missed his cues. Conductor Mahler found full appreciation from the public. After the prelude he had to bow repeatedly to the house, and loud shouts greeted the new man. Herr Mahler is not only an excellent conductor but also a splendid director. . . . He is surely the right man for the present situation. One could not support the ailing director of the Opera more gently yet more realistically than by placing at his side such an artist. Herr Mahler will act as artistic leaven (*Sauerteig*) if we let him assert himself.
>
> Ludwig Speidel, *Wiener Fremdenblatt* (12 May 1897)

With Jahn's deteriorating eyesight impeding his conductorial duties, things took the foreseen course. Mahler took on Jahn's schedule as deputy director on 21 July, two months after his arrival. Three months later, on 8 October, he became artistic director at a salary of 24,000 kronen plus gratuities and pension, with nearly unlimited power.

When opera directors combine within themselves the charisma of their position with the glamor of being a composer as well—as with Liszt in Weimar, Weber in Dresden, Meyerbeer in Berlin, Wagner in Bayreuth, and later Richard Strauss in Vienna—the atmosphere becomes charged with an additional, undefinable quality which, however, is directly felt by the audience and the performers. With no man was that combination of uniqueness and charisma more immediately felt by the public than with Mahler. This was surprising, in that when Mahler arrived in Vienna to take up his position he was actually known only to the musical *cognoscenti*. To musical Vienna at large he was a near unknown, despite his past stewardship in nearby Budapest and despite the fact that he had already composed three symphonies and three *Lieder* cycles. The only glimpse the Viennese had ever had of Mahler's work had been Jahn's staging in 1889 of the Mahler adaptation of Weber's *Die drei Pintos*. Vienna's reception then was only lukewarm despite Hanslick's praise for the performance.

It was in the very nature of Mahler that the fight against him should start immediately, feverishly, tenaciously. Mahler did nothing to calm his critics; on the contrary, his musical superiority, his perfectionism, his lack of desire to understand human nature, his brusque manner bordering on rudeness and arrogance only tended to feed the flames. Be it said, in their honor, that Mahler had two powerful allies: his princely superiors and the public. For ten years, while critics carped, audiences would applaud with unstinting enthusiasm and Prince Montenuovo would support Mahler against one and all.

Mahler took charge, infusing the atmosphere with his artistic totality, and putting from his mind even the image of Anna von Mildenburg, who had hoped that Mahler would call for her as soon as possible. Even if Mahler would have desired to do so, and we have reason to believe that his ardor had cooled by then, it would not have been wise, because reports were already making the rounds in Vienna that Mahler intended to bring his paramour from Hamburg to Vienna. Rosa Papier, in particular, wanted her former protegé at the more prestigious Vienna opera house. Anna von Mildenburg did join the Vienna Opera in February 1898; her renewed proximity, however, did little to rekindle former feelings on Mahler's part, much as Anna would have desired it. But Mahler never failed to pay his respects to Anna's surpassing artistry. Anna's personality also must have been surpassing to have incurred the dislike of Justine as well as of Mahler's later wife, Alma. Justine's presence may, in a remote sense, have contributed to the gradual loosening of ties between Anna and Mahler, because of Mahler's outlook towards his family and his personal life. On the one hand he considered himself paterfamilias to his two sisters; on the other hand, Justine's accommodation to his artistic demands and attention to his well-being without cloying marital ties was a convenient arrangement (perhaps unconsciously so) for the man, the artist, the composer, the director—for all the men that were Mahler. Only the later, irresistible attraction to Alma Schindler overrode all previous conveniences and considerations.

Mahler was directly responsible to and derived his powers from Prince Alfred Montenuovo, the emperor's Lord Steward of the Household, who also administered the opera house as well as the other theater of state, the *Burgtheater*. Prince Montenuovo, mustachioed and bearded, was the perfect image of the Austrian aristocrat, from his mirror-polished shoes to the top of his silvery hair. Unlike the majority of Austrian aristocrats he was a rather cold, unapproachable individual—though also the model of a good administrator, who would defend a position or conviction, once arrived at, to the end, unpopular as it might be. It was primarily the prince's rectitude that, recognizing Mahler's genius, made him stand by him and his decisions for ten years in the face of constant attacks on Mahler for political and religious as well as artistic reasons.

Montenuovo was a man of strong principles, or what he considered principles. His unbending dislike, bordering on hostility, towards the *Thronfolger* (heir to the throne)—Franz Ferdinand and his wife, the former Countess Chotek—is a case in point. Feeling that the heir to the Austrian throne had unnecessarily married beneath his rank, he never missed an opportunity to make the countess, even as a later archduchess and princess, realize that she was lower in rank than her husband. Not even death could change Montenuovo's principles or protocol. After the assassination of the crown prince and his wife at Sarajevo, he ordered the coffin of the princess to be mounted a step lower than that of her husband as their bodies lay in state.

That unbending attitude may have reflected a subconscious attempt at equalization on the part of Prince Montenuovo. Although by the beginning of the twentieth century the Montenuovos were among the noblest families of the realm, Prince Montenuovo must have known only too well the story of his forbears. Marie Louise, the daughter of Emperor Franz of Austria, had been brought back to Vienna by her father after her husband, Napoleon, had been banished to St. Helena. Since her presence as the wife of Napoleon was undesirable during the Congress of Vienna, she was shunted off to the duchy of Parma, there to lord it over her small coterie, led by her dashing equerry, one-eyed General Albert von Neipperg, thoughtfully added to her entourage (it was whispered) by Chancellor Metternich. The drowsy, languid atmosphere of Parma, devoid of all diversions for the vivacious, pleasure-bent princess, found her stymied and bored. This could not escape her ever-present equerry's attention; his ardent advances soon gained the princess's bedchamber, with the upshots tellingly named Albertina and Wilhelm Albert. The mother, fearing a scandal of international proportions should the truth become known, saw to it that the two bastard children remained hidden from sight, from her entourage, and even—especially—from her father, the emperor. Only after Napoleon's death was a marriage with Albert Neipperg legally and officially consummated and her father the emperor apprised of the situation. Emperor Franz, presented with a fait accompli, had no choice but to accept the offspring. Since titles for them were in order, he changed their names from Neipperg (originally Neuberg, meaning "new mountain") to the Italianized Montenuovo and, *voilà*, with the help of a secret loan floated by the financier Baron Rothschild at the emperor's behest, a new Austrian family of aristocrats was born. Marie Louise's grandson was none other than Prince Alfred Montenuovo, the image of unbending rectitude. Yet beneath the prince's stiff exterior there was warmth and understanding for the men he respected, and Mahler was foremost among them. That sentiment was to prompt him to extend his hand to Mahler at their final parting with the words "We are friends." There was no sham or pretense in that gesture, for such was alien to the nobleman; but rather, he appreciated and acknowledged in Mahler an integrity akin to his own. (Indeed, Montenuovo's esteem for Mahler went so far as to allow him to ask the composer's opinion concerning his successor.)

Of the nearly three thousand performances occurring under Mahler's aegis, one-fourth were to be devoted to Wagner. The balance was distributed among the works of Mozart, Beethoven, Puccini, Massenet, Smetana, and a mixture of established and promising composers of many lands. Curiously, fully a fourth of the performances were devoted to ballet, although that art never attained the importance in Vienna which it had in France or Russia. Mahler actually did not care for it, but the public did. To the Viennese, ballet was simply delightful entertainment; this made it possible for that fairly mediocre ballet, *Die Puppenfee,* to remain in the repertory, even under Mahler. Surprisingly, in the matter of ballet Mahler bowed to public preference and mediocrity, for reasons to be seen later. A special place in Mahler's heart was reserved for *Die Fledermaus* by Johann Strauss, which he had already featured in Hamburg and which was to be performed eighty-nine times during Mahler's reign in Vienna.

Mahler had quickly assessed the situation at the opera under Jahn. Some of the great singers were already present and the orchestra was already famous, but the spirit and reality of an ensemble had not yet fully crystallized. Wagner was of course fully established, but Goldmark's time in Vienna, like that of the painter Hans Makart,[11] was past. There existed a vacuum, to be filled with new names, new composers, new singers, and new music. They were not long in coming.

The first upheaval at the opera arose soon after Mahler's ascendency to the directorship. The ensemble roster showed glaring gaps on the one hand, while on the other hand some of the singers, Vienna's favorites among them, had vocally outlived their usefulness and needed to be put out to artistic pasture. Heedless or perhaps even unaware of the outcry to follow, Mahler proceeded to refresh the roster with a group of young singers destined for greatness and world renown. Mahler did not favor the graceful voices which had been Jahn's favorites; he preferred commanding voices in both male and female singers. He counted among such "impressive" singers Anna von Mildenburg, who originally hailed from Vienna but joined from Hamburg, Erik Schmedes from Denmark, Marie Gutheil-Schoder from Weimar, and Friedrich Weidemann and the in-

[11] It is apt to compare the music of Goldmark and the paintings of Makart, because both depicted a glowing sensuous splendor which caught the public's fancy in its day and enjoyed a great success for a limited time before passing on.

comparable Selma Kurz, both of whom hailed from Galicia. Selma Kurz started as a mezzo-soprano. One night Mahler noticed the unusual length of Selma's trill. He timed it and then, through training, prolonged it, extending it to unheard-of length and generating world fame for its owner. Audiences began to wait for the "Selma trill." Other voices who joined Mahler were the Bohemian bass Wilhelm Hesch, Richard Mayr from Salzburg, the German baritone Theodore Reichmann, and Leopold Demuth and Leo Slezak from Brünn.

Other, seemingly unimportant moves changed the atmosphere as well as the tempo of the house. While Jahn had sat, during performance, in one of the boxes in the back of the house, from where he could survey the stage, Mahler sat in the second box of the second tier. From there he not only had a full view of the stage but could descend to it at a moment's notice. Additionally he had a phone installed in the pit for prompt communication with the stage while he was conducting. After incidents in which, to the hilarity of the audience, the opening curtain (in *Lohengrin*) revealed a workman still adjusting the scenery or (in *Freischütz*) the tenor and a chorus girl necking on stage, Mahler also reserved to himself the signal as to when the curtain should rise.

Mahler also moved the conductor's podium back towards the balustrade that separated the orchestra from the audience. Previously conductors had taken their place near the stage so as to better communicate visually with the singers, with the orchestra actually seated *behind* the conductor; usually a broad gangway behind the conductor enabled him to turn to the orchestra if orchestral interludes demanded his attention. Jahn as well as Richter actually sat in wicker chairs amid the orchestra during rehearsals, assuming the relaxed role of paterfamilias with the orchestra rather than the role of "dictator of the baton" that Mahler was to assume.

Armed with Prince Montenuovo's support and his roster of new singers, Mahler's surge began. Ignoring animosities, he exhorted his associated singers, players, and designers to rise to the occasion and surpass themselves in new achievements, overcoming their open hostility or covert reluctance by his own determination and dedication and steely will. There was a burning perfectionism in all that Mahler undertook—a perfcetionism that applied to every phase of opera. Drama and staging were treated as having equal importance with singing in order to achieve unified, well-balanced performances. When the inadequacy of the existing mode of staging became obvious, Mahler, in collaboration with his stage designer, Alfred Roller, went about to make what he considered necessary changes. The painted linear perspective of rooms and landscapes was eliminated as stage design became a specialized art; the "Roller Towers" began to dominate the stage.

On the way to attaining perfectionism Mahler operated with an uncaring and almost naive ruthlessness which brought great admiration for the final artistic product but left many wounds and hostilities in its path. Thus those singers who did not measure up to Mahler's standards fell by the wayside, lending fuel, of course, to the accusations of Mahler's "recklessness." Of the new singers destined for greatness, Erik Schmedes and Leo Slezak were among the most fascinating.

> Mahler engaged my father to the Vienna *Hofoper* [Court Opera] although Erik Schmedes had never sung a tenor role before (he was orginally a baritone). Schmedes had had an operation and while in a plaster cast he began to study tenor roles. Mahler heard about it, telegraphed him. Schmedes sang *Gralserzählung* with an orchestra conducted by Richter.
>
> Schmedes as remembered by his son, writing in
> *Wiener Kurier,* 18 September 1954

Schmedes was not always grateful or even appreciative. But Mahler handled him in his own offhanded way. "Listen, I understand you are badmouthing me up and down. Believe me, this will mean no less work for you." Neither excesses nor excuses were tolerated. When Mahler found Schmedes smoking and drinking in a Vienna tavern, he personally escorted him from the place. When a singer of the old guard remonstrated that he had sung the part under Wagner and knew it well, Mahler peremptorily cut him off: "When you sing under me, you attend rehearsals."

Two of Mahler's prominent singers came from the city of Brünn: Leopold Demuth, who had previously been a pharmacist, and Leo Slezak, whose first métier was that of a locksmith. Throughout his many years at the Vienna Opera there was no question in anybody's mind but that Leo Slezak would win any popularity contest. A giant of a man, of voluminous girth, even in his younger days, he was a superb *Heldentenor* whose repertoire ranged from Mozart to Wagner to Puccini. One of the funniest anecdotes in the Wagner repertoire is ascribed to him: when the swan pulling the boat in *Lohengrin* was moved off-stage before Slezak could set foot on it, he was heard to whisper in *recitativo:* "When does the next swan leave?"

Except in the highest imperial administrative places, Mahler soon found criticism everywhere—but he had the enthusiastic support of the group that was purported to be the most knowledgeable among Vienna opera experts, the youths who nightly inhabited the fourth (top, or *Vierte*) gallery. They might differ as to the merits of one singer vis-à-vis another, but they were of one opinion in their admiration for Mahler, particularly since he had resuscitated the opera by officially removing the claque,[12] closing the doors to latecomers, and, most importantly, restoring

---

[12] The claque before Mahler was a quasi-semiofficial institution to whom free tickets were distributed. Mahler had the singers sign a document that they would refrain from engaging the claque. But although the order became official, singers eventu-

all cuts in opera performances, particularly in Wagner. So strong were their feelings concerning cuts that when Felix von Weingartner, Mahler's successor, again intended to reinstate "customary" cuts, the fury of protest from the denizens of the "fourth gallery" prompted him to abandon the idea.

While he stressed the German repertoire because he considered Beethoven and Wagner supremė, and favored Gluck and Mozart, Mahler was by no means prejudiced against the work of any nation and featured Charpentier as well as Pfitzner and Offenbach, Smetana, Richard Strauss, and Johann Strauss. But in his approach to opera, Mahler, consciously or subconsciously, made a curious distinction. Mozart's operas, Beethoven's *Fidelio,* and the Wagner music dramas remained inviolate, with every note faithfully reproduced. Mozart was recreated in historically and musically correct style, with *recitativos* and a harpsichord for accompaniment restored in accordance with the style as envisioned by Mozart, rather than the out-of-place realism that had begun to distort performances of that master. With respect to Wagner, Vienna under Mahler was the first opera house outside Bayreuth to adhere to Wagner's own principles in performance. This called for complete restoration of all cuts. Furthermore, a false encroaching romanticism in staging Wagner was done away with in favor of an expressionistic approach, more symbolic than realistic and decidedly no longer romantic, its impact reaching into the twentieth century and the stagings of Wolfgang and Wieland Wagner.

However, in the works of lesser masters—Boieldieu, Goetz, Halévy, Mehul, Nicolai, Offenbach—Mahler's compositional and directorial genius asserted itself in the interest of perfection, or what Mahler considered perfection. Even so, all alterations were undertaken only after intensive study of the work and the composer's intentions. It was that total immersion into the composer's intentions which gave performances under Mahler an aura of freshness regardless of how often the work emerged under his baton. At no time did a performance become lackadaisical, hackneyed, or routine, because Mahler's controlled impetuousity never failed or faded. To maintain such standards, Mahler instituted in Vienna a regimen that was previously unheard-of and, at least in the beginning, anathema to the relaxed Viennese spirit. For there was one specific Viennese trait which went against Mahler's nature—namely, the desire to take things easily and slowly, not to rush into anything, not to upset "tradition." Indeed, anything the Viennese wished to remain unchanged, which was most everything, was labeled as "tradition" in order

---

ally circumvented it because some of them could not do without the claque's frenetic and "jubilant" applause, the range of jubilation depending on the sum "contributed" by the singer.

to shelter it from the winds of change. This prompted Mahler's dictum "Tradition ist bloss Schlamperei" (Tradition is only sloppiness).[13]

Such a stern regimen, however, was to bring Mahler inevitably into conflict with the very nature of the Viennese way of life and the peculiar aspects which made the Viennese and Austrian intellect as fascinating as it was exasperating. As Křenek so aptly remarks, in his *Gustav Mahler:* "Vienna offered splendid potentialities for the highest accomplishments as well as the most stubborn resistance to their realization.

This was the legacy of Emperor Franz II and his chancellor, Prince Clemens Metternich, who were haunted by the thought that any progressive notion, once allowed to enter Vienna, would promptly be employed to undermine the foundations of the empire. Thus the most draconian measures were exercised to maintain a fossilized intellectual and emotional status quo because both emperor and chancellor feared that intellectual enlightenment, be it literary, theatrical, political, or journalistic, would adversely affect age-old prerogatives and change the delicate balance of power. This situation had not always obtained. During the reign of the four "Baroque Emperors," [14] for roughly one hundred years, and especially later, during the reign of Emperor Josef II, the arts of all lands flowered in Vienna and progress, under enlightened absolutism, was pursued. Only after Josef II's death in 1790 did regression set in and repressive despotism come to the fore. Amelioration of those regressive conditions had to wait until the mature years of Emperor Franz Joseph's reign.

Surprisingly, the multilingual and multinational Austrian empire was a fairly homogeneous entity. Several factors accounted for such unity. The absence of internal borders brought about a flourishing of intraempire trade; such trade was facilitated by the Danube, which led to trade into the eastern provinces and as far as the Orient. Surely the strongest binding factor was the religious belief—viz., Catholicism, which many of the provinces of the empire shared with the emperor.

As much as he came to love the city, Mahler never became "Viennized," in the sense that he could accommodate himself to the deliberately slow pace and instinctive conservatism of the Viennese. However, he did become acclimated to the extent that he conversed in Viennese dialect and loved Viennese dishes, particularly rich desserts. And when he and Bruno Walter played duet music on the piano, it was Schubert and Mozart

---

[13] To Toscanini, tradition was "the last bad performance."

[14] Ferdinand III, 1637–57; Leopold I, 1657–1705; Josef I, 1705–11; Karl VI, 1711–40. The Habsburg reign continued with Maria Theresia, Karl's daughter, 1740–80; her son Josef II, 1765–90 (1765–80 as co-regent with Maria Theresia); his brother Leopold II, 1790–92; Josef's nephew Franz II, 1792–1835; and Franz's son Ferdinand I, 1835–48. His nephew Franz Joseph, 1848–1916, and Franz Joseph's nephew Karl, 1916–18, brought the Habsburg reign to a close.

that they played more often than anybody else. On such occasions Mahler would go so far, in rare outbursts of genial humor, as to invent Viennese dialect verses to Schubert melodies while they were playing them.

Mahler was the child and beneficiary as well as the captive and victim of all these diverse elements; he was Jewish in religious background, German in upbringing, Bohemian by environment, pan-European in his adult thinking. As brilliant artistic, medical, and scientific achievements enhanced the Austrian image in inverse ratio to its political, diplomatic, and military decline, Mahler became the final gigantic cornerstone of a period which reached a climactic finale with his massive musical canvasses at the sunset of a century, of romanticism, and of a dynasty. Only under Richard Strauss, about twenty years after Mahler and after a devastating world war had decimated the Austro-Hungarian empire into the Republic of Austria, was the Vienna Opera to briefly recapture its supremacy under the most dire circumstances.

When Schönberg, Berg, and Webern eventually ushered in a new age in music, the third wave of musical genius in Vienna, it was on the ruins of that nineteenth-century romanticism which had prevailed long after outliving its *raison d'être*. Few in Vienna were brave or farsighted enough to openly admit the decline and decay, such an admission being totally contrary to the Viennese way of life and thinking. Subconsciously, the Viennese psyche attempted to hide from the facts in the gaiety of the pied-piper music of Johann Strauss and Franz Lehar. Thus Vienna, true to form and to its traditions, indulged itself in plaintive hedonism, a skeptical *joie de vivre,* either extolling Vienna with Hofmannsthal or mesmerized by Schnitzler's word paintings of a degenerating society, pleasure loving amidst a morbid lethargy. A chasm inevitably began to open between the Vienna of Johann Strauss and that of Schönberg. The choice for the Viennese was clear: between Johann Strauss, *Schnitzel,* and *Kaffee mit Schlag,* on the one hand, and the harsh realism of Schönberg and Schiele, on the other. Most Viennese unhesitatingly chose to cling to the past and ignore the present. But even those who wished to face and cope with reality, or at least thought that they were aware of it, later admitted their error. Only the men of music, Schönberg and Webern, intuitively felt the coming of the Great War and in their music mirrored their fears.

The year 1897 was a creative milestone in Mahler's life, because nowhere had he ever previously occupied a position of such magnitude nor had such vast resources at his disposal. With the Opera and the Vienna Philharmonic Orchestra it was to be a decade of triumph and tension—both the result of Mahler's unbending attitudes and reach for perfection.

Mahler's equal adeptness as a composer, brilliant conductor, stage director, and administrator endowed his ten-year regime with an aura unforgotten to this day. It also moved him into a sphere of total influence in modern opera interpretation and production, a historic position similar to that of Max Reinhardt in the German theater. Deep in his heart Mahler possessed the artistic capability to get inside a role, a character, or an entire work and portray feelings and thoughts true to its creator's intention, as contrary to his beliefs as they might be. While in *Die Meistersinger* he revered the serenity and wisdom of Hans Sachs, the spiteful petty intrigue and personality of Beckmesser also received its full measure of attention and characterization. While his heart was with the prisoners of *Fidelio,* he nevertheless immersed himself in the sinister role and thoughts of Pizzaro and thus was also to produce a masterly portrayal of villainy. It was one of Mahler's achievements as a conductor to always maintain a balance of operatic powers, with neither drama nor music nor *mise en scène* dominant or subservient. At any given moment the music might heighten the drama or the dramatic moment intensify the music; the two elements complemented each other. That was no easy task, particularly with an eighteenth-century composer like Mozart, in whose day stage direction or information concerning dramatic interpretation was all but absent. In such a case it was Mahler's intuition coupled with his total immersion into the work, the characters, the times, and the music that brought about such definite interpretations as his productions of *Figaro* and *Don Giovanni.* Thus the opening years of Mahler's stewardship at the Vienna Opera presented a glittering kaleidoscope of his many-sided genius and an impressive list of accomplishments.

1897   Mozart's *The Marriage of Figaro* was "cleansed" of all the non-Mozartian cadenzas accumulated over the years.

Smetana's opera *Dalibor* added Slavic flavor to the repertoire, as did Tchaikovsky's *Eugène Onegin.*

1898   Wagner's entire *Ring* cycle was performed: *Die Walküre* with Anna von Mildenburg as "Brünhilde, *Siegfried* with the newly discovered Erik Schmedes, and *Götterdämmerung* with the Norn scene restored. *Tristan* saw its first uncut performance in Vienna.

Weber's *Der Freischütz,* the father of all German romantic operas, was staged with new lighting, replacing the customary gloomy atmosphere of the wolf's glen scene.[15]

New acquisitions included Bizet's *Djamileh*; Leoncavallo's *La Bohème,* a success despite total disagreement and personal clashes between composer and director; and Rezniček's *Donna Diana,* whose sparkling overture still survives.

---

[15] The night lighting did not meet with public approval, and much of the previous lighting was soon restored.

1899    Mahler produced Haydn's early comic opera *Der Apotheker* [The apothecary], as a bow to the Viennese master.

Lortzing's last comic opera, *Die Opernprobe* [The opera rehearsal], was unearthed by Mahler's whim.

*Der Bärenhäuter* [The bear skinner], by Wagner's son Siegfried enjoyed only a brief success in Vienna.

Rubinstein's *Der Dämon* [The demon] suffered the same fate as Siegfried Wagner's opera.

1900    Tchaikovsky's *Iolanthe*, his last opera, also found little response in Vienna despite Mahler's love for Slavic music.

Zemlinsky's *Es war einmal* [Once upon a time] was Mahler's bow to the music of his time in Vienna and to this friend of Schönberg.

Giordano's *Fedora* was introduced soon after its Italian premiere.

1901    Offenbach's *Hoffmann's Erzählungen* [Tales of Hoffmann] finally reached a Viennese audience. Superstition had kept the opera off the Vienna stage since the night of the disastrous *Ringtheater* fire in 1881 when it had been scheduled to be performed.

1902    Mahler reciprocated Richard Strauss's earlier kindness in performing Mahler's symphonies by conducting *Feuersnot* [Fire trouble].

Mozart's *Zaide*, the unfinished opera of the young (1779) Mozart, and Tchaikovsky's *Pique Dame* [Queen of spades], destined to become one of the composer's most successful operas, were other highlights.

Although only the major acquisitions and productions are here enumerated, the list reflects a staggering amount of activity during Mahler's first five years, the first half of his tenure.

As will be seen later, Mahler's dedication to what he considered the composer's will reflected a considerable departure from either Jahn's or Richter's mode of interpretation. Mahler knew this, of course, and was aware of the risks involved in departing from what was then considered traditional interpretation. But he examined traditions coldly and did away with outworn ones, regardless of criticism or risk. And at that point the positive critics outweighed the nigglers. Remarked Theodor Helm of the uncut *Ring* performances:

Success has justified Mahler; night after night the house is completely sold out, the audience in a mood of reverence and festive excitement. . . . Obviously the performances, every one of them led by the director in person, had been thoroughly rethought and worked over.

Yet the intensity of Mahler's interpretations did take the Viennese by surprise, owing to the obvious differences in conception and tempi between his interpretations and those of the "high priest of Wagner," Hans Richter. Despite Mahler's repeated avowals of fidelity to the composer's intentions and ideals, it was impossible for Mahler not to impart to his performances his own sense of conflict and drama. This should not surprise. It is this mysterious ingredient which the performer—the connecting link between the composer and the listener—brings to a performance that makes performing music the mysterious art it is. In the case of Richter and Mahler, the differences were glaringly obvious. The massive, bearded, blond, blue-eyed giant Richter, like his interpretations, belonged to a ponderous past that was fully acceptable to conservative Vienna because it represented to them the tradition which they knew and understood and in which they felt comfortable. It had been that sense of continuity which had made Brahms immediately and fully acceptable to the Viennese in contrast to the new, Wagnerian element introduced by Bruckner.

In contrast to Richter, the smooth-shaven, finely chiseled Semitic features of Mahler, his tense, quick-silver personality, his sense of excitement and drama, reflected a total departure from the past, a new element, in a city where Richter's interpretations were still accepted as "truth." But Mahler, creator as well as recreator, knew that every century had its own Bible and that interpretations must change with personality, nationality, and the times. Yet in the beginning, despite Mahler's nightly triumphs, the palm was still awarded to Richter.

> Not all themes are equally congenial to [Mahler]. His rendering of the Valhalla motif lacks—not breadth—but calm; on the other hand, when it comes to the oppressive mysteries of the Tarnhelm theme, he gives us an insight rising to a sense of terrifying menace. . . . His treatment of the gods' exchanges in the second scene of *Das Rheingold* is undoubtedly not in the spirit of Wagner. . . . Although often splendid, spirited, and well thought out, Mahler's conducting at times lacks the beautiful balance and continuity of argument and the majestic calm which is the strength of Richter's approach.
>
> Gustav Schönaich, *Wiener Allgemeine Zeitung*

Not all writers, moreover, were as understanding and discriminating as to the nature of different styles and the changing trends in musical conception, or realized that continuity of tradition was no longer the foremost aim in music but was bound to yield to new trends and instincts, such as those which Mahler represented and which prompted him to remark to Alma that it would take fifty years before the world would understand his music. Those trends represented a closed door which the conservative Richter never intended to open and perhaps never even knew existed.

To Mahler continuity of life, not of tradition, was the essence. Thus continuity in the spirit of Brahms, the neo-classicist, was meaningless to Mahler. By outwardly destroying continuity and inwardly infusing his music with new sounds, with tension and excitement, he reflected the continuity of the living spark, the same spark which had inspired Beethoven to break away from the classical mold of Haydn and Mozart, Gluck to abandon Neapolitan opera, and Schönberg to renounce tonality. While Mahler's contemporary, Richard Strauss, reveled in silken, sensuous sounds, the exterior luxuries of his time, Mahler's vision plunged him into depths of despair. In the words of Nietzsche, proclaimed in Mahler's Third Symphony:

> Oh man take heed
> . . . . . . . . .
> The world is deep
> and deeper than the day would think.

The difficulty of intuitive interpretation was dramatically depicted in an episode related by the Viennese music critic and historian Max Graf. Graf remonstrated with Mahler about certain tempi in *Die Walküre* which he considered too fast. Mahler frowned. Graf added apologetically: "I am probably too used to the broad tempi of Hans Richter." Mahler's mood changed from frown to fury: "Stop that. Richter has no idea about tempi." Graf, although taken aback, became angry in turn: "But Richter conducted the first *Walküre* in Bayreuth under Wagner, and therefore must know the Wagnerian tempi." To this Mahler replied curtly: "Maybe he knew the right tempi then. Since then he has forgotten them." Later Graf joined Richter on his way home, and the discussion turned to Mahler's *Walküre* performance. Now Graf asked Richter about Mahler's tempi. Richter heaved a sigh: "What of the music, at the end, is *Feuerzauber*—that was brought out very well by Mahler. But that this end is a transfiguration and a painful resignation—of that Mahler has no idea."[16]

Mahler was, of course, not so thoughtlessly self-centered as not to appreciate Richter's achievements, and we may believe the sincerity of his regret at Richter's departure from Vienna. But soon after Mahler's arrival at the opera, Richter was forced to realize that he no longer was the dominant force in the musical life of Vienna. Before, although Jahn had officially been the man in charge, there had been a convenient division of responsibilities, with Jahn conducting the French and Italian repertoire while Richter was in charge of the entire Wagner program. Since 1875

---

[16] Graf, *Legend of a Musical City*. Surprisingly, the Wagners, both Richard and Cosima, would have agreed with Mahler. Wagner often preferred Bülow, Seidl, or Levi to Richter as conductors. Cosima must have echoed Wagner's opinion when she noted Richter's tempi in her diary: "He sticks too close to his four-to-a-bar." Wagner employed a more plastic, flexible line, which also was Mahler's custom.

he had also been the conductor of the Philharmonic orchestra, and for a number of years he had conducted also the concerts of the *Gesellschaft der Musikfreunde*. Now Richter found himself in a difficult situation. Although Mahler made a sincere gesture to retain Richter at least at the opera after he had resigned from the Philharmonic, the situation became even more untenable when Mahler announced that he would take on the conducting of Wagner. It was at that time that Richter received an offer from Manchester of the position of conductor of the renowned Hallé Orchestra. This brought into focus the triangle of Vienna–Bayreuth–England which encompassed Richter's entire life.

His youthful studies—choir singing in the Court Chapel and, significantly, theory study with Sechter—had taken place mainly in Vienna. His first professional engagement was as French horn player in the opera repertoire of the *Kärnthnerthor Theater*. There he came to the attention of conductor Heinrich Esser, who recommended him to Wagner. Despite the age difference of thirty years, the artistic connection soon became close enough for Wagner to entrust to the young musician the copying of the original score of *Die Meistersinger*. Although Richter became conductor at the Court Theater in Munich in 1868, his connection with Wagner deepened and intensified. He is supposed to have collaborated in the Brussels production of *Lohengrin* in 1870 and participated in the first performance of the *Siegfried Idyll*. Wagner's confidence continued unabated as he directed Richter to prepare the final copy of the *Ring* score. Richter, in turn, moved up to his position as first conductor and director at the Budapest National Theater, which prepared him in stage knowledge for future triumphs. The turning point came in 1875, when he conducted a concert in Vienna. It was so impressive that he was offered the position of conductor of the Imperial Opera the same year, coinciding with Dessoff's retirement from the post. In addition he was also offered the conducting position with the Philharmonic, with which he developed an especially close relationship.

Eighteen seventy-six marked one of the high points in Richter's career. Wagner entrusted him with all the rehearsals in Bayreuth and, as the final glory and honor, chose the thirty-three-year-old Austro-Hungarian to conduct the performances. The following year Richter introduced *Die Walküre* to Vienna, and in 1878 he was elevated to the position of *Hofkapellmeister* (Court conductor). It was through the collaboration of Richter and Jahn that the groundwork was laid for the preeminence of the Vienna Opera. Richter's huge, bearded physique reflected the power he wielded in Vienna. Surrounded by the halo of his close acquaintance with Wagner, he proceeded to raise the caliber of the Vienna Opera. People listened in awe when he conducted Beethoven, Brahms, or Wagner without a score, a rarity in those days. His Wagner performances, in particular, were considered definitive.

By then Richter's fame had reached its zenith. He had been decorated by the King of Bavaria, the Grand Duke of Weimar, and Emperor Franz Joseph. In 1877 his fame reached beyond continental confines, as London invited him to participate in the Albert Hall concerts and share the podium with none other than Wagner. Richter's appearances before London audiences constituted highlights of the season for many years, during which he introduced to England *Die Meistersinger, Tristan,* and the entire *Ring,* in addition to his masterful performances of Beethoven—also, incidentally, without score. Despite his narrow repertoire, limited mainly to the Germans (French music simply did not exist for him), Richter was also fond of English composers and artists and particularly championed the music of Edward Elgar; the composer reciprocated by dedicating his First Symphony to Richter.

Thus one of the concerns of Mahler, upon arriving in Vienna, had been the position, presence and influence of Hans Richter, which he expected to be troublesome in view of the rumors which had reached him prior to his arrival (see letter to Dr. Arnold Berliner, p. 63, footnote). As it turned out, Mahler and Richter were to share Vienna for a relatively brief span of time. The coincidence of Mahler's decision to personally conduct Wagner and the offer from the Hallé Orchestra made Richter decide to sever his Vienna activities completely and transfer his musical work; he divided it, until his retirement in 1912, between Manchester, Birmingham, London, and Bayreuth. Vienna, which had looked forward to another one of those artistic feuds which wet its palate and were discussed and argued by all, was to be disappointed. Mutual respect prevented either man from publicly uttering any derogatory remarks about the other. Richter yielded: Mahler took over.

Despite the splendid accomplishments of Jahn and Richter, a staid atmosphere had invaded the Opera of late, reflected in all departments. The vocal emphasis had been on *bel canto,* scenery had become musty and bedraggled, and stage direction, following "tradition," existed in name only. It took Mahler the comparatively short time of three years to change the house into a Mahler ensemble. Already in 1900 he had engaged the Bruckner disciple Franz Schalk, who was to remain one of the main pillars of strength for nearly three decades. A year later Mahler was able to bring to Vienna his friend and disciple from Hamburg days, Bruno Walter, who had meanwhile gained experience on his own in the opera houses of Breslau, Pressburg, Riga, and Berlin. If the first five years had brought a wealth of exciting premieres to Vienna, the next few reaped no less rich a harvest.

1903    Charpentier's *Louise* was performed in the composer's surrealist conception, along with Wagner's *Tristan und Isolde,* in a new, Roller production, and Puccini's *La Bohème.*

1904    Hugo Wolf's *Der Corregidor* was belatedly, posthumously premiered, while Beethoven's *Fidelio* had a new production.

1905    Featured were Eugène d'Albert's *Die Abreise* [The departure]; Leo Blech's *Das war Ich* [That was I];

Ermanno Wolf-Ferrari's *Le Donne Curiose* [The curious women]

Pfitzner's *Die Rose vom Liebesgarten* [The rose from the garden of love] (after an initial refusal); and

Mozart's *Don Giovanni,* which production saw the first appearance of the "Roller towers."

Audiences, regardless of whether or not they agreed with Mahler's interpretations, loved every minute of them.

His every appearance in the orchestra pit was preceded by the tenseness with which one looks forward to a sensation. The house grew silent when, with quick, firm step, he made for the desk. If a whisper would arise or an embarrassed latecomer sneak in, Mahler would turn around and a dead silence would reign over the intimidated audience . . . everybody was under his spell. Before the opening of the third (last) act, he was invariably received with a hurricane of applause. . . . That was the order of things through the period of his incumbency.

Bruno Walter, *Mahler*

Oddly enough, news of a performance led by Mahler had to be spread by word of mouth or through newspaper announcements, because neither in its placards nor in its programs did the Vienna Opera list the name of the conductor. Mahler and Weingartner are alternatively credited with seeing to it that the conductor's name was included in the program.

Vienna became more than a position to Mahler. He adored the city, as had Gluck, Haydn, Mozart, Beethoven, Schubert, and Brahms before him. Operatically and conductorially, he considered himself at the peak of his career. Audiences were mesmerized by his performances. Such admiration, however, was extended to the artist, not necessarily to the man. If Alma Mahler was willing, during their marriage, to make sacrifices and allowances for him, the public was not, nor were many of the artists with whom he came in contact. An artist might strive to attain Mahler's ideal of perfection, but could and would still retain strong reservations as to the manner in which Mahler attained such perfection. Mahler's silences as well as his torrents could be devastating. In one performance of the *Magic Flute*, Elise Elizza sang one of the three ladies. Her cue was incorrect the first, second, third, and fourth time. On the fifth attempt Elizza's patience was at an end. Instead of addressing the snake on the ground, she sang her cue, at the top of her voice, at Mahler, the conductor: *"Stirb, Ungeheuer, durch meine Macht."* (Die, monster, through my might.) Deadly pause. Instead of producing the expected terror the feared conductor calmly looked at her. "Of course that would suit you. Anyhow, this time your cue was perfect. Let's go on."

Recalls Bruno Walter, in *Theme and Variations:*

> I still can see him, at an orchestra rehearsal of *Götterdämmerung,* rushing towards the trumpet and trombones in a far corner of the orchestra pit, to impress upon them especially a passage in the Funeral March; or quickly using a double-bass chair to climb up to the stage in order to give directions there . . . as, for instance, in connection with the shading of a distant chorus or of music on stage. The orchestra would, meanwhile, remain in hypnotic silence under the spell of a master who, himself spellbound by the intrinsic conception of a work of art, seemed urged by a compelling force to make his coworkers comply with the irresistible dictates of his innermost self.

Occasionally humor would enter into the situation, as at the time when Mahler explained to Tristan that he was to be gloomy and reserved before drinking the love potion and broad and open after drinking it. *"Also vergessen Sie nicht, vorher sind Sie ein Bariton, nachher ein Tenor."* [Don't forget, before you are a baritone, afterwards a tenor.]

With orchestras Mahler was unrelenting. Once during rehearsal he was totally dissatisfied with the famous opening of Beethoven's Fifth Symphony and had the orchestra repeat it over and over again. Finally members of the orchestra became so outraged that some refused to play and others began to pack their instruments. Mahler, now doubly exasperated, bore down on them: "Gentlemen, save your fury for the performance; then at least we shall have the opening played as it should be." The comment itself sheds light on Mahler's conception of the meaning of the opening. It soon became apparent that Mahler was at no time willing to enter into a popularity contest with anybody, be it emperor, artist, critic, or public. The end result was respect and admiration but hardly love, unless one was an artist or a wife with the insight of a Schönberg or an Alma Mahler, respectively.

Mahler's actions and words, unencumbered by and insensitive to the feelings of others, were prompted by two motives, one deliberate, one subconscious. Subconsciously Mahler's dramatic, terse decisions and pronouncements were nothing less than outward manifestations of the inwardly churning volcano of an artist striving for perfection. Mahler had come to realize in opera house after opera house, that the terse, precise word, the succinct phrase, brought the desired results promptly and without the need for lengthy discussion and argument. Mahler apparently never consciously realized the fundamental gap between his admiration for the democratic aspirations of the working class (he once marched in a May Day parade) and his own dictatorial behavior as a conductor.

Mahler's life had drastically changed with his move to Vienna. Prominent before, he had overnight become a man of international musical importance by virtue of his Vienna position. His life-style concomitantly changed, although he did not allow it to affect his basic habits. One could still see him storming along the *Ringstrasse* as people respectfully pointed him out—*Der Mahler*. But he also enjoyed an automobile which the opera management had put at his disposal, as well as that other novelty now at his command, the telephone, which kept him in easy touch with his friends, his home, and the opera. As could have been foreseen, a year later, with Richter removing himself from the Philharmonic, the Opera, and Vienna, Mahler was offered the post of conductor of the Vienna Philharmonic Orchestra. Although he was the man of the hour and the logical choice, the union of Mahler and the Philharmonic was not especially warm or harmonious nor of long duration. But regardless of strife and lack of harmony, Mahler felt "at home" in Vienna and Austria, and two years after his arrival the town of Maiernigg on Lake Wörther in Carynthia was to see much of Mahler because he bought ground there and built a summer home.

Vienna's relationship to its musical life in general and its opera in particular bears brief scrutiny. Prior to Mahler there had been the matter of opera cuts, now fully restored by him. That Jahn as well as Richter had had no qualms in deleting parts of operas in order to cut them to "manageable size" represented one of the more amazing compromises made in the realm of that time. From the exuberant but negligent Jahn one might expect such slighting of the composer's intentions, but from Richter, "the conscience of Vienna's music," who had sat at Wagner's feet and had been anointed by him, such deletions bordered on sacrilege. With Mahler, however, objections came from a different direction. Audiences objected to his added instrumentation in Beethoven's Ninth Symphony and his setting for string orchestra of Beethoven's Quartet in F Minor, opus 95. Undeterred, Mahler shrugged off such objections: "Your Beethoven is not my Beethoven." He was totally convinced of the rightness of his cause, but as the clamor increased he was eventually moved to issue a detailed reply. There was ferment for other reasons also. For while Vienna was artistically enthralled, it was not mollified socially. Here it is worthwhile examining the nuances of the specific position of the Opera in Vienna's musical life.

The Opera was not simply a musical institution to be judged by musical standards alone. It was totally, inextricably a part of Vienna itself, and events there were discussed as much on a social and human level as on a musical one. When Maria Olczewska and Maria Jeritza spat at each other on stage, the incident crowded other, seemingly more important, news off the newspaper pages. And when a singer married the policeman who had assisted her at the scene of an automobile accident, the event furnished material for coffeehouse chatter for weeks thereafter. Non-Viennese may find such attention to trivia surprising in so cultured a city as Vienna, but such was the Viennese attitude to "their" music, an attitude which, in actuality, reflected their interest in gossip more than their attachment to music. In line with such an attitude of involvement, every time a seemingly time-honored tradition was abruptly scuttled, every time one of the old stars, beloved by the Viennese despite a conspicuously fading voice, was replaced by a promising young new singer, murmurs of dissent enlivened the newspaper music columns and the conversation in the Vienna salons and prompted wounded roars from these quarters. Still Mahler went on, undisturbed and undaunted, molding new voices, preparing new stagings, experimenting, reaching new heights. Some of his endeavors met with predictable resistance: all new voices, for example, necessitated guest appearances which overburdened all concerned and did little to ingratiate the newcomer with those who had previously sung the role now being attempted. But Mahler ignored overt and covert disagreements, constantly striving with undiminished hope and enthusiasm which were more often than not rewarded with splendid success. His spirit illuminated all phases of music: the contemporary—Pfitzner and Richard Strauss; the classics—Gluck, Haydn, Mozart, Beethoven; the neglected —Charpentier, Smetana; the out-of-favor—Goetz, Boildieu, Halévy; and, of course, Wagner. His deep insight and conscientiousness created a consistently rich operatic tapestry never equaled before or after him, and his productions of *Don Giovanni, Fidelio, Iphigenie en Aulide, The Magic Flute,* and *Tristan* were forever enshrined in the annals of the Vienna Opera.

The fact that Mahler's tenure in Vienna lasted a full ten years—in Vienna an incredibly long span of time for any director or conductor— speaks for Mahler's genius. But his uncompromising attitude, his undisguisedly harsh judgments and his lack of diplomacy eventually provided the tools which his enemies used to bring him down. Fortunately for all, Mahler himself realized, then, that his time at the opera had ended. Thus the parting was without any of the hostility and bitterness for which the Viennese were hopefully poised.

Emotionally the relaxed Vienna style (*"Mir wern kan Richter brauchen"*—we won't need a judge to settle the argument) was anathema to Mahler from the outset—a tide against which he had to swim for ten years. Yet admiration for his artistic accomplishment reached right into the *Hofburg,* where the emperor saw fit to congratulate Mahler: *"Es ist Ihnen gelungen Herr der Verhältnisse im Opernhaus zu werden"* [You have succeeded in becoming the master of conditions at the opera house.] There may have been a touch of envy in Franz Joseph's congratulatory message to Mahler, because seldom in the long reign of the beloved emperor could he consider himself "master of conditions." At the moment when that mastery was threatened, Mahler resigned. Subconsciously he must have realized the fruits and faults of his attitude, because in his moving farewell to the members of the opera he spoke of "wounds of battle and . . . misunderstandings on both sides." Few of his coworkers realized that his harshness began with himself and the demands he made of himself surpassed anything he asked of others.

Miraculously, during summer vacations he conceived and put to paper his Fourth, Fifth, Sixth, Seventh, and Eighth symphonies, and then found time between rigorous rehearsals and performances to orchestrate and put the finishing touches to those giant works during the ensuing winter seasons, besides making innumerable guest-conducting appearances in his own works and the general repertoire. His Fourth Symphony, begun during the summer of 1899 and finished in 1900, was premiered a year later in Munich and heard in 1902 in Vienna. There Mahler was as much appreciated as a director as he was reviled as a composer. But he was not to be denied. In 1902 his Third Symphony, performed at the Music Festival in Krefeld, brought him overwhelming recognition as a composer. His Fifth Symphony—perhaps the most difficult of conception —was first heard in Cologne in 1904. It was a decided success; yet it left Mahler dissatisfied and subsequently underwent decisive instrumental changes, because the initial score did not conform to the philosophical changes in outlook which Mahler then underwent.

Mahler—the sophisticate, the sensitive thinker, the giant of music— had never bothered to acquire social graces. When a private performance bored him, he would either endure it stonily or leave the room, never to return to the performance. Once, while deep in thought during one of his rapid noonday walks on the *Ring,* Mahler was joined by an amiable musician of slight acquaintance who struck up a conversation. After a few minutes of total silence on Mahler's part he abruptly left his companion, ran after a streetcar, and vanished without as much as an adieu to the perplexed musician. In contrast, to his peers and to the friends and musicians in his small circle, he was open and charming, reciprocating kindness and sympathy.

> One of my fond memories is of a concert which the "Society of Creative Musicians" [presented] . . . and had invited Mahler to conduct. To the deep reverence in which he was held by the young composers, Schönberg and Zemlinsky at their head, Mahler responded with hearty sympathy. Thus the evening . . . was turned into a veritable Mahler celebration. On that evening Mahler was really happy. In the young musicians' unbounded devotion, more beautiful and pleasing to him than the loud acclaim of the great public, he felt the response of the heart to the call of his own heart in his songs. Every one of these striving and talented followers received only impressions of sympathy, of interest, and ungrudging kindness [from Mahler].
>
> Bruno Walter, *Mahler*

Walter had spent two years with Mahler in Hamburg; when Mahler left for Vienna, their ways parted. After four years in Vienna, while Walter was filling a post of conductor at the *Stadttheater* in Riga, Mahler offered him a conductor's position in Vienna, to begin in 1900 when Walter's Riga contract was to end. Walter was dubious with regard to his experience and self-confidence, a far cry from his self-assured attitude at age nineteen when he first met Mahler in Hamburg. He consequently turned down Mahler's offer, to the latter's express disappointment; Walter accepted instead an offer to become "Royal Prussian Conductor" at the Berlin Opera. Only occasionally was he able to travel by train to his beloved Vienna. His stay there was enhanced by witnessing Mahler performances, and he soon became convinced that Vienna was the answer to his plans of artistic growth. Thus when Mahler again approached him and offered him a five-year contract, Walter promptly requested and received a termination of his Berlin contract. As fate would have it, Walter and the tenor Leo Slezak, also destined for worldwide fame, cabled their contract acceptances to Mahler at the same time.

Life in Vienna was to be as variably pleasant and unpleasant for Walter as it was for Mahler. Eduard Hanslick had been succeeded by the equally competent and powerful Julius Korngold [17] as music critic of *Die Neue Freie Presse,* and the equally knowledgeable but extremely conservative Max Kalbeck [18] had become music critic of the *Neues Wiener Tagblatt.* But it was the subtle anti-Semitism of Mayor Dr. Karl Lueger and the outspoken anti-Semitism of Georg von Schönerer which made life less than comfortable for Mahler and Walter. The latter writes in *Theme and Variations* that "two newspapers in Vienna at the time . . . were wholly in the service of anti-Semitism . . . [spreading] . . . lies and calumnies concerning Mahler and myself."

Upon his arrival in Vienna Walter was awed by many things—by the stateliness of the opera director's office, for instance, but even more by the custom of the Vienna Royal Opera House (and also of the Court Theater) of providing a special service for its female singers and actresses. They were privileged to have a carriage service at their disposal, which called for them at their respective residences at a given hour before curtain time and returned them to their home after each performance. But most of all Walter was awed by the power Mahler wielded in his post as opera director of the foremost opera house in the world.

With disciple Walter at Mahler's side, the fury so often unsuccessfully vented against Mahler overflowed to include Walter's work, with the *Neues Wiener Tagblatt* stating in one review that "Walter would not do as the leader of a rifleman's band." Walter succeeded despite vilification, however. At this crossroads in his life he was aided by **Arnold Rosé,**

---

[17] Father of the composer Erich Wolfgang Korngold.
[18] The friend and future biographer of Brahms.

brother-in-law of Mahler, concertmaster of the Philharmonic orchestra since age seventeen, and leader of the famous quartet that bore his name. Rosé invited Walter to participate in chamber music sessions with the quartet at the small but acoustically superb *Bösendorfersaal* [19]; there Vienna's musical elite met, and their response to Walter was warm and gratifying. Walter was to make music with the Rosé Quartet for fifteen years.

Just as Mahler was interested in and drawn to the younger generation of composers as represented by Schönberg, Berg, and Zemlinsky, his zest for knowledge and widened artistic horizons eventually drew him into the circle of a vigorous group of artists whose new perceptions and conceptions of art prompted them to secede from the *Künstlerhaus,* the established artists' organization, and form a new organization aptly called *Sezession;* among them were sculptor **Max Klinger;** painters **Gustav Klimt, Egon Schiele, Oscar Kokoschka,** Carl Moll, Kolo Moser, and Emil Orlik, who painted Mahler; architects **Otto Wagner** and **Adolf Loos;** and theater designer Alfred Roller.[20]

Mahler met Roller at a party given by some of his friends. Roller was a friend of the Schindlers (Alma's parents) and shortly after they made each other's acquaintance the two men became deeply involved in a discussion of the staging of *Tristan.* Roller was enchanted with the music but exasperated with the insipid staging, which, in his opinion, destroyed much of the opera's magnificence. Roller, an artist in his own right and a friend to the great Viennese painters of his day, had given the staging of *Tristan* much thought. When he now expounded to Mahler his viewpoint concerning the function of the stage, Mahler found himself completely in accord. Roller, carried away with his favorite project, then began to unfold before the director of the Vienna Court Opera his vision of the splendor of the opera as it should be staged. Mahler was stirred: "See me tomorrow at the opera." The next day Roller was commissioned to design a new staging for *Tristan.* Roller's slogan, "space, not pictures," was to transform the Vienna opera stage and enlarge it spiritually, visually, and symbolically. His work—it was Roller's first venture into stage design —inspired some and exasperated others. Old-time singers and stage people rebelled against the innovations of the "amateur." Mahler—acting, as he so often did, on artistic instinct—was taking a tremendous risk, which, had it failed, could have had serious adverse repercussions for him. But Mahler's instinct again proved correct; the new *Tristan* was a resounding success and Roller was appointed permanent stage designer.

---

[19] Named after Vienna's famous piano maker, Ludwig Bösendorfer, who had discovered the hall's spectacular acoustics while it was one of Prince Liechtenstein's stables.

[20] Alma Mahler later claimed to have introduced Mahler to these artists, who were friends of her parents.

With Roller a new era in staging dawned at the Vienna Opera. Tradition was done away with, as Roller experimented with light effects as well as scenery. Naturalism, or what had passed for naturalism in German mythology, was discarded in favor of a much more significant element—symbolism. Thus the staging at the Vienna opera of Wagner's operas, combining his symbolism of the *Leitmotif* with Roller's symbolism of light and color, became the standard for Wagner performances throughout Europe.

> The relationship between auditory and visual perception was achieved by means of light and colors; each act of *Tristan* was allotted a particular color as a visible fundamental chord. Passionate orange–red flamed from the sails and curtains on the king's ship; a sultry violet–blue lay over the night of love, whereby the contrary-color stimulus brought about another coloristic and symbolic relationship; the landscape of the delirious and dying hero was swathed in a cold, whitish grey, whose bleakness was relieved by a huge lime tree.
>
> Heinrich Kralik, *Die Wiener Oper*

> The poetically conceived settings seemed to take their colors from the music . . . they translated something of the delicate chromaticism of *Tristan* into the settings and obtained musical effects with vibrations of the air and colors.
>
> Max Graf, *Legend of a Musical City*

> The localities can be described but not the light. When the tent is opening, when morning dawns, when Isolde sinks into the light—these are strokes of genius. Here is the conception of the music of light.
>
> Critic Oscar Bie's review after
> the premiere of *Tristan* with
> Roller's staging

Roller's collaboration with the conductor–director brought about a degree of intuitive interplay which aroused critics on both sides of the footlights. So strongly did Mahler feel about the importance of staging and lighting that even the individual lights above the orchestra stands in the pit constituted for him an intolerable intrusion into the atmosphere of *Tristan* created by Roller's staging. Consequently he had the floor of the orchestra pit lowered so that the orchestra would no longer intrude into the beholder's view.

Nineteen four saw one of the great achievements of the Mahler–Roller era: a production of Beethoven's *Fidelio*. But it was not until *Don Juan* [21] (Mozart's *Don Giovanni*) was produced in 1905 that Roller fully came into his own.

---

[21] The change from the Italian to the Spanish title on the Vienna programs was incongruous, particularly since the opera was sung in German anyway. Mahler disliked the change of title but did nothing to change it back to Italian.

Roller's conception . . . develops gradually; it formulates itself, and the form it assumed in *Don Giovanni* is not even the final one. . . . Here we see a markedly stylized stage picture. There are some architectural focal points in the shape of wooden towers . . . which define the stage space . . . The towers are quite simple, practicable constructions, with openings . . . serving as windows of houses, oriels, or balconies; these are sometimes hung with draperies, a kind of structural *passe-partout* creating an ideal space . . . made just as deep and broad as the purpose of the scene demands. So it cannot happen that the stage turns into a vast wilderness on which a single person makes enormous gestures because he instinctively wants to take up as much room as possible. This caricature of operatic acting is . . . done away with.

Critic Ludwig Hevesi's review after the premiere of<br>*Don Juan* with Roller's staging

Hevesi refers, of course, to Roller's greatest innovation, the "Roller towers," pylon-like structures usually placed on either side of the stage. (Occasionally there were even more on stage than the two usually required.) They always remained on stage but served different purposes as the action might demand. Mahler's *Don Giovanni* interpretations had been among his finest achievements as early as his Budapest days; now, with Roller's staging, the opera became a stage sensation. It was the foremost musical topic of the day, particularly since Mahler had asked the writer and critic Max Kalbeck to revise part of the translation of the libretto and had also done away with some of the ornamental vocal moss that the opera had gathered over the decades and which he considered to be not in the spirit of Mozart. Not all were pleased with Mahler's conception of Mozart, and from the ranks of the traditionalists the lament was quite audible. However, Mahler was to encounter much greater resistance to his music making from another quarter.

## THE VIENNA PHILHARMONIC ORCHESTRA

In line with his intention to sever his ties with Vienna, Hans Richter had resigned in 1898 from his post as conductor of the Vienna Philharmonic Orchestra. To fill the vacancy as quickly and at as high an artistic level as possible, it was a logical move on the part of the Philharmonic to offer the position to the new director of the Vienna Opera, by then an operatic and orchestral conductor of international renown.

At this point the dual function of the Vienna Philharmonic, unique in the world, should be understood. The Vienna Philharmonic and the pit orchestra of the Vienna Opera are one and the same from a musical point of view. Organizationally, however, there is a subtle yet trenchant difference. When playing at the opera house the artists are employed by that institution and subject to the orders of the director. Removed from the opera, in their own headquarters at the *Musikverein* building, the men of the Philharmonic are an entity unto themselves, totally autonomous and subject only to their own democratic decision-making. The conductor chosen and engaged by the Philharmonic Orchestra for their concerts assumes a position totally different from that obtaining in the director–orchestra relationship at the Opera. In the Philharmonic deliberations he is, to this very day, engaged by the artists making up the orchestra as *primus inter pares,* first among equals.

Thus the players making up the Philharmonic Orchestra were in no way obliged to turn to Mahler, but decided as a matter of professional and artistic judgment to engage the man under whose inspired baton they played night after night. Moreover, it was also a matter of convenience. Why engage another conductor, perhaps from halfway across Europe, when an acknowledged genius was in their city? Furthermore, the very fact that Mahler was hailed as a genius made him a gate attraction for the Philharmonic concerts. All of these factors were debated and the decision made even though the majority of the members confessed that their sentiments still lingered with Richter, to whom they had related as pater-familias since he had actually emanated from their ranks. During rehearsals with the Philharmonic Richter would actually conduct while sitting in a wicker chair among the orchestra, a father figure directing his family, or let the orchestra play by itself while he watched from his chair with his arms folded. It was with that past relationship in mind that Mahler tactfully replied to the welcoming speech by the Philharmonic spokesman:

> It is primarily to my regret that such a splendid collaborator as Hans Richter was lost to me. I could not believe that he was really serious in his withdrawal from the Philharmonic concerts, in which he celebrated such well-earned triumphs. I therefore hesitated until the last moment to follow your call, and decided only when I was faced with the absolute certainty that the circumstances which prompted Hans Richter to persist in his decision were irrevocable. Only then could I accept. As I now stand at your helm, I cannot help but express my pleasure to make music with this splendid body. . . .

The history of that "splendid body" was, at that time, as fascinating as it was brief. It is an incredible paradox that in the time of Haydn, Mozart, and Beethoven, Vienna, the "city of music," had no professional orchestra of its own to perform the immortal creations of the men in its midst. The fact that an innate musicianship, reaching into the court and the aristocracy, pervaded Vienna does not veil the fact that all concerts were played by musical amateurs or semiprofessionals at best, bound by no professional bond or organization and engaged only in the loosest contractual manner for individual performances. When Mendelssohn visited Vienna he commented unfavorably on the fact that Vienna had no professional orchestra such as cities like Leipzig, Mannheim, or Paris were boasting. There was, of course, the hoary and respectable *Tonkünstler Societät* (Tone Artists' Society). Today it is remembered mainly because it refused membership to Haydn and only in his old age made him an honorary member. Besides, the *Societät* was mainly a charity organization for musicians, with benefits also extending to the musicians' widows and orphans. Its musical contribution to the Vienna scene consisted of two yearly choral concerts.

Eighteen thirteen saw an alteration of conditions with the founding of the *Gesellschaft der Musikfreunde* (Society of Friends of Music), which exists to this day with undiminished importance in the musical life of the city. Under the patronage of Archduke Rudolf, Beethoven's pupil and patron, *Musikfeste* (music festivals) of oratorios, with as many as one thousand singers, were performed in the Spanish Riding School. Eighteen thirty saw the foundation of its world-famous *Konservatorium;* the erection of its own building, the *Musikverein,* with one of the acoustically finest concert halls in the world; and the establishment of a choral society, the *Singverein;* and the society crowned its growth in 1851 with the appointment of Josef Hellmesberger as its first professional conductor. From then on some of Vienna's greatest musical names were either members of the *Gesellschaft* or conductors of its concerts.

The shift to music making by professionals had begun, imperceptibly but irrevocably. The basis for a first-class professional orchestra was, of course, present, playing daily in the pit of the opera house, and to organize it into a symphonic ensemble was the next logical step. **Franz Lachner** was the logical choice for the job; already in 1833, Lachner, the immensely talented composer and conductor of the *Kärnthnerthor Theater,* had arranged for subscription concerts in which the opera and choral personnel of the opera participated. He had known Beethoven personally, had befriended Schubert and studied with Sechter; but apparently the public was not yet ready to attend concerts on a regular organized basis, and the subscription concerts were discontinued. An eight-year hiatus ensued.

In the summer of 1841, after a successful performance of his opera *Il Templario,* **Otto Nicolai** had become first *Kapellmeister* at the Vienna Opera. Like Beethoven before him and Brahms after him, the German found the Viennese musical climate conducive and settled there for six years. Reserving for himself only a limited repertoire of Mozart and Beethoven and a few new productions, Nicolai and a group of like-minded friends turned their sights on the establishment of a professional orchestra for Vienna. March 28th, 1842 thus became a historic date for Vienna when the first *Grosse Konzert* (Grand Concert), a Philharmonic concert, took place in the *Redoutensaal* (a ballroom and concert hall). Nicolai had accomplished a tremendous feat.

> In these concerts thus far I have brought only thoroughly classical music to performance, and they shall continue in this spirit. . . . I combine for these performances all the members of my orchestra, which will be reinforced by other artists of the city—amateurs totally excluded—in order to reach the number of sixteen first violins. . . . At the *Kärntnerthor Theater* there are now engaged nine first violins, nine second violins, four violas, five cellos, five string basses, three flutes, three oboes, three clarinets, six horns, three bassoons, four drums, two timpani, four trombones, one bass drum, and one triangle. Georg Hellmesberger acts as principal orchestra director and at the same time as member of the Imperial Court Orchestra and professor at the Conservatory of Music; only he is a bit too quiet for my taste.
>
> as quoted by Heinrich Kralik, *Das grosse Orchester*

Nicolai's verve and enthusiasm carried all before him in his primary task; first-class performances of Beethoven. Whatever else he might present in his concerts—Haydn, Mozart, Mendelssohn, Weber, Cherubini, Meyerbeer, Spohr—was intended only to frame the main presentation of the evening, a Beethoven work. Already in his third concert, on 19 March 1843, he reacquainted Vienna with Beethoven's monumental Ninth Symphony, by then almost unknown in the city in which it had been conceived and created. Nicolai demanded perfection from his professionals, and no less than thirteen (!) rehearsals were allotted to Beethoven's Ninth. The performance was a sensational success. When Nicolai decided in 1848 to leave Vienna, his somewhat arrogant prediction came true.

> I believe that for a while these unsurpassed concerts might continue to be excellent without me, but over the long run, without me or without a director who, like me, will give of time and effort [and] possesses energy and perseverance like me, [they] will be difficult to maintain, at least in their present perfection.
>
> Kralik, *Das grosse Orchester*

The predicted sad tale unfolded after Nicolai's departure, as Georg Hellmesberger and others, less energetic and inspired, took their turns at the conductor's podium, only to see the popularity of their concerts fade into oblivion.

The end of the 1848 uprisings saw no improvement in the artistic spirit nor any immediate impulse to reactivate the concerts. And without a personality of the determination and energy of Nicolai (who had died in 1849 at age thirty-nine), Vienna's musical atmosphere remained stagnant. In 1854, **Karl Eckert**, the prominent conductor of the Opera, again attempted the difficult task of assembling an orchestra and thus reviving the Philharmonic concerts. The opening program was as impressive as it was varied.

Weber, *Euryanthe Overture*
Beethoven, Fifth Symphony
Mendelssohn, Violin Concerto in E Minor. Soloist: Henri Vieuxtemps.
Weber, Aria from *Euranthe*
Mozart, Quintet from *Cosi fan tutte*

Eighteen fifty-six saw a major event at the Philharmonic Orchestra. Clara Schumann played the Beethoven E-flat Major Piano Concerto, to the "stormy enthusiasm of the two thousand listeners assembled," according to one report. Such immortal creations as Bach's Concerto for Three Harpsichords in D Minor and Schubert's C-Major Symphony (The Great), Beethoven's Triple Concerto, and Schumann's *Manfred* Overture, however, met with no more than reserved respect. It was a phenomenon beyond explanation that the Viennese should show so little understanding for and derive so little pleasure from the magnificent work of Schubert, this most Viennese of composers. "Aside from many interesting spots there was much length, some harshness, some commonplace, some reminiscences of Beethoven, and in summary, the overall impression of this work could hardly be considered . . . praiseworthy" was a representative comment in the Vienna press on the symphony which Schumann described as being of "heavenly length." Despite Eckert's conscientious effort and preparations, the general public's enthusiasm had not yet been ignited; the Philharmonic concerts had not yet succeeded in taking their place by the side of the Opera to become a vital part of Vienna's artistic life. Part of the reason for such a condition was to be found in Eckert himself, whose direction at the Opera had fallen on hard times despite the magnificent *Lohengrin* performance, which literally moved Wagner to tears. Three more years had to pass before Eckert could again give fuller attention to the Philharmonic. The auspices were still not promising. Eighteen years had passed since Nicolai's first concert, and during those years only twenty concerts by any orchestra bearing the title of "Philharmonic" had been heard in Vienna. Eckert was now more determined than ever. First he set out to prepare a plan which would ensure continuity through financial stability. Suddenly the solution became obvious: concerts by subscription. Energetically he went to work, and the first of four subscription concerts took place on 15 January 1860. Beethoven's Seventh Symphony was the featured work. Eckert's intuition and dedication, coupled with sound business sense, bore fruit, and upon public demand a fifth concert was added. Another important move was the transfer of the concerts from the *Redoutensaal* to the actual home of the orchestra, the *Kärnthnerthor Theater*—from ballroom to opera house. But despite all of Eckert's accomplishments, his days, owing to intrigue at the opera house and the concert hall, were numbered. Fortunately another able man was on the scene. A young, promising conductor, **Otto Dessoff**, had been engaged by Eckert. Dessoff had no qualms about accepting an invitation to conduct the next concert series, beginning an association which was to grow into a long reign as conductor of the orchestra.

The decade of 1860–70 saw the blossoming of Vienna into a metropolis. The medieval walls had fallen, and monumental buildings—the opera house among them—rose on that new boulevard, the *Ring,* in luxuriant splendor, as well as the *Musikverein* building of Theophil Hansen, only one block removed from the *Ring.* The *Musikverein* became the home of the *Gesellschaft der Musikfreunde,* who now approached the Philharmonic Orchestra with an offer of fusion of the two foremost established organizations in Vienna. The orchestra, wishing to retain its independent character, did not accept; but this did not hinder a close and pleasant relationship between the two organizations. The *Gesellschaft* put its magnificent concert hall at the disposal of the Philharmonic, while the orchestra, in turn, obligated itself to provide a number of its instrumentalists for the concerts of the *Gesellschaft.*

March 6th, 1870 witnessed the last concert at the old *Kärnthnerthor Theater,* as the finale of Beethoven's Seventh Symphony closed a historic Philharmonic chapter. The first concert at the *Musikvereinssaal* opened with the *Euryanthe* Overture, which Weber had composed in Vienna and which had had its disastrous premiere in Vienna, but which had become a kind of good-luck charm for orchestral organizations in Vienna. Things musical began to establish themselves in the city. The Philharmonic had "come home" at the *Musikvereinssaal,* and it was Dessoff who was to guide its fortunes over the next five years. His programs abounded with names once bright but now faded: Brüll, Esser, Fuchs, Lachner, Reinecke, Raff, Volkmann; though they also featured brilliance—Liszt—and even genius—Beethoven, Wagner. Brahms made his first appearance in the programs in 1863 with his Serenade No. 2 in A Major. Surprisingly, his Serenade No. 1 in D Major, introduced some years later, proved a source of such a violent dispute that some members refused to play it and, Dessoff, in helpless rage, gored the conductor's score with his baton and departed furiously. It was Brahms who, in a brief address, smoothed the orchestra's artistic temperament. "You have rejected my work and I can only say to you: if you wish to make comparisons with Beethoven, such heights will never be attained again. But my work is the product of my best artistic conviction. Perhaps you will see your way clear that it is not quite unworthy to be played by you." Not only was the Serenade subsequently performed, but Brahms was invited to conduct it in person. From then on the closest of bonds connected the composer with the orchestra. He played his D-Minor Concerto there in 1871 with spectacular success (after its disastrous premiere in Leipzig) and conducted the premiere of his *Haydn Variations* in 1873.

While the talented and musically inspiring but personally somewhat retiring North German Dessoff directed the Philharmonic's musical fortunes, something exciting was happening at the *Musikverein* concerts. That something, or rather that somebody, was Johann Herbeck, the dynamic, fiery, flamboyant, Viennese. Herbeck, practically self-educated, had risen rapidly, and now the only musical post beyond his grasp was the conductorship of the Philharmonic, a position which his enthusiastic following clamorously claimed for their darling. Overnight the cry "Herbeck to the Philharmonic" rent musical Vienna in heated dispute—a favorite pastime, welcomed again in a city which took its musical affairs and scandals personally. Immediately all were embroiled, with Vienna's two most influential critics taking opposite views; Hanslick was pro-Dessoff, Ludwig Speidel pro-Herbeck.

Herbeck was near the short-lived zenith of his career, as *Hofopernkapellmeister* and *Hofoperndirektor* (Court Opera conductor and Court Opera director). Now only conductorship of the Philharmonic could make his life complete. For a while Dessoff sarcastically countered the haranges of the Herbeck clique, but he soon thought better of repartée and intrigue and accepted a position in Karlsruhe. His farewell concert in Vienna turned into a triumphant performance of Beethoven's Ninth Symphony.

Dessoff's departure in 1875 did not spell success for Herbeck. Instead, he was destined to fall victim to the grating sarcasm of Wagner and a cold shouldering by the Viennese public, which, in sudden fickleness, turned against him. April 1875 saw the end of his opera tenure and his return to the *Gesellschaft der Musikfreunde,* a chastened man. There trouble of a different nature awaited him. Brahms had become conductor of the *Gesellschaft* concerts. Vienna was again poised for a battle royal, rubbing its collective palms in anticipation. Battle lines promptly formed, as Herbeck adherents again wanted him in command. Brahms was to have none of such friction, however. Wrote he to his friend, the surgeon **Theodore Billroth**: "Nothing's happened, but the prospects are not encouraging, and I better depart." Brahms bowed out and waited; time was on his side. He was to appear repeatedly at the helm of the Philharmonic and a warm relationship developed between the man from Hamburg and the Vienna Orchestra, a friendship bordering on adoration which lasted to the day of Brahms's death.

Eighteen seventy-six found Brahms again on the Philharmonic podium conducting his *Haydn Variations* and presenting to Vienna a new name from the east of Europe, Tchaikovsky, whom he introduced to Viennese audiences with the symphonic poem *Romeo and Juliet.* This was much to the credit of Brahms, because he and Tchaikovsky never saw eye to eye in their conception of music, with Tchaikovsky referring to Brahms in his diary as "that scoundrel . . . this self-inflated mediocrity."

In 1877 the shadowy spectre of Herbeck rose for the last time. Herbeck having died a disillusioned man, shortly before reaching the age of forty-six, the Philharmonic wished to pay a last musical tribute, with a performance of his D-Minor Symphony, to the man who had labored so assiduously in Vienna's musical vineyard. Yet final success was to elude Herbeck after death; the music, like Herbeck, died ignominiously.

If the critics decided to use restraint in their judgment of the dead Herbeck's work, they felt no such compunctions with respect to Herbeck's protegé, Anton Bruckner, and in December 1877 Vienna witnessed the lamentable spectacle of Bruckner, devoid of support from his former patron or his audience, attempting to conduct his Third Symphony in D Minor, only to bow at the end of the performance to an all but empty hall and worse, upon turning back, to find the members of the orchestra also in full flight. Hardly anybody had remained to witness the emotionally pitiable scene of the composer, alone on stage, placid even in despair, collecting his score and, after a last look at the gaping scene of his defeat, shuffling off the stage. Bruckner's time had not yet arrived. While Germany acclaimed his *Te Deum,* Vienna fled from the man who was Wagner's disciple and Herbeck's protegé.

It was Brahms—the conservative, the epitome of classic continuity— to whom Vienna opened its heart. In the weeks prior to 30 December 1877, as Vienna awaited the world premiere of Brahms's Second Symphony, Richter, wrote Eduard Hanslick, "studied it with loving perseverance and brought it to a performance with a perfection which [did] him honor." Hanslick, who had hailed the First Symphony but with reservations, heaped unreserved praise on the Second, describing it in his *Music Criticisms* (1878) as

> a great unqualified success. . . . extends warm sunshine to connoiseurs and laymen alike. . . . [It is] radiant with healthy freshness and clarity, . . . serenity and cheerfulness, at once manly and gentle, animated alternately by good humor and reflective seriousness. . . . Mozartian blood flows in its veins. . . . Brahms has turned to the spring blossoming of the earth in his Second Symphony.

Brahms had become a Viennese in musical spirit; the Viennese idolized him and Richter's loving interpretations nurtured the infatuation.

The relationship between the Philharmonic and Richard Wagner was of a different nature; it was passionate but of much shorter duration. Wagner had first appeared with the orchestra in 1863 in a concert arranged by his disciple, the pianist and Liszt student Karl Tausig; on that occasion Vienna heard excerpts from *Tristan* and *Die Meistersinger*. Nine years were to elapse before Wagner again appeared at the helm of the Philharmonic to raise sympathy and money for his Bayreuth venture. Three years later, in 1875, Vienna was given its first glimpse at *Götterdämmerung;* the work unfolded so splendidly that Wagner magnanimously praised the Philharmonic as "the best orchestra in the world."

For the Opera and the Philharmonic, 1875 had been a fateful year of decisions. The former favorites' stars had set: Herbeck had resigned from the Opera, Dessoff from the Philharmonic. The threat of a void loomed over musical Vienna. The Opera chose the pragmatic way out, going from glowing idealist Herbeck to coldly calculating businessman Jauner. With the Philharmonic, however, idealism was not so carelessly discarded. They chose, in Hans Richter, one of their own, who had risen from the ranks, had played French horn with them, and had proven himself as a conductor of stature. His first concert for the *Akademische Wagnerverein* (the Academic Wagner Society) had been a success, and a kinship was felt between orchestra and conductor. Jauner had also recognized his genius and appointed him as *Hofkapellmeister*. If Jauner's artistic gaze fastened on Wagner out of opportunism, Richter featured him because he had experienced Wagner's genius. Richter balanced Wagner in equal measure with Brahms; only Bruckner (and Hugo Wolf) went against his grain, despite the former's enthusiasm for Wagner. Somehow Bruckner did not yet fit into that artistic balance that was to be Richter's hallmark. But Richter eventually did justice even to the music of Bruckner, the naive Austrian genius who combined baroque splendor, Schubertian joy, and Wagnerian monumentality in his symphonies.

Richter's sense of artistic balance was apparent in his first concert, when Wagner's *Faust* Overture and Liszt's *Hunnenschlacht* were balanced with an aria from Weber's *Oberon* and Beethoven's First Symphony. Although the season continued with Bach, Haydn, Mendelssohn, Mozart, Schumann, Weber, and, of course, Beethoven, Vienna also became acquainted with music of its own time, such as Berlioz's *Harold in Italy* and Karl Goldmark's *Ländliche Hochzeit* (Rustic Wedding). The Viennese felt secure; both Wagner and Brahms had given Richter their blessing, and Vienna had a new darling. But the city did not always accept the music of its other darling, Brahms. When his Piano Concerto No. 2 in B-flat Major was performed, with the composer at the piano, the performance was hampered, according to Max Kalbeck, music critic and future Brahms biographer, in 1881

> by the uneven, occasionally powerful and massive play, which removed the self-created difficulties without mastering them. . . . the clarity, precision, and fullness of tone were lost in the tumultuous sea of sounds, which Brahms, together with the orchestra, masterfully conducted by Richter, unleashed.

Having reached a new peak of perfection under Richter, the Philharmonic desired to carry its superb music making into localities outside Vienna. Salzburg, the birthplace of the most Austrian yet universal composer, Mozart, was a logical choice. Yet it immediately elicited heated accusations from German sources who intimated that the launching of concerts in Salzburg was a distinctly anti-Bayreuth (i.e., anti-Wagner) move. Despite such objections, the performance, for which conductor Otto Dessoff came from Karlsruhe, was a distinct success. His programming of Wagner's *Faust* Overture together with Mozart's *Jupiter* Symphony proved the baselessness of the German accusation.

Two years later Richter played *Meistersinger* excerpts in Salzburg. Thus Richter felt serenely supreme, secure in his position and in the love of the Viennese. Yet he was not really secure, not in Vienna. When Jauner gave way to Jahn at the Opera, the new director, a brilliant opera musician, beheld the Philharmonic post with covetous eyes. Again it was the critic Speidel who brought the weight of his opinion to bear in favor of Jahn and against Richter, as he had ill-conceivedly done once before when he had favored Herbeck over Dessoff. Confronted with the possibility of strife and dissension within the Philharmonic ranks, Richter yielded the post of his own accord and had the satisfaction of watching Jahn all but make a fool of himself. Jahn, the inspired conductor of the theater was lost on the concert podium. The excitement which he conjured up from the pit gave way to dry, schoolmaster time beating or distorted tempi in front of the orchestra, with his eyes at all times glued to the score before him. Vienna tolerated him on the Philharmonic podium for one year before recalling Richter in triumph. Their respective fields of artistic endeavor now clearly defined, Jahn again triumphed at the Opera while Richter presided over the Philharmonic and *Gesellschaft* concerts. Peace had been restored, but with their roles curiously reversed. Richter, the Wagner disciple from his early youth, had now grown into a guardian of classicism and traditionalism, of whom Debussy said: "He conducts as God would conduct if He had learned conducting from Hans Richter." Jahn, on the other hand, scored operatic triumphs in the Wagner repertoire.

In the Vienna symphonic sphere, meanwhile, the Viennese, who yearned for controversy to enliven their musical lives, continued the senseless Brahms–Bruckner controversy unabashed. In the concert hall the argument polarized into a division between the *parterre,* the main-floor seated section, and the standees, the seated section applauding Brahms while the standees led by Wolf, the brothers Josef and Franz Schalk (respectively pianist/composer and conductor), and **Ferdinand Loewe**, the conductor, hissed Brahms and wildly applauded Bruckner. An interesting position in that feud was taken by Johann Strauss. Although he and Brahms were the closest of friends, it was Strauss who was among the few and the first in Vienna to include Wagner excerpts in his programs and who bolstered Bruckner's sagging ego by sending him a congratulatory telegram on the night of his fiasco in the concert hall. Vienna's love for artistic arguments notwithstanding, however, the Brahms–Bruckner feud went deeper than mere drawing-room conversation. It touched on the conflict between progressive and conservative elements in Vienna, between advocates of experimentation and defenders of the status quo, and between the younger generation and the older, with the sixty-year-old Bruckner becoming, surprisingly, an inspiring figure for the younger generation. Thus the see-saw battle of Viennese opinion continued. After Brahms's Second Symphony his Third was also applauded. When the Viennese heard his Fourth Symphony, however, they rendered a decisive negative verdict. But at least the symphony had received a fair hearing at the hands of Richter and the Philharmonic before being rejected. Bruckner could not even count on such a degree of fairness. The very mention of a projected performance of his Seventh Symphony loosed such a floodtide of antagonism that Bruckner was moved to produce this document of despair, still preserved in the archives of the Vienna Philharmonic Orchestra:

Honorable Committee!

Allow me to petition the honorable Committee to desist for this year from the project, so honoring and pleasing to me, of performing my Symphony in E Major, the sole reason arising from the lamentable local situation concerning competent criticism, which might impede my young success in Germany.

With all due respect,
Anton Bruckner

Vienna, 13 October 1885

The German musical public exhibited considerably greater open-mindedness. The Germans, who played host to one hundred consecutive performances of Johann Strauss's *Fledermaus* after its sixteen-performance fiasco in Vienna, also gave Bruckner a fair hearing and found exaltation in his music. **Arthur Nikisch**, a Bruckner disciple and once a Vienna Philharmonic violinist, conducted Bruckner's Third Symphony in Leipzig and Hermann Levi (a Wagner favorite despite his being a Jew) did the same in Munich, both to enthusiastic applause, and Mahler had a similar success later with Bruckner's *Te Deum* in Hamburg.

It was the combination of favorable German reviews and the insistent clamoring of Vienna's young enthusiasts which finally, in 1886, induced the Vienna Philharmonic to "take a chance" with Bruckner. But if the verdict on Brahm's Fourth Symphony had been one of reluctant rejection, that on Bruckner's Seventh Symphony was utterly devastating, culminating in Gustav Dömpke's critical comment: "Bruckner composes like a drunkard." The clapping, stamping, and shouting of Bruckner's young enthusiasts, led by Hugo Wolf, had not been able to save their hero and his work from defeat; the subscribers fled the hall.

Wolf, in the forefront for Bruckner and against Brahms, was to incur the Philharmonic's wrath and Richter's malice. Wolf had made the mistake of submitting his youthfully extravagant symphonic poem *Penthesilea* (after the drama by Heinrich von Kleist) for the Philharmonic's approbation and performance. Wolf had been entranced by the work, an excitement he was able to transmit to others. Relates his roommate, the future prominent writer Hermann Bahr:

> In the middle of the night the door would open from the adjoining room and there appeared Hugo Wolf, in his long nightshirt, a candle and book in hand, pale and ghostly in the gray, shimmering light, odd to behold with his mystic, solemn motions. . . . He would step into our midst and begin to read . . . from *Penthesilea*. This had such power that our protests were silenced and we did not dare to speak. . . . Never in my life did I hear such reading.

Richter and the Philharmonic were determined not to fall under such a spell but could not resist the temptation of airing the music. Under the pretext of "reading" the score with the orchestra, and with a straight face, Richter made a travesty of the music. To add insult to injury, he commented that he had wanted to look at the music of that Brahms slanderer Wolf. This unkind act of Richter left a deep emotional scar on the sensitive Wolf.

By 1890 the Bruckner tide could be dammed no longer, and Vienna heard his Third Symphony then and his First in 1891. By 1892 Bruckner had the unique distinction of having an entire program devoted to his Eighth Symphony, under the now inspired baton of Richter. Almost overnight he had become "our Bruckner" to the Viennese—though not to all of them. Hanslick still wrote of the composer, in *Music Criticisms,* with a vitriolic pen:

> The listener is crushed under the sheer weight and monotony of this interminable lamentation. . . . Also characteristic of Bruckner's newest symphony is the immediate juxtaposition of dry schoolroom counterpoint with unbounded exaltation. Thus, tossed between intoxication and desolation, we arrive at no definite impression and enjoy no artistic pleasure. . . . There are interesting passages and flashes of genius—if only the rest were not there! . . . The finale, with . . . its confused structure and inhuman din, strikes [one] only as a model of tastelessness. . . . The childish, hymnal character of this program characterizes our Bruckner community. . . .
>
> And the reception of the new symphony? A storm of ovation, waving of handkerchiefs from the standees, innumerable recalls, laurel wreaths [including one from the emperor]. For Bruckner the concert was certainly a huge success. Whether Hans Richter performed a similar favor for his subscribers . . . is doubtful.

On that occasion, however, public opinion overruled Hanslick. The case was no longer Brahms versus Bruckner or even Brahms *or* Bruckner; it had become Brahms *and* Bruckner. Bruckner's Eighth Symphony had been the high point of the composer's life, but it was also the high point of Richter's. Vienna and, through Richter, the Philharmonic slowly became more tolerant of and openminded toward the music of its day. Brahms had introduced Dvořák and Tchaikovsky into the repertoire; Richter widened Vienna's acquaintance with the latter with his performance of his Violin Concerto in 1891 and his Fourth Symphony (performed posthumously) in 1895. An old era was passing; Wagner had died in Venice in 1883 and his father-in-law Liszt in 1886, in Wagner's hallowed Bayreuth. But 1892 brought Richard Strauss and his *Don Juan* to Vienna and the Philharmonic, followed in rapid succession and under Richter's aegis by *Tod und Verklärung* [Death and transfiguration] in 1893, *Till Eulenspiegel* in 1896, and, one year later, *Also Sprach Zarathustra* [Thus spake Zarathustra]. One senses Richter's grasp of the momentum of history in the program for a January 1896 concert, when *Till Eulenspiegel* preceded Bruckner's Fourth. That sequence was particularly significant because the next concert featuring Bruckner's music, in November 1896, was already a dirge for the composer. Barely half a year later, in March 1897, Brahms, hollowcheeked and haggard, jaundiced by cancer of the liver, was to receive his last ovation from the adoring Viennese, the Philharmonic, and Richter, only four weeks before his death.

Sensitive artist that he was, Richter could not have remained unaffected at seeing an era and its giants pass on. Inwardly he may have wondered where his future lay; because in 1897 there was again a meeting of eras, of the old and the new, in Vienna. In the spring of 1897, with Jahn sick, a representative of the new era had grasped the baton of the opera conductor and made his sensational debut. His was not the pontifical bearing of Richter nor the imploring gesture of Jahn, but the tense, nervous fanaticism of another age. A collision seemed inevitable. Richter had never spoiled for a fight, and now he sensed that his era in Vienna was coming to an end. With England beckoning, he folded his Vienna tent and, ever the gentleman, gave way, nobly. His last concert, in March 1898, began with Brahms and Richard Strauss and closed with the *Eroica,* the work which had introduced him to Vienna.

By then many an old conflict—Wagner–Brahms, Brahms–Bruckner —had been settled, but a new conflict was to be met head-on: viz., the old order against the new. The new order was no longer satisfied in continuing the "tradition" of ballasting musical works with mannerisms and oratorical pathos not in the spirit of (and not part of the original intent of) the composer. The time for artistic reassessment—musically, dramatically, emotionally, philosophically—was at hand. Vienna had changed. In painting, the artifice of Makart's overblown, sensuous pseudo-romanticism had given way to the exiting stylistic art of Klimt, the lean expressionism of Schiele, and the profusion of Kokoschka. The over-ornamentation and profusion of the *Ringstrasse* building was now counter-acted by Otto Wagner's spare ornamentation and Adolf Loos's unorna-mented functional design. The overblown romanticism, devoid of reality, in the poetry and literature of a bygone era had been supplanted by a new generation of writers and a new style, ranging from the laissez-faire pessimism of Schnitzler and the soul-searching of Stefan Zweig to the jubilant brilliance of Hofmannsthal. While literature, painting, and architecture had already achieved their new era, music's new master—Gustav Mahler—was standing in the Vienna wings.

## MAHLER AND THE VIENNA PHILHARMONIC

Mahler assumed the helm of the Vienna Philharmonic Orchestra in 1898. As we noted before, the selection of Mahler by the orchestra was as pragmatic as it was logical. But the choice was one dictated by the brain, not by the heart. Thus, all the ingredients for a brilliant collaboration were present—fame and genius on the one hand, one of Europe's greatest orchestras on the other—but the warm relationship that had existed with Richter, an ingredient so important in Vienna, was not present, nor did it ever materialize. Mutual respect in artistic matters and correctness in personal relationships were the best both sides could muster. Such cor-rectness was an absolute must, considering the respective personalities of the orchestra and of Mahler. The Philharmonic, under Richter, had reached a state of perfection which few orchestras could rival and none could surpass. It had established a brief but proud tradition of excellence which had inspired many of its adherents to wish for a certain continuity in the performance of certain compositions, especially those of Mozart, Beethoven, and Brahms. Few wished to realize that the approach to and execution of such compositions by the two men would be as different as their appearance and the eras they represented. As the critic Max Kalbeck noted:

> In place of the tall-standing, blond-bearded giant who stood before the orchestra imperturbable, solidly built, broad and calm, a slender, nervous figure, possessing extraordinary supple limbs, balanced itself on the podium.

Mahler was to hold sway from September 1898 to April 1901. His personality, appearance, and execution sufficed to hold audiences in mesmerized attention, as they willingly fell under his demonic spell. The program of the premiere appearance on 6 November 1898 could not have been chosen with greater care.

Beethoven, *Coriolan* Overture
Mozart, Symphony No. 40 in G Minor
Beethoven, Symphony No. 3 in E-flat Major, *Eroica*

Including the *Eroica* was a stroke of genius, as Richter had said farewell with the same work. Mahler thus attained two goals. It was a sign from him to Vienna that continuity was to be preserved. But also, by means of comparing his performance with Richter's, the audience was put on notice that a different era of interpretation had arrived. Reported the music critic Theodor Helm:

> There was icy silence at the entrance of the new conductor, and even after the towering *Coriolanus* Overture, a breathtakingly dramatic performance, only sparse applause. Mahler's conception of the first movement of Mozart's G-Minor Symphony . . . found the audience more responsive. Then came the charming floating Andante with its delicate ebb and flow; even the most hardened skeptics were conquered, and for the first time there was heartfelt applause. [Note the custom of applause *between* movements.] This was repeated for the next movement, the Minuet. . . . The Finale . . . seemed a little too slow for me, a view shared by the majority of listeners. The climax of the concert, for sheer overall success, was the first movement of the *Eroica* (although it was Mahler's conception of it which most sharply divided opinion *after* the concert). The immediate effect of Mahler's brilliant direction and of the magnificient playing of the Philharmonic was overwhelming, expressing itself in frenetic bursts of applause.

The initial public reserve, even after Mahler's opening success, must be understood if Vienna is to be understood. "Tradition" in Vienna has a significance far beyond the meaning of a mere word in that two thousand-year-old city. Beginning with its Gothic churches and Baroque palaces, tradition is an ever-present fact and factor as well as a *chimère,* a dream into which to retreat from unpleasant realities. In the case of Mahler and Vienna, tradition had an ominous double meaning. It was first the mistaken notion that a tradition of perfection in the performance of Beethoven had been handed down through innumerable interpreters of various temperaments yet had arrived unchanged to the present, an impossibility which the Viennese refused to acknowledge. Beyond that, Hans Richter was considered to be the true and only manifestation of that tradition at the time. Therefore, if one was captivated by the new conductor, praise had to be tempered by fault-finding, by *nörgeln,* that specific kind of carping in which the Viennese were past masters. With respect to Mahler that was not a difficult task, because one could always fall back on the phrase "constant experimentation" (with something the Viennese had come to consider absolute truth, such as Beethoven) or "tampering with orchestration" or, worst of all, "flaunting tradition." Thus the retouching of Beethoven's Fifth and Ninth symphonies, a double crime involving both orchestration and tradition, roused the Viennese.

> There is a tendency to adopt the thoroughly disgraceful system of "overpainting" the works of our great classical composers. What was offered yesterday as Beethoven's Ninth Symphony is a deplorable example of this aberration, this barbarism. A large number of passages were totally reorchestrated, altered in sound . . . against the clearly expressed intention of Beethoven.
>
> Music critic *Richard Heuberger* in the *Neue Freie Presse*

At that point Heuberger and other critics yearning for authenticity simply did not grasp the significance of symphonic development. In Haydn's Esterhazy days the entire orchestra consisted of approximately twenty-eight players. In Beethoven's time the necessary enlargement of the orchestra increased the number of strings alone to twenty-five to thirty players. With the advent of Berlioz, less than a decade after Beethoven's death, the romantic orchestral enlargement allowed for about double that number of strings in the standard orchestra of about ninety players. The logical consequence escaped Heuberger. If the strings are doubled the rest of the orchestra also has to be adjusted to be in balance. It was that balance which Mahler primarily wished to redress in light of the larger orchestra and improved instruments.[22] Such developments, coupled with concert halls possessing a size and acoustics undreamt of by Beethoven, prompted, indeed forced, a sensitive musical poet of the stature of Mahler to redress the imbalance which he heard and felt, be it in Beethoven or in Schumann. Anonymous letters complaining about Mahler's tampering with the orchestration began with his first rehearsals. But Mahler's superhuman artistic efforts all but wrested approval from his audiences in the face of covert complaints and overt press criticism. Such criticism was also submerged in the excitement generated by the orchestra's first foreign venture. There had been a tour of sorts, to Brünn, under Richter. But now the orchestra was to go beyond the empire borders. Paris and its world exhibition was the lure and the aim. And in June 1900 the Philharmonic Orchestra, accompanied by the *Wiener Männergesangsverein* (Vienna Male Choir Society) went there on its first five-concert tour, enthusiastically started but poorly planned and organized. The guarantee fund established by wealthy Viennese music lovers proved totally inadequate, as did the advance preparations. Nor did the French spelling of

---

[22] For example, he allowed the improved trumpets of his days to blow through the choral part of Beethoven's *Ninth,* while Beethoven, who knew only natural trumpets, could allow them to play only single notes.

Mahler's name as *Malheur* (misfortune) help to raise spirits. No public announcements had been prepared; no newspapers, reviewers, or music lovers properly alerted. What last-minute preparations had been made were amateurish and insufficient; the famed Vienna Philharmonic Orchestra was totally submerged in the whirl of the Paris World Exhibition. Mahler was outraged. He had prepared the orchestra with minute care, only to be confronted with total incompetence in administrative quarters. Yet he triumphed against all odds.

> Herr Mahler's orchestra captivated us at once by its display of perfect discipline and by its rare richness of sound. . . . There is no one to touch Mahler . . . a man whose entire appearance bespeaks powerful and nervous will—with his special insight and manner of conducting. . . . Herr Mahler has brought off a success that amounted to a triumph.
>
> Catulle Mendès in the *Neues Wiener Tagblatt*, 22 June 1900.

To this Pierre Lalo (son of the composer Edouard), added:

> We wish to express our regrets that Herr Mahler, one of the most remarkable symphonic conductors of the German school, did not see fit to perform one of his own compositions.

Leaving Paris proved much more difficult than arriving there, because the meager funds available had been exhausted and the concerts had produced a deficit. The entire Philharmonic ensemble was on the verge of becoming stranded in Paris. Again Mahler intervened and obtained the necessary funds for the return trip from the Paris Rothschilds. It has been reported that on that occasion he received a bigger ovation from the orchestra than at any time before or after, gratitude now being added to respect.

Once returned to Vienna, Mahler continued his implacable regime. If closed doors in the opera kept latecomers from disturbing the performance, so would-be early leavers were glued to their seats by a withering look from the conductor. Such was Mahler's personal magnetism that few dared to leave. Regardless of whether one welcomed or criticized Mahler's interpretations, nobody remained indifferent. While Heuberger caviled and Kalbeck reserved his opinion for each individual performance, Hanslick waxed ecstatic over Mahler's Beethoven interpretations, stating that he had never heard the works so clear in detail yet so overpowering in their totality. Boldly Mahler began to present his hero, Beethoven, in the manner in which he, the modern composer, felt Beethoven would have wanted to be played had he lived at the end of the nineteenth century instead of at the beginning of it. The first fruits of such interpretative thinking were served Vienna as early as Mahler's fifth concert in January 1899, when he led Beethoven's Quartet in F Minor, opus 95, in a performance by the entire string section of the Philharmonic. "Defamation" and "treason" were the epithets hurled at the man who dared to tamper with Beethoven. Mahler had anticipated the agitation.

> Chamber music is originally written for private rooms. It is actually appreciated only by the performers. If chamber music is transported into the concert hall, the intimacy is already lost. But more than that is lost. In the large room the voices are lost. They do not speak to the listener with the strength which the composer had intended for them. I give them this strength because I intensify the voices. After all, we intensify an orchestral movement by Haydn, an overture by Mozart. Do we thereby change the character of the work? Certainly not! The fullness of tone which we impart in a work depends on the room in which it is performed. I will perform the *Ring* in a small house with a reduced orchestra; in a gigantic theater hall . . . I must reinforce the orchestra.
>
> quoted in Heinrich Kralik, *Das Grosse Orchester*

All this was grist for the mills of his denigrators, but Mahler, convinced of the merit of his ways, continued headlong on what was to become a collision course. Vienna, in anticipation, streamed to Mahler's Sunday matinees. There they first became acquainted with Bruckner's Fifth and Sixth symphonies, Dvořák's symphonic poem *Waldtaube* [Forest dove] and *Heldengesang* [Hero's song], Richard Strauss's *Aus Italien* [From Italy], and Mahler's own First and Second symphonies and *Lieder eines fahrenden Gesellen* (sung by Selma Kurz). Tickets for Mahler's second season were in such demand that additional evening concerts were arranged. If interpretation and its visual aspects were the main novelties of the Mahler concerts, the repertoire, with the exception of his own works, continued within the established framework, presenting old as well as new works in first performance.

Mahler was the sensation of Vienna. In the pit and on the podium his position was secure, his reputation unchallenged, his adversaries at bay. But genius cannot stand still. The reasons for the striving of genius are veiled in mystery, and one cannot even surmise but only wonder at the deep wellsprings which inevitably gush forth and propel the mind. Mozart could have safely lived in gray mediocrity to the end of his days, filling an orchestral position in the ensemble of the Archbishop of Salzburg, had such a position sufficed and composition remained a pleasurable sideline. But he had to thrust himself into the maelstrom outside the pale of patronage and compose his imperishable masterpieces. Gluck could have remained in the comfortable and profitable field of Neapolitan opera (which he had early mastered), his nest feathered by the dowry of his Viennese merchant bride; no one knows what compelled him to become the mighty reformer of opera who halted the downward trend of a form which had fallen into disrepute. Similarly, Beethoven could have remained famous and feted had he confined his symphonic output to his first two delightful symphonies, his reputation buttressed by his incredible pianistic prowess at improvisation. But the *Eroica* welled up in the innermost crevices of his soul, and music was never to be the same again.

Mahler was to be as important an innovator in his time, but he was equally concerned with attuning music to the times in which he lived. His interpretative concern was with Beethoven, who had possessed neither the hearing ability nor the instrumental or orchestral means to do justice to his visions. Mahler the composer was fully aware of those handicaps in Beethoven's creative life and times and went about trying to rectify them, mainly through orchestral reinforcement and reinstrumentation. He had historical precedents for his endeavors: had not Mozart, upon Baron von Swieten's urging, added clarinet parts to Handel's *Messiah* and written added accompaniment for *Acis and Galatea* and *Alexander's Feast?* Mahler, however, did not hide behind precedent when the storm broke. Through the press, he went before the public and spoke his mind:

> Since due to certain utterances by a part of the public the opinion might arise that certain arbitrary changes in some details in the performance of Beethoven's work, particularly the Ninth Symphony, have been undertaken by the conductor, it seems apt not to withhold a clarifying comment on that point.
>
> Due to his hearing defect, leading into total deafness, Beethoven lost indispensable contact with reality, with the physically sounding world, at that time in his life in which the mightiest conceptions pressed for a means of expression. . . . Equally known as this fact is the other, that the quality of the brass instruments of his day totally excluded certain tonal sequences needed for the building of melody. This very lack, in due time, has brought about the perfection of those instruments, and not to use them now to the best possible ends in performance of those works of Beethoven would be an outrage.
>
> Richard Wagner, who, throughout his life, in word and deed, passionately endeavored to save the presentation of Beethoven's works from a nearly unbearable negligent performance, pointed in his essay "On the performance of Beethoven's Ninth Symphony" . . . to the way in which [Beethoven's] intentions could be followed by all modern conductors and expressed in a closely corresponding performance. The director of today's. concert has done just that in the fullest conviction gained by experiencing the work, without essentially going beyond the guidelines set by Wagner.
>
> This is definitely in no way a case of reinstrumentation or alteration, let alone "improvement," of the work of Beethoven. The long-practiced augmentation of the string instruments has, already for some time, brought in its wake an increase of wind instruments, solely to serve to increase the volume, but without assuming a new orchestral role. In this point as in all others, . . . [it] can be proven by us through the score (and the more studied in detail the more compelling the proof) that the conductor

was solely concerned with the pursuit of . . . Beethoven's intentions to
the seemingly most insignificant detail [and was] far from becoming
arbitrary, . . . but [was] also uninfluenced by any "tradition." . . .

Mahler's remarks were intended to serve a double purpose: on the
one hand to explain his action, but also to underline his disagreement
with the traditionalists demanding a return to Richter's interpretations,
emphasizing instead the need for departure from pontifical statement in
the name of Beethoven and a return to the rugged vitality of the master.
In brief, Mahler attempted to fulfill what he believed would have been
Beethoven's intentions had he had at his disposal an orchestra of the
caliber of the Vienna Philharmonic. While audiences applauded his performances wildly, his antagonists remained unmoved and the critics continued to see only willful, arbitrary change.

The artistic collaboration continued unabated through Mahler's third
season despite the lack of close understanding between the orchestra and
Mahler, a condition that had existed with Richter and was to exist again
with Weingartner. Bruckner's Fifth Symphony finally received a hearing,
as did Beethoven's Ninth in the Mahler instrumentation as well as Mahler's own delightful Fourth Symphony. Bruckner's Fifth elicited a new
controversy, brought about by the composer's own indecision as to which
version was official. Purists complained about cuts in the one performed
by Mahler, but all had to admit that the brass chorale in the finale (re-
putedly added by Franz Schalk), as interpreted by Mahler, gave the work
a solemnity never before heard.

But the fates were against the Philharmonic–Mahler collaboration.
In 1901 he suffered a severe hemorrhage due to overwork. Even Mahler's
determined energy could not sustain a Philharmonic concert in the afternoon and a *Meistersinger* performance in the evening. Doctors prescribed
immediate and total rest, and Mahler left for Abbazia (near Fiume, then
in Italy, now in Yugoslavia), walking painfully and laboriously with two
canes. Josef Hellmesberger and Franz Schalk conducted the remaining
concerts of the season.[23]

Josef Hellmesberger was the youngest member of a proud Viennese
musical dynasty. His grandfather Georg (1800–1873) had been a leader
in early Philharmonic undertakings, as well as a music educator who
counted such illustrious violinists as Josef Joachim and Leopold Auer
among his students. Josef Hellmesberger, Sr. (1828–93), Georg's son,
destined to become the most famous member of the family, was leader of

---

[23] Alma Mahler claims that owing to his illness the Philharmonic orchestra "ruthlessly and unceremoniously" replaced him with Hellmesberger, an act which
Mahler regarded as treachery, and that the orchestra did not even give Mahler
the courtesy and consideration of allowing him to submit his resignation. In view
of the success of Mahler's tenure with the Philharmonic, Alma's statement appears
to be not in line with the facts.

the famous quartet that bore his name, concertmaster of the Vienna Philharmonic and the Opera orchestra, and conductor of the concerts of the
*Gesellschaft der Musikfreunde* and director of its famed conservatory.
Josef Hellmesberger (1855–1907) also became a prominent Philharmonic violinist, ballet conductor at the opera, and conservatory teacher
as well as the composer of lovely, unpretentious music.[24] Despite his
excellent credentials and knowledge, young Hellmesberger was a failure
at his new post because his limited conducting experience as ballet conductor at the opera had in no way prepared him for the exacting task
involved in occupying the helm of one of the world's great orchestras. He
soon relinquished the post to a number of guest conductors but occasionally returned as guest conductor.

As for Mahler, he had made up his mind to resign from the Philharmonic, because he had reason to believe that his reelection would not receive the unanimous approval that he demanded. The relationship never
having been close, the parting was not difficult and Mahler's letter of
resignation was a formality.

[24] Two more members of the Hellmesberger family achieved relative fame. Georg
(1830–52), brother of Josef Sr., was a prominent violinist and composer before
his untimely death. Ferdinand (1863–1940), son of Josef Sr., became solo cellist
in the Opera orchestra and was also professor at the conservatory.

# Vienna (The New Spirit, 1901-1907)

## THE MAHLER ERA OF THE VIENNA OPERA

POSITIVELY AS WELL AS NEGATIVELY, 1901 was a significant year for Mahler. He acquired property in Mayernigg at Lake Wörther, a favorite vacation spot of Brahms and later of Alban Berg; he witnessed a belated performance of *Das klagende Lied,* but resigned from the Philharmonic; he composed the Rückert songs and had his Fourth Symphony premiered in Munich. And, most important of all, he met Alma Maria Schindler, the daughter of a painter, the late Anton Schindler, and the step-daughter of another, Carl Moll.

That second major female acquaintance, after Anna von Mildenburg, was to precipitate a crisis in the Mahler household, which then consisted of Gustav and his sister Justine, who presided over their Vienna home as she had done in Hamburg. Their close relationship had resulted in a kind of "spiritual marriage," with one feeling responsible for the other's welfare and feelings. Justine was deeply disturbed when she realized that in the company of newly acquired artistic friends Gustav had met Alma Schindler and was captivated by her.

Twenty-year-old Alma was as unusual in her own way as Mahler was in his, and the attraction soon became mutual, despite the fact that the composer was then twice as old as Alma. She was possessed of stunning good looks, which, four years earlier, had strongly impressed **Gustav Klimt**, much to the disapproval of her stepfather.[1] Aside from possessing attributes of beauty, Alma, a pupil of the composer **Alexander Zemlinsky**, had proven to be a composer of promise. Alma had already published nine songs, with sophisticated texts by, among others, Heine, Dehmel, and

---

[1] Alma was always to be attracted by and attractive to men of the highest caliber of intellect and achievement, with Klimt being one example. After Mahler's death she became the companion of painter Oscar Kokoschka and later the wife of architect Walter Gropius and of writer Franz Werfel.

Rilke. The combination of such attributes and accomplishments in so young and sparkling a creature immediately kindled Mahler's interest.

Mahler had met Alma at a dinner party at a mutual friend's house and had invited her to visit him at the opera. When she arrived, the rehearsal for *Tales of Hoffmann* was in progress. Despite her resolution not to be intimidated by the great conductor, Alma sat spellbound. Mahler was the moving spirit behind all aspects of the rehearsal. He conducted the superb orchestra, took exception to the too-revealing costume of one singer (which had to be stitched up immediately), and commented on the scenery and staging; no detail escaped him. His presence was so all-consuming that Prince Liechtenstein, the Imperial Theater Intendant, once commented, half in earnest and half in jest, to Mahler: "There's really no need for you to shift scenery yourself." If Alma had been determined to hold to reservations about Mahler and not to be overawed by him, a performance of Gluck's *Orfeo ed Euridice* changed all that. Upon Mahler's invitation, Alma, her mother, and Mahler had met in the opera foyer before the performance. Since Mahler's presence among ordinary mortals immediately elicited stares and whispers, he suggested that they retire to his private chambers. Surprisingly, Mahler and Alma's mother immediately enjoyed each other's company. A visit by Mahler to the Schindler home was arranged.

Friends looked at this budding friendship with a jaundiced eye. Perhaps owing to his innumerable contacts with opera singers of the opposite sex, Mahler had acquired a dubious reputation. Yet Mahler's and Alma's mutual feelings blossomed quickly. On their first winter walk, Mahler blurted out a proposal of sorts. "It's not so simple to marry a man like me. I am free and I must be free. I cannot be bound or tied to one spot. My job at the opera is simply from one day to the next." Alma, despite her youth, answered maturely: "Of course. Don't forget that I am the child of artists and have always lived among artists and also, I'm one myself. What you say is obvious to me" (Alma Mahler, *Memories and Letters*).

Subconsciously, almost unthinkingly, Mahler had decided that they should get married. It did not even occur to him that Alma might not agree. But, equally subconsciously, Alma had known that she wanted their lives to be joined, recognizing as she did the superior being in the man she had barely met. Neither of them may have considered at that moment that subsequent clashes were inevitable at several levels: middle age versus youth, artist versus artist, Jew versus Catholic. No greater contrast could be imagined between Gustav—demonic, schizophrenic, self-centered, eccentric, naively ruthless, inspired, and Alma—beautiful, understanding, spirited yet devoted, self-sacrificing yet proud. Shortly before their wedding an event took place which illumines a dark corner in Mahler's psyche. One day, while on a concert engagement in Dresden, Mahler received a letter from Alma informing him that she would have to curtail letter writing because of her preoccupation with composition. The inference that anything could be more important than being in touch with him, or even of equal importance, so infuriated Mahler that he shot back an epistle forbidding her to do any more composing. There were to be no other lares and penates in his household besides himself. Alma was to be his helpmeet: she was to share his triumphs and anguishes, his hells and despairs; she would bear his children, supervise his household, copy his music, pay off his debts, and be a sounding board for his inspirations; but no longer would she create in her own right. Alma, totally devoted to this genius-to-be-her-husband, totally bound up in love and admiration, acceded tearfully to Mahler's dictum. She never composed again, but the renunciation remained an open wound throughout their marriage. On the other hand, it did not occur to Mahler to acknowledge Alma's painful sacrifice. Only years later did Mahler become aware of the cruelly monstrous demand he had inflicted upon Alma, so typical of his lack of understanding for the feelings of others. The burden of that guilt became so weighty that it induced temporary impotence and was one of the reasons for Mahler's seeking out Sigmund Freud.

As far as Justine was concerned, Mahler acted as secretively and deviously about his engagement to Alma as his sister acted with regard to her own love life. Justine had also found fulfillment in Vienna; she had met **Arnold Rosé**. They had fallen madly in love but the illicit affair needed to be kept from Mahler—who, had he known about the affair, would, Justine knew, have taken immediate steps to have her removed from Vienna. The relationship had to be kept a total secret from her mighty brother, whose puritanical ideas (as far as his sister was concerned) would not tolerate the love that bound her to Rosé. Meanwhile, Justine could not fully enjoy her love affair because of the spiritual relationship of trust and interdependence between her and her brother. Slowly, however, Mahler began to see through the web of evasions and intrigue. When, finally, inevitably, the veil was lifted from the lovers' secret, he went into a rage and insisted that Justine and Rosé either marry or break off immediately. Surprisingly, Mahler drew a distinct line between Rosé the man and Rosé the musician, and as far as the musician was concerned Mahler continued to listen to his opinion and advice.

Mahler himself had equal reason to be secretive. For one thing, Alma had become pregnant during their engagement; besides which, his sister's jealousy gave him pause. Other troubles beset their romance. Alma strongly disliked Mahler's close friends, a closely knit group of "insiders" which included Guido Adler and Siegfried Lipiner. They had seen young singers and other damsels come and go and therefore refused to take seriously or even acknowledge this latest "interlude" with a twenty-year-old girl, thus infuriating Alma. After a five-month courtship and ten-week pregnancy, Mahler and Alma, with her delighted mother's blessing, were married on 9 March 1902 in one of Vienna's most imposing sacred edifices, the *Karlskirche* (Charles's Church). A day later Justine was married to Arnold Rosé.[2]

After his marriage great changes occurred in Mahler's life. Of course he continued to advise and mingle with disciples and young composers such as Zemlinsky, Schönberg and Pfitzner, but relationships to old friends changed. While he retained a life-long friendship with Guido Adler and Victor Adler, his attachment to Anna von Mildenburg and correspondence with violinist/friend Natalie Bauer-Lechner faded. He did experience a period of greater productivity, if for no other reason than that Alma removed from his shoulders the day-to-day problems which he had detested and neglected and which had thus been left to the inept handling of sister Justine. He also began to travel more, concertizing and conducting in ever widening circles throughout Germany, Holland, and Italy.

The marriage to Alma produced two children; Maria Anna ("Putzi") born on 3 November 1902, whose death on 5 July 1907 was one of the most terrible blows in Mahler's life; and Anna Justine, born 15 July 1904. The latter was to prove a gifted sculptor; and, like her mother, she knew how to bring out the best in the men she met. Apparently she also *met* the best, because she married, in turn, the composer Ernst Křenek, the publisher Szolnay, and the conductor Anatol Fistoulari.

It was in 1902 that Richard Strauss and Mahler, the two giants of their time, became friends. Strauss had been of great assistance to Mahler by performing his First Symphony. Now Mahler reciprocated by performing Strauss's opera *Feuersnot* at the Vienna Imperial Opera, although he did not have a high regard for that early work. Both negatively and positively, it was to be an evening which Strauss would long remember. Elated and stimulated by the numerous curtain calls which had been accorded him, Strauss appeared in the box which Alma Mahler and Pauline Strauss occupied. Already during the performance Pauline had made numerous allusions to her dislike of her husband's opera. She considered it shoddy and lacking originality, partly pirated from Wagner, and altogether a pretense of an opera. When Strauss, flushed with the excitement of the moment, asked for her opinion, she, according to Alma, flew into his face. "You thief—get out of my sight. I'm not going with you. You disgust me too much." After a lengthy and heated argument she decided that they should join the others in the festive dinner prepared for them, with Richard meekly bringing up the rear. Alma disliked Richard Strauss because of his constant, meek deference to his wife and his equally constant preoccupation with money matters. In inevitable comparison with Mahler, Strauss's image, for her, shrank considerably. She was joined in her opin-

[2] The ties between the two families were extended even further when Mahler's younger sister Emma married the cellist Eduard Rosé, Arnold's brother.

ion by Franz Schalk. He knew Strauss well and whispered into Alma's ear: "The sad fact is he's not putting on. It's the real man." Schalk and Alma were not alone in their opinion.

> I remember . . . exhausting rehearsals with Richard Strauss. . . . I went to his home in Garmisch. . . . He really was a very simple family man, entirely devoted to his temperamental wife. He was really a henpecked husband. . . . I sang a lot of his Lieder, and often his wife Pauline would listen. Some of the Lieder seemed to bring back happy memories to them both, and Pauline would run to him, throwing her arms around him, saying with sobs of touching sentimentality, "Do you remember, Richard?"—and he would have tears in his eyes, too. They were a strange couple. They fought like mad. Needless to say, Pauline always started these fights. . . . He said to me when I departed: "You have seen a lot which you will find strange in this house. But believe me, all the praises in the world are not so refreshing as my wife's outbreaks of temperament.
>
> He was so accustomed to meeting people who adored him, bowed before him in reverence. He did not like it; he was a thoroughly straightforward man—and his Pauline was like a draft of fresh water.
>
> Lotte Lehmann, *Time*, 17 August 1953

The year 1901 passed for Mahler in many-sided preparations, and rehearsals for his Fourth Symphony and *Das klagende Lied,* to be performed on 12 January 1902. It marked the first time that Alma attended all rehearsals and performances. Although pregnant, she also accompanied Mahler on what was to be their concert honeymoon in St. Petersburg. Mahler was then beset by many ills, fever, a cough, and a sore throat, but his concerts were tremendous successes. While Mahler suffered under the harsh Russian winter, Alma enjoyed herself watching people skating on the frozen river Neva. So thick was the ice that a temporary train line had been laid across the frozen river.

Alma also watched with fascination her husband's attitude in his meetings with aristocracy—which varied, depending on the nature of the meeting. In artistic matters he would brook no interference and resisted pressure regardless of how high the rank of the person. When a young soprano, wishing to be engaged at the opera, presented Mahler with a card from none other than Archduke Franz Ferdinand, recommending her, Mahler pointedly tore the card in two, then sat down at the piano and turned to the soprano: "Now show me what you can do." (*"Österreichische Illustrierte Zeitung,* 24 May 1931). On another occasion, Prince Montenuovo, the Imperial Theater Intendant, recommended to Mahler an opera by an aristocratic amateur (Count Zichy?):

> "His Majesty is interested in the work."
> Silence.

"What do you think of the opera?"

"What opera, Your Excellency?"

"The Hungarian one which I recommended to you."

"Oh that one. . . can't do a thing with it. It's a piece of trash."

"But I told you, His Majesty . . . "

"Oh, if His Majesty orders a performance then I will perform it with the notice "Upon Highest Order.""

"You can imagine that His Majesty won't expose himself [i.e., to undue publicity]."

"Then I am expected to bear the onus. No, that's impossible."

"That means. . . ?"

"That the Imperial Opera will never perform the work as long as I am the director in charge."

"That's your final word?"

"My very final one, Your Excellency."

"Then, my dear director, at least give me that in writing, send me a report which I will pass on—I don't dare convey this myself."

Alma Mahler, Erinnerungen und Briefe

Reports Mahler: never did the prince get a letter as quickly as that one. But Mahler's attitude shifted completely when he was meeting aristocracy on a social level. In such circumstances he stiffly observed all the time-honored conventions of the Austrian caste system.

Only four months after his marriage, Mahler, his stunning bride at his side, had arrived in Krefeld at the invitation of the *Allgemeine Deutsche Musikverein* [General German Music Society] to conduct the first complete performance of his Third Symphony. It turned into a triumphant success, with Richard Strauss leading the ovation. The evening turned into an equally momentous one for the bride, as she felt the first stirrings of a child in her womb. It was also in Krefeld that Alma witnessed a degrading scene, as a composer of great promise debased himself before Mahler in an attempt to have his opera performed at the Vienna Opera. Hans Pfitzner came to Mahler's suite, pleading with him for a performance of his opera *Die Rose vom Liebesgarten* [The rose from the garden of love]. Mahler did not care for it and enumerated his reasons for refusal in cold, terse, almost brutal terms: the libretto was poor, the symbolism obscure, the work much too long. Pfitzner remonstrated, explained, pleaded, but Mahler was unmoved. Pfitzner left crushed.

The summer brought a return to their place in Maiernigg, where Gustav looked forward to peace, solitude, and composition. "I am a summer composer," he once exclaimed to Walter. He worked on his Fifth Symphony in between taking endless walks in solitude. Mahler's relationship to Alma had by then taken a peculiar turn. As he lost himself in his music, he became faintly estranged from her, as though he were afraid of her youth. The fear expressed itself in an overbearing, schoolmasterish attitude which abjured all beauties and pleasures of life, except for the pleasures of the spirit and energy-sapping walks. To everyone's surprise and slight embarrassment, Anna von Mildenburg also decided to spend the summer nearby. Anna (Alma coyly refers to her as Madame M) apparently had not given up hope of a rekindling of Mahler's feeling for her. Alma relates that Mahler was by then "disgusted" with Anna—which must be assumed to be an exaggeration, because Mahler's esteem for Anna's artistry never wavered.

Maiernigg was an unvarying routine for Mahler. Up at 6:30 in the morning, he took a steep walk to the "composer's hut," which was in the forest and high above their villa. Breakfast, usually frugal, was consumed in total solitude on a bench and table in front of the hut in the quiet of the forest—furtively served by a maid who was mortally afraid of Mahler and ran the moment she had deposited the tray on the table in front of the hut. It was the perfect retreat, and Mahler longed for it throughout the long and busy opera season. The inside of the hut consisted of a huge desk and chair, a piano, and some crude bookshelves, with Goethe and Kant lined up alongside the complete music of Bach. At midday Mahler would descend back into humanity, changing from his ragged clothes into "society clothes" or going directly to the lake for a swim, where Alma would soon join him. After his swim and sunbath he would feel invigorated and return for a meal. Lunch, like most meals in the Mahler household, was a frugal and exact affair, expected by Mahler at the precisely prescribed time. Restlessness could be curbed only for the duration of the meal; then were resumed the long walks on which he expected Alma to accompany him at his rapid pace, regardless of whether she was tired, otherwise preoccupied, or pregnant. If he was not walking he was rowing—anything to keep from standing still. Sometimes, like Beethoven, he would suddenly stop, stand motionless, then whip out a notebook, write down a musical idea, reflect on it, beat its time, pore over it. During those intervals, which lasted sometimes for minutes, sometimes for hours, he forgot everything about him, including Alma. If they had visitors in the house during such periods of musical meditation, conversation was carried on in whispers, because no oral sound escaped Mahler's delicate hearing and the break in his train of reflection infuriated him. Thus the summer days at Maiernigg were totally given over to musical creation; outwardly serene and undisturbed, they were inwardly pulsating with demonic intensity.

Autumn saw the completion of his Fifth Symphony. With Alma as his sole audience, Mahler premiered the work for her on the piano, a rare occurrence. The performance took place, upon his insistence, in his hut in the forest.

The winter season passed with much time consumed in orchestration of the Fifth Symphony but with Mahler not otherwise varying his routine or his attention to his opera duties. He rose at seven in the morning, was at the opera at nine, lunched at one. When Mahler arrived home for lunch, the first course had to be on the table. He would storm into the house, race to the bathroom, wash his hands, and sit down to lunch. After the meal he took a rapid walk, usually along the *Ring;* punctually at five, he took tea. Evenings were spent at the opera house, where he came to each performance and remained for at least part of it. Alma would usually call for him and would unobtrusively wait if he was still involved with opera affairs.

On 3 November their first child was born. The child's awkward position in the womb gave rise to anxiety for some time, and Mahler, for once helpless, frantically walked the streets of Vienna. When he was informed that the child was born and well he broke into tears. But when Alma told him that the child had "seen the light of the world first with its posterior," his demeanor changed to one of roaring laughter. "That's my child— showing the world right away the part it deserved." Her name was Maria Anna, and during the brief span of her young life (she died of scarlet fever and diphtheria in 1907) she remained a withdrawn child whom Mahler loved dearly.

One of the difficulties Mahler experienced vis-à-vis Vienna soon began to appear, in that he refused to "Viennese" himself. He would regularly visit the coffeehouse at the Hotel Imperial, mainly to scan what the music critics had to say about the previous night's performance or concert, but to spend two hours over lunch or an afternoon enjoying a cup of *Schale Gold* (coffee with enough milk or cream added to give it a golden color) was not his idea of how to spend the day. By their own choice, Gustav and Alma increasingly retired within the circle of their close friends.

In 1902 Richard Strauss arrived in Vienna to conduct some concerts in which his wife was to sing. Alma relates a delightful incident which sheds more light on the state of affairs in Strauss's personal *commedia domestica:*

> He was still the much debated, eccentric composer and she was an unbridled, ambitious wife. She sent word to me . . . to come and see her. I went and found her in bed. There was a concert that evening at which she was supposed to sing, but she did not rise from her bed. Then the door burst open and Strauss came in with a little case in his hand. "I've got your ring, now you will get up, won't you?" And [Pauline] got up at once and the concert came off, an expensive one for Strauss; for it was a large diamond ring.

Despite their different musical and philosophical outlooks, Mahler and Strauss enjoyed each other's company. Their arguments and conversations would range from scandal to opera singers, from the merits of Beethoven's earlier versus later creations (Strauss: "The spontaneity of youth is worth all the rest"; Mahler: "Such a genius could only get better as he grew older") to such esoteric topics as Mommsen's *History of Rome*. A topic of which Strauss and Mahler never tired was opera and opera singers. At that time Strauss loved *bel canto*, while Mahler followed Wagner's dictum on singing. The roles were destined to be reversed later on, when Mahler heard the magnificent voices of the New York Metropolitan Opera Company whereas Strauss wrote music for Vienna's German singers, like Mildenburg (*Klytemnestra*) and Gutheil-Schoder (*Elektra*).

Yet there always remained an unbridgeable gap between the two men, simply because they lived in different worlds: Mahler deeply involved, Strauss forever remaining on the surface of things.

> I had quite a pleasant time with Strauss yesterday; but there is always with him that frigid, blasé feeling. However, he made me a present of his latest publication (Berlioz's *Treatise on Instrumentation*, with comments of his[3]). . . . He promised me further a score of *Salome*. . . . But, as I said before, a little more warmth would be preferable to all this.
>
> Mahler to Alma, 10 November 1905

The one topic on which Mahler and Strauss would never see eye to eye was Strauss's attitude toward money, or rather his craving for it. Strauss was never particular about where he conducted (including John Wanamaker's department store in New York), as long as it was lucrative. Said he to Mahler: "When I've collected enough money I'll settle down in peace and compose." Mahler was skeptical about such an outlook: "By that time he'll be close to losing his soul," he remarked to Alma.

Although Mahler admired the operatic creations of Mozart, Beethoven, and above all Wagner, he was never seduced into composing opera himself. And although his Wagner interpretations were considered the marvels of their time, Mahler's music remained uninfluenced by the Wagnerian idom—a rare exception at the time, when some were actually afraid of Wagner's influence yet few could escape it. When Mahler once invited Goldmark to a Wagner performance at the Opera, Goldmark apprehensively replied: "I never listen to Wagner. I'm afraid of getting too much like him." Mahler's reply was typical. "You eat beef without becoming an ox." Yet the thought of eventually writing an opera must have been in the back of his mind, because when he was asked, in later years, why he had never composed an opera he thoughtfully replied to the effect that the world had to get Wagner out of its system before the time for "something else" arrived.

In his constant effort to present the old alongside the new, Mahler in 1903 staged a new production of Weber's *Euryanthe*. The opera had never been a success in Vienna despite its romantic score, owing mainly

---

[3] Berlioz's treatise was actually so all-encompassing that Strauss was mainly restricted to adding the instruments which had entered the symphony orchestra since the days of Berlioz.

to Wilhelmina von Chezy's clumsy libretto. Mahler was quite taken with the music, which, he felt, foreshadowed *Lohengrin*. He had attempted to improve on the libretto, but, in contrast to his work on Weber's *Die drei Pintos,* he met with little success. Instead, the novelty of the year turned out to be Gustave Charpentier's *Louise.* Mahler attended to the rehearsals and the staging with his customary enthusiasm. However, when he invited Charpentier to attend the premiere, the composer did not agree with Mahler's conception. He took over the direction of the work himself and revamped its staging in near-surrealistic fashion. The singer playing the role of the seducer had to be equipped with electric wiring, because Charpentier wanted his glowing heart exposed when he opened his cape. In keeping with such staging, light effects seem to have been as important to Charpentier as the music on which he had worked feverishly and in abject poverty after he and his literary friends had concocted the libretto in one night. To everyone's surprise, Mahler in no way resented Charpentier's interjections at that late hour. He completely entered into the composer's spirit and intention, and *Louise* enjoyed as tremendous a success in Vienna as it had in Paris.

It was not the first time that a composer had disagreed with Mahler's ideas of staging his work. Leoncavallo considered himself "critically wounded" and his opera *La Bohème* "chopped to pieces." That time Mahler did not agree with the composer, and they had an unpleasant scene during rehearsals. Upon his departure Leoncavallo thanked the stage manager but not Mahler; Mahler, in turn, completely avoided the composer. He did not even bother to bow with the composer after the performance and had his customary between-acts tea in a singer's dressing room.

Nineteen hundred and three found Mahler in other parts of Europe again. He conducted his Second Symphony in the cathedral of Basel after conducting his Third Symphony in Amsterdam, where he befriended the conductor Willem Mengelberg, who was destined to become one of the great Mahler interpreters of his time. There was tremendous excitement during the Basel rehearsals of the *Resurrection* Symphony, and the performance in the candlelit lofty house of worship turned into a triumph for Mahler. Composer Oscar Nedbal knelt and kissed Mahler's hand after the performance.

Despite her husband's initial refusal to perform Hans Pfitzner's *Die Rose vom Liebesgarten,* a friendship grew between Pfitzner and Alma, perhaps, subconsciously, because of the frustrations both had suffered at the hands of Mahler. Pfitzner held a high opinion of Alma's musical comprehension and sent her his String Quartet in D Major for her opinion, which he valued. During the summer, Mahler, while working on his Sixth Symphony, also had occasion to study the Pfitzner quartet and, after a thoughtful perusal, pronounced it, to the astonishment of all, the work of a master. It became the opening wedge in Mahler's reconsideration of Pfitzner's work in general and *Die Rose vom Liebesgarten* in particular. Alma had always held the work in high esteem, and she now urged Mahler to restudy and reconsider it. Mahler did so and later announced that he would produce the opera—much to the satisfaction of Alma, who felt herself vindicated in her appraisal of Pfitzner. Said Pfitzner of Mahler: "There is love in him. What greater measure can a man possess but love."

Mahler's reconsideration of Pfitzner's *Die Rose* was not the only one of his artistic turnabouts. In 1904 Vienna witnessed a belated, posthumous performance of Wolf's *Der Corregidor;* Alma called it a "debt of honor." As predicted and feared by Mahler, the "opera of songs" was not a success, despite Wolf's ravishing music. Criticism of a different kind was also leveled at Mahler in connection with the Wolf opera, because many felt that his initial refusal to perform the work was the final disappointment which drove Wolf over the brink into insanity. Such criticism rests on dubious grounds, however, because venereal disease was the main factor in Wolf's demise and would inevitably have brought about his disintegration regardless of other influences.

Mahler's stand vis-à-vis the genius of Wolf is enigmatic. Despite their early companionship and shared admiration of Wagner, and despite Mahler's belated performance of *Der Corregidor* in later years, he cared neither for the man nor for his work. Of the latter he said: "Of Wolf's songs I know only three hundred forty-four. Those three hundred forty-four I do not like." The purist in Mahler may have resented Wolf's life-style, and the feeling carried over into artistic consideration. Mahler and Wolf had been friends since student days at the *Konservatorium der Gesellschaft der Musikfreunde* in the late 1870s. At that time, Mahler, Hugo Wolf, and Rudolph Krzyzanowsky shared a room. All were sensitive budding composers and very conscious of noise. Consequently, when one composed the others had to either go to bed (without snoring), sleep on a park bench, or walk the streets for the duration of the inspiration. In true Bohemian fashion, the three often found themselves on the brink of starvation, and only music lessons and packages from home kept them alive. Their room sharing came to an abrupt end, however. Once the three had scraped up the money for some tickets to *Götterdämmerung*. Their excitement upon their return to the room carried them to such vocal heights that the landlady gave them notice on the spot and waited in the room until they had departed (in the middle of the night) with their meager belongings.

In 1880 a summer engagement as *Kapellmeister* for performances of light summer fare at the spa of Bad Hall became available. Wolf stonily refused it as beneath his artistic standing; Mahler accepted and conducted operettas throughout the summer. Subsequently Mahler and Wolf drifted apart. After Mahler became director of the Vienna Imperial Opera, Wolf came to visit him. He had the score of *Der Corregidor* with him and all but demanded that Mahler stage it. Mahler had been concerned about Wolf's inability to get the opera performed; that concern had prompted him to write to their mutual friend Natalie Bauer-Lechner on 3 September 1895:

> Tell Wolf to send *me* his opera, if he can't place it anywhere else. If it is in my power I will effect (*durchsetzen*) the performance, i.e., if it is *worth performing*. The last comment you need not tell him, or disguise it in less dubious form.

But now his former friend's bearing, the vehemence of his speech, his glowing eyes, his entire countenance made Mahler suspicious and uneasy. When he attempted to evade the issue Wolf's voice rose to an unusually shrill pitch as he restated his insistence. They had started on an even footing: they had shared a room as well as the joys and vicissitudes of early musical life. That Mahler, who had reached the pinnacle of musical attainment in Vienna, would have the effrontery to reject his friend's opera after the possibility of performing it had been held out to him was, to the exhausted and frustrated Wolf, the ultimate defeat. Mahler at that point pressed a hidden bell; a secretary appeared, announcing the pre-arranged message: "The Intendant wishes to see you at once." Mahler excused himself and left; Wolf departed, crushed and raving. Shortly thereafter Wolf would announce to his anxious and dismayed friends that he had dismissed Mahler and that he, Wolf, was now the opera director. He was committed to an asylum shortly thereafter. On 10 March 1904, a year after Wolf's death, Vienna heard the official premiere of *Der Corregidor*.[4]

The premiere of Mahler's Fifth Symphony had been set for 25 October 1904 in Cologne. But earlier in the year Mahler had scheduled a run-through rehearsal with the Vienna Philharmonic. The work's initial weaknesses—particularly the overscoring of the percussion, which nearly drowned out the balance of the instrumentation—became apparent to him. Upon Alma's urging he removed much of the percussion. Yet despite rescoring, success eluded him in Cologne. The picture brightened considerably once Mahler arrived in Amsterdam. That city, thanks to Mengelberg's efforts, had become a "Mahler city." Only there could it have happened that a concert should consist of two performances of Mahler's Fourth Symphony. First Mahler conducted the work; then, after the intermission, Mengelberg followed suit, with Mahler sitting in his box listening to Mengelberg's interpretation. This raises an interesting question,

---

[4] It was actually the second performance in Vienna. A trial performance on 18 February 1904 of a revised version had not pleased Mahler, who, in the March performance, restored the opera to its original form.

recently touched on in an article by Harold C. Schonberg.[5] Contrary to the recent remarks of Henri-Louis de la Grange, witnesses' comments [6] lead us to believe that Mahler was constantly conscious of tempo continuity and would not have approved of Mengelberg's exaggerated *ritenutos*, which Harold Schonberg observed in a Mengelberg recording of the Fourth Symphony. We therefore wonder whether, at the above-mentioned performance, Mahler endured Mengelberg's distorted dynamics with inward cringing or whether he was carried away by the magic of the occasion. Mahler's report to Alma seems to express his delight—with the audience, at least, if not with Mengelberg.

> It was an astounding evening! The audience from the start was so attentive and understanding and the response was warmer with each movement. The enthusiasm increased the second time and at the end was something like in Krefeld. . . . I really believe now I shall find Amsterdam the musical home for which I had hoped in stupid Cologne.

Success, however, was still far from assured. The performance of his Third Symphony in Vienna in December 1904 was well received, although in January Mahler had complained to Alma: "It is appalling what they make of my work in my absence. Strauss is absolutely right to conduct his own work on all occasions."

By this time Mahler began to become more and more introspective, totally immersed in and absorbed by his musical labors and his work at the opera and unaware of things and people around him if they were outside his artistic sphere. At social gatherings, if he attended them at all, he became unaware of others who wished to address him and was without any social graces or consideration for others' feelings. Such blindness extended even to Alma, who understood but suffered. Such suffering through neglect could have been ameliorated had she been able to immerse herself in music as she had done before meeting Mahler, but her husband's dictum forbidding her to continue musical activities had deprived her of such an outlet; despairingly, she yet held to his dictate and to her promise. This was regrettable, because Alma had been a sensitive artist, beginning to assert herself under the tutelage of Zemlinsky when she met Mahler. Her artistic judgment remained clear, as her diary indicates:

> 26 January 1905. Concert yesterday: Zemlinsky–Schönberg. My surmise was correct. Zemlinsky, in spite of many charming little inspirations and imposing knowledge, had not the strength of Schönberg, who, for all his wrong-headedness, is a very original fellow . . . his talent was beyond question.

[5] "Would Mahler Have Raised The Roof?" *The New York Times,* 16 September 1973.

[6] "The Life and Music of Gustav Mahler," presented on radio station KFAC, Los Angeles, William Malloch, producer.

Through Zemlinsky Alma had come to meet and know Arnold Schönberg. Zemlinsky had great respect for Schönberg, a respect which Alma in her younger years did not share but which Mahler established in her.

Mahler's relationship with other prominent men of his day reflected personal as well as artistic considerations. His relationship with Wolf had cooled; Reger's polyphonic complexities left him cold; he underestimated Puccini and almost totally neglected French impressionist music. He could never warm to Pfitzner. Although he had relented and performed (and even praised) *Die Rose vom Liebesgarten,* Pfitzner's personality went against his grain, particularly since he paid much attention to Alma. Alma reciprocated artistically because she finally had found a kindred soul who would listen to her songs and discuss them on an artistic level. Mahler resented Pfitzner's and Alma's making music for hours but continued to invite him to their home. Despite Mahler's reluctance to widen the circle of their friends, particularly in view of the fact that Alma was pregnant with their second child, new friends and acquaintances now entered their lives, among them the German poet and dramatist **Gerhart Hauptmann** and the *Burgtheater* actor Josef Kainz. Mahler and Hauptmann found that they had many interests in common and hence engaged in endless talks. Hauptmann and his paramour, the actress Margarete Marschalk (who also appeared in some of his plays), were the exact opposites of the Mahlers in one particular. While the Mahlers lived frugally in every respect, Margarete bragged to Alma about their eight servants and all but berated her for not living a more luxurious life. Despite the imminent arrival of their second child, the Mahlers (with the Rosés) attended Hauptmann's play *Der Grüne Heinrich,* with Kainz playing Heinrich. Alma was enchanted both with the play and with Kainz's interpretation. The next day Alma's labor pains began. While she was writhing in pain, waiting for the arrival of the midwife, Mahler read Kant (!) to her.[7]

Regardless of how he acted when with Alma or what attitude he might assume when in the company of strangers or friends, Mahler was at his most relaxed and genial when playing with his two small daughters. With them he would spend a great deal of time, singing to them, dancing with them, and telling them stories.

That summer Mahler finished his Sixth Symphony and the *Kindertotenlieder* [Songs of dead children]. Alma was never favorably inclined toward those songs, because she knew that the poet **Friedrich Rückert** had written the verses to bewail the loss of his own child. With Mahler's children alive and well and playing outside, she felt that Mahler might anger

---

[7] As far as his own health was concerned, Mahler was a gullible hypochondriac. Every cure that had benefited some friend he too had to try, any medicine that had presumably helped somebody else he also had to take and apothecaries counted him among their best customers.

the gods. So strong was her resentment of the songs that even her critical judgment of their artistic validity was clouded and she could not bring herself to acknowledge their greatness. Before the end of the summer, Mahler's composer's hut resounded with his playing of the Sixth Symphony to Alma. Alma felt chilled when he spoke about the symphony, because she felt that the work, together with the *Kindertotenlieder,* was a true mirror of his life and fate—a withdrawal into gloom, darkness, and tragedy.

To explore the timbres and textures of his Sixth Symphony, Mahler arranged for a reading rehearsal with the Philharmonic. He found himself displeased with the sound of the bass drum, which he considered too subdued for the crashing effect he had intended to be produced by it. To achieve the intended sound he had an enormous sound box constructed, over which he had hide stretched. It was so huge that the regular drumsticks were useless and Mahler decided that clubs would be used. Finally the cue came and the percussionist raised the club and pounded away, but all that emanated from that monster of wood and hide was a dull thud. To the barely hidden amusement of the orchestra, Mahler had the passage repeated; the result was the same. Unconvinced, Mahler took the club from the player's hand and tried it himself, with the same result. Now the laughter in the orchestra was undisguised. Thereupon the original bass drum was brought back and, by comparison, produced a gratifyingly thunderous sound.

The premiere of the Sixth Symphony took place on the occasion of a music festival of the *Vereinigte Deutsche Musik Gesellschaft* in Essen. After the performance Mahler was so moved and aroused that he broke into uncontrollable sobbing in the presence of Alma and some close friends who had come to witness the occasion—Richard Strauss, Mengelberg, Ossip Gabrilovich. Strauss was critical of the performance, viewing it only from a showman's perspective and unable to grasp the vaster aspects of Mahler's macabre vision. Indeed, Strauss never quite fully grasped the stature, historic position, and impact of Mahler. He thought highly of Mahler's opera production but had deprecatingly called him a "celebrity" when Mahler's Second Symphony had a resounding success in Vienna.

Life in the Mahler household continued to revolve in total imbalance around the life, figure, thoughts, and habits of Mahler. While he was constantly and consciously aware of Alma's spirit and beauty, he was, for example, totally oblivious of her work, her tremendous responsibilities, or even her clothes. It was thoughtlessness born of overconcentration. If he needed clothes or shoes he would, as a matter of course, order them from the finest tailors or bootmakers, but somehow it never occurred to him that Alma, in her position as the wife of the director of the Imperial Opera House, might also be in need of a proper wardrobe. Had she had the necessary monies at her disposal to acquire a wardrobe he might have taken that for granted also, but it never occurred to him to inquire into the matter. When they were invited to formal dinners and Alma had no proper clothes she would simply remain at home and he would go alone, without bothering to inquire as to the reason for her absence. On the other hand, he rigidly demanded that the house and his meals and recreation be arranged to his precise wishes and convenience.

All matters and all people had to be subordinated when Mahler composed. Nobody stirred, nobody played an instrument, nobody sang in the house until Mahler emerged, his smile signifying accomplishment amidst total concentration. If nobody's welfare, including Alma's, counted, neither did his own. All that mattered was his work, and the tattered clothes, the haggard look, the unkempt mane attested to it. Alma, deprived of her music for the sake of the genius who was her husband, suffered most.

The basic reason for such thoughtless lack of interest could be found in the fact that Mahler always, inevitably, became totally immersed in and absorbed by the project of the moment. In 1904, for instance, it was *Fidelio* which was to go into production. Roller was in charge of redesigning the settings, and Mahler's world consisted only of the world of *Fidelio*. There was no time for anything else; *Fidelio* was to be his operatic monument forever. He was everywhere; no detail escaped him, be it the grouping of the chorus, the changing of the libretto, Roller's design, or the lighting. As was to be expected, it was in the music that his influence became everlasting, through the master stroke of the placing of the overtures. Starting the performance fittingly with the *Fidelio* Overture, he placed the *Leonore* overtures between the acts, leaving the *Leonore* No. 3 to open the final act. It was at that time a well-kept secret that it was not originally a spiritual motive which prompted the insertion of the *Leonore* No. 3 before the final act, but rather Roller's request for more time to effect the necessary change of scenery. It turned out to be the intuitively right move. Beethoven, whose inspirational thoughts transformed themselves immediately into music, had been greatly hampered by the often unwieldy libretto. So great had been his frustration that he had felt impelled to relate the drama in his own, symphonic terms and in the course of doing so conceived four overtures. To have the *Leonore* No. 3, in itself a symphonic poem descriptive of the drama, introduce the last act turned out to be a stroke of genius on Mahler's part, which established a tradition. Many feel that Beethoven's "magnificent failure," as some in the Vienna press called it, was brought about because he wished to impart too many of his cherished ideals—heroism, loyalty, marital love, faith, justice, triumph over tyranny—to what was to be his only operatic effort. Mahler was able to feel artistic empathy with Beethoven's aims and ideals despite the semi-comic level of the opera, which prevails until the appearance of the tyrant Pizzaro. Consequently Mahler emphasized the heroic aspects, aided by his inherent sense of the dramatic.

By then the Vienna Opera had reached a new zenith under Mahler's direction. Surprisingly, the new acquisitions of the 1903–4 season were sometimes of lesser interest than the redesigned standard operas of the repertoire. In the process of the Mahler–Roller collaboration no detail was overlooked, be it music, libretto, scenery, lighting, or direction, in the attempt to achieve a harmonious interplay among all these components. What Mahler achieved in music Roller paralleled in stagecraft.

As Mahler's fame and influence grew he became the champion of musical causes and youthful composers, particularly that of his young friend Arnold Schönberg. The first occasion for Mahler to defend the young composer came about when Schönberg's Quartet No. 1, opus 7, was performed in 1905. While in his previous chamber-music ventures Schönberg still hewed to an impressionistic line which already had been the subject of much controversy, the String Quartet in D Minor was made of sterner stuff; Schönberg was exploring uncharted fields. The performance took place in the intimacy of the *Bösendorfersaal*. The audience had expected a departure from what it considered the norm (viz. Brahms's chamber music), but what it heard could, in their opinion, be considered only as a joke, and silently, patiently at first, they treated it as such. Finally, inevitably, the bubble of tolerance burst when one critic sprang from his chair and demanded that the music stop. The next moment the scene became one of bedlam and of angry shouting and yelling such as the sedate *Bösendorfersaal* had never before witnessed. Mahler would have none of it. He strode determinedly toward the worst offender, but before the two could face each other the man was forcibly removed. Alma Mahler remembers the man's parting words: "You needn't get so excited, I hiss Mahler too." Another time, when the audience again became unruly during a performance of Schönberg's Chamber Symphony in 1906, Mahler sternly asked for silence and at the end applauded until all dissenters either had been quieted or had left. Mahler's staunch support of Schönberg was doubly startling in that he admitted to Alma: "I don't understand his work, but he's young and he may well be right."

At the opera, Franz Schalk's early promise was recognized by Mahler, who appointed him conductor. Mahler later regretted the appointment of Schalk, whom he came to consider uninspired and pedestrian. By openly indicating his dislike for Schalk and embarrassing him before his fellow artists at the opera, he turned a friend into an enemy. Be it said of Schalk that in later years he was to become a most valuable member of the opera, which he was called upon to lead alone as well as in collaboration with Richard Strauss.

In the nonmusical world it was the relationship between Mahler and Gerhart Hauptmann which deepened. Their philosophy and outlook on life made them kindred spirits, and in discussions with Pfitzner it was no rarity for Mahler and Hauptmann to make a common front against

Pfitzner, who easily became rattled and would leave in confusion. There was never a meeting of the minds between Mahler and Pfitzner, be it on the subject of Wagner, politics, poetry, or music. Pfitzner, whose most mature work in subject matter and musical conception, *Palestrina* (1917), harks back to the past (a logical consequence of portraying the great six-teenth-century polyphonic master), simply could not comprehend Mahler's soaring flight of spirit, and confided to his confidant, Alma (of all people!), that he doubted whether Mahler's creations were music. Mahler, on the other hand, despite his personal dislike for Pfitzner, gave his opera his finest effort and was soon caught up in its special qualities, so different from those in his own work.

The Mahler–Hauptmann friendship soon extended to Zemlinsky and Schönberg, to whom Mahler introduced the dramatist. Upon their urging, Mahler accepted the presidency of the "Composer's Club," an avant-garde group, and he aided their efforts by having them perform some of his music, such as the song cycle *Des Knaben Wunderhorn*. At one concert Mahler personally conducted Richard Strauss's *Sinfonia Domestica*. But despite his best efforts, the club soon faded away. Still, Mahler was never concerned about lack of activity. Jointly with Richard Strauss, he con-ducted at the Alsatian Music Festival; and, of course, every free hour was devoted to composition. He was feted and admired, and his performances, especially of Beethoven's Ninth Symphony, brought audiences to their feet in frenetic acclaim. Only in Germany did he find an occasional cold shoulder, indicative of prevailing sentiments. Despite his embracing of Catholicism, in Germany he remained *"Der Jude Mahler"* and was either ignored, if possible, or attacked under the guise of musical criticism.

By 1905 Strauss had put the finishing touches on *Salome,* his first mature opera (after *Guntram* and *Feuersnot*), with *Elektra, Rosenkava-lier,* and *Ariadne auf Naxos* waiting in the wings, to be created within the next seven years through Strauss's inspired collaboration with Hugo von Hofmannsthal. Mahler, in an early discussion with Strauss, had op-posed a composition based on Oscar Wilde's play on moral, ethical, and religious grounds; despite his opposition, Strauss nevertheless asked him to listen to it. Thus, one day Strauss, Mahler, and Alma went to a piano shop and listened while Strauss sang and played *Salome* for them. Most composers attempting to present a semblance of their work make a mess of it (with Tchaikovsky's playing for Rubinstein of his piano concerto in B-flat the classic example), but not so with Strauss; he played and sang in a masterly fashion. Mahler was fascinated. Regardless of Strauss's often boorish behavior and materialistic outlook, Mahler realized that he sat in the presence of a masterpiece and a genius. The only peculiarity at the time was the absence of the "Dance of the Seven Veils." Mahler com-mented on it, and Strauss replied laughingly that he would compose it later. Mahler always felt that it was the least inspired part of the opera, because it had been composed at another time and in another spirit. *Salome* was premiered in Dresden on 9 December 1905. Mahler wished to perform the opera in Vienna and urgently wired Strauss for the score, only to find himself stymied by the censor. The censor's stated reasons for disallowing a performance of *Salome* are a unique document of Vienna's underhanded, repressive policies, smacking of the medievalism of old, which still persisted in the face of Emperor Franz Joseph's avowed liberalism. The memorandum of refusal to Mahler stated, among other things:

> The first objection is to the repeated references in the text, expressed or implied, to Christ. . . . All these passages would have to be deleted. A further difficulty arises from the fact that John the Baptist is brought on stage. . . . But apart from these textual objections, I cannot reconcile myself to the repellent nature of the entire subject matter and can only say again: events which allude to the sphere of sexual pathology . . . are not suitable for presentation on the stage of our Court theaters.

After so outright a refusal, however, the censor hedged on his decision, which he did not wish to become known to the fullest. Consequently he had the temerity to suggest to Mahler:

> I should like to leave to your discretion, in the interest of all concerned, the desirability of adopting the attitude toward the press that the question whether or not the suppression of *Salome* is final still remains open.

Mahler was furious and responded first with an official *communiqué* to Strauss:

> The office of the director of the Court Opera House is in receipt of an intimation that the censor's department objects to the release of the libretto of the opera *Salome* on "religious" and "ethical" grounds and that "the General Intendancy of the Court Theater is not in a position to grant permission for this stage work to be performed."
> I take the liberty of communicating this decision to you, while expressing at the same time my most lively regrets that, under these circumstances, I am unfortunately compelled to refrain from performing your work.

This was followed by a personal note, assuring Strauss of Mahler's abiding faith in the work.

> I cannot refrain from telling you what an overwhelming impression your work made on me at renewed reading. This is your best so far! I would even say that nothing you have written thus far compares to it. As I have known for a long time, you are the perfect dramatist.

Later Mahler and Alma traveled to Graz, the provincial capital of Styria, to witness *Salome*'s Austrian premiere. Richard Strauss was to return to Vienna at a later, critical time to save the opera from disaster after World

War I. But in 1906 he railed against the Viennese for not allowing Mahler to stage *Salome*. He combined his criticism with a *caveat* to Mahler not to waste his talents and strength on the thankless task of running the opera house—an utterance that was to prove quite pertinent a year later.

If Mahler's winter schedule was totally different from his summer timetable, it was no less intense. He rose at seven o'clock in the morning. An urgent bell brought the maid with breakfast and the newspaper, both quickly devoured. There followed approximately two hours of orchestration of the music he had conceived in the isolation of his summer hut. Nine o'clock found him at his desk at the opera, scanning the mail. When his assistants arrived he was already *au courant,* giving instructions with rapid-fire intensity. The results of such unrelenting drive were the 1906 orchestration of his Seventh Symphony and a new production of Mozart's *Die Entführung aus dem Serail* [The abduction from the seraglio]. In the new production of *Don Giovanni* in German, Roller had exhibited for the first time his new stage device, the "Roller Towers," which, after initial resistance, became a sensation because of the ingenuity of their manifold and flexible applicability; they became a Roller trademark. The next production, *The Marriage of Figaro,* was as dear to Mahler as was its creator. During his entire tenure in Vienna, *Figaro, Don Giovanni, Fidelio,* and *Tristan* were reserved by Mahler, to be conducted by him only.

Alfred Roller had by then begun a campaign of self-aggrandizement and experienced surprising initial success, partly as a result of Mahler's indulgence of his whims. Since he had originally been a protegé of Mahler, everybody assumed that all his arrogations had the approval of the director. When Roller, during a new production, also assumed the role of ballet master, the man in charge of the ballet brought his rage and outrage directly into the office of the Imperial Theater Intendant, Prince Montenuovo, thereby going over Mahler's head. The prince confronted the director, who for better or for worse, defended Roller's actions. The scene ended unpleasantly, with the prince openly showing his annoyance with Mahler. Furthermore, not all agreed with the novel stagings, and Mahler's opponents, their courage now bolstered, accused him of novelty for novelty's sake, their main target being Roller's ubiquitous "Towers." Mahler replied, undeterred:

> All modern art must serve the stage. . . . What matters is the collaboration of all arts. There is no future in the old standard clichés; modern art must extend to costumes, to props, to everything that can revitalize a work of art.
>
> *Illustriertes Extrablatt,* 9 September 1903

Meanwhile, Mahler's daring experimentation with new, untried, and sometimes disappointing voices at this most illustrious of opera houses only tended to further fan the flames of opposition and intrigue against the director. Now his selections were discredited, because it was felt he was being "swayed by his subjective preferences rather than by his artistic convictions." Opposition was also fanned by Mahler's lack of consideration for others' feelings. Petitions and letters of complaint kept up the pressure against him. "One constantly hears the artists complain that the director frequently disregards . . . the most elementary rules of courtesy . . . which has already cost the Court Opera many valuable and all but irreplaceable members." That complaint was coupled with a statement aiming at the heart of the petitioners' purpose, viz., that a "competent and unprejudiced man" be installed and invested with adequate power to avoid such errors of judgment on the part of the director.

Within the bureaucracy such complaints fell on sympathetic ears—until they reached the top of the ladder, Prince Montenuovo. Despite occasional disagreements, the prince understood the director, appreciated his artistic aims, and admired his courage. Besides, Mahler seasons at the opera, with every performance of a new or restaged work conducted by the director in person, invariably produced a cash surplus, an unheard-of miracle in a theater which had constantly depended on court subsidies despite the Viennese predilection for opera. Thus the strongest efforts on the part of Mahler's detractors were doomed to failure. Knowledge of this state of affairs and of Mahler's unique position had become the talk of Europe:

> It may be counted to Mahler's credit to have incurred [nobility's] displeasure; for it proves that his pride yields to no man, that he will not curry favor with the aristocracy. . . . He will not defer to anyone's wishes in the choice of a new opera. . . . To be sure, he is supported in this attitude by the constitutionalism of the monarch, who will never act without consulting his advisers.
>
> Munich press report, 1904

The incredible zest and zeal which Mahler brought to his work as director as well as composer can be gleaned from the fact that from 1901 to 1905, at the very height of his directorial work at the opera and with all the worries and tensions and responsibilities, which every day brought with it, he found the inner strength and physical drive to create three symphonies.

As previously alluded to, there had been founded in Vienna by Zemlinsky and Schönberg, the short-lived *Vereinigung schaffender Tonkünstler* (Society of Creative Musicians), with Bruno Walter a member and Mahler its honorary president. But it was Schönberg who was the moving spirit and the most outstanding and controversial member of the group. The relationship between Schönberg and Mahler had not always been that close, particularly since Schönberg, in youthful arrogance and overexuberance, had called the older man incompetent. Thus when they had met face to face for the first time in 1903 the situation was awkward, but the occasion momentous. The Viennese music critic and historian Max Graf described the event in his *Legend of a Musical City*:

> Soon after the performance of the quartet [in D Minor] [Schönberg] brought me a sextet, *Verklärte Nacht*. The music sounded new, the harmonies unusual. Since I did not trust my judgment, I gave the score to Gustav Mahler, at that time opera director. Mahler wavered in his opinion, as I had done, and asked Arnold Rosé to play the sextet with his musicians, in Mahler's office. He invited me [and Schönberg] to come to this private performance, and we were both enthusiastic. Mahler said to Rosé: "You must play that!" and Rosé played it at the next chamber music evening, to the great displeasure of the Viennese public, who hissed loudly.

The enthusiasm of the conservative Rosé for Schönberg's music was surprising. He had rejected an offer to perform the quartet by Hugo Wolf; yet he continued to champion Schönberg. During one concert when, as expected, the audience openly expressed its displeasure with *Verklärte Nacht,* the men of the Rosé ensemble rose as if acknowledging enthusiastic applause instead of open hostility, and then sat down to replay the entire work before the stunned audience.

There eventually developed a close understanding between Schönberg, who both revered and youthfully rebelled against his elder, and Mahler, who was deeply concerned about Schönberg's progress despite occasional tensions. Alma writes:

> After dinner, Mahler, Schönberg, and Zemlinsky would go to the piano and talk shop—at first in all amity. Then Schönberg let fall a word in youthful arrogance and Mahler corrected him with a shade of condescension—and the room was in an uproar. . . . Schönberg leaped to his feet and vanished with a curt good night. Zemlinsky followed, shaking his head. As soon as the door had shut behind them, Mahler said: "Be sure never to invite that conceited puppy again." On the stairs Schönberg sputtered: "I shall never cross that threshold again." But after a week or two Mahler said: "By the way, what's become of those two?" I lost no time in sending them an invitation, and they, who had been waiting for it, lost no time in coming.

> *Memories and Letters,* 1946

Eventually the day arrived when Schönberg effusively acknowledged Mahler's stature:

12 December 1904

My dear Director,

I must not speak as a musician to a musician if I am to give any idea of the incredible impression the [Fifth] Symphony made on me: I can speak only as one human being to another. For I saw your very soul, naked, stark naked. It was revealed to me as a stretch of wild and secret country, with eerie chasms and abysses neighbored by sunlit, smiling meadows, haunts of idyllic repose. I felt [your symphony] as an event of nature which, after scouring us with its terrors, puts a rainbow in the sky. . . . I shared in the battling for illusion; I suffered the pangs of disillusionment; I saw the forces of evil and good wrestling with each other; I saw a man in torment struggling towards inner harmony; I divined a personality, a drama, and truthfulness, the most uncompromising truthfulness.

I had to let myself go. Forgive me. I cannot feel by halves. With me it is one thing or the other.

In all devotion,<br>Arnold Schönberg

Mahler reciprocated with equal warmth. When Schönberg requested a loan of 300 to 400 gulden ("I am completely penniless at the moment and have to pay the rent"), the money was promptly forthcoming. Even on his deathbed Mahler was to worry about Schönberg; "Who will take care of him when I am gone?" he inquired of Alma. Mahler's concern actually outlived his death. An endowment set up by Mahler to benefit a different promising composer each year selected Schönberg as its first recipient.

How different this attitude was from that hardened but ambivalent one which he bore toward Richard Strauss, which ranged from disgust for the man to unreserved praise for the genius. Strauss's materialistic approach to most everything (aroused and encouraged by his wife) and his lack of a personal conception of romantic feelings (though these were eloquently expressed in his music) aroused Mahler's ire, for to him romantic conception and philosophical dialectics were necessities of being. In a moment of arrogance bordering on naiveté, Mahler wrote to Alma on 17 December 1901: "I can't do a thing for him, for while I see him as an entity, he sees only my pedestal." Despite such deprecating remarks, he was totally aware of Strauss's genius. After hearing Salome in Berlin in 1907, Mahler extolled it to Alma: "It bears the stamp of genius . . . undoubtedly one of the most magnificent [works] that has been produced in our time!" Nevertheless, Mahler persisted in distinctly separating the man from his work. "Under that heap of rubble there is a volcano living and working, a subterranean fire . . . no mere fireworks. This is probably true of Strauss's entire personality. This is what makes it so difficult to separate the wheat from the chaff in him."

At this point a comparison forces itself upon us, viz., that between the character of Strauss and that of a genius of another century—Mozart. How close a resemblance one finds with respect to their simultaneous human shallowness and musical depth! Mahler's disgust at Strauss's crudely materialistic attitude alongside his admiration for his genius bring to mind the memoirs of Karoline Pichler, the daughter of a Vienna court councilor in whose house Mozart performed his immortal music. "No outstanding spiritual force . . . an everyday turn of mind, insipid jokes . . . and yet, what depth, what world of fantasy, harmony, melody, and emotion!"

Mahler shared with the eighteenth-century genius, whom he revered as did Strauss, a sense of drama. While Strauss in his creations reveled in operatic drama, Mahler shied away from composition for the musical theater. Rather, his sense of drama manifested itself in tone drama (as early as *Das klagende Lied*) and was expressed even more intensely, and on a higher spiritual level, in his symphonies. Nevertheless, in those symphonies Mahler unquestionably drew on his experience with the stage— on which, incidentally, Mozart's most dramatic work, *Don Giovanni*, was one of Mahler's most beloved and most inspired recreations.

Mahler also had in common with Mozart the desire to perform his own music and the conflict arising from that desire. Just as Mozart's repeated absences from the orchestra of the Archbishop of Salzburg constituted one of the reasons for his eventual dismissal, so Mahler eventually found his superiors in Vienna taking umbrage at his repeated and prolonged absences as the demand for his personal appearances and his compositions increased. In 1905 alone, he took time out from his directorial and conducting duties in Vienna to conduct his compositions in Hamburg, Strassburg, Berlin, Triest, and Breslau. He had been recognized as a composer to such an extent that a German publisher had offered and paid him the then enormous sum of 15,000 marks for his Fifth Symphony. At that point an action of Mahler's proved his unbending integrity. Once he had arrived at the realization that the work should be reorchestrated, he also realized that parts of the work or perhaps the entire work would have to be reprinted. Since that would have caused the publisher considerable hardship, he returned the entire fee even before he began to revise the symphony's orchestration.

Mahler's trail was now widening into a broad avenue of success. His Vienna position was as secure as Viennese conditions would ever permit, and his fame was spreading, as a conductor as well as a composer. Willem Mengelberg, at the helm of the Amsterdam Concertgebouw Orchestra, had led the way; now Germany, Russia, and France were clamoring for Mahler's appearances. In Vienna, in December 1905, his Fifth Symphony, under his direction, registered a triumph.[8] Suddenly he was found worthy of musicological discussion. In Vienna, Richard Specht and Mahler's long-time friend Guido Adler were in the forefront of Mahler enthusiasts in the German-speaking world. In France, Romain Rolland admired Mahler,

[8] It was the last new Mahler work Vienna was to hear under his baton; all others had posthumous premieres. Not until 1912, one year after Mahler's death, did Vienna hear his Ninth Symphony under Walter, who also conducted the Vienna premiere of *Das Lied von der Erde*. The Seventh had to wait until 1916, when Weingartner conducted it, and the Eighth was not heard in Vienna until Franz Schalk performed it in 1918.

although he admitted to not understanding the powers that drove him. He particularly felt that Mahler's opera activities in Vienna intruded into the composer's world and impeded his efforts: "he has no time to dream." There was truth in that observation, although Mahler, strictly apportioning his time, "dreamt" during the summer months in the seclusion of his "composer's hut." Yet Mahler was to come to the same conclusion two years later, at which time he acted accordingly.

Aside from his directorial duties and compositional efforts Mahler took little active part in the affairs and events of his time, although, prompted by an all-consuming curiosity, he followed them assiduously, voraciously reading newspapers, magazines, pamphlets, and books. People never failed to fascinate him, *if* he considered them to be on his intellectual level. By then Mahler's personality was unquestionably beginning to show signs of outward strain contrasting with an inner calm: rudeness would collide with compassion, efficiency with absentmindness, deep despondency with exuberantly high spirits. Depending on with whom one spoke, he was the tyrannical director or the gentle guide, the man basking in mass adulation or the hermit of the "composer's hut." Inconsistencies in his musical evaluation also became more pronounced, largely as a result of his immersion in the work of the moment. While it was, for example, understandable and proper to pronounce Strauss's *Salome* a great masterpiece, it was less appropriate to state that "*Rienzi* is ultimately Wagner's greatest work." Such mildly schizophrenic tendencies were bound to enter also into Mahler's art, whose pendulum swung from the massive orchestration of his symphonies to the spare instrumentation of his orchestral songs.

Descriptions of the Mahler of those years reflect these tensions and the collision of elements within the man. Max Graf described the diminutive giant in these terms:

> When the house grew dark, the small man with the sharply chiseled features, pale and ascetic looking, literally rushed to the conductor's desk. His conducting was striking enough in his first years of activity in Vienna. He would let his baton shoot forward suddenly, like the tongue of a poisonous serpent. With his right hand, he seemed to pull the music out of the orchestra. . . . He would let his stinging glance loose upon a musician who was seated far away from him, and the man would quail. Giving a cue, he would look in one direction, at the same time pointing the baton in another. . . . He would leap from his conductor's chair as if he had been stung. Mahler was always in full movement, like a blazing flame. Later he became calmer. Evidently he controlled himself, which only augmented his inner tension.
>
> *Legend of a Musical City*

That controlled manner was likewise observed by the musicologist Ludwig Schiedermair in 1900:

Mahler's manner of wielding the baton . . . is singularly free of the ruling passion of striving for effect. . . . Mahler does not go in for nervous gesticulation; there is no extravagant bobbing up and down, no body motion that degenerates to the level of a stage pose.

Blaukopf, *Gustav Mahler*

Bruno Walter, in a portrait of Mahler in his later years, depicts him as masking total control with outward calm:

The external pattern of Mahler's conducting became infinitely simplified in the course of years. . . . Gradually his stance and gestures became quieter; his conducting technique became so intellectualized that he achieved musicianly freedom combined with unfailing precision quite effortlessly by a simple-looking beat, while keeping almost still. His enormous influence on singers and instrumentalists was conveyed by a look or the sparest of gestures, where before he had exerted himself with impassioned movements. Towards the end his conducting represented the image of an almost eerie calm.

Bruno Walter, *Gustav Mahler*

Most people watching such explosive or contained intensity in the opera pit or concert hall would attribute little physical strength to the man's small body. Few realized that, although Mahler was not an athlete, he possessed a tightly muscled body. Once he stopped a rehearsal of *Das Rheingold* to inquire why Wagner's directions were not followed. Freya was to be carried off by Fafner and Fasolt. When the two giant basses looked astounded at Mahler and declared this to be an impossible feat, Mahler leaped on stage, lifted the singer (Freya) high up in the air, and carried her about the entire stage.[9] Such stamina had been acquired by Mahler through his favorite pastimes—swimming, bicycling, hiking, and mountaineering—all undertaken with the intensity so typical of all of Mahler's activities, albeit restricted to the summer months. There are echoes of these various summer-month activities in his music, such as the cow bells in his Sixth and Seventh symphonies and the inclusion of Ländler melodies in his music.

The intensity with which his activities were carried on and the discipline those activities reflected went hand in hand with an inconsistency already touched on. He could never be quoted, because he reserved the right to change his opinion the following day. This likewise held true with respect to his work, interpretation of which was a matter of artistic intuition rather than hard and fast planning. Such intuition, unencumbered by the restriction of any particular "school," flowed from tradition, trends, musical genius, and personal insight, and inevitably became

[9] *Österreichische Illustrierte Zeitung*, 24 May 1931.

identified with what is known as "Mahler style"—which, upon scrutiny, does not really exist but is rather manifested as a constant renewing, as each work is individually conceived.

The leanness of Mahler's body carried over into his living habits. Meals remained frugal. "Drunkenness was an abomination to him, as were filthy language and indecency," observed Roller. Cigars were his daily companions, a glass of beer his evening companion. Whisky and brandy were out of bounds, and wine limited to an occasional glass or two of German or Italian vintage. Alma relates that a moderate amount of wine was sufficient to put him into a delightfully relaxed, humorous state of mind, as did a quick visit to the Café Imperial, where, over a cup of famed Viennese coffee, he would scan the Viennese musical reviews, his face a strange mixture of intensity and amusement.

Alongside Mahler's musical development was evidenced a continual preoccupation with a plethora of other interests: literature (Goethe, Dostoievsky), philosophy (Nietzsche, Kant, Schopenhauer), psychoanalysis (Freud), Austrian politics (Victor Adler), and even physics, reflecting a constant desire to seek, explore, understand, interrelate. Such delving into many phases of life and thought brought about understanding as well as tolerance, a tolerance which did not always extend to all aspects of music and musicians. While he was an open Wagnerian and a reserved Bruckner adherent, he never joined Wolf's open forum of harangue against Brahms (whom he also viewed with reservations but performed beautifully). Although by his own admission he did not wholly comprehend Schönberg's musical intentions he supported his efforts fully; but he spoke in deprecating terms of Sibelius. And although the French-impressionist world of sound may have been alien to Mahler's German tendencies, he nevertheless made Debussy heard for the first time in America by performing his *Iberia* and *Rondes de Printemps*. Finally, while he grew to detest Wagner's pompous writings ("One really has to forget their existence, to give Wagner's genius his due"), he proceeded to become the greatest Wagner interpreter of his day.

## THE VIENNA CURTAIN DESCENDS

The last two years of Mahler's Vienna presence were years of feverish activity and achievement in all fields of musical endeavor, in part because 1906 was the one hundred fiftieth anniversary of Mozart's birth, a celebration that was a "must" in Vienna for artistic as well as psychological reasons. Mahler was, of course, in his element, and Vienna, which had treated Mozart so shabbily during his lifetime, saw an opportunity to make belated amends.

The world will never know what demon drove Mozart back to Vienna. Had he been a mediocre musician, his hometown of Salzburg would have provided him with a meager lifetime position there as it had done for his father, Leopold. But Wolfgang was irresistibly drawn to the *Clavierland* (as he exuberantly described Vienna to his father in the early 1780s, a time when he was flushed with his early [and passing] success as a pianist), against the advice of Count Arco ("You allow yourself to be far too easily dazzled by Vienna. A man's reputation here lasts only a very short time") as well as that of his father ("The Viennese public . . . cannot even understand what seriousness means"). In Prague he was feted as never before; his operas and his symphonies were enthusiastically received ("*Die Prager verstehen mich,*" he remarked: "The people of Prague understand me"), but back he went to Vienna, the city which had lived up to Count Arco's assessment of it and which eventually totally neglected Mozart. Why did Mozart venture back to Vienna? Was it because the city had charmed him even in its negligence, as it was to charm many before and after him? Or was it in order to prove to Vienna that his was a mastery beyond compare? If so, the attempt was in vain: Vienna listened to Salieri and Kozeluch, while Mozart went to an anonymous grave. Vienna had attempted, belatedly, to make amends of sort. A statue of the composer had been erected, with Mozart draped in a clumsy stone mantle.[10]

Now, in 1906, was an ideal time for Vienna to honor "its" Mozart in the concert hall and on the opera stage. Mahler had anticipated the Mozart year with his presentation of *Don Giovanni* in 1905. In 1906 he lost no time, and in January *Die Entführung aus dem Serail* was ready. In March a new *Marriage of Figaro* was staged in a new German translation by Max Kalbeck (the original Italian libretto was by Lorenzo da Ponte). In June the Mozart remembrance continued with Roller's staging of *The Magic Flute,* with Vienna's star, Selma Kurz, singing a sensational queen of the night, Georg Maikl as Tamino, and Marie Gutheil-Schoder and Anton Moser as Pamina and Papageno. *Cosi fan tutte,* the fifth Mozart production in one year, completed the cycle. During all that feverish activity Mahler had visions of composing in the stillness of his composer's cottage at Maiernigg; but it was not to be. "By gracious command of his Majesty" he was summoned to conduct a gala performance of *Figaro* in Salzburg, which had also shunted Mozart aside in life but now wanted all the world to remember that he had been its native son. Mahler's *Figaro* was a superlative production; twenty years later, the critic Julius Korngold's reminiscence in the *Neue Freie Presse* would note how vast projects could, in the mind of a genius, simultaneously move to fruition.

---

[10] The statue originally stood behind the opera on *Mozartplatz.* After World War II it was removed to a charming garden spot in the *Burggarten,* next to the Imperial Court; in itself an irony, in light of the neglect Mozart suffered at the hands of his sovereign.

*Figaro* in Salzburg: the words conjure up an imperishable memory. Gustav Mahler came to Mozart's town in 1906. Visions of a new symphony crowded in on him, but he came, happy in this premonition, in a mood not far from exuberance. A much-thumbed volume protruded from his coat pocket: it was *Faust*. The theme of the medieval metaphysician, which was to dominate the first part of the symphony—it was the Eighth—had taken shape. Now the parallel passages from Goethe were waiting. . . . It was in this mood that he was inspired by the tiny theater to perform a miracle of artistic genius. . . . This *Figaro* of his at Salzburg was the ideal *Figaro* in its enchanting grace, its light-winged conversational tone, and the incomparable balance of the entire ensemble. No one who was present on that occasion can ever forget it.

The truly superhuman extent of Mahler's Mozart effort can be gleaned when we realize that while producing all those stagings Mahler had also restaged *Lohengrin* in the new Roller design and traveled to Antwerp and Amsterdam to conduct his own music and to Essen for the premiere of his Sixth Symphony. In the autumn he went to Berlin, where Oskar Fried also conducted Mahler's Sixth Symphony, and then back to Breslau to conduct his Third Symphony; and late in the year he conducted another performance of the *Sixth* in Munich. All the while, on his desk, in his pocket, on his mind, were a ninth-century Latin text and Goethe's *Faust*. His Eighth Symphony was taking shape. To that task Mahler dedicated himself as soon as time permitted him to rush back to Maiernigg.

Despite Mahler's strenuous and dedicated efforts, all did not go well. The Mozart revivals and restagings, though among the crowning achievements of his tenure in Vienna, received critical acclaim but did not fill the house or the opera coffers. The production of a new opera, *Le Juif Polonaise,* an important contemporary work of the French composer Camille Erlanger, was an outright failure. The coincidence of financial and artistic failures was a new and distressing experience for Mahler. In a drastic turnabout and revision of plans, he shelved planned new productions by Max von Schillings and Zemlinsky and instead resourcefully ressurrected Rossini's *Barber of Seville,* barely bothering to blow the dust off the old scenery. Vienna did not care; they flocked to listen to Selma Kurz's coloratura, and Mahler breathed easier as box-office receipts rose, to the satisfaction of all concerned. The appearance of Caruso in 1906 and 1907 also helped box office. True to his principles, Mahler demanded on those occasions that the entire cast sing in Italian.

At the beginning of 1907 Mahler again requested a leave of absence to respond to conducting invitations from Berlin, Amsterdam, and Frankfurt. Mahler's enemies took advantage of his absence to resume their open war against him, and Vienna promptly began to engage in one of its favorite guessing games.

People in Vienna seem to have gone quite crazy. The newspapers here are continually inserting telegrams from them, saying that I have sent in my resignation, that I have piled up an enormous deficit, that I have become impossible, etc., etc.

Mahler to Alma, 15 January 1907

But Mahler put aside the latest Vienna tempest, because the overriding matter in his life then was the creation of his Eighth Symphony, for which he had decided on part two of Goethe's *Faust* as a fitting climax. Mahler's recourse to Goethe is not surprising, for Goethe had assumed the same awesome importance for him in poetry as had Wagner and Beethoven in music. Many among Mahler's close circle of French friends —Paul Painlevé, George Piquart, Paul and Sophie Clemenceau—whom he saw frequently in Paris as well as in Vienna, were Goethe admirers, a factor which contributed to their close friendship with Mahler over the years. They would together make pilgrimages to Goethe shrines; and whenever they would meet in Vienna, Mahler would regale them with operas by Wagner, Beethoven, and Mozart.

The attacks on Mahler, however, continued with increased ferocity. For the first time, the influential critic Korngold joined Mahler's foes. While fully acknowledging the accomplishments of Mahler and the magnificence he had brought to the Vienna Opera, Korngold maintained in the *Neue Freie Presse* that

> side by side with this . . . sprouts a crop of Court Opera juveniles that is unpromising, if not totally dispensable. Mahler's predilections for rising talent . . . have favored a collection of mediocrities. . . . There is half a tenor here and half a bass there, and the two of them still do not make a whole singer.

Along with this criticism was that emanating from those who had enjoyed the *Barber of Seville* because it had presented a star singer, a beautiful coloratura, and *bel canto,* all the things Mahler had wished to do away with and for which the Viennese were still yearning. Mahler shrugged off his critics and went on to prove *his* point with a production of *Die Walküre* that was admiringly considered "total art" by his critics and whose influence was to reverberate half a century later on the Bayreuth stage. One month later, in March 1907, Mahler presented his ultimate conception of opera production, Gluck's *Iphigénie en Aulide.*

If one considers opera as the artistic product of three contributors— composer, poet, and stage designer—then in Gluck's time the composer was ignored by the *castrati,* who, unencumbered by artistic principles, imposed their own vocal aberrations on opera. The poet was equally driven from the scene, because the story was dispensed with in *pastiches* which strung arias together with total disregard for continuity. These vocal acrobatics were abetted by elaborations of stage design and stage craft which enticed the eye and, together with the *castrati's* impudent insertions, catered to an ignorant public, intent only on aural and visual effect and totally devoid of artistic appreciation. What Gluck had to say in the preface to his major reform opera *Alceste* could have been said by Mahler:

> I resolved to divest [opera] entirely of all those abuses, introduced either by the mistaken vanity of singers or by the complaisance of composers, [which] . . . made . . . the most splendid operas . . .    ridiculous and wearisome. I have striven to present music . . . without interrupting the action or stifling it with a useless superfluity or ornaments. . . . Thus I did not wish to stop an actor in the greatest heat of a dialogue in order to wait for a tiresome *ritornello,* nor hold him up in the middle of a word on a vowel favorable to his voice, nor make a display of the agility of his fine voice in some long-drawn-out passage. . . . In short, I have sought to abolish all the abuses against which good sense and reason have long cried out in vain. . . . Furthermore, I believed that my greatest labor should be devoted to seeking a beautiful simplicity, and I have avoided making displays of difficulty at the expense of clearness.

What Mahler had begun in *Die Walküre* was taken to a logical conclusion (and in complete harmony with Gluck's principles) in the Mahler–Roller collaboration. Scenery was reduced to its basic elements. Just as Gluck had departed from the frills of Neapolitan opera, so Mahler eliminated the meaningless vestiges of a mistaken conservatism in favor of the spirit of the composer. The music again became the essential ingredient, hand in hand with the story.

But Mahler's renewed artistic successes could no longer still the vociferous voices of his detractors, particularly when, shortly after staging *Iphigénie,* he again left Vienna to concertize in Brünn, St. Petersburg, and Rome. The request for three additional days in Rome was particularly vexing to Prince Montenuovo, because it would have meant Mahler's staying away beyond his allotted period of absence. The prince openly displayed signs of annoyance, commenting on slumping box-office receipts due to the director's repeated and prolonged absences. Outwardly calm, Mahler had by then already considered taking a decisive step, which he must, moreover, have already discussed with Roller.

> At the opera there is really great confusion, thanks to the usual Viennese love for mischief. . . . It seems that all forces are now uniting to bring about [Mahler's] downfall. If people only knew how glad he is to go.
>
> Roller to his wife, April 1907

"How glad he is to go." The phrase clearly indicates that Mahler had already made up his mind to resign from his post while his opponents still strained to accomplish that end. It also indicates that Roller may have been privy to communications which had reached Mahler from New York, some as early as 1903. Mahler, world famous and much sought after, would have no problem relocating himself.

Mahler deliberately did nothing to put an end to or counteract the crisis.

> You see, that's what they are now doing to me: if I wanted to remain seated, all I would have to do is lean back firmly and I could hold my own. But I am not offering any resistance, and so I shall finally slide off.
>
> Bruno Walter, *Gustav Mahler*

Shortly thereafter he informed his disciple of his resignation with the words: "In the ten years at the opera I have completed my cycle." Mahler had arrived at a point in life at which the composer overshadowed the conductor. He needed more time to "dream."

Prince Montenuovo, meanwhile, casting about for a successor to Mahler, was running into difficulties. The main problem was, of course, that only a conductor of world stature could be considered for so prestigious an institution as the Vienna Imperial Opera, and one was not easy to find. Felix Mottl had been approached but had bowed out with a polite "Thank you, but no thank you." Vienna itself was having second thoughts by then, and the *Neue Freie Presse* commented ominously: "We let the man go, for it was time to prove once again how carelessly we husband our cultural resources." The situation had become difficult for both parties, because there had been harsh words from Prince Montenuovo concerning budgetary overruns and tart rejoinders from the director. Although there had not yet been any official word issued from either side concerning the severing of relations, it was considered a fait accompli in Vienna.[11] But now Prince Montenuovo had second thoughts concerning the retention of Mahler. His tentative inquiries concerning a new director had been fruitless. After Mottl, Nikisch had also refused, and so, initially, had Weingartner. But Mahler had arrived at a point of no return. His time in Vienna had ended.

Montenuovo was seemingly not immediately aware of Mahler's resolve. Although the prince had originally reproached Mahler for his repeated absences (for, in his words, "advertising your symphonies"), he was now willing to concede Mahler's argument that such appearances were like showing the flag and actually enhanced the prestige of Vienna—i.e., that of the opera as well as of Mahler. In subsequent conversations, however, Mahler made his resolve abundantly clear to the prince, at which time he also informed him that his determination to conclude his tenure in Vienna had prompted him to sign a contract with Heinrich Conried of the Metropolitan Opera in New York.

To make sure that no misunderstanding arose between him and the prince, Mahler conveyed his plans and requests in a follow-up letter to Prince Montenuovo.

---

[11] Mahler had once before submitted his resignation in 1905, when the Vienna censor had prohibited a performance of Strauss's *Salome*.

Your Highness,

Forgive me for troubling you with a letter in reference to our conversation of yesterday. My future relations with the Royal Opera House were clearly defined, but it did not occur to me (or, rather, I forgot) to raise the question of my personal interests; that is to say, of what view your Highness takes of my future in the financial sense. As a decision on this point has become a matter of immediate concern, allow me to place before your Highness what I regard as desirable in view of the alteration of my circumstances.

1. As regards my pension: I am entitled to retire on a pension of 5,500 florins at the end of my tenth year of service (on 1 May of this year). Until recently I might well have counted on claiming the higher pension of 7,000 florins to which a further three years' service would have entitled me.

My way of living has been planned on that basis—for I am not by any means past my work, nor has your Highness ever hinted that my retirement was other than premature—and also I have entered into commitments which I must meet in any case, such as insurance policies for the benefit of my wife and children and the building of a house in the country. It would weigh very heavily on me for the rest of my life, if through unforeseen circumstances and . . . no fault of mine I were to be deprived of advantages on which I had every reason to count; and I therefore request that I may be granted the pension of 7,000 florins assured me by decree after thirteen years of service.

2. In order to wind up my present household and way of life with a quiet mind, . . . I request the payment of 10,000 florins in final compensation. . . . What I ask . . . is more or less the same as was granted at that time to my predecessor.

3. The assurance in the event of my death for my wife and two children the pension for widows and orphans, as laid down by royal statute. (Your Highness was kind enough to draw my attention to this point.)

In expressing frankly and in full what I should desire in the event of my departure, I rely on the kindness your Highness has always shown me and which at our last meeting your Highness was good enough to express. It is not for me to champion my own cause by alluding to the manner in which I have carried out my duties during, one might well say, war years.

I ask your Highness's forgiveness for the liberty I take and with the expression of my gratitude beg to remain your Highness's obedient servant,

Mahler

Prince Montenuovo's reply was evidence of the magnanimity of this true nobleman as well as of his high regard for Mahler. Although he refers to having put Mahler's requests before the emperor, it was his own recommendation which secured the benefits for Mahler.

Semmering, 8 October 1907

Dear Director,

I did not until yesterday receive the definite and official intimation that Weingartner consented to take up the appointment on the 1st of January 1908.

I make haste to inform you of this, as I have been keenly aware of the suspense in which you have been kept. My only consolation is that your freedom comes within the appointed time, for you told me yourself in Vienna that difficulties on account of your American engagement would not arise until *after* the last of January. I have arranged everything satisfactorily with W. He will come to Vienna at the beginning of September. I am glad to be able to tell you also that your three requests have been put before His Majesty and that, after handing over your office on 1 January 1908, you will be granted:

I. a pension of 14,000 kronen, instead of the pension to which you are entitled under your contract;

II. a sum of K. 20,000 in full compensation; and lastly,

III. Your wife after your death will be entitled to the pension of the widow of a Privy Councillor (although you did not rank as such), in accordance with the Statute of Court Pension.[12]

It gives me great pleasure to have been successful in settling all this in accordance with your wishes.

Please treat W.'s appointment as strictly confidential for the time being. I do not wish the matter to be made public until what I consider the proper moment has arrived.

— Conried now need delay no longer in making your engagement public. Please inform him of this.

Cordial greetings,
Montenuovo

Mahler had signed a contract with the Metropolitan Opera in June 1907. Since the emperor's (and Prince Montenuovo's) decision was not to be announced until the late autumn of the year, the overlapping months allowed Vienna to play its favorite guessing game (Will he stay? Will he go?). As can be gleaned from Prince Montenuovo's letter, his intensified efforts to find a Mahler successor had snared a worthy bird—Felix Weingartner, who lost no time in communicating with Mahler.

Bad Kreuth, 22 August 1907

My dear Mr. Mahler,

What only lately appeared incredible has now come true; I am really to be your successor in Vienna. There is much I might say, but may I confine myself to the expression of one brief wish?

[12] 2 kronen = 1 florin. Hence, Mahler received exactly the amounts he had requested.

I learn from the newspapers that you are going to reside in Vienna.[13] My wish and hope, then, are that the friendly relations which have existed between us, but which seem to have lapsed for several years, may revive, and thereafter continue without interruption.

I look forward with warmth to seeing you again in Vienna, and hope that it may be soon. Until then I remain, with my best wishes,

Ever most sincerely yours,

Felix Weingartner

All these events, however, were overshadowed by a series of catastrophes which were destined to totally alter Mahler's physical, spiritual, and musical life beyond anything his often morbid thoughts had ever envisioned or dreaded. Having settled his affairs in Vienna, Mahler and his family returned to Maiernigg for a much longed for vacation. But rest and relaxation continued to elude him. Alma needed an operation and the younger child took sick with scarlet fever, which the older girl soon also contracted. To everyone's consternation, the older child failed to improve. When the danger of suffocation became acute a tracheotomy was resorted to, the operation being performed at Mahler's summer home. It was to no avail. The child, choking in agony, lived only one more day. It was a crushing blow to Mahler. He had loved the child dearly and deeply, had held long conversations with her, had played and danced with her, reliving in the child a youth which he had never known. The void for Gustav and Alma was a nearly unbearable one.

Yet fate had not played its last trump card in that fateful year 1907. Alma's mother, whom Mahler also loved dearly, had come from Vienna to help and to comfort, but was striken by a heart attack. A doctor was summoned; he examined her and also Alma, diagnosed that the strain had affected Alma's heart as well, and prescribed complete rest. In a seizure of morbid humor Mahler jocularly remarked to the doctor: "You might as well examine me too." The doctor saw nothing humorous in the request under the circumstances and he began to examine Mahler, who was then lying on a couch. When the doctor straightened up, his face was grave. "You have no cause to be proud of a heart like yours." He had been the first to diagnose Mahler's heart disease. Mahler heard the verdict behind the casual remark; he immediately returned to Vienna, where two heart specialists, Dr. Blumenthal and Professor Kovacs, confirmed the first doctor's findings. Mahler listened grimly as the Vienna specialists forbade him to walk fast, to walk uphill, to ride a bicycle, or to engage in any strenuous activity. Walks were to be restricted to five minutes, and all walking had to be deliberate. This to Mahler—who had gloried in mountain climbing, swimming, and rapid walks.

---

[13] Prince Montenuovo had not revealed to Weingartner the news of Mahler's New York contract.

Yet Mahler obeyed. The life that he had lived was forcibly forgotten; restrictions and compromise became the order of the day. "Compromise"— once Mahler would have rejected the term in the sharpest possible language; now compromise was to become a way of life. Then and there a part of Mahler's spirit began to wither. There were yet to be great moments in his life, but the Mahler of yesteryear had ceased to exist.

Aside from Alma, Bruno Walter was then one of the few whom Mahler took into his confidence with respect to the profound changes which the discovery of the heart ailment was to impose. The mountains, the lakes, the long walks, all of which had been witnesses to his musical fecundity, were no longer to play a part in his life. Worst of all, death, which had occupied Mahler's mind as a philosophical and esoteric concern whose mysteries fascinated him, now loomed as a sinister reality, one whose shadow was to profoundly alter Mahler's attitudes and outlook during the remaining years of his life. However, in a musical sense, fears that the regimen imposed on him would stifle his artistic impulses proved unfounded, for it was during those years that Mahler's greatest creations, his Eighth and Ninth symphonies and *Das Lied von der Erde*, were born, eventually to be performed to world acclaim—the Eighth under Mahler's direction, the others posthumously.

A final, magnificent performance of *Fidelio* on 15 October 1907 before a half-empty house (because of the animosity of the local opera clique) marked the end of the Mahler era at the Vienna Opera. And on 24 November he said adieu to Vienna in a performance of his *Resurrection* Symphony at a gala concert of the *Gesellschaft der Musikfreunde*. There Mahler was greeted by emotional applause, which swelled to a veritable hurricane at the end and moved him to tears. The Philharmonic and the *Singverein* participated in the ovations, which was doubly remarkable because Mahler's relationship with the Philharmonic had always been on a level of cool correctness. The entire audience remained in their places, and Mahler was recalled thirty times. As men wept and women waved handkerchiefs, the shouts of "bravo" reverberated through the magnificent hall. Two weeks later, two hundred persons, the musical intelligentsia of Vienna, assembled at the *Westbahnhof* to bid farewell to Mahler, and as the train left the station the emotional scene of the last concert repeated itself on a quieter but perhaps even more deeply felt scale. As the outskirts of Vienna sped by, Mahler looked back at fond and tortuous memories alike without regret. On his last day at the opera, he had fastened this farewell letter to the bulletin board of the house:

Honored Members of the Court Opera:

The time of our working together has come to an end. I leave a working community that has become dear to me and bid you all farewell.

Instead of a complete, rounded whole, such as I had hoped for, I leave behind the incomplete, the fragmentary, as a man seems fated to do.

It is not for me to judge what my work has meant to those for whom it was intended. But at this moment I can honestly say, I have tried my best, I have set my aims high. My endeavors were not always crowned with success. No one is so exposed to the perverse obstinacy of matter, to the malice of the object, as the interpretative artist. But I have always pledged all I have, putting the aim above my person, my duty before my inclinations. I did not spare myself, and therefore felt I could ask others to exert their full powers.

In the thick of the fray, in the heat of the moment, neither you nor I could escape altogether injuries or misunderstandings. But when our work was successful, a problem solved, we forgot all our troubles and felt richly rewarded, even if the outward signs of success were lacking. We have all of us made progress, and with us the institution we sought to serve. Accept my heartfelt thanks, then, all who have supported me in my difficult, often thankless task, who have aided me and fought by my side. Accept my sincere good wishes for your future careers and for the prosperity of the Court Opera Theater, whose fortunes I shall continue to follow with lively interest.

Even at that point of final farewell, the wrathful personal animosity of some was not mollified, and the next day Mahler's letter was found torn and crumpled on the floor.

Mahler's departure from the Vienna musical scene decisively ended the period of supremacy of the Vienna Imperial Opera. Weingartner's tenure after Mahler was an expected anticlimax. There was a rekindling of the Opera's greatness with the appearance of Richard Strauss in Vienna after World War I, when the dismemberment of the Habsburg empire threatened the very foundations of the now tiny republic of Austria and its *Staatsoper* (State Opera). While Strauss, in dual directorship with Schalk (1919–24), saved the Opera and although under such dedicated men as Franz Schalk, Bruno Walter, and Clemens Kraus it remained one of the most distinguished opera houses in the world, the influence it had exerted throughout Europe and the world became a thing of the past. Just as Wagner's Bayreuth had become a relic, so the supremacy of the Vienna Opera had passed into history, soon to be followed by the Habsburg's double eagle, its aristocracy, its parade of flamboyant playboy officers, and an entire era which had overstayed its welcome and its raison d'être.

In the last analysis, two factors combined to bring about Mahler's resignation: his own artistic intransigence, and the realization that the composer in him could no longer spare time for the conductor–administrator. Thus it was Mahler more than any of his determined denigrators who brought the Mahler era to a close. The compensations in Vienna had been many: artistic acclaim in the opera house, the beginnings of recognition as a composer, and his marriage to Alma, which, besides adding the dimension of love to his life, made possible a degree of order, a reduction in his debts and, importantly, his introduction to a new circle of artist friends. To the very end, his princely superior responded nobly to the artist whom he respected and whom he considered a friend.

Felix Weingartner, upon assuming the directorship at the opera, was to discover to his surprise that the many decorations and honors which Mahler had received during his ten years in Vienna had been left in the director's desk. Abandoned? Forgotten? Rejected? We shall never know.

# Post–Vienna (1907–11)

## THE NEW YORK METROPOLITAN OPERA COMPANY

THE MAHLERS HAD FLED MAIERNIGG, where the ghost of their daughter pursued them, but the farewell from Vienna, the city with which Mahler had always maintained a love–hate relationship, was difficult. Now, having rid himself of the daily annoyances of the opera directorship and basking in the glow of farewell triumphs and ovations, Mahler knew that he would miss the city as he began his trek to the New World.

A long line of European musical greats had preceded Mahler to America. Tchaikovsky had participated in the opening of Carnegie Hall; Johann Strauss, Verdi, and Bülow had celebrated America's independence with the Bostonians; Dvořák had witnessed the greatest triumph of his life when New York made the premiere of his *Symphony from the New World* a musical event of the first order and a rousing success; and Richard Strauss had had the short-lived satisfaction of a *Salome* performance in New York. Mahler looked forward to his work at the Metropolitan with great anticipation because it was an entirely different opera house from the one he had known. In Vienna the watchword had been "ensemble." The finest pit orchestra in the world—the Vienna Philharmonic—played in Vienna, and took pride in achieving that near-perfect integration between them, the soloists, and the chorus that made Vienna unique among opera houses throughout the world. New York under Heinrich Conried, on the other hand, prided itself on its ensemble of soloists: Olive Fremstad, Antonio Scotti, Johanna Gadski, Geraldine Farrar, Enrico Caruso, Feodor Chaliapin—voices unexcelled in artistic caliber anywhere in the world.

A word should be said about the matter of artistic management in that era. In contrast to the situation prevailing today, when singers and conductors have become nomads equally at home at the Vienna Opera, La Scala, Covent Garden, or the Met (and thus genuinely at home nowhere),

at the beginning of the twentieth century each opera house had its "stable"
of famous names, who considered their specific opera house "home." Thus
Caruso might triumph in Vienna but considered New York his artistic
home, while Leo Slezak, though he got rave notices at the Met, considered
himself a Viennese artist.

Heinrich Conried, attempting to entice Mahler to come to the Met,
had first offered him a contract covering eight months out of the year for
a fee of 180,000 kronen. Mahler demurred, considering the engagement
too long. Thereupon Conried shortened the time to six months; but
Mahler insisted on a still shorter time. They eventually agreed on three
months for a salary of 75,000 kronen, with all expenses, including travel-
ing first class and first-rate hotel accommodations, paid.[1] Mahler was to
conduct mainly Mozart and Wagner and stage three new productions, but
he was also free to do a number of concerts. Mahler was determined to use
the glorious voices of the Met to their, and his, fullest artistic advantage.
He had entered into a contract with the Met in full realization of his
value, since his name represented a world standard of opera and every
opera house would receive him with open arms. He was determined to
amass an amount of money which would enable him to retire to composition with only an occasional conducting stint, and at the same time provide
his family with the financial security which had eluded them thus far—
although, with Montenuovo's help, his Vienna arrangements had begun
to provide a measure of security. He would give New York his best—
Wagner, Mozart, Beethoven—and reap a harvest of dollars in return. It
was in such a spirit that Mahler had signed a contract with Conried to
come to New York.

Heinrich Conried, who had succeeded Maurice Grau as director of
the Metropolitan Opera Company in New York in 1903, was a fascinating
figure, often in a negative sense. German-born, Vienna-trained, he was
shrewd, bold, and tactless. As a man of the theater he knew it from the
acting, managerial, and directing vantage points, but he knew little of the
musical side of the serious musical theater, his previous experience of and
in that form having been limited to the lighter vein of Johann Strauss
and Karl Millöcker, produced in German, in New York. Thus, while he
was capable as a manager, he was ignorant as an impresario. Theater
instinct and his innate shrewdness carried him forward in the face of
stringent critical appraisal in the New York press; by yielding on one
point to gain the next, he was able to hold his own. In the matter of voices
and who should sing what role when, he pliably accepted audience preferences. Yet he manipulated his position in such a manner that singers were
obliged to sign contracts with him personally instead of with the Metro-

---

[1] With the Austrian krone pegged at $0.20, this amounted to $15,000 for a three-
month engagement, a not inconsiderable sum in 1908. (Source: World Almanac,
1910)

politan Opera Company. Thus he acquired a hold on artists which, among other things, obliged them to participate in an annual "manager's benefit." Needless to say, Conried saw to it that the occasion of a sold-out house would be chosen for such a benefit performance.

His production of *Parsifal* proved an outstanding test of Conried's boldness, instinct, and tenacity. In order to bring *Parsifal* to the Met he fought Bayreuth and the appeals of the Wagner family to that end to the *Kaiser* and the Catholic and Protestant clergy, in civil court suits and through public petitions to revoke his license, all aimed at keeping *Parsifal* from being performed at his opera house. Yet, through instinct and his acumen for business as well as art, he prevailed, and triumphed. Henderson of the *Sun* hailed it as "better than any production ever given in Bayreuth." To Aldrich of the *Times* it was "the most perfect production ever made on an American stage." Having achieved an artistic success and whetted public appetite, Conried waited one month and for an SRO house before announcing a manager's benefit performance of *Parsifal,* and then pocketed the box-office receipts of the sold-out house. Conried also nourished the myth of his having "discovered" Caruso. Caruso had actually been engaged two years prior to Conried's ascendancy to the directorship, but he was not immediately available to the Met. When Maurice Grau, meanwhile, retired and the contract lapsed, Conried renegotiated it. It constituted one of his accidental master strokes.

Another giant of the day, the German conductor **Felix Mottl**, served under Conried's aegis. His natural field of endeavor was the Wagner repertoire, of which he was considered the foremost exponent since the tempestuous **Anton Seidl**. It had been the trio of Mottl, Seidl, and Richter, all graduates from Wagner's personal tutelage, who had ruled over the Wagner repertoire until the advent of Mahler and Toscanini.

Conried was to stop at nothing for the sake of publicity for the Metropolitan and money for his own pocket. The height of his managerial manipulations occurred in February 1905. At an excellent *Fledermaus* performance (which was, incidentally, a benefit performance for the manager), he inflicted the supreme indignity on the star cast under contract by "inviting" them to present a "concert" during the second-act ballroom scene. There Scotti sang an aria from Verdi's *Falstaff;* Fremstad *Les Filles de Cadiz* by Delibes; Eames, Plançon, and Nubio the Trio from Gounod's *Faust;* and Nordica (the great Wagnerian!) was pressed into the Quartet from *Rigoletto* with Caruso, Homer, and Giraldoni. Artistic disapproval did not keep Conried from repeating the farce one year later with Johann Strauss's *Zigeunerbaron,* when such greats as Caruso, Eames, Fremstad, Journet, Scotti, and Sembrich were led on stage as prisoners of the hero Barinkay and forced to "sing for their freedom," the phrase itself an ironic reflection of actual conditions. There was a storm of critical outrage, but Conried took home a $20,000 profiit.

On the other hand, Mozart, in Conried's opinion, was not good box office. Consequently, during the year 1906, when Europe, with Vienna in the forefront, celebrated the one hundred fiftieth anniversary of the master's birth, the Metropolitan Opera all but ignored the occasion by presenting but two performances of *Don Giovanni*.

But there were events which were beyond the control of Conried. In April the Met was on tour in San Francisco when the earth heaved and the city buckled. In the ensuing holocaust, the touring company of the Met lost all its costumes, scenery, and properties. The worst loss was suffered by the musicians, most of whose instruments were damaged beyond repair.[2]

It is ironic that circumstances should have brought Conried low at the very time when he was on the verge of becoming worthy of the Metropolitan. One was Oscar Hammerstein's glorious four-year season in his new Manhattan Opera House, which boasted such stars as Luisa Tetrazzini, Maurice Renard, Nellie Melba, and Alessandro Bonci. The other was his own declining health. Conried pluckily readied himself for another production intended to rock New York to its foundations—the American premiere of Strauss's *Salome*. If its artistic value may have escaped him, Conried was nonetheless convinced of the work's shock value and saleability because of the critical furor it would create and the subsequent curiosity it would arouse. Indeed, its commercial value seemed so obvious to him that he selected the premiere as his annual "manager's benefit." The reviews of *Salome* ranged from the kindest comment of "deadly bore" to "degenerate," "moral stench," and "operatic offal." Public, private, and press pressure prompted the dropping of the work at a great loss to the Met—after Conried had lined his pockets from the sold-out performance of the curious first-night crowd.

This was the man who, at the end of his tenure, his good health ("for days at a time, Mr. Conried was too sick to transact any business"—the *Sun*, 17 March 1907) and his career, concluded a contract with Gustav Mahler to conduct at the Metropolitan. The conditions at the house at that time were confusing. Giulio Gatti-Casazza had been unofficially approached to step into the office of director should Conried be unable to continue, in part because it had been rumored that Toscanini would not conduct in New York without his presence. But the man in nominal command was Conried, and at the end of his career he once more covered himself with glory by securing the services of one of Europe's most illustrious conductors—Mahler—for the Metropolitan Opera. What added to the general uncertainty was the fact that Mahler's contract went beyond Conried's tenure. Also, the presence of such diverse talents and personal-

---

[2] Upon the return of the demoralized company to New York, Marcella Sembrich, one of the most beloved Met members of her time, gave a benefit concert which yielded $9,000 toward the restoration of the musicians' instruments.

ities as Mahler and Toscanini at the same institution might, it was felt, prove a source of conflict. At that point Toscanini proved himself to be gracious. "I am happy to find myself with an artist of Mahler's worth. I hold Mahler in great esteem, and infinitely prefer such a colleague to any mediocrity," he wrote to the Metropolitan. Unfortunately that ray of good will was soon obscured by the thunderclouds of conflicting artistic aspirations and interpretations.

The Met's uneven artistic image and Conried's increasing inability to serve at its helm prompted a group of millionaires, led by Otto H. Kahn, to buy out Conried's contract with the Met, in the hope of being able to institute a new policy and pursue loftier artistic aims. But it was not in Conried's nature to simply bow out and fade away. The remainder of his contract specified one more "manager's benefit," and since receipts from those benefits usually approximated his yearly salary, Conried was not going to let the opportunity slip away. Since no sure-fire performance to guarantee a full house was available at the time, he devised the idea of a gala concert as the only fitting means of signaling his passing from the scene. The program he arranged was certain to guarantee the desired sold-out house: Mahler was to conduct the *Leonore* Overture No. 3, and the balance of the evening's program had practically the entire company participating in excerpts from *La Boheme, Madame Butterfly, Die Meistersinger, Faust,* and *Il Trovatore.* Management, at least, rose to the occasion: the stage eventually resembled a garden of flowers, and Conried was presented with an inscribed silver cup eighteen inches high. His receipts from the evening amounted to nearly $20,000.[3]

Mahler was uneasy about the changeover from Conried to Gatti-Casazza. According to a letter written in April 1908 to the impresario Emil Gutmann, his unsettled future plans paralleled those of the Met. According to that letter and Alma's recollections, he had been offered the managerial position, and his refusal had led to the engagement of Gatti-Casazza and Toscanini, then artistic director and conductor at *La Scala.*

The day appointed for their departure to New York found Mahler and Alma in Cherbourg, boarding a tender at night to bring them to the liner *America,* which, bathed in light, was awaiting them. A choppy sea did nothing to ease Mahler's apprehension about sea travel. Alma laughingly recalls: "There was a rough sea, and he endeavored to avoid seasickness by lying rigidly on his back in his bunk like a cardinal on his tomb, neither eating nor speaking until the dread sensation had passed."

Mahler's first appearance in the pit of the Metropolitan Opera on New Year's Day, 1908, was anticipated as a major social and musical

[3] Upon his death in 1908, funeral services for Conried had the distinction of being held in the Metropolitan Opera House. It was a signal honor, to be bestowed on only two other men: Leopold Damrosch, conductor and manager, in 1885, and the tenor Richard Tucker in 1975.

event in New York. He made his debut with *Tristan,* with the admirable Heinrich Knote and Olive Fremstad in the title roles. Fremstad, guided by Mahler, sang Isolde for the first time. Although Mahler had been unsuccessful in having Roller engaged for the event, the debut proved spectacular, and the *Sun* spoke of a performance "filled with vitality and voicing a conception of high beauty."

His next production—of *Don Giovanni,* three weeks later—exuded all the incomparable splendor for which his Vienna performances of that opera had been famous. He particularly reveled in the roster of great voices at his disposal: Antoni Scotti as Don Giovanni, Alessandro Bonci as Ottavio, Feodor Chaliapin as Leporello, Emma Eames as Donna Anna, Johanna Gadski as Donna Elvira, and Marcella Sembrich as Zerlina. Only at the Metropolitan, with its nearly unlimited financial resources, was such a roster possible. His productions of *Die Walküre* and *Siegfried* in February 1908 and of *Fidelio,* with the Roller setting, in March equally showed him at the zenith of perfection. New York was ecstatic.

Mahler had mellowed in a way in which Vienna audiences had never had an opportunity to observe him; the realization that overly strenuous activity would be detrimental in view of his heart ailment unquestionably was a factor. His demeanor with respect to singers was softer and more gentle; and there also occurred a loosening of the purist attitude which had been so strongly in evidence in Vienna. Those who had witnessed Mahler's Wagner zeal in Vienna were perplexed and distraught at his acquiescence to cuts in Wagner's operas. Mahler was, of course, not the only one to eventually allow cuts in Wagner operas. Toscanini, in his later Wagner performances, was also not above tampering with them. Seidl, during his celebrated New York appearances, had introduced the custom. Curiously, audiences did not raise a whisper at such butchering habits. Yet a storm of protest would erupt if a hair on Beethoven's head was touched—if so much as a section of the Beethoven orchestra was reinforced. Such attempts were considered tantamount to sacrilege, comparable, according to New York *Tribune* music critic Henry Krehbiel, to "tampering with the Bible or Shakespeare, or an attempt to have Michelangelo's Moses stand up."

Actually a majority of the New York opera audience of Mahler's day paid litle attention to scenery, story line, *recitativo,* or continuity. In a throwback to the worst habits of Neapolitan opera audiences, the opera public waited en masse for *bel canto* or for one of Caruso's big arias, of which they never could hear enough. Caruso, without question, dominated the scene. It was never Destinn and Caruso, or Farrar and Caruso, but Caruso and — — —.

In any case, in his changed world and with his changed mental attitude, Mahler no longer objected to cuts which he would have considered outrageous in Vienna. For the man who was accustomed to long walks, swimming, and mountain climbing but who was now forced to spend much of his days in bed in order to save his heart and his strength for the evening's performance, aesthetic considerations took on a different order of importance. Thus, in New York, the Mahler who had attended to every phase of opera in Vienna simply was no more. Now he rose from his bed only to attend rehearsals and evening performances.

Despite such precautions, Mahler began to age visibly. Once an official, within hearing distance of Alma, spoke of Mahler as her father! Yet the Mahlers were determined to make the best of the situation and of New York. Although the language barrier presented difficulties, Mahler liked America and Americans; their easygoing openness and friendliness bridged many handicaps and made the Mahlers feel welcome. Mahler took a special liking to one New York institution—the subway. Although New York society would have been happy to put their carriages at his disposal, and although he certainly could have afforded a taxi, he preferred to ride the subway whenever possible.

Before Mahler's return to Europe at the end of the season, his plans to return to New York the following season were firmly established. It was a logical decision: no other position of interest to him was available; the compensation he received from the Metropolitan furthered his plans to provide financial security for his family as speedily as possible; and the work load was comparatively light. Although he had produced seven operas during one season he had been required to conduct only nineteen performances, a fraction of the number he had led in Vienna (in addition, there, to performing administrative duties). Thus in May he returned to Europe in good spirits and, as always, devoted himself to composition and performances of his own works during the summer months: the First Symphony in Wiesbaden, the premiere of his Seventh Symphony in Prague, plus concerts in Munich, Berlin, Hamburg, and Paris before visiting Vienna.

After Vienna Mahler settled down in Toblach, where, in the course of his last three summers, he composed *Das Lied von der Erde,* the Ninth Symphony, and the fragments of his Tenth Symphony. While in Vienna he had had a surprising meeting with a ten-year-old genius. His name was **Erich Wolfgang Korngold**, the son of **Julius Korngold**, the influential critic of the *Neue Freie Presse* and for many years a strong supporter of Mahler. Mahler was deeply impressed when the boy submitted to his scrutiny a cantata entitled *Gold.* He predicted a great future for the *Wunderkind* but his prophecy was to be only partially fulfilled.

In Toblach friends visited the nearly eremitic couple, and amidst the lively conversation with such friends as **Gabrilovich**, **Decsey**, and **Walter**, Mahler thawed and relaxed and seemed his old self again. But the mountains, to Mahler's distress, had to remain landscape, because his doctor had been quite specific concerning his patient's activities and the thoroughgoing Mahler went so far in obeying his doctor's orders that he attached a pedometer to his leg to carefully measure his walking distance and regulate his gait. The resignation expressed in Hans Bethge's translations of Chinese poems answered to something in his spirit, so he affixed a first, tentative title to his latest composition: *The Song of the Affliction of the Earth.*

In September 1908, before his return to New York, Mahler conducted the first performance of his Seventh Symphony in Prague, where he had a joyful reunion with friends Klemperer, Bodansky, Berg, and Gabrilovich. All of them were put to work correcting mistakes in the orchestral parts. As with those of Bruckner, Mahler's symphonies, beginning mainly with the Fifth Symphony, were subject to constant revision, particularly in instrumentation, because Mahler was much concerned with balance. There was, however, a major difference. Bruckner had usually reacted to advice from friends or critics, whereas Mahler was his own most severe judge and made corrections on his own initiative.

On the return journey to New York, their three-year-old daughter went with the Mahlers this time. They stayed at the Savoy Hotel, where many of the Metropolitan's stars also had their New York residence. Once immersed in rehearsals Mahler enjoyed a great improvement in his health, and his productions of *Figaro, Fidelio,* and *Pique Dame* [Queen of spades] were exciting evenings. The Tchaikovsky work proved especially exhilarating, with Eames, Farrar, Scotti, Sembrich and young Leo Slezak in the cast. *Fidelio,* with Roller's Vienna staging and the *Leonore* No. 3 before the last act, made a deep impression.

But while his productions were acclaimed, the situation behind the scenes began to become unpleasant. Conried was dying, and Gatti-Casazza had taken over his place and had brought Toscanini to the Metropolitan also. The latter, for reasons of his own, made it a condition that he should open with *Tristan* and that that particular opera should remain his responsibility. (Surprisingly, the Italian Toscanini had shown a strong affinity for Wagner and had introduced most of the *Ring* as well as *Tristan* and *Parsifal* at *La Scala* in Milan; his special request for *Tristan* therefore, was no surprise.) Mahler demurred and, while still in Europe, had expressed his dismay in a letter to the Met.

> I took particular pains with *Tristan* last season, and I think I may say that the form in which the work currently appears in New York is my brainchild. If Toscanini—for whom, unacquainted though I am with him, I have the highest respect—were to take over *Tristan* before my return, an entirely new stamp would inevitably be put on the work, and I would be in no position to resume direction of it in the course of the season. I must therefore beg you most earnestly to reserve the direction of this work to me.

Apparently his protest carried weight, at least for that particular season, because Toscanini did not conduct *Tristan* but *Götterdämmerung,* and that before Mahler's arrival in New York. The actual opening performances of the two musical giants were fully in keeping with their heritage: Toscanini opened with *Aida* and Mahler with a new production of Mozart's *The Marriage of Figaro,* on 13 January 1909. For some time Toscanini and Mahler worked separately and successfully, with Toscanini presenting two minor works by Puccini and Catalani plus a major performance of the Verdi *Requiem,* a splendid production of *Falstaff,* and *Cavalleria Rusticana,* with Caruso singing Turiddo. Mahler introduced Eugène d'Albert's *Tiefland* (although Alfred Hertz conducted the performance); the production received mixed reviews but high praise for the cast, which included Erik Schmedes from Vienna.

Even with such giants at the helm and the outstanding productions at their hands, turmoil at the Met continued, particularly since the status of the director had not been clearly defined at that time. After much factional infighting, an arrangement was worked out for coadministration between the singer Andreas Dippel and Gatti-Casazza, with Gatti-Casazza being declared top administrator of the institution and Dippel ending up in a somewhat subordinate role.

At that time the dim situation at the Metropolitan was brightened by Mahler's premiere presentation of Smetana's *Verkaufte Braut* [Bartered bride], with Emmy Destinn singing Marie (in German) and with special dancers imported from Prague and also drawn from New York's Bohemian circles. Enhanced by Mahler's memories of his Bohemian background and his affinity to that particular work, the opera was an immediate and brilliant success. "A specimen of genuinely artistic comic opera," wrote W. J. Henderson in the *Sun.* Even the dour Krehbiel found it a masterpiece, presented with "vivacity and lustiness." Here again a change must be noted to which Mahler, in his Vienna days would not have consented. Although New York had not known the opera, its overture had been a concert-hall favorite. As a bow to latecomers who nevertheless would not wish to miss their favorite overture, the overture was played between the first and second acts (!) instead of before the opera, where it properly belonged. Another splendid performance of Mozart's *Figaro* received applause. The work had been carefully honed by Mahler in twenty (!) rehearsals, an unheard-of number in New York, although in Vienna Mahler would have insisted on an even greater number. In a new staging by Dippel the opera received a performance which only the Met, in all the world, could have produced, with Emma Eames as the Countess, Marcella Sembrich as Susanna, Geraldine Farrar as Cherubino, Adam Didur as Figaro, and Antonio Scotti as the Count. Performing under Mahler's subtle guiding hand, the exquisite cast was acclaimed for its "fine unity of style." Even the orchestra received a rare accolade for its "clear, accurate, elastic, and transparent" playing, a surprise for New York but basic for Mahler. Then came the *Tristan* performance, of which Mahler said: "I have never known a performance of *Tristan* to equal this." Even the press went beyond petty complaints and tepid praise and awoke to Mahler's genius; the *Sun* rhapsodized:

> There was an Isolde last night [Fremstad] who may sometimes remember with a great glow of joy her performance of May 12, 1909. A superb, a queenly, a heroically tragic Isolde this, but she was not alone in her glory. . . . Mr. Mahler hurled all petty restraints to the four winds . . . and turned loose such a torrent of vital sound as he had never before let us hear . . . the crash of the death motive when Isolde raised the cup to her lips was cataclysmic.

It was to be Mahler's last *Tristan* performance in New York. Next it was Toscanini's turn with the same opera, this having been one of the contractural conditions of his coming to New York. Toscanini's version also received much praise. In contrast, his much-heralded *Meistersinger* interpretation met with the objection that the Italian conductor lacked the required affinity for "German thought, custom, and feeling." But on one point the press was unanimous, viz., that the Viennese Leo Slezak was a masterly Walter in every way. This had not been Slezak's first appearance, but it was certainly the highlight of his season with the Met. It was an irony that Slezak, whom Mahler had discovered and nursed to prominence, should have his greatest triumph in New York under Toscanini's direction. But it was not to be long before Slezak would be united with his mentor. The occasion: Tchaikovsky's *Pique Dame,* the opera which was also to constitute Mahler's farewell appearance at the Met on 21 March 1910.

Mahler's three outstanding successes in three months in opera-conscious New York may have belied the fact that he had lowered his standards; but, his personality had unquestionably changed. The reasons, in retrospect, are obvious. The loss of his daughter, the spectre of death, inevitable maturing, and his presence in a strange country all contributed to a certain mellowing. Mahler's fierce zeal and dedication in Vienna had necessarily meant overwork; in New York he was no longer capable of overwork. Thus in a constant tug-of-war between perfection demanding overwork and a frail body and heart, the body prevailed. But the New York public was ecstatic.

Meanwhile, "that other opera house" was no less acclaimed. Oscar Hammerstein, Sr.'s, Manhattan Opera Company stole a walk on the Met by premiering Strauss's *Elektra.* Mahler went to hear it and was appalled by it, but to everyone's surprise New York liked it, primarily because of Hammerstein's magnificent staging.

By then the Met repertoire had disintegrated. Surprisingly, the initial fears that the ever stronger Gatti–Toscanini influence would be inimical to the Wagner repertoire never materialized, but the general level of repertoire was lowered. Mozart, for example, again suffered almost total neglect, although Mahler could have given New York *Don Giovanni* and *Così fan tutte* performances of Viennese splendor. Even some of Toscanini's performances, it was charged, lacked the incisiveness of the previous year. However, with the uncontested ascendancy of Gatti-Casazza during the 1910–11 season (his avowed goal being to make the Met one of the great opera houses in the world), standards rose to the point where the Met was awarded its first two world premieres in rapid succession: Puccini's *La Fanciulla del West* [The girl of the golden West] and Humperdinck's *Königskinder* [Royal children], on 10 December 1910 and 28 December 1910 respectively.

By then Mahler had left the Metropolitan Opera for what he hoped to be greener American fields. His disappointment was to be severe, and deadly.

## THE NEW YORK PHILHARMONIC

To understand the dilemma and decline of Mahler in New York, the cultural and financial context of that era—the first decade of the twentieth century—bears brief investigation. The public may have enjoyed the great performances of those times, but their financial contribution amounted to virtually nothing; the financial powers that made artistic life happen in New York were not the public, nor impresarios nor theater managers, but rather men of great wealth who philanthropically provided the not inconsiderable sums needed to support such ambitious undertakings—along with their wives, who administered the wealth made available by their spouses. Thus it was the fortunes of such as August Belmont, Andrew Carnegie, John D. Rockefeller, J. P. Morgan, Joseph Pulitzer, and George R. Sheldon that financed most artistic endeavors in the city.

It was particularly Mrs. Sheldon of the influential ten-member "Guarantee Committee" of the New York Philharmonic Orchestra who convinced all concerned that "there is now not only willingness but desire on the part of the Philharmonic Society for radical changes in its organization and methods." The popular conductor Wassily Safonoff had outlived his usefulness. The Russian showman/conductor was among the first to conduct without a baton, and the graceful arabesques his hands had traced while conducting had mesmerized the matrons in the audience. "He was recalled a dozen times, cheered, pelted with flowers, and made so much of . . . that his eyes filled with tears, presumably of happiness," writes Richard Schickel in *The World of Carnegie Hall*. Despite previous successes in Vienna and London, Safonoff had been largely unknown in America until the orchestra had plucked him from among a number of guest conductors. Now that a world-famous name loomed on the American horizon, his oblivion was preordained. As coincidence would have it, the New York Philharmonic Orchestra was in need of a new conductor, due to its sad pecuniary circumstances.

Despite its comparatively brief history, beginning with its first concert on 7 December 1842, the New York Philharmonic could point to impressive achievements under such world-renowned conductors as Leopold Damrosch, Theodore Thomas, Anton Seidl, Edouard Colonne, Sir Henry Wood, Victor Herbert, Felix Weingartner, Richard Strauss, and Willem Mengelberg. Whereas under Damrosch, Thomas, and especially Seidl the financial fortunes of the orchestra had constantly improved, the period of guest conductors during the years 1903–06 had brought about a distressing financial decline despite the array of impressive, world-famous conductorial "names." The New York Philharmonic had originally been founded on self-governing principles similar to those which still prevail in the Vienna Philharmonic; in New York, however, that approach did not work and the orchestra found itself in financial straits. It was at that point that the energetic Mrs. Sheldon enlisted the financial support of other music-minded millionaires to rescue the orchestra, on condition that the orchestra was willing to abandon its independent status and agree to a governing directorial committee of ten members, thus turning the orchestra into a subsidized organization. On 6 February 1909 the orchestra was handed what amounted to an ultimatum by Mrs. Sheldon and her advisory group, "suggesting" radical changes in the orchestra's organization; in return, all deficits would be absorbed for three seasons (1909–12). It meant the end of democratic rule within the orchestra: the conductor was thenceforth to be selected by the committee and he was to have the power to engage and dismiss musicians if he found them unacceptable according to his musical standards.

Considering its situation, the orchestra had no choice but to accept these terms; on their acceptance hinged the support which guaranteed the continuation of the orchestra's existence. Thus, on 12 February, only six days after Mrs. Sheldon made her "suggestion," the old order of the orchestra collapsed and the new arrived. The governing committee, chaired by Mrs. Sheldon, consisted of Ruth Dana Draper, Henry Lane Eno, Ernest H. Schelling, and Nelson S. Spencer, all acquaintances and associates of Mrs. Sheldon's group; Richard Arnold, Felix Leifels and Henry P. Schmitt, members of the orchestra; and Mrs. Harry Payne Whitney and Mrs. Samuel Untermeyer, musically interested socialites. Upon acceptance of the committee's terms the orchestra also found out that a conductor had already been chosen without consultation with them. The man: Mahler.

It had been a welcome change for Mahler when the women of the governing committee, led by Mrs. Sheldon and Mrs. Untermeyer, approached him with the suggestion of taking over the musical direction of the New York Philharmonic; Mahler was delighted. At the final concert of the season on 27 March 1909, Andrew Carnegie in person presented the departing Safonoff with the usual laurel wreath and a shower of compliments. But the real drama of the evening first unfolded when unbeknownst to all except the innermost circle, Carnegie also called on the "retiring" concertmaster of the orchestra, Richard Arnold, and showered the "beloved nestor" with kudos and flattery. Arnold was, in fact, being demoted from that important post into the ranks of the orchestra. He had always led the opposition to any attempt at reform; and by then Mahler had been engaged and he had expressed himself against having the leader of the reactionary faction occupying the foremost chair in the orchestra. The fact that Arnold retained a seat in the all-powerful governing-committee, however, did not bode well for Mahler.

Nonetheless, four days after Arnold's retirement, with American-born and European-educated violinist Theodore Spiering installed in the concertmaster's seat, Mahler ascended the Philharmonic podium in a special concert, conducting Schumann's *Manfred* Overture and Beethoven's Seventh Symphony in Carnegie Hall, New York's foremost musical showcase.

The cornerstone to that illustrious building—one of the latest ventures in philanthropy by the steel and railroad magnate Andrew Carnegie—had been laid on 13 May 1890. Since its first concert series,[4] the "Music Festival in Celebration of the Opening of the Music Hall," which lasted five days, from 5 to 9 May 1891, Carnegie Hall has welcomed the musical greats of the world (with occasional visits from such nonmusical luminaries as Woodrow Wilson, Winston Churchill, William Jennings Bryan, Mark Twain, and Georges Clemenceau), and is one of the world's most prestigious concert halls.

The opening festival's main interest centered around one of the great romantic names of the day, that of Piotr Ilyich Tchaikovsky.[5] The Russian composer had accepted the orchestra's invitation to conduct reluctantly because of a morose tendency for restless homesickness, but he was overwhelmed by American hospitality and amazed at some of our peculiarities, like Walter Damrosch rehearsing his orchestra in shirtsleeves or Carnegie's embracing him without kissing. "Here men never kiss," commented Tchaikovsky in his diary. But he could not help enjoying himself, despite repeated onslaughts of melancholy and depression.

[4] There had been previous concerts in the building by pianists Franz Rummel, Arthur Friedheim, and Leopold Godowsky, but they were given in the Lyceum Hall in the basement of the building.

[5] Tchaikovsky appeared in four concerts. Among the music he conducted was Beethoven's *Leonore* Overture No. 3, his own *Marche Solenelle,* and the *Te Deum* of Berlioz.

Amazing people, these Americans! Compared with Paris, where at every approach, in every stranger's kindness, one feels an attempt at exploitation, the frankness, sincerity, and generosity in this city, . . . [offered] without hidden motives, and its eagerness to please and win approval are simply astonishing and, at the same time, touching.

America was equally charmed. Damrosch, meeting Tchaikovsky at the first rehearsal (at which Tchaikovsky received an ovation from the orchestra), recalled: "In all my years of experience I have never met a great composer so gentle, so modest . . . as he. We all loved him from the first moment." Tchaikovsky's first appearance was a social as well as musical triumph for the new hall. *The New York Times* considered the hall "ample, well-placed, well-planned, and well-equipped," while the *World* quipped that "for the display of gowns its advantages are greater than those of the Metropolitan Opera House, and its facilities for conversation are certainly no less."

Tchaikovsky had started the parade of the immortals. Among those who followed were pianist Ian Paderewski ("the largest receipts ever realized by a piano recital in this or probably any other country," wrote Richard Schickel of one of his appearances), Antonin Dvořák, pianist Moritz Rosenthal ("made us forget Rubinstein"), composer/pianist Teresa Carreno ("a strong woman, playing her instrument strongly"), pianist Josef Hofmann ("Women and men fought one another . . . to gain entrance to the hall"), and violinists Eugene Ysaye and Bronislaw Hubermann.

The 31 March concert at Carnegie Hall was actually not Mahler's first orchestral appearance in America. He had previously taken over Walter Damrosch's "Symphony Society" for a three-concert series, the first of which comprised Schumann's *Spring* Symphony in B-flat, the Prelude to *Die Meistersinger,* Beethoven's *Coriolan* Overture, and the overture to Smetana's *Bartered Bride.* Public and critical response was as extravagant as it had been to his operatic work:

> As a conductor Mr. Mahler scorns to cultivate any devices, picturesque or otherwise, to attract attention to his personality. . . . He conducts with the utmost simplicity of gesture, but at the same time he exerts an influence almost hypnotic. . . . His readings were those of a master musician in whose highly developed intellectuality keen appreciation of the subtlest phrases of emotion and forceful dramatic feelings are combined in extraordinary well-balanced proportions.

For his own part, Mahler was less than ecstatic about the orchestra, and he did not hide his distaste. Although the ensemble carried 115 members on its roster, this was merely a fictitious figure, because no more than 60 players ever presented themselves at rehearsals. The laissez-faire attitude of the members also did not meet with Mahler's standards. Some members attended rehearsals irregularly or did not stay for the full rehearsal time, which Mahler felt was necessary to achieve the excellence he demanded. In the second concert, Mahler's interpretation of Beethoven's Fifth Symphony was reviewed as "rough handling," mainly because American audiences were not accustomed to the robust masculinity of the work, which Mahler understood and reproduced. That basic though minor clash of opinion should have been an omen to the governing ladies of the Philharmonic, but they were blinded by the splendor of Mahler's reputation—reinforced by the third concert, featuring Mahler's Second Symphony, a success despite the orchestra's total apathy as displayed in the performance.

Mahler's first appearance with the Philharmonic seemed to fully bear out the ladies' judgment when Mahler masterfully conducted Wagner's *Siegfried Idyll* and *Tannhäuser* Overture, Beethoven's Seventh Symphony, and Schumann's stirring *Manfred* Overture. Mahler soon began to shape the orchestra to his musical taste. Having installed a new concertmaster, he made changes in the woodwind and brass sections and reduced the number of basses from fourteen to eight, more emphasis to be given to the celli. Concerts were increased from the customary eighteen to forty-six per season.

Whatever attributes Mahler may have possessed, tact and diplomacy were not among them. His first announcement of goals—"to raise popular musical standards in this country [and] weld the orchestra into an effective instrument"—was not conducive to winning him friends. Nor were subsequent statements more ingratiating. "It will be my aim," he proclaimed, "to educate the public . . . in a manner which will enable those who may not have a taste for the best to appreciate it later." He would play novelties (so dear to New York audiences) only "if the music were worthy." Nor did the manner in which he addressed the orchestra endear him to them. Long ago, in his early operatic ventures in Laibach and Olmütz, Mahler had learned that the firm, assertive command produced better results than entreaties or discussions. Thus, regardless of place or orchestra his stentorian *"Ruhe, bitte"* (Silence, please) resulted in attentive but resentful silence.

It was not long before Mahler encountered an unrelenting foe in the influential music critic of the New York *Tribune,* **Henry E. Krehbiel.** Krehbiel, who also happened to be the first chronicler of the New York Philharmonic and program annotator of the orchestra, had become somewhat of a crotchety (he was fifty-five years old at Mahler's arrival) self-appointed guardian of musical standards in New York. In his reviews, which resemble American echoes of Hanslick's pieces, something of a double standard was maintained. Thus, while he not only did not object to cuts in Wagner operas but, in fact, had been an ardent admirer of Seidl and his truncated type of Wagner music making, any change in orchestral instrumentation on Mahler's part, or any interpretation different from the "norm," was iniquity, sacrilege, and crime all rolled into one. And when Mahler went so far as to forbid Krehbiel to write program notes to his (Mahler's) symphonies (Mahler hated the idea of program notes), thus indirectly impugning Krehbiel's ability to comprehend such music, Krehbeil threw down the gauntlet.

> There is no reason why [Mahler] should be a prophet of the ugly, as he discloses himself in the last movement of the Symphony in D. He makes that plain by interrupting a painfully cacophonous din with an episode built on a melody which is exquisitely lovely and profoundly moving.
>
> New York *World,* 16 December 1909

There was no denying that Krehbiel, like Hanslick, knew his music— which made him an even more intrepid foe to reckon with. He considered himself the keeper of New York's tradition of Beethoven performance, and Mahler raised his musical hackles.

> The famous cadenza in the first movement [of Beethoven's Fifth Symphony] . . . Mr. Mahler phlebotomized by giving it to two oboes and beating time for each note—not in the expressive Adagio called for by Beethoven, but in a rigid Andante. Thus the rhapsodic utterance contemplated by the composer was turned into a mere connecting link between two parts of the movement. Into the cadence of the second subject of the third movement, Mr. Mahler injected a bit of un-Beethovenian color by changing the horn part, so that listeners familiar with their Wagner were startled by hearing something like Hagen's call from *Götterdämmerung* from the instruments which in the score simply sustain a harmony voice in octaves. In the finale Mr. Mahler several times doubled voices (bassoons and cellos) and transposed the piccolo part an octave higher. Here he secured sonority, which aided him in building a thrilling climax but did not materially disturb Beethoven's color scheme. The question of the artistic righteousness of his act may be left to the decision of musicians.
>
> New York *Tribune,* 13 December 1909

Mahler's *Coriolan* interpretation incurred further Krehbiel wrath.

> The performance . . . was dramatically lurid. All through the evening the tympanist bombarded the ears of the hearers.
>
> New York *Tribune,* 17 December 1909

Nor was Mahler's *Pastorale* interpretation to his liking.

> Mr. Mahler is not satisfied with the thunder of Beethoven's kettledrum, so he has added another pair with a part of their own. The fact that Beethoven was in his day an innovator in the use of the kettledrum, and

might have written three parts or four if he had been so disposed, might be offered as a plea for the preservation of the purity of the classic text. But under the present conditions it would be idle to offer it.

New York *Tribune,* 15 January 1910 [6]

The summer of 1909 saw Mahler back in Toblach, absorbed in the composition of his Ninth Symphony (to be completed in New York in 1910) and the planning of his Tenth. It was an illuminating indication of the prevailing American sense of musical inferiority, that a famous European conductor like Mahler was not expected to remain in the country between seasons or to settle in the United States. Thus Mahler's departure for Europe once the season was ended was expected, as was his return in autumn at the beginning of the next season. This also held true for Josef Stransky, Mahler's successor. A paragraph in the latter's contract with the New York Philharmonic even contained the specific clause that the transportation of his luggage upon his arrival in the United States and at the time of his departure would be an expense to be borne by the Philharmonic.

With Toscanini now fully in charge as musical director of the Metropolitan, Mahler was free to devote himself in his second season to his preferred task of conducting the Philharmonic. In the beginning Mahler did not consider the ensemble to be on a par with Europe's finest orchestras, but under him the orchestra went from "good" to "excellent"; the seed which such grand men as Theodore Thomas and Leopold Damrosch had sown came to fruition under Mahler. It was also under Mahler that the orchestra began to tour on a limited scale. And Mahler insisted that the full complement of the orchestra—all ninety members, if needed—play every concert, be it in Carnegie Hall, Buffalo, or Providence, Rhode Island. This was contrary to custom then. The Boston Symphony Orchestra, for example might reduce its orchestra by as much as one-third when on tour. This was, of course, detrimental to the performance of the larger nineteenth-century works of Bruckner, Wagner, or Richard Strauss. Mahler's touring performances with the Philharmonic thus became a revelation for the cities visited, because audiences were now able, for the first time, to hear Berlioz, Wagner, Strauss, or Debussy at their most sumptuous.

At the same time, Mahler became acquainted with and interested in the music of American composers, then still European-educated and influenced, such as Charles M. Loeffler and Edward McDowell. Surprisingly, Mahler was to include his own music only sparingly in Philharmonic

[6] Embittered and frustrated, Krehbiel could not even bring himself to make peace with Mahler at the time of Mahler's death (as Hanslick had after the death of Wagner). In a virulent article (New York *Tribune,* 21 May 1911), he reviled the departed composer, only to be rebuked by his peers.

concerts, restricting himself to the *Kindertotenlieder* and the American premiere of his First Symphony.

Returning to Europe at the end of the New York concert season, Mahler attended a Paris performance, arranged by Gabriel Pierné, of his Second Symphony. Again Mahler, who had also attended a rehearsal of his symphony, was baffled by the insouciant behavior of the chorus, who came and went whenever they pleased. But he was deeply gratified by the first-rate performance which Pierné presented. Pierné also entertained the Mahlers, with Debussy, Dukas, and Fauré present. According to Alma Mahler, Debussy and Dukas had disliked the Mahler work and had walked out of the performance. (Such discourtesy on their part is to be doubted, since the composer was present.) Mahler, in turn, felt bored with Dukas's *Ariane et Barbe Bleu* but nevertheless had the courtesy to compliment the composer. Here again we encounter a changed Mahler—because in his Vienna days it would have been Mahler who would have walked out if a performance had bored him. In Paris Mahler also made the acquaintance of Auguste Rodin, who did the famous bronze bust of Mahler and another one in marble for himself. The composer and the sculptor enjoyed each other's company. Rodin was fascinated with Mahler's head—which, he said, was a composite of Franklin's, Frederick the Great's, and Mozart's. (The curator of the Rodin Museum actually did label the Mahler bronze "Mozart" for many years.)

When Mahler finally reached Vienna, a letter from Engelbert Humperdinck awaited him. It must have gladdened his heart, and might have had far-reaching consequences for Mahler and for German music had Mahler lived to act on it. The letter, dated 30 May 1909, was marked "Confidential" and read:

Honored Master!

You have no doubt already learned from the newspapers of the proposal to establish a second opera house in Berlin in response to a long-felt need of the capital of the empire . . . . a building is to be erected as much as possible after the pattern of Bayreuth . . . . the opening could take place in the spring of 1911.

We still, however, lack what is more important than all else: the future director of our Richard Wagner Theater, who must be not only a man of proven attainments and firm will, but above all a great artist and, in short, combine all those qualities which are summed up in the name: Mahler, a guarantee in itself of an artistic program unsurpassable in its range and excellence. And as the bearer of this name is at present within reach, I venture, my dear Master, to ask whether you would be disposed to answer our call and to take this great work in hand. The position of general director which we have in mind would naturally in your case be furnished with the most far-reaching powers—similar to those you had at your command in Vienna. I can therefore well believe that the task of giving life to a new and unique enterprise would perhaps have charm for you.

I scarcely need to say how delighted I should be personally to know that you were at the head of it. . . . I await an early and, I hope, favorable reply and remain, with the assurance of my lasting esteem, yours most sincerely,

E. Humperdinck

Alma Mahler, who quotes the letter in her memoirs, gives no inkling as to Mahler's attitude toward the grandiose project described by Humperdinck. Actually it would have been difficult for Mahler to have become involved with it, because he was at that time firmly committed to conduct the New York Philharmonic.

November 4, 1909 was the date set for New York to hear Mahler conduct the reorganized Philharmonic Orchestra,[7] for which Mrs. Sheldon's committee had signed Mahler to conduct forty-six concerts during the 1909–10 season. The first performance opened appropriately with Beethoven's *Consecration of the House* Overture, to the prompt disapproval of Krehbiel ("a composition written 'to order' . . . [which] therefore belongs to the class awkwardly called 'occasionals'—of which, as a rule, little is expected"). The overture was followed by the *Eroica* Symphony, Strauss's *Till Eulenspiegel* and Liszt's *Mazeppa*. It was to be one of the last occasions when the American critics were kind to Mahler. "Scarcely within memory of man had the wind choirs played so nearly in tune and with such brilliancy and precision," rhapsodized Richard Aldrich in the *New York Times*, who looked forward to further transformation of the orchestra. Henry T. Finck of the *Post* seconded the motion. Particularly interesting was the allusion to the past by the *Sun*'s W. J. Henderson, who spoke of the orchestra's "emerging from the mists which surrounded it last season, an encouraging demonstration of the achievements of a good conductor in the matter of dynamics, attack, and nuance."

Two December performances brought about the first of a long series of criticisms, doubts, and grumblings. One was the American premiere of Mahler's First Symphony, which drew mixed notices. Henderson enjoyed it:

Neither the subject matter nor the manner of its treatment will tax the analytical power of the average listener. The subject matter indeed is thoroughly melodious, unaffectedly simple and directly presented.

But another critic considered the work "a very radical departure from tradition, received with what might be described as courteous applause, much dubious shaking of heads and no small amount of grumblings." The

---

[7] It was apparently the reorganization of the New York Philharmonic which confused Alma Mahler and left her under the impression (as expressed in her memoirs) that a "new" orchestra had been formed and put at Mahler's disposal.

other performance, a stirring rendition of Beethoven's Fifth Symphony, saw increased shaking of heads. The reason for this was to be found in the unwillingness of the New York audience to accept anything but the "accepted version" of Beethoven—a slicked-down, so-called romantic reading, probably established by Anton Seidl, which was perhaps controversial in its day because of the conductor's "irreverence," but had long since been accepted. Mahler's searching rediscovery of the score met only with accusations by the press, led by Krehbiel, that he was "taking liberties with Beethoven . . . approaching the domain of sheer license or even whimsicality . . . [which] takes him from the spirit of Beethoven's intent." In retrospect it borders on the ludicrous that the man who had given the world a new and truer picture of Beethoven should have drawn the public's and the critics' most pointed arrows in response to his Beethoven renditions.

One of the highlights of the season was a concert which included Rachmaninoff's Third Piano Concerto in D Minor, with the composer at the piano and Mahler conducting. Rachmaninoff then disliked America, but he pointedly enjoyed the high level of music making under Mahler's baton. Thus he had written to a cousin in Russia concerning the United States:

> In this accursed country, where you are surrounded by nothing but Americans and "business," "business" they are forever doing, clutching you from all sides and driving you on. . . .

But he was the astute musician when speaking of Mahler.

> Mahler was the only conductor whom I consider worthy to be classed with Nikisch. He devoted himself to the concerto until the accompaniment, which is rather complicated, had been practiced to perfection. . . . According to Mahler every detail of the score was important—an attitude too rare among conductors.

In light of the personalities of these two European giants—both were austere and withdrawn; neither man was ingratiating in dealing with the public—it is understandable that they would each intuitively respect the other's uncompromising attitude with respect to music making.

Mahler could not expect an equally intuitive grasp of musical values, however, on the part of the governing committee of the Philharmonic. Since he naively expected just that, he was bound on a headlong collision course. Had the ladies not been blinded by Mahler's fame and reputation—had they investigated the history of his personal relationships with others and learned of his intractability and rigidity and his demand for uncompromising compliance, they would have realized that they had not engaged a conductor pliable to their ignorant yet adamant requests and naive musical approaches. "Those simple wealthy ladies," writes Richard Schickel in *The World of Carnegie Hall,* with little knowledge of music and no real love for it . . . were simply not the people to deal with such a temperament. For them music was merely a pleasurable activity, in a category with charity balls and shopping exhibitions.

Although Mahler had mellowed to a point, he was not to be budged by the committee's demands, which ranged from the stupid to the naive to the arrogant; nor did he particularly care what the press and public said about him. He was a musician, he was dedicated to a musical vision, and if others could not see the light—so much the worse for them. To Mahler's uncompromising stand was added a lack of social graces. The ladies could tolerate a mediocre conductor with a flamboyant personality and ingratiating manner, a man to be exhibited at charitable affairs amid superficial chitchat; but they could not abide an unapproachable, defiant, diminutive giant.

To such conflicts were added numerous minor incidents. There was, for example, the incident with pianist Josef Weiss. Mahler had invited Weiss, his friend, to America; he considered him to be one of the great pianists of the day. Mahler first arranged for a chamber-music session in which Weiss and two players of the Philharmonic would rehearse the Brahms Trio in E-flat Major, opus 40. But Weiss's playing became so arrogantly unrestrained that the other two players refused to continue the rehearsal. Weiss took that as a personal affront and left abruptly. Thereupon Mahler took to the piano, and peace was restored. Later Mahler invited Weiss to play the Schumann A-Minor Concerto at the next Philharmonic concert. But Weiss's egotism and eccentricity again made a shambles of the dress rehearsal, which threatened to develop into a musical tug-of-war between soloist and conductor. At one point Weiss complained that a woodwind cue was too loud even though Mahler found it quite in order. As Weiss continued to complain, Mahler admonished him to confine his attention to his own instrument. At that point Weiss hurled the piano part at the conductor, shouting that he was the conductor's equal in a performance and entitled to express his views. In a moment the rehearsal hall was a scene of pandemonium. The orchestra members, fearing that Mahler was being attacked, flung themselves at Weiss, who continued to protest. Mahler stood his ground. Thereupon Weiss shook off his tamers and stalked out. Mahler, determined to play the announced concert, luckily found out that Paolo Gallico knew the work and was available, and rehearsals hastily began anew. But Mahler had not heard the last of Weiss. Bent on establishing a basis for a lawsuit for compensation which he intended to institute, Weiss made an appearance at Carnegie Hall on the night of the concert and straightfacedly announced his intention to play the concerto. Mahler refused to have any part in such mockery, whereupon Weiss made the announcement: "I came from Germany for this concert and I did not play. . . . If I am not paid I will have to go to court."

What brought matters to a crisis was the appearance of Ferruccio Busoni to play the *Emperor* Concerto under Mahler. History has not accorded Busoni the importance that he was to have for Mahler, both as a composer and as a pianist. A disciple and admirer of Liszt and his style, Busoni represented the formidable virtuoso precision of Liszt, but on a more intellectually refined level. It was therefore not surprising that the two intellectuals, Mahler and Busoni, both admiring, and excelling in their execution of Beethoven should have had much in common. Since Busoni was to play the *Emperor* Concerto with Mahler, the two men subjected the score and its then current interpretation to their joint scrutiny and found that the work, over the years of the performance in America, had accreted a number of crowd-pleasing additions, totally unfaithful to the spirit of Beethoven. With the characteristic impulsiveness and dedication of intellectual purists, Mahler and Busoni decided to rid the work of all its acquired musical gingerbread and present it to New York in the spirit and style in which, they felt, Beethoven would have wished to have it played.

It was on the occasion of a rehearsal for that particular performance that the ladies of the Philharmonic directorate decided to pay a visit. They did not care for the music making of two of the greatest masters of their time and, in consequence, subjected Mahler to an inquiry which disintegrated into a stormy session, with the ladies voicing their displeasure and Mahler replying in equally unvarnished language of the tersest kind. The nightmarish scene, totally unimaginable today, ended when one of the ladies, totally devoid of tact and knowledge, had the temerity to tell the foremost Beethoven interpreter of her time: "No, Mr. Mahler, this will never do," upon which she departed in a huff and in tears. The fact that the critical reception was favorable did nothing to assuage the ladies. Nor did the realization that such musical giants of the day as Rachmaninoff and Bülow were in accord with Mahler's ideas soften the mood or raise the horizons of the self-willed female members of the committee. In the performance of his own music Mahler fared no better. After the tepid reception accorded his First Symphony, the performance of the *Kindertotenlieder* fared even worse, although Dr. Ludwig Wüllner, a New York favorite despite his fading voice, presented them.

With the battle lines clearly drawn, a drastic step from either side was expected. It was therefore with considerable surprise that the Philharmonic's subscribers were informed that the season had been a satisfying one and that Mahler had been engaged for another year. The paying audience seemed to feel differently, because the next program, devoted to Bruckner, Strauss, and Pfitzner, drew the smallest audience at a Philharmonic concert in fifty years. Such rebellion was actually directed not against Mahler the man but against the program of "contemporary" music, but since Mahler had selected the program it was in essence a vote against Mahler, the conductor. The "I know what I like" syndrome prevailed. Its reverse ("I like what I know") was demonstrated by the wave of humanity which crowded Carnegie Hall for the last concert of the season, Beethoven's Ninth Symphony. Mahler, seemingly undeterred, continued to bring fine contemporary music to New York audiences, with Chabrier, Debussy, and Enesco appearing on the programs. They received the city's cold shoulder as expected, while a program featuring Berlioz, Strauss, and Beethoven earned rave notices.

Mahler had upheld his standards in New York and departed for Europe, looking forward to a pleasurable summer and particularly to the premiere performance of his Eighth Symphony in Munich. April 1910 found him again at his European haunts; a concert in Paris (his Second Symphony), Rome, Vienna (for a conference with his publishers). In June there were concerts in Leipzig, Munich, and Cologne.

While still on tour he was informed by New York that the number of his concerts there for the coming season had been increased from the planned forty-five to sixty-five. Mahler promptly replied by letter, objecting to the increase in his schedule and demanding additional compensation of $5,000, which he later reduced to $3,000 upon the advice of friends. It was that demand which prompted the ladies of the committee to begin a secret search for another conductor, "in case Mahler continued to be too demanding." When Mahler, at the request of the Philharmonic committee, eventually stated his terms for the 1910–11 season—$30,000 for ninety concerts—his demands were considered too high, and correspondence was begun with Weingartner without Mahler's knowledge.

Mahler meanwhile had returned to Toblach to work on his Tenth Symphony. His absorption was total, his mien remote and withdrawn. Alma, near the end of her strength, finally lost her self-control and in a violent scene accused Mahler of using her, controlling her, and neglecting her in his self-centered absorption and isolation. The dam broken, her verbal torrent swept over Mahler. Her life existed only as a reflection of his own; she felt unfulfilled and wasted. Her emotional explosion cleared the air and awakened Mahler to the injustice he had inflicted upon her over the years. The shock may have been responsible, along with a throat infection, for Mahler's collapse—which, however, was of brief duration. Relates Alma:

> One night I awoke suddenly. I called out to Mahler. There was no answer. I ran to his bed and found it empty. I rushed onto the landing and there found him lying unconscious with a lighted candle beside him. I carried him to bed . . . sent our servant to fetch a doctor . . . and meanwhile gave Mahler what stimulant for the heart I had in the house. He came around quickly.

But the nagging guilt persisted, and after much hesitation and delay he contacted Sigmund Freud. A deep reluctance, perhaps fear, prompted Mahler to cancel three appointments with Freud before keeping one in August 1910. Ernest Jones relates the circumstances of their meeting.

During the summer of 1910, Gustav Mahler was greatly distressed about his relationship to his wife, and Dr. Nepallek, a Viennese psychoanalyst who was a relative of Mahler's wife, advised him to consult Freud. He telegraphed from the Tyrol to Freud, who was vacationing that year on the Baltic coast, asking for an appointment. Freud was always loathe to interrupt his holidays for any professional work, but he could not refuse a man of Mahler's worth. His telegram making an appointment, however was followed by another one from Mahler countermanding it. Soon there came another request, with the same result. Mahler suffered from the *folie de doute* of his obsessional neurosis and repeated his performance three times. Finally Freud had to tell him that his last chance of seeing him was before the end of August, since he was planning to leave then for Sicily. So they met in a hotel in Leyden and then spent four hours strolling through the town and conducting a sort of psychoanalysis. Although Mahler had had no previous contact with psychoanalysis, Freud said he had never met anyone who seemed to understand it so swiftly. Mahler was greatly impressed by a remark of Freud's: "I take it your mother was called Marie. I should surmise it from the various hints in your conversation. How comes it that you married someone with another name, Alma, since your mother evidently played a dominating part in your life?" Mahler then told him that his wife's name was Alma Maria, but that he called her Marie! . . . This analytic talk evidently produced an effect, since Mahler recovered his potency and the marriage was a happy one until his death, which unfortunately took place only a year later.

In the course of the talk Mahler suddenly said that now he understood why his music had always prevented him from achieving the highest rank through the noblest passages, those inspired by the most profound emotions, being spoiled by the intrusion of some commonplace melody. His father, apparently a brutal person, treated his wife very badly, and when Mahler was a young boy there was a specially painful scene between them. It became quite unbearable to the boy, who rushed away from the house. At that moment, however, a hurdy-gurdy in the street was grinding out the popular Viennese air *"Ach, Du lieber Augustin."* In Mahler's opinion the conjunction of high tragedy and light amusement was from then on inextricably fixed in his mind, and the one mood inevitably brought the other with it.

Ernest Jones, *The Life and Work of Sigmund Freud*

It is not firmly established whether Mahler saw Freud because he wanted to understand himself better, in order to alleviate his guilt feelings concerning his attitude toward Alma, or simply to encounter Freud intellectually. The two men found each other fascinating—Mahler in an intellectual, Freud in a clinical sense.

I analyzed Mahler for an afternoon in Leyden. If I may believe reports, I achieved much with him at that time. . . . [During] a highly interesting expedition through his life history, we discovered his personal conditions for love, especially his Holy Mary complex (mother fixation). I had much opportunity to admire the capability for psychological understanding in this man of genius.

From Freud's letter to a pupil, translated by
Theodor Reik in *The Haunting Melody*

Freud had analyzed, explained, calmed. His mind at rest, Mahler even sought out and played Alma's songs, exiled from his presence for ten years. Immersion in creation, after his session with Freud, had another beneficial effect: a passionate rekindling of his relationship with and feelings for Alma. Thus his words on the final existing page of his Tenth Symphony: "To live for thee! To die for thee! Almschi [Mahler's pet name for Alma]!"

An incident that occurred at about that time sheds light on another side of Mahler and proves him to be capable of generosity and even selflessness. Austria's foremost music publishing house, Universal Edition, had agreed to publish Mahler's first four symphonies, and Mahler looked forward to receiving his first royalties. But at that point Universal Edition made a strange request of Mahler: they asked him to forego royalties until five times the original sum mentioned had been earned by his symphonies. The reason was that they also wanted to publish the complete set of Bruckner's symphonies, but could not do so unless Mahler forewent his royalties for the time being. Although Mahler would gain no benefit from the publication of Bruckner's work, he immediately agreed to the proposal out of reverence for the symphonist who had once been his mentor and idol. Spurred by the temporary loss of expected income, Mahler now realized that it was time to look at life objectively, put his financial house in order and use his considerable American earnings wisely. It is ironic that money matters did not fully enter Mahler's mind until he had said adieu to Vienna. Then, confronted with two realities—higher earnings and a diseased heart at age forty-seven—serious considerations with respect to money matters came to the fore. The irony lay in the fact that at a time of ebbing health and, as a result, subconsciously lowered musical standards, he was able to earn substantially more money than ever before.

With retirement from conducting also beckoning as a distinct possibility, his thoughts constantly returned to Vienna ("where the sun shines and the grapes grow," Bruno Walter quotes him as saying), regardless of whether he was working in New York, Paris, or Munich. Already in Munich Mahler showed deeply disturbing signs of illness and weakness, but he had subdued them in his intense search for the ultimate musical expression of his life, the performance of his Eighth Symphony. After the historic Munich performance, the task before Mahler was a monumental one as he looked forward to another season with the New York Philharmonic and a tour ranging from New York to Seattle. With financial matters under control for the present and the future, Mahler, despite the doctor's dire prognosis concerning his heart, went vigorously to work on his Tenth Symphony and busied himself with plans for the 1910–11 season with the New York Philharmonic.

# Finale

IN THE AUTUMN of 1910, Mahler embarked at Cherbourg for his last Atlantic crossing to America. The journey took from 15 November to 25 November, which afforded Mahler ten days of much-needed rest and relaxation.

The 1910–11 season started auspiciously with Schubert's C-Major Symphony (*The Great*), which shared the program with *Also sprach Zarathustra* and two Bach suites in a (much-criticized) Mahler arrangement, with Mahler conducting from the harpsichord.[1] The surface calm obtaining in his relationship with the directors was deceptive, because the ladies of the committee would not rest until they had broken Mahler to their will and curtailed his power of programming without interference. They were aided by a tactical mistake on the part of Mahler, who allowed a man in the orchestra to act as an informer for him. When that situation was found out, Mahler lost the indispensable support of the orchestra. Now the search for a successor proceeded in earnest. The name of Franz Kneisel, eminent violist and leader of the famous quartet bearing his name, was bandied about. But he was in no way the conductor of eminence that the Philharmonic demanded.

If the noisy, vengeful clique led by Henry Edward Krehbiel needed additional ammunition in their vendetta, Mahler, in his pursuit of excellence in performance, gave them what they had been looking for in his performance of Beethoven's Seventh Symphony. To achieve a balance more in keeping with a large modern orchestra and a large modern hall, he doubled the woodwinds for the performance. It was the "sacrilege" Krehbiel needed to shout "desecration!" the next day. History was repeating itself. Mahler, undaunted, pursued his programming, presenting also a number of works by much-loved American composers—Chadwick, Hadley, Loeffler, MacDowell. But the time for reconciliation had passed, and

---

[1] Mahler's "harpsichord" in New York was actually a Steinway piano with its timbre altered to resemble that of a harpsichord.

the proceedings unfolded with the relentless inevitability of a Greek drama. With Krehbiel and his ilk screaming for Mahler's scalp, he was peremptorily summoned before a board meeting in the sumptuous home of Mrs. Sheldon. There Mahler had to defend his artistic aims before a group of New York matrons who were parading as protectors of art—and who then proceeded to character assassination. A curtain, pulled open, revealed an attorney who, without Mahler's knowledge or consent, had taken down all of his heated comments and statements. With triumphant glee the ladies watched the breaking of a proud spirit—the demeaning of one of the world's musical geniuses.

Mahler left the meeting frustrated, furious, and fatigued, having surrendered in writing his prerogatives with respect to programming. The matrons of the committee had arrogated unto themselves the power to veto any program selection that did not suit their musical tastes. Mahler's predicament at that moment was great. On the one hand, his contracts with American institutions, first the Metropolitan, then the Philharmonic, had brought him, for the first time in his life, a material situation bordering on wealth. At the same time, ominous throat trouble had begun to beset him again. The following day he awoke feverishly, with a sore throat, shaken by chills. Alma called a physician, who counseled rest, but a series of scheduled concerts demanded Mahler's attention and he conducted them, ignoring the doctor's advice. During the last concert Mahler complained about severe headaches and overall weakness, but he insisted on finishing the evening. One reason why Mahler was so anxious to conduct the concert, even against the advice of his physician, was the premiere of *Cradle Song at the Grave of My Mother* by his friend Busoni. The date was 21 February 1911, and it was the forty-eighth concert of the season. It was to be the last concert of Mahler's life. New York, which at first had seemed to Mahler a new musical paradise, had become his personal hell.

Mahler miraculously felt much improved after the concert; even his temperature was near normal. He attributed it to his severe perspiration while conducting, which presumably had ejected the toxins from his body. But it turned out to be no more than a deceptive calm. Soon a renewed flaring brought on tonsillitis, which Mahler's weakened heart and generally weak mental and physical condition could no longer combat.

New York now became concerned about Mahler's health. From the policeman on duty at his hotel to the lights of New York society and musical circles, all inquired into Mahler's state of health. The warmth of their newly found friends, offered to two people alone in a foreign land, was balm to the Mahlers. Alma was deeply touched: "Never in my whole life have I met such genuine warmth of heart and delicacy of feelings as in America." One member of the committee summoned up a belated show of graciousness, stating that in her opinion Mahler was "the greatest conductor in Europe and America today. . . . we have been fortunate in keeping him as long as we have."

Despite such protestations, however, Mahler's sickness was a stroke of luck for the committee, because it provided them with the opening they needed to rid themselves of this impatient, ill-tempered, impossible little man. They had shopped around in earnest for a replacement, a "name" conductor worthy of the orchestra. But now their past strategy backfired. No one who had witnessed the humiliating blows dealt to one of the world's most celebrated musicians and composers cared to fill the position.

The ladies finally settled for the talents of Josef Stransky. Perhaps more than any other act, the selection of Stransky attested to the narrow musical horizons of the ladies of the Philharmonic committee. But Europe was not fooled and cast a cynical eye at the proceedings. "Stransky . . . ranks as an excellent dilettante," observed the *Hamburger Fremdenblatt* on 31 May 1911, adding that he had been hired "through mistaken considerations."

Meanwhile, ominously and despite rest on Mahler's part, the symptoms of his affliction did not wane and his strength began to ebb alarmingly. Soon Alma had to spoon-feed him, and when he was reading, page after single page had to be removed from books and handed to him because he was no longer strong enough to hold an entire book. When Mahler finally yielded and agreed to a blood test, the devastating truth was established—a streptococci infection. Various healing methods were gingerly attempted without result. With the New York medical community stymied in their efforts to help Mahler, it was decided after consultations that Mahler was to go without delay to Paris and undergo thorough bacteriological treatment. Unobtrusively, coffers were packed. At the appointed time a stretcher was waiting, but Mahler waved it aside and, leaning heavily on his doctor's arm, stiffly walked to the elevator. Mrs. Untermeyer, Mahler's unwavering supporter among the women of the governing committee, was waiting at the ground floor, her automobile and chauffeur at Mahler's disposal. The marvelous personnel of the hotel had thoughtfully cleared the lobby to spare Mahler, who hated to be stared at, embarrassment. Mahler was promptly put to bed once aboard ship, and his doctor and friends bade him a brief farewell for the last time. The cabin was filled to capacity with flowers and farewell presents from American musical and society friends. Mahler by then was too weak to do anything and had to be dressed, fed, and walked. Busoni was aboard ship and amused Mahler with funny bits of counterpoint and an occasional bottle of choice wine— a gentle sign of his devotion. During the crossing Mahler insisted on getting up, regardless of his weak condition, to half walk/half be carried on the boat deck. The thoughtful captain reserved a special part of the deck for Mahler to move about undisturbed.

On arrival in Cherbourg the captain saw to it that the Mahler party alighted before disembarking of the passengers was begun. An official of the steamship company saw to Mahler's conveyance from the boat to a railroad compartment, while Alma attended to their forty pieces of luggage in French customs. When she informed the inspector on duty that Mahler was gravely ill, all formalities were immediately dispensed with and the party was waved through.

Mahler, Alma, and their attendants reached Paris in the graying dawn and sped in desperate haste to the Hotel Elysée. There Mahler experienced what seemed to be a miraculous recovery. Laughingly he reminded all within reach of his voice he had always maintained that Europe would have a restorative effect on him. Suddenly he was excited and animated; he dressed and shaved himself; he was hungry. He asked to be taken for a drive through Paris. Alma recalls: "He got into it as a man recovered . . . he got out of it as a man at death's door." On the verge of total collapse, Mahler, was rushed back to the hotel and an urgent call for a doctor went out. Mahler morosely asked Alma's mother to be buried in Grinzing beside his daughter but without fanfare or ceremony, with the tombstone bearing only the single word "MAHLER." "Anyone who comes to look for me will know who I was and the rest do not need to know." Instinctively he knew that the end was near. This did not keep his mind from occupying itself with thoughts of his Tenth Symphony, because the thought of leaving work unfinished made him disconsolate, and with no future to look forward to, he conjured up the past.

As soon as the Parisian specialist had ended his examination, he arranged for the removal of Mahler from the hotel to a nursing home. Feverish excitement in Mahler now alternated with lapses into total weakness. "There he lay, tortured victim of an insidious illness, his very soul affected by the struggle of his body, his mood gloomy and forbidding," wrote Bruno Walter. Mahler looked up at Walter's concerned face as the latter bent over him. "I have now but one desire—to take enough digitalis to support my heart."

Dr. Chantemesse, the celebrated bacteriologist, proved a disaster. His interest turned out to be wholly clinical, his manner absurdly lacking in sensitivity. "Madame Mahler, come and look," he beckoned her, adjusting the miscroscope. "Even I have never seen streptococci in such a marvelous state of development." Mahler's deadly bacteria were in a "marvelous state" while the patient was left to die! In view of the visibly deteriorating situation, Alma wired a famous specialist of the Vienna Medical School; he sped to Mahler's bedside and arrived the following morning. The Vienna doctor, Professor Chvostek, first of all calmed Mahler, then took steps to speed Mahler to Vienna. Mahler's face lit up with joy. To see Vienna once more! He could not leave too quickly. An ambulance sped him to the railroad station, the doctor by his side. But all Dr. Chvostek was able to accomplish was to fool Mahler for a little while. In an unobserved moment he confided to Alma: "No hope, and may the end come quickly. If he survives the whole nervous system will go . . . you don't want to wheel a senile idiot about." Along the journey, German and Austrian journalists requested reports on the state of his health, and Mahler, mentally fresh, was keenly aware of their complimentary presence and interest.

Finally—Vienna. Mahler's eyes shone as an ambulance sped him to the Löw sanatorium. Soon his vast room and veranda were filled with flowers. He inspected the card of each arriving basket and bouquet, and his haggard face showed a smile when one basket bore the inscription "From the Philharmonic." The difficulties of years past receded as he treasured the card from "my" Philharmonic. But the belated joy did not last. His keen sense of awareness dimmed. When he failed to recognize his sister Justine, she fled from the room in despair. Eventually only Alma's name was on his lips. His emaciated body was plied with radium and oxygen, but death came stealthily and the groaning agony lasted for hours. As with Mahler's idol, Beethoven, nature vented its fury in a thunderstorm as greatness, once again, passed on. His last word: "Mozart."

> The burial . . . turned into a demonstration of loyalty quite comparable to the impressive funerals Vienna had granted its musical heroes of the past. However, there was also a sense of irreparable loss, of silent despair . . . [as well as a sense of] mystic exaltation, felt by many but understood by but a few, at the historic moment of Gustav Mahler's passing . . . that rainy May day, which had started so somberly, only to end consolingly in sunshine with the jubilant song of the nightingale.
>
> Redlich, *Gustav Mahler*

## REFLECTIONS

> Mahler was sick when he returned to America. The colossal fees which had been offered to him lured him. The man, whose slender body held immense, flaming energy, and who constantly worked under great pressure, believed that his already weakened heart could do justice to the flood of concerts . . . [and] that large lumps of gold could be gained quickly. . . . There is something tragic in the fate of this man of supreme willpower . . . his was the temper of the capitalistic age.
>
> *Tägliche Rundschau*, Berlin, 21 May 1911

> Gustav Mahler was one of the last great idealists of our time . . . who in his art reached for the unattainable, who, on his way to the impossible, attempted to conquer the possible.

There was something repulsive about him, he was an ugly little human creature and one had to look closely to discover that it was exactly in that seeming repulsiveness where lay the magnetism, . . . power, high spirit and grace, all of them a specific form of expression and spiritual beauty.

Once under his spell, the public remained faithful to him. . . . He played the orchestra like a virtuoso. . . . What a splendid leader of temperament . . . unbending in his art, bestowed with such rare magic of personality, he attracted after repelling. . . . This star is now extinguished. If Vienna only knew what it had lost, how much poorer the city has become through the death of this master whose last breath belonged to Vienna.

*Neue Freie Presse,* Vienna, *Feuilleton,* 21 May 1911

Mahler is dead and Vienna mourns. Thus read the obituaries and articles in the newspapers of Vienna. . . "One of the greatest sons of our city!" "One of the most charming men!" "The director who raised our opera to unheard-of heights!" . . . and this is only a small sampling.

Such [is] "Viennese mourning." It expresses the feeling of superficiality, regret perhaps [of a city] which committed an injustice . . . which no longer can be redressed.

Vienna has always mourned thusly. When a man lives he is attacked . . . only after he is dead does one bemoan the fact that he no longer serves mankind. . . . There is little love and little faithfulness, but much deceit to be found in the Viennese tear . . . [and] the "mourning Vienna" which drove him away. . . . They found him ugly and bizarre . . . now his profile is noble and his music original. It is always the same. One must be dead to be able to live comfortably in Vienna.

Truly, few can mourn as well as the Viennese. If I were one of the greats of the world I would write in my death notice, "Under no circumstances will I allow expressions of sympathy from the dear Viennese."

*"Adagio," Sonn- und Montagzeitung,* Vienna, 22 May 1911

He was demonic, neurotic, demanding, selfish, noble . . . sarcastic, unpleasant . . . irascible, impatient, exuberant . . . and a genius . . . [who] did not live long enough to see his eventual triumph in the only thing that really mattered to him: his own music.

Harold C. Schonberg, *The Great Conductors,* 1967

# THE WORLD OF MAHLER: A Pictorial Biography

# The Faces of Mahler

*Gustav at age 5 (1865)*

*Gustav at age 16 (1876)*

*The bearded Mahler (1881)*

*Mahler with moustache (1884)*

*Mahler clean-shaven (1892)*

*Mahler's most famous photographic portrait, taken in the director's office of the Vienna Opera (1899)*

Mahler on his way to the Opera, with hat in hand, as was his custom (1904)

The famed bronze bust by Rodin in the foyer of the Vienna State Opera

Pen-and-ink silhouette of Mahler conducting
(artist unknown)

Drawing by Fritz Gareis caricaturing
Mahler's vehement conducting gestures

Two sketches of Mahler by Hans Schliess-
mann. Above: a caricature of the withering
look Mahler gave concert or opera latecomers;
below: a silhouette of Mahler asking for more
volume

*Three of the famous silhouettes by Dr. Otto Böhler, showing Mahler's expressive gestures in the opera pit*

*An advertisement by a Vienna dealer in recordings, showing Mahler surrounded by the images of some of his greatest singers. The caption reads: (left) "Why pay the great salaries?" (right) "furnishes us with the most beautiful voices without background noises"*

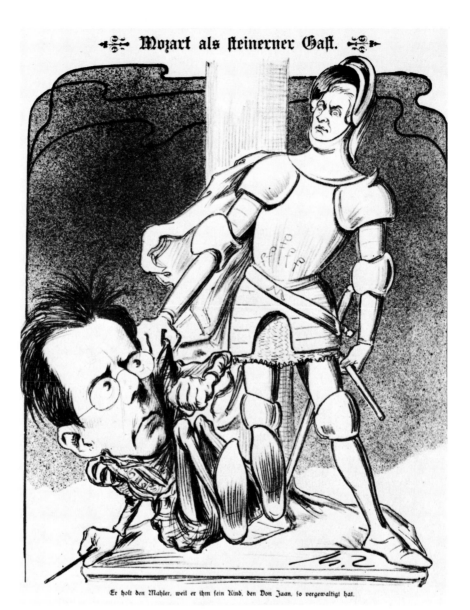

Er holt den Mahler, weil er ihm fein Kind, den Don Jaan, fo vergewaltigt hat.

*A sarcastic newspaper caricature of Mahler's* Don Giovanni *performance, entitled "Mozart as the Stone Guest." The caption reads: "He [Mozart] comes for Mahler (depicted as conductor in period costume), because he has raped his child, Don Juan."*

Newspaper caricature alluding to Mahler's alleged "borrowing" from other composers, entitled: "Mahler's Metamorphoses." "After the performance of his last symphony, several critics noted that Mahler could not free himself from the memories of the masters he esteems. . . . At each new performance of his work, Mahler now presumes that he resembles, in facial expression and attitude, the composers who have influenced the particular composition." From top left clockwise: Wagner, Liszt, a Viennese Beethoven, Schubert, Meyerbeer

# The Mahler Family

*Marie Mahler, Gustav's mother*

*Gustav Mahler with his sister Justine*

*Karlskirche in Vienna, where Gustav and Alma's wedding took place*

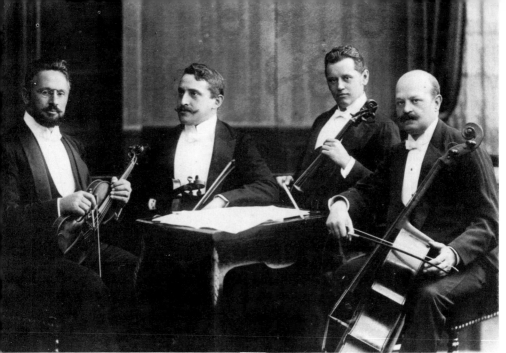

*Arnold Rosé (left) and his world-famous quartet: Paul Fisher (second violin), Anton Ruzitska (viola), Friedrich Buxbaum (cello) (1910)*

*Alma Mahler, née Alma Margarethe Maria Schindler, 1879–1964 (1909)*

Self-portrait of Oscar Kokoschka
with Alma Mahler

Kokoschka at the time of his acquaintance with
Alma

# Mahler and His Time

*The Cathedral of St. Stephen, the spiritual and geographical center of Vienna*

Emperor Franz Joseph of Austria, 1900. The emperor congratulated Mahler on "having made himself master of the situation at the opera," a condition which hardly ever prevailed in Austria under Franz Joseph's regime.

The German dramatist Gerhart Hauptmann. Mahler and Hauptmann became close friends who engaged in lengthy discussions on theatrical and philosophical topics.

*The German author Thomas Mann, who felt that Mahler "embodied the most serious and sacred artistic purpose of his age"*

*Arthur Schnitzler, the oldest of the Vienna literary triumvirate (the others were Arthur Schnitzler and Stefan Zweig) of Mahler's day*

*Hugo von Hofmannsthal, the young genius who became the librettist and close collaborator on Richard Strauss's operas. He expressed himself derogatorily to Strauss with respect to Mahler's music, considering it "heterogenous, vague, and hybrid."*

*Stefan Zweig, the poet and writer, who also collaborated with Richard Strauss, here in animated conversation at a Vienna coffeehouse. After Hitler's invasion of Austria he emigrated to South America. He died by his own hand on 22 February 1942.*

*Karl Kraus, writer and critic, whose magazine Die Fackel became the literary conscience of Vienna in his time*

*Hans Richter, conductor at the Vienna Opera and the Vienna Philharmonic, who was the musical power in Vienna before the arrival of Mahler. After Mahler became director of the Opera, Richter resigned his Vienna positions and retired to England.*

Felix von Weingartner, who succeeded
Mahler as director of the Vienna Opera

Hans von Bulow, the great German conductor.
He praised and recommended Mahler as a conductor but disparaged him as a composer.

*Johann Strauss and his friend Johannes Brahms at Strauss's villa at the spa of Ischl in 1895. Brahms idolized Strauss and his music; Strauss could do no more than respect the music of his friend.*

*Anton Bruckner, composer, Wagner apostle, and one-time teacher of Mahler at the Vienna University. Mahler's early ardor for Bruckner's music cooled in later years.*

*Hugo Wolf, the famous song composer and friend of Mahler during their conservatory days. Many felt that Mahler's refusal to perform Wolf's The Corregidor drove the already sick Wolf over the brink into insanity.*

Richard Strauss, the ambitious composer of sensuous music. Already famous at a time when Mahler was still struggling for recognition, Strauss assisted Mahler in the performance of his music. A life-long love-hate relationship developed between the two famous composers.

Bruno Walter, the conductor, who became a devotee of Mahler's music. He met Mahler while still a young struggling musician, and a life-long friendship developed.

Willem Mengelberg, the famous conductor of the Concertgebouw Orchestra in Amsterdam. It was through Mengelberg's efforts that Amsterdam became a "Mahler City" in Mahler's time.

Arnold Schönberg, as depicted in watercolor by Egon Schiele

Alban Berg, composer, student and friend of Schön-berg, and enthusiastic admirer of Mahler

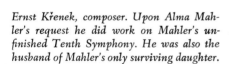

Ernst Křenek, composer. Upon Alma Mahler's request he did work on Mahler's un-finished Tenth Symphony. He was also the husband of Mahler's only surviving daughter.

Gustav Klimt, one of the foremost painters of the "Secession" group. Despite the great age difference between them he was an early admirer of Alma Mahler and remained a life-long friend of the Mahlers.

*Egon Schiele, self-portrait. Although he died at the untimely age of 28, he was one of the foremost Viennese expressionist painters and likewise a member of the "Secession" circle; he was also a close friend of Klimt and Schönberg.*

*Sigmund Freud, as Mahler knew him. Although they met only once (in a session which lasted for hours), the two men admired each other greatly.*

# The Mahler Stage

A sketch on wood by B. Strassberger of a performance of Aida. Note the position of the conductor, who conducts the singers while leaning against the stage, with the orchestra behind him. A path behind him allowed him to step back to conduct the orchestra in orchestral interludes.

The gilded Musikvereinssaal, where the Vienna Philharmonic concerts are given. Acoustically the hall is one of the finest in the world.

Alfred Roller, the stage designer of genius, who contributed greatly to the visual success of Mahler's stage productions at the Vienna Opera

Amalie Materna, as Brünhilde in Die Walküre by Wagner. Materna became so formidable a Wagner interpreter that Bayreuth needed her and other Viennese Wagner singers.

Erik Schmedes, tenor, here seen as
Loge in Das Rheingold. He was one
of Mahler's major discoveries.

Anna von Mildenburg, in her role as Walküre in
Die Walküre. A deep love interest developed
between her and Mahler in Hamburg. Although
Mahler's love for her cooled in Vienna, he never-
theless invited the splendid singer to the Vienna
Opera.

*Above, Selma Kurz, the foremost coloratura soprano of the Vienna Opera in Mahler's time*

*Right, Marie Gutheil-Schoder, one of the greatest dramatic singers on Mahler's roster*

Enrico Caruso, the celebrated Italian tenor, seen here in his famous role as Radames in Aida. He sang triumphantly under Mahler in Vienna as well as New York.

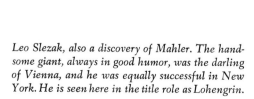

Leo Slezak, also a discovery of Mahler. The handsome giant, always in good humor, was the darling of Vienna, and he was equally successful in New York. He is seen here in the title role as Lohengrin.

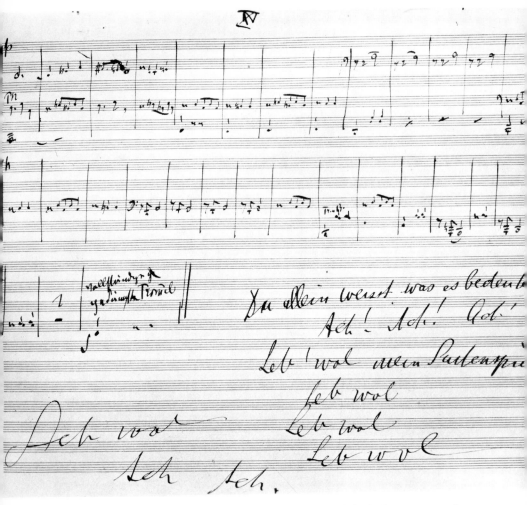

The final page of Mahler's unfinished Tenth Symphony. The final comments read:

You alone know what it means
Ach! Ach! Ach!
Farewell, my lyre!
Farewell
Farewell
Farewell

# The Creator

# The Romantic Century

## THE BIRTH OF ROMANTICISM

"I AM NOT SATISFIED with my works up to the present time. From today I mean to take a new road." Those words from Beethoven to his friend and factotum **Wenzel Krumpholz** ushered in the romantic era in music. Thus two years later that "new road" led to the creation of the *Eroica* (the Symphony No. 3 in E-flat, opus 55), even cursory comparison of which with earlier work will illuminate Beethoven's giant stride into a new age. Aside from the doubled length of the work as compared with Haydn's or Mozart's symphonic creations, the self-willed opening immediately impresses and astounds, as does the logical spiritual integration of the first and second movements. The daring innovation of a funeral march was in itself an advance of gigantic proportions, spiritually as well as musically. Haydn would never have dared to include a funeral march as a second movement (or as any movement, for that matter), because Haydn's position was totally different from that of Beethoven. Haydn was an *entertainer* who composed music on the highest level for the entertainment of his princely patrons. And therein lies the key; entertainment precludes such a concept as a funeral march because it turns a jaundiced eye at any display of strong or deep emotion in symphonic music. Thus Haydn's or Mozart's second movements traditionally featured an Adagio or Andante in charming contrast to the lively opening Sonata allegro.

Perhaps even more trenchant was Beethoven's innovative introduction of the Scherzo into the symphony. Gone was the scraping and bowing of the graceful minuet, which had found temporary haven in the symphonies of Haydn and Mozart (and those of the early Beethoven) after having been driven from the palaces of the French nobles in 1789. Its measured grace is abandoned in favor of the throbbing vitality of the *Eroica's* Scherzo. Beethoven's only adherence to tradition in that movement is in the ABA construction scheme that is followed—and there, a rousing hunting theme for three horns in the middle (B) section replaces the mildly contrasting trio of the minuet. Beethoven had shed the livery of the princely entertainer and had emerged as a *composer,* unencumbered by princely commands and commissions. It comes therefore as no surprise that the final movement of the *Eroica* should be the apotheosis of heroic music instead of a formalized, lively, applause-getting rondo.

This was, of course, not the first intimation of Beethoven's *Sturm und Drang.* Clearly the opening theme of his Piano Sonata, opus 13 (*Pathétique*) had introduced the romantic notions of pathos and emotion into music, and his opus 27, no. 2 (*Moonlight*), had clearly given notice in the very title, *Sonata quasi una fantasia,* that Beethoven intended to leave behind the classical form which had so pleased Haydn and Mozart and into which they had continued to pour the inventions of their musical genius. But it was with the *Eroica* that Beethoven entered upon the "new road" of romanticism.

The nineteenth-century romantic spirit soon pervaded all fields, from art to philosophy, and all nations, from France to Russia. In the arts it appeared first in poetry, next in painting, and eventually, belatedly, in music. Yet music was to become the strongest expression of the romantic spirit—essentially a nineteenth-century phenomenon under whose umbrella widely diverging styles of music were embraced. Greater contrast in musical concepts and execution can hardly be imagined than that between Berlioz and Mendelssohn, Wagner and Brahms, Brahms and Tchaikovsky, or Chopin and Liszt.

Basically, what all romantic composers had in common was their expression in some form of a revolt against classicism. Although all professed veneration for the classics, even in revolt, such veneration was extremely variable. Berlioz disliked Bach and Handel, while admiring the symphonist in Beethoven and the opera composer in Gluck. Wagner, although he put the finishing touches to some of Gluck's music and even edited Palestrina, believed only in Mozart and Beethoven. Mendelssohn became a romantic bridge to the classical past, while Schumann, creating in the image of the past, strove for new tonal directions. Brahms, disavowing and turning away from the neo-German aspirations of Wagner and Liszt, was happy to be recognized as the logical extension of the Viennese classical past.

Contrasts did not end there. In the process of gathering the faithful under its umbrella, romanticism allowed the extrovert and introvert, the flamboyant and the reticent, to live side by side. Thus the intimate works of Chopin and Schumann coexisted with Liszt's flamboyancy and Weber's virtuosity. Verdi remained the quiet musician, deeply rooted in the soil and tradition of his native Italy, while Wagner bent German mythology to his purposes and molded music to his image. Mendelssohn respected and observed the order and harmonies of the past, while Schumann sought to break away from them. Berlioz and Wagner paid lip service to the past. They all proclaimed Beethoven their god, but built musical temples of their own.

As form changed, so did sound and so did harmony. As we observe the succession—Haydn–Mozart–Beethoven–Schubert–Weber–Berlioz— we realize that with the classical composers form was uppermost in their mind, while with the romantics sound became supreme and form was forced to adapt to sound and emotion. Extramusical matter, be it poetry, painting, or mood, found expression in music and became increasingly important, despite Mendelssohn's dictum that good music does not become more significant or intelligible through poetic interpretation, but that, on the contrary, it becomes less significant by virtue of losing its musical depth.

To express romantic ideas and images, not only the form of music but also its most expressive vehicle, the orchestra, had to be changed and enlarged. As Beethoven had found the sonorities of Haydn and Mozart insufficient to his vision, so history repeated itself after his death. A wealth of new orchestral sound and expression was made available when, through Berlioz's novel ideas of orchestral sound, virtuosity became the hand-maiden of romanticism. What Paganini had accomplished on and for the violin and Liszt on and for the piano, Berlioz unleashed in the orchestra.

Many a cherished symbol of the magic of the past was forced to fall, to give way to the excitement of the moment. If 1789 had been an out-ward, explosive manifestation of political change and revolt, 1800 was the turning point for the emancipation of the musical spirit. The indi-vidual and individuality reigned supreme.


## THE ROAD OF ROMANTICISM


To fully appreciate the divergent influences and developments of which the romantic era was the result, it is necessary to retrace our steps a few centuries back from the year 1800. The very fact that Luther, Michelan-gelo, and Palestrina were contemporaries [1] gives us some idea of the tension and turmoil of the period. No greater contrast can be imagined than that obtaining between these three giants of Protestantism, Renaissance art, and Renaissance church music, respectively. While the Roman school of music and one of its major masters, Palestrina, desperately, defiantly clung to what they considered virtuous musical art, Protestantism had brought about a revolution which extended into many fields seemingly

---

[1] Martin Luther, 1483–1546; Michelangelo Buonarotti, 1475–1564; Giovanni Pier-luigi da Palestrina, 1525–1594.

unrelated to religion and brought about new alignments and developments. The artistic freedom of the Renaissance coincided.

The music of the church of Rome now found itself attacked and threatened from all sides. From Germany the hymn challenged the dominance of the Mass. Even on its home ground, Italy, the dominance of sacred music was threatened. In worldly Venice, the secular madrigal vied with the solemn motet; in Florence, the magnificence and richness of the newly devised art form, opera, threatened to draw audiences away from the church, which vainly attempted to match its splendor.[2] Worst of all, no longer did all musical roads lead to the Sistine Chapel and the Schola Cantorum. While the church of Rome continued to be important musically, its eminence was weakened because patronage proliferated throughout the crowned and princely courts of Europe, thereby changing the musical face of the Western world. Artistically, politically, and religiously, the outlook changed from heliocentric to geocentric, from heaven-centered to earth-centered. No longer was mankind totally concerned with the question: "Where am I going from here?" The question which became much more intriguing was "Where did I come from?" The Renaissance dawned.

In the arts, many of these changes were initiated not by artists but by patrons. And just as music had been ordered by the patron and composed and performed for the patron, so changes were instituted mainly from the outside. Even if on rare occasions the composer dared to initiate changes, he had to tread lightly in order not to offend his patron, be it church or aristocrat. Those powerful institutions or individuals had no qualms about imprinting their particular stamp of taste on their time and its artists. What Hindemith was to call *Gebrauchsmusik,* music that served a specific everyday purpose, was not an invention of the twentieth century but was rather a response to the age-old demand of the patron to have music written for a Mass, a wedding, a dance, or a banquet.

There were, of course, at all times instances of daring or inspiring individualism. The position of the *castrati* of the seventeenth and eighteenth centuries, for example, became so powerful that they could securely impose their will and whim upon a composer or sponsor and dare to include into an opera any aria or costume they pleased. There arose, however, developments which greatly fostered the eventual emergence of individuality. One was the social shifts of patronage, from church and landed aristocracy to monied aristocracy or well-heeled bourgeoisie, who were neither sufficiently educated nor so ruthlessly self-willed as to impose their preferences and tastes on the composer. A second was the separation

[2] Opera was actually a latecomer to the age of the Renaissance. By 1600, when opera began in Florence, the other great artists of the Renaissance had long since created their masterpieces, while music still wallowed in medieval polyphony. Opera was not truly to bloom until the Baroque era.

of composer and performer, brought about by new demands from a new patronage. Until the nineteenth century, performance of a composer's work was left mainly to the composer himself. Such were the tastes, demands, and expectations of the time that the composer was all but forced to present a new composition at each concert—which, for example, prompted Mozart to compose twenty-three piano concertos for his *Akademien* (subscription concerts) and Haydn ninety-two symphonies for the entertainment of the princes Esterhazy. A trend which had begun in the eighteenth century—the emergence of the virtuoso performer—came to fruition in the nineteenth century and was to greatly influence individualism and romanticism. No longer was a performance impossible because the composer's genius had outdistanced his pianistic or violinistic prowess; a virtuoso stepped in and accomplished the task. Soon the relationship was reversed, with the virtuoso approaching the composer with a commission for a virtuoso vehicle.[3]

Change manifested itself in areas other than music; manners, thinking, and dress were affected. It had been symbolic of Haydn's rank and position at the Esterhazy court that he wore at all times the light blue, silver-embroidered livery of his aristocratic patron. Mozart, when concertizing before the crowned heads of Europe as a *Wunderkind,* did so attired in a nobleman's attire, complete with *Dreispitz* (three-cornered hat) and miniature sword, while in the employment of the Archbishop of Salzburg, he was seated, according to his rank, with the kitchen help.

But Beethoven would have none of this. Gone overnight was the oppressive, restrictive contractual patronage, gone the livery, gone the bowing and scraping. He had ceased to be an entertainer "writing to order" for princely patrons' pleasure or for bored bourgeosie; he had become a professional composer on a free-lance basis. No longer did he present his music for aristocratic pleasure but rather for the enjoyment of an ever-growing (although not always appreciative) public—a public which was turning away from houses of worship and more and more toward the concert hall and the opera house for its musical enjoyment. He was to be his own master, which Mozart had unsuccessfully tried to be. Only in his last three symphonies had Mozart, bereft of pupils and patrons, been able to create symphonies "for the world." But Beethoven succeeded where Mozart failed: in the end it was the princes of Vienna who put themselves at Beethoven's disposal, without any binding commitment on his part. He repaid them with verbal insults and immortal music. And in the end he did not even care whether anybody heard his last sonatas and quartets. That trait removed him even further from the classical concept

---

[3] A case in point was Paganini's commissioning of a viola composition from Berlioz; the result was *Harold in Italy.* Paganini, who expected a virtuoso vehicle, never performed it.

and into the romantic orbit. No longer need the composer dilute his life and art with lesson giving, choir singing, and organ playing; with Beethoven, being a composer became a full-time profession as well as an art. The weekly symphony for the princely visitor or the demanding patron was no longer. Where in the past revolt had been a rare exception, with Beethoven it became part of his art in the desire to create different, challenging music, flauntingly colorful, and perhaps freely dedicated to a patron out of respect but no longer the property of a specific patron.

Along with this assertion of individuality, however, we find the emergence of a powerful surge of nationalistic identification and expression, with Wagner flaunting Teutonic mythology and the world around him bursting into nationalistic song, starting unexpectedly from the eastern end of Europe, where Glinka and Dargomijsky laid the groundwork for an entire flock of inspired amateurs, destined to become masters in their own right. Pronounced, even revolutionary nationalism raised its voice in Smetana's *Ma Vlast* [My country] and Sibelius's *Finlandia,* while Debussy called himself *musicien français.*

Yet regardless of the purposes which music was made to serve, there was no question in the romantic's mind, be he poet, dramatist, or musician, that music had become the supreme, unifying expression of nineteenth-century romanticism, having been raised to that supreme position from its previous lowly status as the handmaiden of poetry, which had been its function as late as the time of Mozart or Haydn. It was therefore Beethoven to whom the romantics paid homage, because it was he who had shattered the classical shackles of formalism and opened the romantic gates of emotion and mystery. In the process, however, music was in a sense cheapened, because it was to be called upon to depict extramusical matter. "Program music" had been born. Beethoven had been embarrassed by the implication of program music in his *Pastorale* Symphony, which prompted him to state in the heading that the work was "more an expression of feeling than a painting." Yet as the nineteenth century progressed, the innate poetry of music, its address to basic emotions such as elation, sorrow, or joy, no longer sufficed. In a mistaken longing for a joining of music and poetry, the "symphonic poem" was born.

Symphonic creation, hand in hand with its reproductive instrument, the orchestra, had expanded to unheard-of proportions, with Richard Strauss and Gustav Mahler taking it to its extreme tonal and technical limits. Yet the careful observer could not help but notice that many a symphonic composer filled the first movement emotionally to the brim and in the next three movements went through the traditional motions of making contrasting and delightful but seldom meaningful music. The idea thereby arose of making the first movement an independent, self-contained creation. Thus Liszt announced his novelty.

Programmatic music was, of course, not new. As early as 1540, the composer Clément Jannequin had depicted the battle of Marignano in *La Bataille,* with all tone painting done by human voices! In 1689, Johann Kuhnau published his *Biblische Historien,* musical descriptions of the Old Testament, for the keyboard, and in the eighteenth century Antonio Vivaldi described nature in four miniature violin concertos known as *The Four Seasons.* Even young Johann Sebastian Bach vented his feelings of sadness in an early programmatic composition, *Capriccio on the Departure of a Beloved Brother.* But Liszt was not to be satisfied with such naive attempts at program music. He felt impelled to call on the muses of Victor Hugo (*Ce qu'on entend sur la montagne*), Byron (*Tasso, Lamento e trionfo*), Lamartine (*Les Preludes*), Hugo (*Mazeppa*), Schiller (*Die Ideale*), Goethe (*Faust*), and Dante (*Divina Commedia*), and to avail himself of the genius of Michelangelo (*La Notte*) and the talents of Kaulbach (*Hunnenschlacht*), expressing their sublime thoughts in blatant musical terms. The results, although musicologically significant, were less than impressive as musical and artistic accomplishments.

> When Liszt, the most gifted virtuoso of our time, grew tired of triumphs won with other people's compositions, he set about to surprise the world with large compositions of his own. . . . In Liszt's case it was his intention that the composer should overshadow the virtuoso. . . . It seems more likely that the musical world has suffered, in the virtuoso's abdication, a loss [for] which the composer's succession can hardly compensate. . . . Well aware of his insufficient power of invention, Liszt habitually elaborated on the melodies of others in transcriptions, fantasies, etc. . . . Now, suddenly, he has resolved to come out with great and profound compositions. . . . Too intelligent not to recognize his most obvious shortcomings, he has chosen to approach music from an angle where, inspired by external ideas, it occupies the comparative intellect and stimulates poetic and picturesque fantasy. . . . A musician cannot but find this method hazardous from the very start, since it demonstrates that music is only the afterthought. . . . Liszt's symphonic poems do not flow from the pure fountain of music; they are artificially distilled. Musical creation does not come freely and originally with Liszt; it is contrived . . . intelligence, poetry and imagery in abundance, but no musical essence. Liszt belongs to those ingenious but barren temperaments who mistake desire for calling. . . . Only those who do not know the works of Berlioz or Richard Wagner could mistake Liszt for a musical discoverer or reformer.
>
>    Eduard Hanslick, in a review of Liszt's *Symphonic Poems,* 1857 [4]

As the desire for emotional expression and exhibitionism spread, Berlioz was to musically depict a decapitation in *Symphonie Fantastique* and Tchaikovsky, in the *1812 Overture,* described Napoleon's retreat from Moscow in such explicit terms as to virtually drain the work of musical content. In that great Italian achievement, opera, music had always been

---

[4] The reference to Wagner was remarkable, coming as it did from the era's most virulent critic of Wagner's.

the dominant ingredient. In opera the poet and the librettist had no illusions as to their position vis-à-vis the musical score; they knew and accepted the fact that the story stood or fell with the success or failure of the music. Hardly ever, with the exceptions of Gluck and Wagner, was that dominance challenged. Setting out from that premise, so basic to opera, the symphonic composer felt that the same dominance would be retained in his musical sphere. Mistakenly, he felt that tying music to poetry would not only intensify but also "aid" the poetry. Little did he realize that in the process the music would be reduced to an adjunct of the poetry. Furthermore, the entire undertaking became a limiting experience of the spirit because hearing the music always evoked the initially stated extramusical thought without permitting the listener to engage in his own interpretation. Music thus became a two-dimensional experience, deprived of the infusion of individual interpretation and shackled to the initial inspiration of the poet or painter. Only if the listener was fortunate enough to be unfamiliar with the extramusical premise was he able to give himself freely and fully to an interpretation of his own, unencumbered by any preconceived image.

The romantic age also witnessed the proliferation of the composer—specifically, his emergence as writer, critic, and musicologist. In the past the spectacle of the composer who was such "by the grace of God" was common. Haydn and Mozart, the composers of immortal music, were mortals who often acted and spoke in the coarsest manner; later, Bruckner was to represent a throwback into that era and that type of composer. The liberalism and romanticism of the nineteenth century fostered a totally different type of composer. Beethoven had already used the term "science of music," and Weber had tried his hand at writing a novel. But it was left to the later romantics to arrive at a higher intellectual plateau. Thus the earnest, informed, and critical comments of Schumann in his newly founded periodical *Neue Zeitschrift für Musik* and the acid-tipped reviews and articles of Berlioz in the famed and feared *Journal des Débats* opened new musical, literary, and critical vistas, to be explored also in the writings of Liszt and, to an even greater extent, of Wagner. "Gone were the mere musicians; there were only artists in the service of the romantic ideal," wrote Alfred Einstein in *Music in the Romantic Era.*

Despite the intrusion of extramusical matter into the musical fabric, instrumental music became the supreme expression of the nineteenth-century romantic age. In a sense the romantics became captives of sound per se, recognizing and embracing the power of its magic. No thought was given to the inevitable: viz., that the infatuation with sound carried within it the seed of its own destruction, in that the public would eventually grow tired of massed sound per se and would revolt, just as in the seventeenth century surfeit with polyphony had led to the emergence of a new art form—opera.

The romantic vocal contributions, the Lied and opera, were a further expression of this romantic love affair with sound. Comparison of most preromantic operas with Wagner suffices. In an eighteenth-century opera a basic, tame, musical score generally lends harmonic support to soaring voices. With Wagner the orchestra churns, roars, soars, laments, sings; in other words, it participates, it becomes a partner within the dramatic or comic context of the score.

Having reached such an illustrious, elevated plateau, the composer felt lonely and almost isolated in its esoteric atmosphere. What better way to return and resume contact with the earth and life than by way of folk song. Those who embraced the folk song most eagerly were the Germans, who did so in near-veneration. Schubert, Schumann, Brahms, Wolf, Richard Strauss—all drew on German folk songs for their inspiration, as did Mahler in his song cycles and symphonies. Such use of folk music served another purpose: it helped restore earthiness to otherwise grandiose music. Again Beethoven had led the way. While his stentorian voice spoke of heroic battle, of the triumph of light over darkness, his spirit's flight was such that contact with the earth, with earthy excitement, joy and mirth, was never lost.

The contrasts and contradictions of the romantic era manifested themselves on other levels. After an undeserved hiatus of one hundred years, Bach was being "discovered" by the romantics. Mendelssohn's rendition, in 1829, of the St. Matthew Passion in a distorted, mutilated, romanticized version intended to "render it practical for the abilities of the performers" (according to Carl Friedrich Zelter) spurred the renaissance. Such total misinterpretation of the aims and spirit of Bach should not be considered surprising at a time when virtuosity had gained the upper hand—when "spirited" was more important than "spirit," when the chamber music of Mendelssohn, Schumann, and Brahms received only a respectful hearing while the masses flocked to the exhibitions of often outrageous virtuosity in orchestral, piano, or violin renditions and the names of Liszt, Paganini, Herz, Thalberg, Tausig, Sarasate, Vieuxtemps, and Wieniawsky drew large and insatiable crowds. Nowhere was the initial combination of gigantism and virtuosity more apparent than in Berlioz's music, for which he had fashioned the virtuoso orchestra.

If romanticism basically represented revolt against classicism, the generation gap was neither as deep nor the animosity as strong as the word "revolt" might indicate. Haydn, placid and pleasant, was tolerated with a tinge of envy. "Heavenly harmony resides in [Haydn's] sounds, so free of traces of boredom, so productive of gaiety, zest for living, [and] childlike joy . . . what a service he has thereby rendered, especially to the present age . . . when men are so seldom inwardly satisfied." Thus Schumann appraised "Papa Haydn," although he also patronizingly added that one could not learn anything new from the old master, who was "no longer highly interesting for the present day." His strict adherence to the form he had created, his high spirits and childlike wit, and, above all, the absence of "emotion" in his music meant that that music held only limited attraction for the romantic set. With Mozart the romantics were forced to be a bit more careful and selective in their judgments and utterances. They acknowledged in passing his music's beauty, polish, balance, and purity; his G-Minor Symphony, with its hollow-eyed pathos, was recognized as being "airy and graceful." But what aroused the romantics' interest was Mozart the dramatist, the man of the stage. Without any desire for deeper understanding, they often brushed past *Marriage of Figaro* and *Cosi fan tutte* but avidly fastened their sights on *Don Giovanni,* a malevolently romantic work which aroused their morbidly romantic emotions.

For Beethoven they built an altar and burned incense to the "liberator" of romanticism. To them that diminutive German with the lisp, the pockmarked face, the unkempt hair, the provincial manners, and the boorish behavior became the embodiment of everything romanticism stood for: mystic, rebel, revolutionary, liberator. Their pleasure was mixed, however, because Beethoven disturbed as well as roused with his drive, his often brutal force, and his wildly slashing innovations. His young contemporary, Schubert, was at first strongly critical of the older man. "His eccentricity unites the tragic with the comic, the pleasant with the repulsive, heroism with bluster, the saints with the harlequin . . . driving a man to distraction instead of leading him to love."

While Schubert later imitated Beethoven in form and instrumentation, he did not follow him unto the plateau Beethoven reached with the *Eroica* but preferred to remain in the calmer valleys of Haydn, Mozart, and the lyrical Beethoven. The gentler nature of Schubert abjured the highly dramatic and the grossly tragic. If melancholy or passion were plumbed in Schubert's late symphonies, it was done within a strictly Schubertian conception with still strong adherence to Vienna's classical image, tinged with a romantic lyricism far removed from Beethoven's earthshaking musical quakes. While in symphonic, piano, and chamber music Schubert had to serve his apprenticeship, he arose in the field of Lieder as fully clad as Pallas Athena from the head of Zeus. It was a field in which he was destined to become the first of a long line of romantic minstrels. Although under Salieri's tongue-lashing Schubert was to pursue the fata morgana of opera throughout his brief life, the Lied was the ideal vehicle for his romantic aspirations. As can be observed with other romantically disposed composers, Schubert lacked the ingredient which had emerged as one of the strongest attributes in Beethoven's creative life, as attested to in his sketch books: viz., the will, the power to rework what had been forged in the white heat of creation and, most of all, limit in space, in size, and in length what had emerged. Beethoven's inspiration did not flow nearly as freely as Schubert's; Beethoven had to wrest each theme, each phrase, from the giants who inhabited his soul. It was precisely his free-flowing, almost overflowing inspiration which undermined Schubert's creative powers and kept him from exercising tighter control.

But such control was not needed in the Lied. The poem's length provided the measure, the framework into which Schubert, beginning with his first song, poured his inventive melodic genius, surpassing in the process all the Lieder creations and creators who had preceded him. The marvel of Schubert's Lieder music is that it did not become the handmaiden of poetry or merely lend its harmonies to melting *bel canto.* Rather, the music became part of an artistic fabric complementing and enhancing the poetry, and in the process raising the poet's creation to new, heretofore undreamt of heights of artistic expression. The form, meanwhile, became the specific genre of expression of the romantic era, with Schumann, Wolf, Brahms, and Richard Strauss drinking deeply from Schubert's well.

Another member of the early Vienna romantic triumvirate succeeded in a field in which Beethoven failed magnificently and Schubert miserably —viz., opera. Carl Maria von Weber[5] succeeded in romantic opera because he appeared on the scene at the exact time at which Germany, weary of the predictable, artificial *bel canto* of Bellini and Donizetti, was tiring of foreign operatic products. The stage had held an early magic and charm for Weber, but it was not until 1820 that he fulfilled his calling with the first truly German romantic opera, *Der Freischütz,* which marked a total departure from the prevailing Italian repertoire. Others had attempted opera along the same lines, but Weber's romantic genius and penchant for the dramatic stage carried him through where others had failed. *Der Freischütz* proved to be not only the opera of the hour but the opening operatic work of the German romantic age, which was to culminate in the music dramas of Wagner. The mysticism so dear to German sentiments became musical reality in the Weber opera—it had the magical tension of the supernatural, the triumph of love, honor, and purity, the romantic rustling of the German oak forests. Its Berlin reception in 1821 was a veritable triumph.

Eighteen hundred twenty-three found Weber in Vienna and in the company of Beethoven and Schubert. Barbaja, the impresario of the prestigious *Kärnthnerthor* Theater, had commissioned an opera from Weber, for which the Vienna author Wilhelmina von Chezy provided the libretto. The opera, *Euryanthe,* failed, owing mainly to the inadequate libretto, and Weber went on to London, the success of his opera *Oberon,* and an early death.

---

[5] The "von" in Weber's name does not denote the customary aristocratic lineage, but was rather the result of his father's charlatanry. The older Weber added the "von" to his name in order to impress others in his devious dealings, and the son continued it, although without the father's devious intentions.

Another setback to the romantic movement could be observed in Vienna. Beethoven's unrelenting perfectionism so influenced the fields of symphonic and chamber-music writing (as was the case later with Wagner in the operatic field) that to escape it was virtually impossible. Thus imitation, conscious or unconscious, was inevitable. Some sought new ways, succeeded, failed. Mendelssohn proved the classical romanticist. Schumann strained toward a freer romanticism. Chopin deepened the piano's expressiveness, while Liszt widened its virtuoso potential. Berlioz sought virtuosity on the vaster scale of the orchestra.

In the music of Mendelssohn, neither the classical nor the romantic element disturbed the other, both being subject to grace and symmetry, even in passionate passages. Although Mendelssohn, too, could not escape Beethoven's symphonic influence, it was not the powerful Beethoven who pointed the way for Mendelssohn but rather the gentler one of the *Pastorale* and the Eighth symphonies, which found a romantic echo in the younger man. Berlioz, meanwhile, followed the passionate path of the *Eroica,* the Fifth, and the Seventh symphonies. The contrast between the two younger romantic masters becomes particularly obvious in their "titled" symphonies. While Berlioz in his *Harold in Italy* and *Symphonie Fantastique* became unabashedly programmatic, Mendelssohn, in his *Scottish* and *Italian* symphonies, follows Beethoven's lead.

Robert Schumann followed a different romantic path. A romantic revolutionary, he strove for novel sounds, a new form of originality within the legacy of the enlarged form bequeathed by Beethoven. Like Mendelssohn he was a pianist. But while for Mendelssohn the piano was a graceful virtuoso instrument, it became for Schumann a total means of expression, as it was to become for Chopin. Both Chopin and Schumann imparted a depth of romantic feeling into their piano compositions which stood in marked contrast to the shallow brilliance of Liszt and his school, as well as the older virtuoso creations of Weber.

Form actually became of less importance as romanticism grew. It could be diffused, as in Schumann's *Fantasies* and *Novellettes;* it could follow along established lines, as in his symphonies; or it could be sharply defined, as in his song cycles. Schumann, who started as a pianist and a composer for the piano, was in a sense fortunate that his pianistic career was forcibly ended owing to a self-inflicted "accident" to his hands.[6] Thus a benevolent fate all but drove him to composition, resulting, during his first year of marriage to Clara Wieck, in the creation of his First Symphony and a great number of Lieder. Already in his First Symphony (in

[6] It was on 14 June 1831 that Schumann informed his mother in a letter of a "strange misfortune." In an attempt to give his fingers greater individual dexterity in playing, he had invented a device consisting of a suspended sling in which he would hang one finger while practicing with the others. The result was a partial laming of his right hand which abruptly ended all dreams of piano virtuosity.

B-flat Major, the *Spring*), the romanticism is no longer *Tonmalerei* (tone painting) but is fully invested with romantic feeling within the context of its motto, *"Im Thale blüht der Frühling auf"* [Spring blooms in the valley]. Schumann was growing away from the clarity and purity of classicism, and he reached a new romantic high point in his Piano Concerto in A Minor. During the four years of its creation (1841–45), Schumann had turned a corner in his growth as a composer. While Mendelssohn wrote two "pretty" virtuoso concertos, presumably for his own use and in themselves a far cry from the classic, balanced beauty of his Violin Concerto, Schumann had opened the door to the great piano concertos of the nineteenth century. No longer was the solo instrument "featured" in the virtuoso sense of a Paganini, nor did it possess Mozart's limpid balance or Beethoven's dramatic dialogue. Instead the solo instrument became part of the musical fabric of the work—a bright thread within the fabric, interwoven in a way which created a new balance, a new romantic sense of expression, a new fusion within the concerto. The piano set the style and the pace: romantic and free-flowing but eschewing virtuosity.

Despite his avowed admiration for Beethoven, Berlioz was the one romantic symphonist who was to stray farthest from the classical mold. This was practically predestined by time, location, background, and penchant. The time was one of revolt, the location was French, the background Latin, the penchant Italian. Thus Berlioz's development as a romantic composer was farthest removed from the German (northern) form and formality of Beethoven. The titles of his composition alone—*Roman Carnival* (originally the overture to his opera *Benvenuto Cellini*), *Harold in Italy, Romeo and Juliet*—indicate Berlioz's fascination with Italy. In keeping with the aforementioned factors, the treatment of the (avowedly programmatic) subject matters is freer, the use and treatment of the orchestra bolder, than anything that had theretofore been composed. It tries the imagination to realize that such free, bold works as *Harold* and *Symphonie Fantastique* were composed within a decade after Beethoven. No longer does Berlioz hide behind the phrase "tone painting"; rather, he presents his vast narrative canvases with a consummate mastery of orchestral color. Schumann was both repelled and fascinated by Berlioz's music, calling him a "raging bacchant" and "that terror of the Philistines" in the same breath. But while he, the northerner, took exception to many facets of the music of the southerner, in his discussion of the *Symphonie Fantastique* he nonetheless exclaims:

> Berlioz must be heard; even a view of the score is not sufficient. . . . there are strange disguises that even the experienced ear cannot clearly imagine after the eye has merely seen the notes on paper. . . . the whole exerts an irresistible charm . . . despite the many things that are offensive and unfamiliar to the German ear. In each of his works Berlioz has proven dif-

ferent, has ventured into a new field. . . . he shines like a lightning flash but he also leaves a smell of brimstone behind him. . . . It seems as if the music wished . . . to raise itself to unrestrained speech, to a higher poetic kind of punctuation (as in Greek choruses, in the language of the Bible, in the prose of Jean Paul).

Schumann, *Neue Zeitschrift für Musik,* 1839

Franz Liszt's aforementioned position relative to program music followed different lines and arguments. Although he professed his belief in "renewal of music through its inner connection with poetry" and gave the world numerous compositions with poetic (programmatic) titles, he never intended to express the poetic thoughts per se. Instead he let his own penchant for the romantic flow freely, usually unencumbered by the poet's vision or by announced titles. By then the stream of music was about to divide, and Liszt was to become the instrument of such a division. We have already observed that symphonic structure and texture had become respectively larger and louder. At the same time, Liszt's fusion of music and art—the symphonic or tone poem—had given rise to twelve consecutive compositions by him in that genre.[7] The form subsequently rose to a position of great popularity with fellow composers and audiences alike— with composers because they could express a thought or a mood in concise form, and with audiences because they could enjoy a comparatively brief and supposedly meaningful composition (if the composer's programmatic notes were to be trusted and taken at face value) instead of yawning through often ponderous hour-long symphonies which had little to say. All of Europe welcomed the idea of the symphonic poem and followed Liszt's lead. The Bohemian Smetana wrote memorable and popular symphonic poems, as did the Russians Tchaikovsky, Rimsky-Korsakov, and Moussorgsky; the Frenchmen Dukas, Saint-Saëns, and Franck; Finland's Sibelius and Italy's Respighi.

If Liszt championed the fusion of the arts, there was one musical intellectual who totally disavowed it—the influential music critic of Vienna's *Neue Freie Presse,* Eduard Hanslick. Hanslick assessed the musical scene in general and Liszt's position in it quite realistically. From an admirer of Wagner, whose *Tannhäuser* he praised, Hanslick soon changed to become one of the most outspoken and eloquent critics of Wagner and Liszt and their neo-German school. Hanslick's major musicological contribution, *Vom Musikalisch Schönen* [On the beautiful in music], was to be decisive in bringing to awareness the cleavage in music in the romantic era. In polemicizing against Liszt's vulgar emotionalism and bombastic musical rhetoric in his crude attempts at fusion of the arts on the one hand, and against Wagner's "music of the future" and "endless melody" ("formlessness exalted to a principle") on the other, the conservative

---

[7] To be followed by a thirteenth in Liszt's old age.

Hanslick reminded the romantic movement of his day that music within itself cannot express precise or definable emotions or thoughts, and that to express feelings such as anger, despair, hate, love, or pity was totally beyond Liszt's pretentious and artificial proclamations. He thus sought to restore music to its original conception as an artistic entity sufficient unto itself, which takes on additional extramusical meaning only because the composer so wills and indicates it and the public is willing to accept it as such. It was thus to a great extent Hanslick's polemics which bared to full view the basic cleavage within the Western musical world, with Berlioz, Liszt, Wagner, and Wolf on one side and Schumann, Mendelssohn, Chopin, and Brahms on the other (and with Bruckner somewhere in between, he having accepted Wagnerian sonorities into his giant but unquestionably romantic symphonies).

Anton Bruckner, to whom we will address ourselves at length later, remained an anachronism throughout his life. Although he pursued the concept of pure, absolute music (as did Brahms) and made use of the tonal sonorities of Wagner (which incurred him the wrath of Brahms and Hanslick and the admiration of Mahler and Wolf), Bruckner intuitively set himself apart as a throwback into an earlier period. In an era which had witnessed the emergence and crystallization of musicology and music criticism, participation by the composer in the literary, artistic, and political life of his time, Bruckner remained the untutored composer, uninterested in all phases of life and art. He continued into the nineteenth century the by then outmoded form of the Mass, which retained vitality only because of his deeply religious spirit which pervaded it. Yet there can be no doubt that the sweeping spirit of the romantic age dominates his music as well as an aura of the mysticism of the noble fool, the provincial Parsifal, as the splendor of Bruckner's sonorities attests to a true spirit of genuinely felt romanticism, worlds apart from the bombast of Liszt.

Like Bruckner, Brahms was also isolated in his time, but in a different sense. While Liszt broke with the symphonic past and dealt mainly in images, while Wagner broke with the operatic tradition in creating his music dramas, Brahms ignored opera and derided "program" images. Whereas Wagner (successfully) and Liszt (less so) explored new frontiers, Brahms reached back into the classical period for inspiration, for he saw his role as that of a nineteenth-century continuation of the classical tradition, a position which endeared him to the conservative Viennese. He had not always seen himself that way; as a young man his romanticism had been fostered and influenced by the older Schumann, under whose influence he came for a while. But already with his opus 15, his Piano Concerto No. 1 in D Minor, Brahms veered into the classical orbit, although near-pathological fear was to prevent him for nearly twenty more years from attempting a symphony. (Until then his only forays into the symphonic field were his two Serenades, opus 11 and 16.) Yet the struggle between the classicist and the romantic in Brahms never ceased. The classicist in him caused him to settle permanently in Vienna, while the summers saw him roaming through Europe, the hallmark of the romantic. The classicist in him venerated the structure of Bach, the controlled passion of Beethoven, the clear directness of Schubert; the romantic delighted in the folk songs of Germany, the folk music of Hungary, the waltzes of Vienna. Alfred Einstein (*Music in the Romantic Era*) sees Brahms as having been dominated by "the perception of the greatness and unaffected happiness of the past, the sorrowful renewal of this happiness and the resignation of the man born too late."

It was the desire to uphold and perpetuate the greatness of the past which prompted Brahms to sign (together with his friend, the violinist Joseph Joachim, and others) the ill-timed *Manifesto* against neo-German music in general and Wagner in particular. By the time Brahms and Wagner met in Vienna in the home of a mutual friend, the face of music had changed. Already in 1834, Liszt had stated: "Art has left the heart of the temple and, broadening out, has had to seek in the outside world the stage for its noble manifestations." Owing to tendencies previously touched upon, as well as to the apparatus demanded by "new" compositions, music had moved out of the church. Where the church had once been the fitting setting for the musician, such a setting no longer sufficed (except for Bruckner). No longer could its spiritual or physical confines accommodate the composer and his work. Instead, it was the opera house and the concert hall which became the workshop, experimental proving ground, presentation forum, and battlefield for the composer.

Again Beethoven had shown the way. His *Missa Solemnis,* no longer a solely spiritual work dedicated to the church, had physically outgrown church performance, as had Berlioz's *Requiem* (which was not even spiritually linked to the church), with its aggregate apparatus of a gigantic orchestra, (110 strings, 16 timpani, four brass bands, a solo tenor, and a mixed chorus of hundreds of voices).[8] The same held true for Rossini's *Stabat Mater,* Brahms's *German Requiem,* and Verdi's *Requiem.*

In opera also a vast change had taken place: no longer was it primarily a vehicle for patrician amusement. Mozart's *Magic Flute* had already moved into Schikaneder's *Theater an der Wien,* and with Beethoven, Weber, and Rossini, opera became a vehicle for the masses. Wagner was to provide the German romantic capstone with his music dramas, irrevocably ending the tradition of the set *recitativo*/aria sequence and supplanting it with a totally new, structured work. Its "endless melody," mingled with the lavish orchestral sound, was so penetrating, so overwhelming that only few, Verdi and Moussorgsky among them, could es-

---

[8] Although both the Berlioz and the Brahms works were initially performed in churches.

cape its influence. Yet, as Hanslick observed, Wagner's art was an end, not a beginning.

However, in the last instance, the true spirit of romanticism, at least in the German context, did not repose in virtuosity, orchestral voluptuousness, or operatic splendor, but in the voice—or more specifically, in the Lied. Here the fusion of music and poetry was logical because it occurred naturally. The flood tide of the German Lied began with Schubert, who, as we have seen, emerged without groping, search, or development. With his first song creations, *Erlkönig* and *Gretchen am Spinnrade,* there emerged the accomplished master. Surprisingly, no great master appeared through Schubert's influence or shortly thereafter. Instead, Lied development had to bide its time until the advent of Schumann, who wrote blocks of song cycles filled with romantic light and fervor, as delicate as *Mondnacht,* as dramatic as *Die beiden Grenadiere.* After Schumann a stream of Lieder composers—Franz Abt, Robert Franz, Carl Loewe—was nurtured on German soil. Even Wagner expressed his admiration for Mathilde Wesendonck in *Five Poems for Female Voice.* Yet it seems that after Schumann the Lied was again biding its time until the advent of Brahms. In song Brahms left the classical pose and became the romantic, a mood which otherwise often escaped him. No phase of the Lied, be it an arrangement of a folk song or a song of medieval splendor or romantic exuberance, remained untouched by his thought and treatment.

Two diverse pillars of the German romantic age demand attention; Hugo Wolf and Richard Wagner, diverse in the sense in which their musical productivity progressed, yet kindred in spirit. If Schumann walked in the path of Schubert's song, although with intensified depth and sensitivity, and Brahms glorified folk song, the phenomenon of Wolf was remarkable for his versatility of song expression. True, Wolf was wholly bound up in the limitations of the Lied. Symphony and opera were beyond him, but within the realm of the Lied he proved himself a master. Like Schubert, all Wolf needed was a poem to stir his musical imagination. Once artistically aroused by Eichendorff, Goethe, or Mörike, he would retire into near seclusion and create song cycles in which the deep intensity of his own feelings gave rise to miniature masterpieces of grace, passion, and delicious humor. In the late years of his brief life, he was particularly attracted to Italian and Spanish texts. Their warmth, gaiety, and romanticism inspired him to write the *Italienisches* and *Spanisches Liederbuch* and that "opera of song," *Der Corregidor.*

The man whom Wolf idolized and in his critiques of Brahms constantly held up as the ideal composer—Richard Wagner—was of much tougher fibre than his disciple. In his earlier periods Wagner vascillated between romanticism and grand opera. With *Rienzi* he wished to outMeyerbeer Meyerbeer in a pompous and supposedly grand manner, after having unsuccessfully tried his hand in lighter operatic fare with *Die Feen* and *Das Liebesverbot*. Surprisingly it was not the milestones in German opera—Mozart's *Magic Flute*, Beethoven's *Fidelio*, or even Weber's *Freischütz* (generally considered the forerunner of German romantic opera) —that were the models in Wagner's basic operatic development but rather the late Beethoven in his most powerful, most dynamic expression, the Ninth Symphony. It was concomitant with Wagner's philosophical approach to opera to find that Beethoven's need for expression could no longer be satisfied by instrumental means alone.

Opera strategy and direction, particularly in libretto selection, caused much of Wagner's early confusion. Only slowly, step by step, did he turn to romantic mythology in *Der fliegende Holländer*, *Tannhäuser*, and *Lohengrin*. *Lohengrin* marks both an end and a beginning. On the one hand, the traditional time-honored insertion of the aria at given intervals begins to vanish with *Lohengrin*, the only remaining aria in that opera being the *Gralserzählung*. At the same time, *durchkomponiertes* (a German term for which there is no generally-accepted English equivalent but which is adequately translated as "continuously set." [Grove] ) music drama is waiting in the wings of Wagner's mind, coming to full fruition in *Der Ring des Nibelungen*. The aria disappears and "endless music" pervades as the role of the orchestra becomes integral and paramount in the development of the music drama (with only the *Leitmotif* acting as a roadsign) and the composer overwhelms the poet (despite claims by Wagner adherents declaring Wagner, the poet, to be the equal of Goethe and Schiller). The transformation which Wagner accomplished in opera was no hurried development, occupying twenty-six years as Wagner labored from *Das Rheingold* in 1853 to *Götterdämmerung* in 1874. Weaknesses are apparent (and Hanslick was quick to point them out), but in historical overview all of Wagner's musical innovations, in orchestration as well as orchestral involvement and staging, were romantic in the sense in which most of the German revolt against the established past—the classical in orchestral music, the Italian in opera—was romantically inspired.

But Wagner's churning mind, while evolving the style that was to revolutionize opera and while creating the *Ring* tetralogy (Wagner actually designated it as a trilogy and prologue) paid homage to the romantic spirit of the age with two more immortal masterworks in the Wagnerian romantic, neo-German conception: *Tristan und Isolde* (1857–59) and *Die Meistersinger von Nürnberg* (1862–67). *Tristan*, composed during and supposedly inspired by Wagner's affair with Mathilde Wesendonck,[9] must be considered the acme of all of his romantic efforts as, in inspired chromatic cascades, Wagner relates his own story of love and denial. How different is the concept of *Die Meistersinger*.

---

[9] Wrote Wagner to Frau Wesendonck on 21 December, 1861: "I shall be eternally grateful to you for the fact that I have written Tristan."

Only so incredible a genius as Wagner could have conceived two such divergent masterpieces in succession. There can be no question that *Meistersinger* is a totally romantic work, yet it is worlds apart from the seering neoromantic Germanism of *Tristan und Isolde.* While *Tristan* is universal in conception, *Meistersinger,* Wagner's only comic opera among his mature works, is devotedly, lovingly German, in the tradition begun by Weber's *Freischütz.* Few tragic tones are heard; no eternal conflicts cry out for redemption. Wagner cannot laugh freely—satire, at least, must be injected—but on the whole the German heritage is emphatically, romantically, joyfully portrayed, uniting baroque conception and lavishly romantic settings and music.

Finally, in the last stage of his life and at the end of the romantic era, Wagner speaks, nearly preaches, in *Parsifal,* of religion, compassion, and beauty. *Parsifal* is the musical sublimation of the mysticism of the church.

At this point romantics of many lands come to mind: Paganini, the romantic fiddler; Chopin, the romantic of the piano, who extended its limits into the inner spheres, worlds removed from Liszt's pseudoromantic virtuosity; Verdi, the Italian antipode of Wagner; the Slavic nationalists (Borodin, Moussorgsky, Smetana, Dvořak), who enriched Europe's romantic musical repertoire with their own brand of lavish orchestration, reflecting oriental infusion as well as vivacious or melancholy melodies and rhythms. But they bear lesser reference in these chapters, which were intended to bear witness to the musical legacy to which Mahler fell heir.

## ANTON BRUCKNER

We recoil in horror before the rotting odor which forces its way into our nostrils from the dissonances of this putrefactive counterpoint. Bruckner's imagination is so incurably sick and unhinged that such a thing as rules in chord progressions and sectional structure simply do not exist for him. Bruckner composes like a drunkard.

Gustav Dömpke, *Wiener Allgemeine Zeitung,* 22 March 1886

Everything flows planless, disorganized, and violent into hideous length. . . . It is not impossible that the future belongs to such a nightmarish caterwauling style, a future which we therefore do not envy.

Eduard Hanslick, *Neue Freie Presse,* 23 December 1892

Mahler's feelings for Vienna were not dissimilar to those of Wagner. Wagner longed for and loved Viennese performances of his operas; yet he derided Johann Herbeck's efforts, which made them possible. He pressed for Viennese performances even though he encountered there the most outspoken, the most vitriolic, and incidentally, the most intelligent critic of his work, Eduard Hanslick. He loathed the city but could not do without its singers. In Vienna Wagner also found his most tenacious antagonist, Johannes Brahms; his greatest interpreters, Hans Richter and Gustav Mahler; and his greatest disciple, Anton Bruckner.

Although he embraced Wagner's musical idiom, Bruckner was never a man of his time. Yet the miracle that was Bruckner must be comprehended to understand the miracle that was Vienna, to understand that period of Mahler's youth. In Bruckner there was embodied and blended, truly through the grace of God, the splendor of Baroque, the Schubertian Austria, and the grandeur that was Wagner, all buttressed by his faith. Max Graf vividly describes Bruckner, whose lectures he attended:

> All of us greeted the old musician by solemn trampling [a sign of respectful applause] . . . much to Bruckner's joy. He wore his Upper Austrian loose jacket of homespun fabric. His big head was close shaven, and innumerable wrinkles furrowed his face. . . . I stopped smiling when I saw his face, humble and blissful . . . refulgent with celestial light. . . . From a nearby church the *Angelus* sounded, and when that little bell rang, Bruckner interrupted his lecture, knelt down, and began to pray. . . . I have seen hundreds in ecstatic prayer, but I have never seen anyone pray as Anton Bruckner did. He looked to be transfigured, illuminated from within. He looked like an aged saint. . . . Having finished his prayer, Bruckner stepped up to the music blackboard on the wall, and began his lecture.
>
> Max Graf, *Legend of a Musical City*

His earliest environment, St. Florian, a magnificent monastic Baroque edifice in Austria with a majestic organ, was to put its stamp on the young schoolmaster. One characteristic of Bruckner was to transmit itself strongly to both Mahler and Schönberg—the use of folk song in their compositions, perhaps an expression of a yearning to belong to a romantic past they were destined to leave behind. Bruckner saw no discrepancy in including these charming folk dances in the scherzos of his Baroque musical edifices, their slow-footed round dance rhythm contrasting oddly with the massive orchestral sound of the rest of the work. Another, no less significant, influence made itself felt in Bruckner's life. The musical world of Johann Strauss was by no means far apart from that of the symphonic giants. Bruckner was Strauss's personal friend, and Strauss was one of his few supporters when Bruckner's music was cynically derided. Wagner loved the music of Strauss and was not above incorporating a waltz into *Parsifal*. Liszt enthusiastically played Strauss, and Mahler performed *Die Fledermaus* while still in Hamburg.[10]

---

[10] Operetta played an important part in the life and livelihood of the neo-Viennese school. In their younger years, Mahler and Zemlinsky, much to their disgust, conducted operettas in summer theaters in order to stay alive, and Schönberg copied and orchestrated hundreds of pages of Viennese operettas for the same reason.

The infectious charm and lyricism which pervades the waltz at its peak, under the reign of Johann Strauss the younger, had been part of the Vienna scene long before Strauss. It actually had been Schubert who introduced the waltz into Viennese music. Schubert had remained untouched by Beethoven's sense of drama. Instead he made his symphonic creations, structurally molded after Beethoven, into truly Viennese lyrical/romantic creations. Whereas Beethoven had enlarged the symphonic form, Schubert loosened it. It was melody—an ingredient so abundantly present in Schubert—that mattered, and symphonic form became an elastic, adjustable feature of secondary importance.

The miraculous continuity of the Viennese school is exemplified in the career of **Simon Sechter**. The musical creations of Sechter are negligible. And the fact that he religiously composed a complicated fugue each day remains no more than a historical curiosity. Today, as in Schubert's day, Sechter's fame rests primarily on the fact that he was a scholar and teacher of counterpoint; and his greatest claim to glory rests in his connection with the names of Schubert and Bruckner. Schubert at his creative peak visited Sechter to arrange for lessons in counterpoint, but death interfered after one lesson. Bruckner became one of Sechter's last pupils. Just as Johann Josef Fux, the prolific master of the eighteenth century, had passed on his polyphonic heritage to bloom again in Sechter, so Sechter had transmitted the Viennese tradition to his pupils Schubert and Bruckner; it later found an echo in Mahler's style and Alban Berg's *Lyric Suite*. Other prominent musicians, Lachner and Nottebohm among them, were proud to call Sechter their teacher. Thus Schubert, Sechter, Bruckner, and Mahler constitute, in **Felix Salten's** words, a "living entity" (*Wien und die Musik*).[11]

Thus romanticism along with Baroque, *joie de vivre* along with piety and pessimism, lyrical song along with dramatic tempest continued side by side in unbroken continuity in what Schönberg called "our hated and loved Vienna." Bruckner's contribution to continuity was accidental yet important because, despite Wagnerisms, Bruckner, in every possible sense, lived in the past. Both Brahms and Bruckner, living to the threshold of the twentieth century, reached back into the past, yet the differences between them were enormous and significant. First of all, Brahms took an interest in the world about him; he collected musical manuscripts, he read, he followed politics. Musically Brahms reached back to the classics in general and Beethoven in particular. Bruckner, mentally fossilized, took no interest in the world about him. His concerns ranged between the narrow confines of fear of Hanslick, Brahms, and Richter on the one hand and religion on the other. While the companions of Brahms con-

---

[11] It would be a total misunderstanding of such continuity to construe it as conformity, however. Mahler's counterpoint is far removed from Sechter's and even further removed from Fux's.

sisted of the social and artistic elite of Vienna—the composer Goldmark, the sculptor Tilgner, Johann Strauss, the pianist Grünfeld, the surgeon Billroth, the critic Hanslick—Bruckner was alone save for his disciples, who pulled him musically hither and yon to "improve" his works; and sundry damsels young enough to be his grandchildren, with whom he was adolescently infatuated. Musically Bruckner reached farther back than Brahms; he was—another anomaly—a Baroque composer writing at the end of the nineteenth century. Yet there can be no doubt that Bruckner, together with Mahler, formed a mighty link in the chain leading to the neo-Viennese school.

Bruckner, the timid schoolmaster, was destined to return to his birthplace in death. He is buried under the mighty Baroque organ in the abbey of St. Florian. This was as it should be, because his voice of expression was not the heavy Austrian accent of the provinces, with which he lectured, but the voice of the organ of St. Florian, through which he spoke with authority and eloquence. Bruckner had come to Vienna upon the urgent advice of Vienna's then most influential musician, the conductor Johann Herbeck, but despite his consummate knowledge Bruckner faced only setbacks and defeat, which, coupled with his lack of belief in himself, brought him to the brink of a nervous breakdown. His only accomplishment in Vienna was the attainment of a lowly position at the university as instructor in counterpoint—not a main subject in the curriculum of the institution, but an elective to be studied by future musicologists. In his limited sphere of musical development, Bruckner infused the Schubertian heritage with an organist's splendor, injecting folk dances into his symphonies, but raising them to a level which was uniquely his own, and combining naive early romanticism with Wagnerian sophistication.

Bruckner the man presented a father image to the young Gustav Mahler. Mahler may have subconsciously yearned for it, because his own father, not particularly sensitive to begin with, had to attend to the needs of a total of eleven children and thus worried about Gustav only in times of urgency. Bruckner, though he grew slowly to maturity (in matters of relationship between the sexes he remained a juvenile throughout life), was quick to appreciate the budding genius in young Mahler. Despite an age difference of thirty years, a friendship developed. Musically their relationship developed along the lines of that between Beethoven and Haydn. The fermenting mind of Beethoven had rejected the conservative objectives of Haydn: "Haydn taught me nothing." But a basic sense of respect for Haydn's achievement never deserted Beethoven, and when he was congratulated on his Mass in C he replied: "It is no *Creation*," alluding to the monumental oratorio of the then aged Haydn. Mahler's position vis-à-vis Bruckner developed along similar lines. Although he presented Bruckner's compositions in splendid concert performances, he became disillusioned with Bruckner's rigidity.

Yet, considered in his historical context, Bruckner appears less of an anomaly. He was born in the last years of the Emperor Franz [1768–1835], in a period in Austrian history characterized by Ernst Decsey in *Bruckner, eine Lebensgeschichte* as "medievalism grown old and gray, fearfully shut off from Europe, held motionless in intellectual stagnation." Since all views from the outside world were barred, people sought diversion in scandal and gossip, and in whatever oddities could be glimpsed through the censor's curtain. Bruckner was no exception. Although he never exhibited any awareness of matters of state, or of international politics and diplomacy, he took an exaggerated and agitated pleasure in the morbid events of the day; the exhuming of Beethoven's remains for reinterment in a grave of honor, the return of Emperor Maximilian's body from Mexico. Thus Bruckner reflected the anachronistic petrification of Emperor Franz far more than the relaxed liberties espoused by Emperor Franz Joseph.

Bruckner's mental horizons were not raised when the autocratic Emperor Franz died and the 1848 revolution subsequently dispensed with Metternich, and the mentally feeble and epileptic Ferdinand ascended the Habsburg throne. Instead, reactionary forces, abetted by the court *Camarilla* (the reactionary court party) and the entrenched Jesuits' religious teachings, brought on an even tighter reign. With the revolution clubbed into temporary submission in Vienna and the Italian, Hungarian, and Bohemian provinces and the *status quo ante bellum* supported by the strongly Catholic middle and peasant classes, repression soon reigned rampagingly. Bruckner, though, did not have to face challenges from censor or police; his devout Catholicism assured him a life free from authoritarian pressure, intimidation, or threat. In that sense he was more fortunate than even Johann Strauss, whose early, mild enthusiasm for the revolution remained suspect for many years and whose operettas occasionally ran afoul of the censor. All those who, purposely or accidentally, left the narrow artistic path delineated by the regime promptly felt the wrath of the imperial censor. None suffered more than Austria's greatest poet, Franz Grillparzer, although he had openly declared: "My devotion to Austria is part of my being." Yet Grillparzer nevertheless felt the brunt of the impossible relationship between author and censor. When he inquired of the censor, whom he knew personally, why his play *König Ottokar's Glück und Ende* had not been released for two years, the censor admitted that he personally had kept the play from being performed. When Grillparzer inquired as to what the censor had found objectionable, dangerous, or subversive, the censor enigmatically replied: "Nothing at all—but I thought: after all, one cannot be sure." Thus each censor, each police official, was a power unto himself, beyond reproach or recourse.

Unsurprisingly, music did not escape the censor's wrath either, and Wagner, a political as well as musical revolutionary, was a logical target.

The *Hofoper* was unable to stage *Tannhäuser* because the censor considered the lewdness of the ballet unfit for virginal Vienna's eyes and ears. So much had censorship become a part of Viennese life that Eduard Hanslick could innocently declare:

> After the storm of the revolutionary years had abated and peace had returned . . . the ardent desire for relief and reconstruction through art, and the need for music and the theater, began once more to be felt.
>
> Hanslick, *Musik in Wien, 1848–88*

Artistically as well as politically, democratic premises and promises had again become empty illusions as the "normalcy" of censorship and repression was restored. Another aspect of that "reconstruction through art" should be illuminated. Until the advent of Brahms, Bruckner, and Mahler, Vienna, in a hiatus between musical waves of genius, filled its musical paunch with the worst kind of virtuoso trash available. Chopin was brushed aside: "He plays with none of the dash and daring which generally distinguish the artist," remarked a Viennese newspaper. A similar fate befell Schumann. Only toward the middle of the century, through the founding of the Vienna Philharmonic by Otto Nicolai in 1842, the reconstitution of the Vienna Conservatory, and the appearance of dedicated musical minds such as the Hellmesberger family, was an element of depth in music introduced in Vienna. The outstanding musical achievements of Johann Herbeck as well as those of Hans Richter have been discussed in a previous chapter. It should be noted, however, that Hanslick's observation sheds light also on another aspect of Vienna's musical history —the preference for the conservative element. It was that preference which made Vienna and its conservative spokesmen, Hanslick and Richter, take Brahms to their hearts, but revile Bruckner and Wolf. It says much about Vienna's prevalent conservatism that Schumann remained unperformed in Vienna as late as 1859, although he had been honored throughout Germany for twenty years, while Bruckner was, at best, ignored.

It was regrettable that Bruckner entered Vienna at an inauspicious time, a time of conflict. One is reminded of the entrance of Mozart into Paris at the most ferocious time of the Gluck–Piccini "war." In the ensuing uproar, Mozart was left to cool his heels during the Parisian winter in the antechambers of Paris nobility. Bruckner suffered an even worse fate. To be ignored was bad enough; to be drawn into the conflict was disastrous. The conflict this time was, of course, again one of ideologies: Wagner versus Brahms. The battlefield was Vienna, the time 1864. The situation had become extremely tense. After a magnificent *Lohengrin* performance in 1861, *Tristan* was dropped by the Vienna Opera as a result of intense intrigue. The war of nerves and politics was fed by Vienna's most influential critic and Wagner's most literate adversary, Hanslick.

The fact that Hanslick was also a great friend of Brahms only tended to compound a difficult situation.

Despite the tense atmosphere, fueled by Hanslick's acrimony and Wagner's disparaging remarks directed at Brahms and Hanslick, Brahms fully appreciated the opera composer. Richard Specht, the Vienna music critic, recalls Brahms's comment: "I once told Wagner that I am the best Wagnerian alive. Do you think that I am so narrow-minded that I cannot be charmed by the gaiety and greatness of *Die Meistersinger?* Or so dishonorable as to keep it a secret that I think that a few measures of his work are worth more than all the operas written since?" That amazing lack of personal animosity on the part of Brahms is also borne out by Hanslick. "Often I heard him [Brahms] defend Wagner vigorously. . . . He knew and appreciated fully the brilliant aspect of Wagner, while Wagner speaks with but little respect for Brahms." But disciples and protagonists on either side could not be stilled, and the tension grew beyond détente or reconciliation.

This was the atmosphere in Vienna into which Bruckner entered in 1868, at the age of forty-four. Of course Vienna was not new to Bruckner. For six years he had diligently traveled between St. Florian and Linz, later between Linz and Vienna. We have no inkling of whether he liked the city. In Bruckner's peculiarly isolated state of mind, he seems not to have been stirred by the beauty of the Baroque city. Musically it was the heritage of Haydn, Mozart, and Beethoven, and practically the urging of Herbeck and the presence of Sechter, which had prompted the many wearisome journeys to and his eventual taking up of residence in Vienna. Otherwise Bruckner's intellectual aspirations and contacts were nil; as a result, his integration into the life of the city was, on any level, totally absent.

The question then remains—Who influenced whom? Did the city, with all its charm, exert a power on the composer? We think not. It will be more important, we think, to ascertain what influence Bruckner may have exerted musically on Vienna, on his contemporaries, and on the musical generation to follow. For years, before Bruckner's arrival, there had been two connections between Bruckner and Vienna, one tenuous, one strong: the advice and encouragement of the conductor Johann Herbeck, who eventually prompted Bruckner to move to Vienna, on the one hand; and the teachings of Sechter. From available material we must realize the importance of the link which Sechter represented. When Schubert realized that "for the first time I now see where I am lacking and how much I have yet to learn," he turned to Sechter, who was then forty years old and had already acquired a reputation as one of the foremost theorists of his time. When Bruckner moved to Vienna Sechter was already dead one year, but in the six years prior to Bruckner's move, Sechter had implanted in him, through correspondence and lessons, many of his ideas about music theory. So firmly were Sechter's teachings on harmonic root progressions implanted in Bruckner's mind that they were to constantly show up in his symphonies, which Hanslick was to point out again and again with vitriolic glee.

Brahms's position in Vienna, on the other hand was serene and secure. Bülow's reference to the "Three B's" had ensured that Brahms's position was fortified beyond the reproach of his contemporaries. Vienna had found Brahms harmonically less venturesome and thus easier to digest and absorb. His works also conformed to the length established by Beethoven and thus required no additional concentration beyond that afforded symphonies of "established" length. Brahms saw himself as the keeper of the classical tradition, but he also represented, and knew that he represented, the sunset of that tradition.

Bruckner's position in musical history is still less firmly established than Brahms's. He maintained the classical form but extended it to an unheard-of length, uncomfortable for the Vienna of his day. He adored Schubert's lighthearted Austrian spirit but was incapable of expressing it, except for deliberate Austrian insertions into his symphonic scherzi. He was an apostle of Wagner, whose extended sounds he adapted to the orchestra, but he also punctiliously applied Sechter's strict counterpoint. He knelt at Bach's altar yet was a votary of Wagner. All of these contradictions were, of course, the result of accumulation over a number of years. (We avoid the term "development," in that, unlike composers like Haydn or Mozart, who developed musically in the course of writing symphonies, Bruckner showed no further development after his symphony No. 1.)

Hanslick, surprisingly, looked at Bruckner's initial conservatism benignly. Bruckner's subsequent alignment with Wagnerian expression had curious consequences: Hanslick, for one, furiously forgot about all of Bruckner's conservatism in the light of his Wagner adulation. Vienna's musical youth, on the other hand, enthusiastically sided with Bruckner because of his Wagnerian leanings, ignoring, in turn, Bruckner's strong conservative ties with the past. But it was Hanslick who had the ear of the public as the music critic of *Die Neue Freie Presse*. Thus the public was informed only of Bruckner's efforts to destroy the classical form, of the corroding Wagnerian influence on his work, and of his "dry formalism" as compared with Brahms, the composer of classical proportions and heir to the mantle of Beethoven.

Similar accusations were to be leveled against Mahler, particularly as far as form was concerned, by some who seemed shocked at Mahler's reckless, relentless innovations. Such critics were either ignorant of or chose to ignore the fact that the ingredients of Mahler's innovations had all been employed before. Expansion in length had been explored by Schubert and Bruckner, expansion in movements by Beethoven and Berlioz, polyphony by Bach and Fux, and the inclusion of voices by Beethoven. It was the novel use of these devices which ensured for Mahler his unique place in history. The further Mahler moved from Beethoven in the use of his material, the more his unique style and genius become apparent.

One constant criticism of Mahler pertained to his use or rather misuse of themes, and to their lack of development. Much had been made in musicological analysis of the relative importance and proper position of main and secondary, male and female, and assertive and lyrical themes. Again, changes in Mahler's symphonies with regard to continuity of themes and succession of movements were not new. Schubert had already exploded the myth of the greater importance of the main theme in his B-Minor symphony. Compared with the secondary theme of the first movement, given over to the celli, the first theme in the oboe shrinks into insignificance. Of course, Schubert was not the equal of Beethoven as far as the effective use of themes was concerned, because Beethoven was unsurpassed in this regard, particularly with respect to the terseness and brevity of his themes. Only Tchaikovsky comes to mind in equal thrift concerning the use of themes. Just as Beethoven's opening signature in his Fifth Symphony is a shining example both of the utmost brevity and of ingenuity of development, so Tchaikovsky's folk-tune theme in the fourth movement of his F-Minor symphony is a marvel of simplicity and brevity.

Bruckner, like Schubert, did not have that gift of gradation and variation in repetition and development so ingeniously displayed by Beethoven and Tchaikovsky. It was left to Mahler to take as simple and naive a theme as *"Frère Jacques"* and raise it, in his First Symphony, to the proportions and sinister implications of a relentless funeral march. There exist many examples attesting to the difficulty of development of an extended theme, regardless of its position within the symphonic structure. An extended theme may and usually does become an entity in itself, so well rounded, so complete, that it resists variation and development. Depending on the composer's intentions (and ability), this may become a dilemma, as in the Schubert theme just mentioned; a tedium, as with Bruckner; or deliberate, as with Mahler, the difference being that with Schubert and Bruckner we have a minor dilemma overcome—in Schubert's case by melodiousness, in Bruckner's by overpowering grandeur—while with Mahler it amounted to an innovative change of style. Thus, while with Mahler the symphony in its most extended form (if it can still be called a symphony at all), was maintained, the style and with it the spirit of the work underwent profound changes. Historical similarities of form were ended in all but name. Just as the sonatas of Handel and Beethoven had nothing in common but the name, so the symphonies of Mahler no longer bore any resemblance to the symphonies of Haydn, Mozart, or even Beethoven.

To understand the musical paradox of Bruckner one must realize the nature of the man and his activities. Thanks to Sechter, Bruckner's occupation with theory, harmony, and counterpoint was pervasive. It became important to him not only to know these subjects in consummate fashion but to prove to himself, over and over again, that this was the case. Thus he constantly, compulsively submitted to qualifying exams which were regularly given in Vienna. At one of them in 1861, Bruckner so impressed the examining panel of Hellmesberger, Dessoff, and Sechter (whom Bruckner was to succeed as teacher of theory) with his theoretical knowledge that Hellmesberger exclaimed to his colleagues: "He should have examined *us*. If I knew half of what he knows I'd be happy." Yet such mastery tended to make Bruckner its prisoner, all but forcing him to hold without deviation to the theory he learned from Sechter. How different to observe the genius of Schönberg, who could teach classical theory and even publish a *Harmonielehre* (harmony manual) at a time when he had already left behind the Elysian fields of classical harmony and tonality. Bruckner, on the other hand, could at no time extricate himself from Sechter's meticulous teachings; he faithfully applied Sechter's dicta and saw fit to pass them on, in turn, to his students. How strong the influence of Sechter's concepts had been on Bruckner may be gleaned from the fact that he remained rockbound within them even after having entered Wagner's harmonic realm. Through such near-religious steadfastness was Bruckner able to communicate Sechter's principles to such students as the composer Camillo Horn, the conductor Franz Schalk, and his disciple Gustav Mahler.

What added to Bruckner's being an anomaly in his time, aside from his speech, behavior, dress, and musical principles, was his position with respect to his faith. Bruckner's Catholicism was total, so absolute that it permeated not only his life-style but also his work. Despite his admiration for Wagner, the Mass occupied a position within his thinking and creation totally out of context with its diminished importance in his time. Yet, as so often, Bruckner went against the tide to such an extent that it is often assumed that his religious music assumed greater or at least equal importance in Bruckner's mind vis-à-vis his symphonic creations. Therefore, when he suggested that his *Te Deum* be added as a finale to his Ninth Symphony should he be unable to finish it, this can be interpreted only as an act of faith and not, as assumed by some, as an imitation of the choral finale of Beethoven's Ninth Symphony, as much as Bruckner admired that work. Brahms, although not nearly as devout as Bruckner, felt the urge to write a spiritual work but could not reconcile his spiritual feelings with the tightly controlled text and spirit of the Mass; thus, when he wrote the work that was to make him a figure of world stature over night, the *German Requiem,* he felt obliged to choose his own text. Long before Brahms, another young genius, Franz Schubert, in a rare show of artistic independence and defiance, had composed his first Mass, in F Major, to German texts of his choosing (hence the subtitle *Deutsche Messe*), paying only lip service to tradition by heading each part of the Mass with a Latin title. How closely the church attempted to control the music for its service can be gleaned from the fact that Gounod as late as the year 1855 was censored because he had added phrases to the text of his *Messe Solenelle* (St. Cecilia Mass) that were extraneous to the prescribed original text.

Despite the depth of his belief, Bruckner was unsuccessful in re-kindling a trend. Brahms's expression of faith was emotional rather than sacred. Mahler, despite his deep attraction to the mysticism of Catholicism, was incapable of writing a major religious work for two reasons: the spirit of the times and his religious heritage. The closest he would come to spiritual expression would be the inclusion of Klopstock's *Aufersteh'n* [Resurrection] into his Second Symphony and, of course, *Veni, Creator Spiritus*, the first part of his Eighth Symphony—to which Mahler often referred as his "Mass."

Yet Bruckner intuitively realized the viability of the Mass within its set pattern and put it to his own use. It is the beauty of the Ordinary [12] of the Mass that, within its unchanging text, it gives the composer full rein to create a sacred work of anywhere from half an hour to two hours' length. Bruckner, while in awe before the classical examples, adapted the form to his concept. Here we find a curious analogy between Bruckner and Schubert. Schubert, although fully aware of the classical symphonic examples, let his own symphonic creations occasionally lapse into near formlessness. On the other hand, in the creation of his Lieder he was constrained by the length of the poem to be set to music. Bruckner faced a similar dilemma. In enlarging the classical symphony he failed (if he ever intended) to create a new form, and only too often became enmeshed in repetition. However, in the Mass, benevolently confined by its text, Bruckner could enlarge without running the risk of formlessness. Thus, adhering to classical heritage he created a last flowering of the ancient sacred form in the nineteenth century. Yet, curiously, in that last glow of an art form which had dominated the scene for three hundred years, Bruckner again presented a paradox: a new, enlarged form of the Viennese classical Mass, endowed with the glowing splendor of a long-bygone Baroque.

[Bruckner] displays a splendor and brilliance in his orchestral and choral color contributions which is comparable to the glow of the glorious colors in Rubens's paintings. In this sense we recognize Bruckner's Masses [as]

[12] Of the two parts of the Mass, only the Ordinary, with its unchanging text, is usually set to music. The Proper, whose text changes daily, is chanted in time-honored Gregorian chant. Thus the musical listener actually hears only half a Mass.

. . . the direct descendants of the Viennese school. They correspond perfectly to the elaborately and imaginatively organized ceremonies of the Catholic service: altars shining in brilliant light, priests in gold vestments,
flying banners, incense, ringing bells, processions.

Max Amer, *Bruckner als Kirchenmusiker*

As the finest example of Bruckner's splendor and surprising drama one
might cite the *Resurrexit* from his Mass No. 3 in F Minor (*The Great*).
The altars were Viennese, but the service was medieval and the splendor
baroque.

In view of his literary noninvolvement and intellectual naiveté, it
must be considered one of the great musical achievements of Bruckner
that he could be attracted to the point of adulation to Wagner's musical
vision without becoming engulfed in Wagner's pseudoreligious trappings
—which, had Bruckner understood them, would have been abhorrent to
him. Thus *Parsifal* deeply affected Bruckner's musical sensibilities, while
he was totally oblivious to what Nietzsche termed "Christianity for Wag-
nerians." We may assume, therefore, that it was Bruckner's innate religious feelings that prompted him to stay free of the framework of the
stage; his "staging" remained within the altar area. His admiration for
Wagner did not lead him to follow that master into the realm of the
stage, where Bruckner would have proven himself innocent to the point
of disaster.

Yet, in his intuitive reaching out and groping for direction, Bruckner
did spadework for Mahler's ultimate total expansion of the classical/
romantic symphonic form. Thus a definite pattern of creation—expansion—
doom emerges within Vienna's musical history and the history of the
symphony.

| | |
|---|---|
| Haydn<br>Mozart<br>Young Beethoven | Emergence and perfection of the classical sym-<br>phonic style |
| Mature Beethoven<br>Schubert | Expansion to romantic length and emotional ex-<br>pression—Beethoven dramatically, Schubert lyr-<br>ically |
| Bruckner | Renewed enlargement of the classical form,<br>reaching in both directions; Bach and Wagner |
| Brahms | Broadening of the classical form within Vienna's<br>classical concepts |
| Mahler | Final total expansion, in harmony, length, tim-<br>bre, and structure, of the symphonic form |
| Schönberg | Negation of the Vienna classical concept; reten-<br>tion of romanticism and conscious use of Vien-<br>nese melodies |

Although Bruckner's deep religious convictions did contribute to his preoccupation with the Mass, the bulk of his work was, of course, devoted not to the church but rather to symphonic creation. In assessing Bruckner's creations and his position within the historical development of the symphony, we promptly run into a stumbling block: whether to consider him by consulting the *Originalfassung,* the original version or versions of a given symphony, or a revised version. A further dilemma arises: *Which* original or revised version? [13] Bruckner was often so unsure of himself and on the other hand so eager to please, that any suggestions for improvement or any adverse criticism after a performance would send him scurrying back to the manuscript for revision. And the complications do not end there. Which is the original, which the authorized, and which the final version? Where should the researcher turn if only revised editions exist because the original version or versions have mysteriously disappeared? When notations in a hand other than Bruckner's are observed, are they there by permission of the much-plagued composer or at the whim of the notator?

Beneath such problems lies the composer's humbleness of background, which was reflected in his attitude toward others and toward his own music. The former was characterized by almost constant bowing and scraping in the presence of others; the latter by intimidation disguised as vacillation or uncertainty. Bruckner never outgrew his provincialism, which made him an immediate target of ridicule and a constant outcast amidst the moribund sophistication of Viennese society.

The greatest offenses committed by Bruckner's friends in their attempts to "improve" his scores usually consisted of cuts made in the music in order to bring the performance time down to "manageable length." On the heels of these well-meant yet outrageous attempts followed a tampering with orchestration, a substituting of different textures of their own instead of the orchestral color intended by Bruckner. In one instance, Joseph Schalk had the temerity to inform his brother Franz on 10 January 1885:

> Recently I went over the score of [Bruckner's] Seventh Symphony with Löwe with regard to some changes and improvements. . . . Nikisch has insisted on the acceptance of our desired cymbal clash in the Adagio (C Major 6/4 chord) and also on triangle and timpani, which pleases us immensely.

In the face of such arrogance, the regrettable fact remains that neither the music nor its acceptance were enhanced. Here again, in the matter of orchestration, heritage is an influence worthy of consideration. Bruckner grew into the symphonic field from the organist's bench. This ac-

[13] For a detailed listing of original versions and revisions, consult H. F. Redlich, *Bruckner and Mahler,* pp. 42–43.

counts for his massive orchestration, in which he pits choir against choir in clear-cut fashion. That concept was often glossed over by Bruckner's "arrangers," a point which eventually began to annoy Bruckner, although he seems to have been too timid to object strongly to it. On that point it was the young Mahler who most respected the older composer's intentions. When Bruckner entrusted his young friend with the arrangement for the four-hand-piano score of his Third Symphony, in collaboration with his roommate and fellow musician Rudolf Krzyzanowski (and under Bruckner's and Epstein's supervision), Mahler did so without changing the structure, a respect seldom evinced by other coworkers. It was a relief for Bruckner to have found Mahler, because until then the brothers Schalk and Ferdinand Löwe had done the "arranging." They were destined for important roles, but in Bruckner's day they were aspiring conductors and Bruckner disciples. Yet their zeal was often misplaced, much to his silent despair.

All this makes it extremely difficult today for conductor and listener alike to plumb the "real" Bruckner, because in attending a Bruckner performance, conductor and listener may find themselves using different scores of the same work. The problem of revisions is compounded by the time factors involved. How is one to approach and assess the First Symphony, when the first version was composed in 1866, Bruckner's forty-second year, and the second in 1891, twenty-five years later! (In that regard, many a callous musicologist will assert that it really does not matter, on the shopworn ground that Bruckner wrote only one symphony—nine times.)

We further realize that Bruckner's First Symphony was actually preceded by two others, the *School* Symphony in F Minor of 1863 and the Symphony No. 0 in D Minor of 1863 (revised in 1869). These are never listed in official catalogs of his symphonies but must have given Bruckner some experience toward writing his First Symphony, even in its first, "Linz" version. Analogously, Brahms's two Serenades for Orchestra did contribute toward the conception of his First Symphony, which, incidentally, found Brahms at the same age as Bruckner was when he composed his First Symphony. Parallels between Bruckner and Brahms do not end there. Although Brahms's attempt at a first symphony was far superior to Bruckner's, the two composers' basic styles of symphonic form and expression are already clear in their respective first symphonic attempts.

The only times when Bruckner descends from his established ardor/passion/piety/exultation level of emotional expression are in his symphonic scherzi. There his roots in his Austrian heritage are most apparent, as he descends from the grandiose conceptions of his gigantic movements to the small-scale themes and tone pictures of the Austrian countryside. This pattern is evident in his first symphonic scherzo, and is brought to its highest level in the "Hunting" scherzo of his Fourth Symphony. The scherzi won Bruckner approval by the public for their melodiousness and by the musical world for their clarity. Even the bold trumpet in the scherzo of his Seventh Symphony was applauded.

Thus the position of Bruckner is remarkable in many respects, vis-à-vis Brahms on the one hand and Mahler on the other. Brahms represents a continuation of the North German heritage, sublimated through the music of his adopted Vienna—Beethoven and Schubert. Bruckner also emanates from Beethoven and Schubert; yet, while Brahms was destined to be the last of his line, Bruckner was to link, in his music, Beethoven and Schubert, blended with Baroque splendor and Wagnerian grandeur, to Mahler and the generation of Viennese masters to follow. The link from Mahler's side to Bruckner must also be acknowledged. Mahler's compositorial activity centered around the symphony, as did Bruckner's. On that point Mahler had, of course, a tremendous advantage in experience. While Bruckner's knowledge was mostly "book learning," Mahler created out of actual conducting experience and experimentation. A century earlier, a similar opportunity for freedom of experimentation had enabled Haydn to develop and establish a "Viennese tradition" of the classical symphony. It now helped Mahler to create the last, final, and total expression and expansion of postromantic symphonic form. Where Bruckner had succeeded merely in widening the form and superimposing Wagnerian harmonies with Baroque overtones upon an established style and tradition, Mahler's style emerges as totally his own.

# The Creations

## MUSICAL GROWTH

It is questionable whether Mahler can be considered a pupil of Bruckner, although he did attend Bruckner's university lectures. The definition "disciple" might be more apt, especially with respect to Mahler's younger years. Yet there can be no doubt that, despite their different backgrounds, ages, religions, and outlooks, there is a common bond in the creations of the two. Křenek put it into perspective best:

> Both composers have in common . . . a propensity for the monumental simplicity of fundamental themes, a sense of the magnitude of gesture. . . . The actual sphere of common interest for Bruckner and Mahler was undoubtedly their admiration for Wagner.
>
> Ernst Křenek, *Gustav Mahler*

Mahler's early admiration for Bruckner changed drastically in later years. But at age thirty-two he was still able to perform Bruckner with conviction and enthusiasm,

> Honored Master and Friend:
>
> Hamburg, 16 April 1892
>
> At last I am so fortunate as to be able to write to you that I have performed a work of yours. Yesterday (Good Friday) I conducted your splendid and powerful *Te Deum*. Not only the entire public but the performers as well were deeply moved by the mighty architecture and the truly noble ideas. . . . You would have been happy with the performance. I have seldom seen a group of performers work with such enthusiasm as yesterday. . . . Bruckner has now made his triumphal entry into Hamburg. I press your hand most heartily, honored friend, and I am, in the true sense of the word, *your*
>
> Gustav Mahler

Now that I have worked my way through Brahms, I have fallen back on Bruckner again. An odd pair of second-raters. The one in the casting ladle too long, the other one not long enough.

From Mahler's letter to Alma, June (July?) 1904

Twelve years later, however, as we can glean from Mahler's letter to Alma, he had outgrown that phase of adulation. What had happened in the interim was a period of artistic growth for Mahler. He had never been an admirer of the classicist Brahms and had outgrown most of Bruckner's simplism. Both had been giants of the nineteenth century and had died with the century (Bruckner in 1896, Brahms in 1897), while Mahler reached well into the twentieth century.

All I can say of [Brahms] is that he's a puny little dwarf with a rather narrow chest. Good Lord, if a breath from the lungs of Richard Wagner whistled about his ears he would scarcely be able to keep his feet. . . . It is very seldom he can make anything of his themes, beautiful as they often are.

From Mahler's letter to Alma, June (July?) 1904

The irritation which caused Mahler's petulant remarks on Brahms may have had its origin in Brahms's attitude toward the younger man—first manifested in Brahms's resentment of the pro-Wagnerian tendencies of the young Mahler (which lost Mahler the coveted Beethoven Prize in respect to *Das klagende Lied*), and subsequently expressed in the marked distinction made by him between Mahler the conductor and Mahler the composer. Thus, Brahms felt that Mahler's Mozart interpretations were the best he had ever heard; yet he dismissed Mahler's own symphonies as *Kapellmeister Musik* [Conductor's Music]. Still, when Mahler the conductor needed help in order to obtain a position in Vienna, Brahms spoke up on his behalf.

It is worth noting that just as Brahms, in disagreement, had been an admirer of Wagner, so Mahler appreciated some of the particular art of Brahms. Mahler, destined to become the Beethoven of his time as far as freedom of the spirit was concerned, was particularly taken by one of Brahms's most inspired yet most traditionally structured works of his middle period, the *Variations on a Theme by Haydn* (opus 56a). One can understand how Mahler was fascinated by the undercurrents of the composition: the freest of forms—variation—structured according to time-honored rules, the contrast between North-German formality and Viennese lightness. Neither is it surprising that Brahms's antagonist and Mahler's idol, Wagner, was equally impressed with a set of variations from Brahms's earlier period, the *Variations and Fugue on a Theme by Handel* (opus 24), and was moved to comment: "One sees what can still be done with the old forms in the hands of one who knows how to deal with them."

In 1824 Schubert had lamented to his friend Schober: "Sometimes I endure miserable days. . . . I sit here alone in the depths of Hungary— whither, alas, I have been lured without a single person with whom I can exchange an intelligent word." Fifty years later Mahler was to equally lament his sorrow and solitude, also from the "depths of Hungary." In both cases it had been a matter of livelihood to give piano lessons to members of families of Hungarian noblemen. While Schubert found eventual solace in his dalliance with the chambermaid on the premises, Mahler was already engulfed in the struggles and doubts that were to beset him throughout his life. If Mahler's utterances of that day seem exaggerated in their romantic wallowing, we must not lose sight of the fact that this impressionable youth was at a crossroads: still a product of a romantic era in whose strong grip he found himself, but already striving to extricate himself from that very influence on his path to a first plateau of early maturity. How many youths of eighteen could already point to having composed a complete opera, *Ernst von Schwaben* (later destroyed by the composer), or attain a romantic depth of feeling expressed in these lines:

> Oh my beloved earth, when, oh when, wilt thou take the abandoned one to thy breast? Behold, Mankind has banished him from itself, and he flees from its cold and heartless bosom to thee, to thee! Oh care for the only one, for the restless one, Universal Mother!

These lines, written on 18 June 1879 amid the mentally arid surroundings of Hungary, are of surpassing importance, as they forebode the spiritual world in which Mahler was to dwell to the end of his days. One need only to compare the above with the second song from *Das Lied von der Erde* (*Der Einsame im Frühling*, conceived thirty years later) to realize the mental maturity of the young Mahler. Of course Mahler's spiritual mold had not yet been cleansed of mental dross, had not yet attained the elevated spiritual level of 1909. Thus we find him wallowing in morbidity and dejection, in the company of like-minded friends such as Hugo Wolf and Hans Rott. In the long run, Mahler proved in many respects the strongest of the trio, with the other two dying in insanity.

That innate strength appears in particularly high relief when we realize that Mahler survived in the face of suicides and insanity, not only among close friends but within his own family. He emerged from an unhappy childhood with an uncaring, often ruthless father; from a tortuous first job away from home, which he endured with stoic impassivity; and, last but not least, from hunger and poverty—which did him lifelong physical harm—inured and toughened in spirit, even if hallucinations and melancholy were to be lifelong companions. All this he overcame or at least coped with and absorbed into his restlessly inquisitive mind and mysteriously charged creative processes.

As we have previously mentioned, Mahler had destroyed a number of his compositions, which, he felt, were below the standards to which he began to aspire.[1] A strong romantic bent was, of course, still part of Mahler's intellectual make-up. Thus, *Das klagende Lied* was a natural outgrowth of that thinking and that period at the end of the nineteenth century. It actually represented a major part of his early life. Having tested his earlier experiments or, in his opinion, his failure in them and having fanatically destroyed them, he found fruitful seed in *Das klagende Lied* because he not only preserved it (subject to later revision) but unquestionably we can find early signs of later works in it, indicating that Mahler, in *Das klagende Lied,* had found an early plateau from which to expand. From such romantic beginnings and classic elements, the desire for form, no matter how enlarged, made itself increasingly felt and brought conflict into Mahler, the composer's, world. In that concept the pronouncement of Schönberg including Mahler among the classical composers acquires new meaning. As Mahler matured and his visions and interests widened to include philosophical thought, religious concepts, and new poetic vistas, his musical conception grew from near-unbridled diversity into philosophically inspired channels, with the symphony becoming the structure most applicable to his visions. Thus attention to form began to take precedence over romantic content so that there would be a vessel in which to express his cosmic contemplations.

Yet romanticism persisted. If the sense of form of Beethoven was the guiding structural principle, the romanticism of Schubert and Bruckner, particularly in the early symphonies, is clearly and joyfully present. Neither is it surprising to encounter fantasy à la Berlioz, since Mahler intensely and fruitfully studied the Frenchman's wizardry of instrumentation and flaming romanticism. Thus Mahler's creative path suddenly took a direction into the symphonic field and into it he poured his very being. All that had preceded it, the love affairs and, more importantly, the melodies evoked by them, were now reflected and sublimated in his first symphonic creation and in three others to follow. It is significant in this context that the song theme of *Ging heut' morgen übers Feld* is heard in the first movement of the First Symphony. The sum and substance of his young life and experiences—of love and erotic consummation, of sorrow and rejection—are incorporated.

The *Wunderhorn* poems struck a similar chord. Intuitively an interrelation between song cycle and symphony had suggested itself for the Wunderhorn songs and Symphonies No. 2, 3, and 4, as it had been between *Lieder eines fahrenden Gesellen* and his First Symphony. Even if Mahler's fame rests today mainly on the strength of his symphonies, the

---

[1] This conclusion is being challenged by some musicologists who feel that Mahler simply lost interest in those compositions. Subsequently they fell into neglect and were lost. Bruno Walter, however, distinctly remembers and describes such a destruction of music by Mahler. (see page 259)

song cycles were an innate part of him as is witnessed by the fact that they occupied him for over two decades between 1880 and 1904. From then on Mahler was careful to establish a continuity among his symphonies, either in individual or cyclic progression. Surprisingly, the cohesion of the progression is one of philosophy, or emotion expressed in music. Thus the words in those symphonies (2, 3, 4, 8) of Mahler which contain vocal parts, do so almost incidentally because in the end it is less the spoken word than the emotion of the music which carries them, moves the spirit and conveys the message. Program music, in the sense in which Mahler's contemporary, Richard Strauss, indulged in it, was anathema to Mahler and words only incidentally served in support of emotion in music.

That romanticism and simplicity of the people, strongly influencing Mahler in his early years, were counterbalanced by the intellectual impact of Nietzsche and Goethe. The depth of Nietzsche's thinking, the conflicts he expressed, were so akin to Mahler's that they remained with him for much of his life. Musically Mahler also embraced Nietzsche, and the stark contrasts of calm splendor and orgiastic ecstasy in his music parallel Nietzsche's concept of the "Apollonian" and "Dionysian" aspects of life. So deeply was Mahler impressed with Nietzche's philosophy that he included an excerpt from his *Also sprach Zarathustra* in his Third Symphony.

In so sophisticated and complex a human being and composer, a binding musical/historical fact soon became apparent. The Danube style of music, the musical idiom of the provinces, established in the seventeenth century by Heinrich Schmelzer (1623–80) and which so clearly shines through in the compositions of Haydn, Schubert, and Bruckner, again found its place in the compositions of Mahler—in the second movement of his First Symphony, in the first movement of his Fourth Symphony, and in the *Ländler*-type melody of the Ninth. Actually Mahler's sophisticated and open mind was nurtured by any and all influences, be they the military sounds of early youth, the dances of the Austrian countryside, or the melodious sounds of his beloved Vienna. Thus his Third Symphony offers a humorous excerpt with bass drum and cymbals in the march movement, and his Fifth Symphony the echo of a Viennese waltz. All these influences and their sublimation combine to put Mahler in proper perspective—not as the end of a romantic line nor as the beginning of a new era, but as the important link between late romanticism and the new expression of the twentieth century; and, equally important, as a true binding link in the tradition of Vienna's music—Haydn, Mozart, Beethoven, Schubert, Sechter, Bruckner, and Brahms, and through Mahler and both Strausses to Schönberg.

At this point of investigation of Mahler's historical position and musical and philosophical outlook, a comparison between Beethoven and Mahler clamors for recognition. Beethoven straddles the eighteenth and nineteenth centuries, leading the way from the classicism of Haydn and Mozart to classic romanticism, leaving the form and sound of his illustrious contemporaries to amplify and augment in both departments and usher in a new era in music. Mahler straddles the ninteenth and twentieth centuries and again augments and enlarges on anything the music of the romantic century had achieved before him. Through his contributions, to be discussed at appropriate points, he led music into the twentieth century.

Both giants, one at the opening of the century, the other at its close, moved the spirit of their time. Berlioz was able to enlarge on the achievements of Beethoven within the decade following the German master's death. Mahler was the end of that line of development. No further enlargement in any direction whatsoever was possible after his symphonic giantism. On the contrary, Mahler actually witnessed the reversion of the trend to a new musical age as Schönberg's compositions briefly crossed Mahler's path before his untimely death. Surprisingly, both men followed the impulse of their time and temperament without giving thought as to the consequences which would ensue in the wake of their expanded thinking, sound, and form. In Beethoven's time there appeared to be sufficient room within the established harmonic system for enlargement in all directions and dimensions. Mahler, on the other hand, did not realize that there would no longer be space for further expansion in sound and form. Only subconsciously did he gain awareness of that fact. Consequently his sounds left the established harmonies, in which Richard Strauss still luxuriantly reveled, and grew more subdued; they were still lavish but reflected a clear descent from the heights of sonority observed in his Eighth Symphony.

That the romantic element was not wholly considered a thing of the past by Mahler, at least in his first four symphonies, is proven in the repeated utilization of themes, melodies, and rhythms dear to romanticism— in dances, folk songs, marches, be they triumphant, funereal, or military. Mahler was avowedly fond of military music, which he had repeatedly heard in early youth. The military band of the garrison of Iglau unquestionably had an impact on the impressionable mind of the receptive child. Echoes of those early impressions found their way into many of his works and their marches:

I Symphony, Third movement: "Feierlich und gemessen"
II Symphony, First movement: "Allegro maestoso"
III Symphony, First movement: "Kräftig"
V Symphony, First movement: "Trauermusik"
VI Symphony, First movement: "Allegro energico"
VII Symphony, First movement: "Langsam. Allegro"

The funeral marches of the First and Fifth symphonies extend into two spheres, the military as well as the romantic preoccupation with death. In a number of songs which deal with soldiers or military life, such as *Der Schildwache Nachtlied, Der Tambourgesell,* and of course, *Revelge,* childhood remembrances are transmitted into the ghostly terror of relentless marching. Those strongly pronounced rhythms, at a time when Wagnerian chromaticism and Debussy's impressionism deemphasized strict rhythms in favor of luxuriantly flowing sound sequences, made Mahler's creation doubly striking and enigmatic to early audiences.

Mahler's rapidly developing maturity in musical creation was signified by the use of bygone musical splendor. It became so important that, beginning with his Fourth Symphony, it began to dominate his musical thinking, as he introduced his unique style of counterpoint. There again it was not a copy of Sweelinck's or Frescobaldi's or even Bach's polyphonic treatment but a counterpoint distinctly Mahler's. With his Fifth Symphony the contrapuntal change in Mahler's style amounted to a revolutionary development. One of the most spectacular features of Mahler's symphonies and one of the points most open for discussion and controversy is the matter of instrumentation. One is often under the impression that for Mahler the fulfillment of his visions and their translation into musical terms required the grandeur of mammoth sound.

While Beethoven or Wagner were called revolutionary, in a musical sense, in their day, today the aura of classicism surely applies to their creations. Mahler, despite the time lapse since his death in 1911, has not yet reached the lofty realm of the "classical" composer to which Schönberg had already alluded. Mahler had felt that it would be fifty years before the public would grasp his ideas and the importance of his position in musical history. "Now they deride me; later they will build a monument to me," he said to Walter upon leaving Vienna in 1908. Surprisingly we again find his position similar to that of Beethoven in his day. While Beethoven opened the door to romanticism, it should never be overlooked that he also, at the same time, was the epitome and incarnation of Vienna classicism. Mahler, in his day, proved to be a similar bridge. While he clearly embodies the sunset of romanticism, he equally clearly points the way to a new generation of composers who were determined to leave worn-out tonality behind. It is therefore not surprising that his sounds are still meaningful and overpowering as they come to be recognized as masterpieces between periods, moving and stirring in themselves but also pioneering in the context of history. While the initial impact of some of Mahler's contemporaries paled and faded, with Reger a typical example of such demise and Rachmaninoff and Strauss beginning to be less favored by a surfeited public, Mahler's intrinsic personal involvement in every musical phrase he wrung from his tortured mind continues to excite and amaze—because he sought not simply to make sensational music, but to create musical documents of humanity, of evocative power, of love, of life, and of beauty. In trying to do so he reached back into the past, to

Bach for polyphonic impetus, to Beethoven for form, to Bruckner for giantism, to Wagner for the *Leitmotiv*. Mahler, to whom symbolism was as significant as it had been to Bach and Wagner, fully understood the intrinsic iconography which could be imparted into his symphonies through the symbol of the *Leitmotiv*. Whether it was fate, death, or love, all were utilized in an orchestration which was exciting and gigantic as it was meaningful, beginning with his first symphonic work. Combined with his rhythmic utterances, sometimes bordering on the coarse and blatant, Mahler made startling music in a world beginning to tire of its overblown harmonies, hysterical utterances, and outsized lengths and straining away from a tonality which was about to outlive its usefulness. Although critics would take repeated exception to Mahler's gargantuan orchestras, few would deny his genius for orchestration. The song technique, so obviously valued in his first four symphonies, was to be abandoned in Mahler's more mature Fifth Symphony, in which contrapuntal texture became the means of expression superseding a more naive conception ("naive" pertaining to folk-song spirit, not to Mahler's treatment) of thematic material.

Surprisingly, in a number of his symphonies (the Second, Third, Fourth, and Eighth) and in *Das Lied von der Erde,* Mahler acknowledges and enlarges on a dictum of Liszt (more validly employed in his own work) pointing to a fusion of poetry and drama with music. Where Liszt failed, achieving instead a superficial, coarsely conceived pseudofusion, where Strauss was unable to reach beneath surface sounds, Mahler, in a constant, unfulfilled quest (like Beethoven), expounded on and expanded the idea. In the process he opened a new field of musical/philosophical expression, barely tapped before him. In that process he upheld the idea of Wagner's *Gesamtkunstwerk,* total artistic achievement, in a field which the opera composer had pronounced dead—the symphony. Such an obituary on Wagner's part had been highly premature, since Brahms, Bruckner, Strauss, and Mahler went on to historically noble achievements in the symphonic form. Curiously there was less a succession than a series of individual achievements: Brahms jubilated in classicism supreme, Strauss by extension of nineteenth-century harmony to its farthest possibilities; Bruckner combined the Beethoven/Schubert classic/romantic structure with Baroque splendor and Wagnerian harmonies, while Mahler exulted in the supreme fusion of philosophical expression and music.

Equally important is the philosophical expansion of the Lied in Mahler's treatment. While *Lieder eines fahrenden Gesellen* and the *Wunderhorn Lieder* fall within Schubert's and Schumann's concept of the song cycle, Mahler's *Das Lied von der Erde,* a "Symphony of Songs," expounds a philosophy of farewell with a cohesiveness never before attained in any previous song cycle.

After his first two symphonies, Mahler found himself in a curiously isolated position—showing neither Wagnerian nor Brahmsian influence but also unmoved by the emergence and influence of non-German impressionism. Mahler, ignoring all the main currents of the time, now turned fully unto his own road, which was eventually to leave behind the sonata and symphony of the romantic age, doomed to destruction, and establish vast edifices of his own musical/architectonic invention to house his thoughts clamoring for expression. That diversity at the sunset of the nineteenth century foreshadowed the complexities in the arts of the twentieth century. No longer was identification of style as simply accomplished as had been the case in prior centuries. Despite the inescapable overlapping of style periods, the early eighteenth century still clearly presented the Baroque, and the end of the same century the Vienna classic period. If the nineteenth century produced romantic, classicist, neo-German, and nationalistic trends, thus beginning a movement of diffusion, no trends were to be observed in the individualistic diversity of the twentieth century. Even Schönberg's school was to be open to divisiveness. While Schönberg and Alban Berg still found a bridge from late romanticism to atonality, Anton Webern was to leave romantic thinking completely behind to become the first true master of atonality. As for Mahler, the shell of his development broke to reveal his churning philosophical mind as well as the direction his work was going to embark on.

> The real Mahler emerges where the symphonic form breaks down under the stress to which he had subjected it. The passage just before the entrance of the chorus in the last movement of the Second Symphony is such a break. It is one of the most inspired and awesome passages of musical literature; where the horrifying silence is interrupted only by fearful tremors . . . and by the appalling calls of distant trumpets announcing the Last Judgment. . . . Music . . . acts out its own agony, hopelessly witnessing the collapse of its overstrained structure.
>
> Ernest Křenek, *Gustav Mahler*

If the finale of the Second Symphony provided the break with the past, it was the Third Symphony which opened to Mahler his true philosophical destiny of a Dionysian and cosmic outlook. If the trite phrase of Mahler's "philosophical music" is to be taken at face value, then the Third Symphony is the window to Mahler's future as a composer and to his thinking.

The emphasis in Mahler's activities shifted decisively after the Fourth Symphony: from a famous conductor who also composed to a composer who was also a famous conductor. Mahler's music actually brought about more controversy than Richard Strauss's, as Mahler began to make headway in gaining acceptance as a composer of stature. The term "*Kapellmeistermusik*" had lost its validity—because during the remaining ten years of his life Mahler grew into his historic position and mission as the most powerful link into the twentieth century. After the turn of the century he would still be enough of the renowned director, conductor, and *regisseur* to lend splendor to the "Mahler Era" of the Vienna Imperial Opera House for seven years and grow in conductorial stature to be lured to America. But intuitively he knew much sooner than he admitted to Bruno Walter that his conductorial period was ended.

Mahler's accomplishments clearly bear out this assessment. We witness the volcanic symphonic change to modern polyphony in his Fifth Symphony, the somber tragedy of his Sixth and his enigmatic Seventh, followed by the monumental expansion of form, height of expression, and depth of feeling in his Eighth. Then, intuitively, the Farewell in his *Das Lied von der Erde* and the Ninth Symphony. We can only surmise what agonies seized him during the composition of his Tenth Symphony, which was destined to remain fragmentary. When we further consider that these works were conceived during brief summer holidays in a life otherwise brimming with directorial and conductorial duties, that they emerged out of a human being plagued by family catastrophe, ill health, and the constant spectre of death, the creative genius of Mahler looms giganticly. The time factor mentioned above must be kept in mind in order to avoid the misconception that these symphonic and song creations erupted within the time span of a decade (1901–11). Because, as we indicated, only a limited number of months within that decade could be devoted to composition in a life consumed by events of secondary importance.

> I am not . . . speaking of my activities in opera or as a conductor; they are, after all, of an inferior order.
>
> Mahler to Alma, Berlin, 14 December 1901

But even some of those activities, such as the world premiere of his Eighth Symphony in Munich with Mahler conducting, took on the significance of a milestone in musical history.

If one expected further elaboration on the form after the early symphonies, such expectation would have to bide its time until the "middle symphonies," wherein Mahler would look structurally toward the Viennese classic conception on the one hand and progress to a new polyphonic concept on the other. This makes those three symphonies among the more difficult to comprehend and at the same time his most progressive symphonies, conceived in pure instrumental style, to the exclusion of "the word." The complete departure from previous technique is promptly heralded by the introduction of that intricate and novel polyphony which was to play a major role in future compositions. Yet, although the human voice is mute in these works, the vocal past is not forgotten. Thus we hear a quotation from *Nun will die Sonn' so hell aufgeh'n* from his *Kindertotenlieder* in the first movement of the Fifth Symphony, *Revelge* in the funeral march of the *Fifth*, and *Tambourg'sell* in the *Nachtmusik 1* of his *Seventh*. Mahler's device of depicting a demise, a sunset, a darkening, a farewell, by modulation from major to minor also links the sixth and seventh symphonies. This is, of course, not a new device, and was employed long before Mahler. Again Mahler expanded the meaning and usage of an age-old device into symbolic higher meaning.

Mahler's symbolic visions of sound set his music far apart from Richard Strauss, who used sound to very different purposes. Strauss painted the realities of life, its splendors, passions, and cruelties, but they always remained surface images and surface sounds, painted by a master of such a dazzling orchestral palette that their very excitement and color variegation made one forget that the view was shallow and the vision limited. When depth was attempted, as in *Also sprach Zarathustra,* it became Lisztian sham on a more sophisticated sound level. Mahler had no time or use, in his music, for the sunrise or sunset per se. To him the moment of sunset was not a spectacle but a symbol of the end of life and the power of evil over light, and to that end his mammoth orchestra had to make available every conceivable sound texture. In contrast to Strauss, who remained purposely earthbound, Mahler roamed the heavens and, more often, hell. A Strauss crescendo might lead to an avowal of love, to mischief, or to comic relief; with Mahler it led to triumph or disaster, never to domestic bliss or an Alpine thunderstorm. Only in *Das Lied von der Erde,* where personal relationships (friendship and farewell) enter into the music, does the chamber-music sound justify its existence in the world of Mahler.

To realize his ghostly visions—the dread of disaster, the dream of earthly bliss—Mahler constantly experimented with the inclusion of new instruments to satisfy his need for special sounds: the somber tenor horn in his introduction to the Seventh Symphony, the delicate cowbells in his Sixth Symphony, the guitar and mandolin in the *Nachtmusik* 2 of the Seventh Symphony. Vaster vistas for the musical eye were also sought by the use of the offstage orchestra. Some scholars attribute such features as the offstage orchestra to an innate theatricalism, acquired as a result of Mahler's operatic activities. While such an influence is undeniable, its use by Mahler goes beyond theatrics and again approaches symbolism as well as a realistic probing into new tonal textures. Thus massed horns in a basically trite melody (opening of the Third Symphony) become a stirring call to life, while the chirping of a solitary mandolin affects the listener and evokes man's mournful, saddened retreat from life (*Das Lied von der Erde, Der Abschied*). Yet the same instrument, used with harp and tambourine, mirrors the plays of youth (*Das Lied von der Erde, Von der Schönheit*), while the delicate bell sounds of the celesta underline the word *"Ewig"* and accompany it into eternity, again in the *Abschied* section. By then Mahler had acquired a dexterity of refinement and a virtuosity of subdued orchestral treatment which, to a great extent, shunned the sonorous extravaganzas and the steep peaks and deep valleys of sound of previous symphonies. In working out his orchestrations, usually during the winter months in Vienna, Mahler again was an example of the "constructive" composer, who revamped and reforged the original image innumerable times before he achieved its satisfactory realization. In some instances, such a realization might never be achieved to the satisfaction of the creator. Thus Mahler resembled the burning desire for perfection of Beethoven and the multiple efforts at revision of Bruckner, although Bruckner, as we have seen, revised for different reasons. The preserved manuscripts of Mahler attest to the fastidiousness with which he attended to every facet of orchestration, dynamics, and effects, by making innumerable marginal notations, often during rehearsals, with an assistant in attendance to take down all of his comments and admonishments, over and above already written comments.

The tragic and disconcerting events of 1907 were bound to have a physical effect on the man and through it a mental and psychological one, since he suddenly found himself drastically curtailed in all of the physical activity dear to him. These mental and psychological effects, in their positive as well as negative consequences, totally changed the direction of Mahler's thought, philosophy, and artistry. One effect was a loosening of Mahler's stringent perfectionism (in performances in America); another was a spirit of contemplative sadness.

> If I am again to find my way back to my own self I shall have to deliver myself up to the terrors of solitude. . . . That I must die is no news to me. But without attempting here to describe to you or to explain that for which there are perhaps no words at all, I merely want to say to you that, at one fell stroke, I have lost everything of clearness and assurance that I had ever won for myself and that now, at the end of my life, I must learn anew how to walk and stand.
>
> Mahler to Bruno Walter, July 1908

As one follows Mahler's rise to creative eminence, one cannot help but take notice of certain basic features which, if they did not constitute the whole of Mahler's style, certainly contributed greatly to it. They illumine Mahler's heritage as well as his legacy: the influences that shaped his creations and the elements and developments that shaped his musical life, as well as the accomplishments which he bequeathed.

a. The legacy of Beethoven, Schubert, and Bruckner. From Beethoven the dramatic gesture, from Schubert the lyric jubilation; from Bruckner Baroque solemnity. From Beethoven the steely determination; from Schubert and Bruckner, the inspired use of Austrian romantic folk songs and dance tunes.

b. His subconscious affinity and allegiance to class continuity. His use of classic devices even at a time when what he termed "symphony" was far removed from classic models.

c. His musical/religious affinity and identification, primarily with Catholicism, pointed up in his use of the chorale, a hallmark of the Baroque whch he shared with Bruckner; but also with the hymnal of Protestantism.

d. The military march influence, attributed to youthful experiences. That influence was later to express a multitude of emotions. Combined in massed brass and drum sound, it gave a solemn, majestic sonority to initially trite statements and expression to Mahler's predilection for monumental sound.

e. An affinity to and identification with nature, its sounds and sights, found in bird cries, Alpine melodies, and the sound of cowbells in his music.

f. The Jewish/Slavonic heritage, irrevocably present despite innumerable, acquired layers of Central and Western European culture and impressions, and despite Mahler's lack of interest in matters Jewish.

g. Superimposed upon all these, Mahler's greatest and most enduring musical achievement, his personal counterpoint.

The original impetus and point of departure for such application of counterpoint was Mahler's increasing preoccupation with the music of Johann Sebastian Bach. Some of Mahler's statements ("They will understand me in fifty years") may have been an expression of artistic solidarity with Bach, whose music had to bide its time before full recognition and honor were bestowed. Bach's influence—the Baroque splendor of his music, never far from Bruckner's and Mahler's minds—may also have acted to counter excessive romanticism. Mahler's progressive fugal treatment, touched upon first in the Adagio of his Fourth Symphony and fully expressed in his Fifth Symphony, reached its climax in the towering fugue *Ductore sic te praevio* [Our faltering steps with sureness guide] in the first section of his Eighth Symphony.

How and where were these influences applied? Again there is a vague similarity with Beethoven with respect to periods of creation.

a. (up to 1900) *Das klagende Lied*; Symphonies One to Four; song cycles *Lieder und Gesänge aus der Jugendzeit, Lieder eines fahrenden Gesellen, Des Knaben Wunderhorn*; strong romantic flair. Introduction of song elements into symphonic form. The world of Dionysus (Pan) vividly reflected in Mahler's music. Nature prominent in all its aspects.

b. (up to 1906) Symphonies Five to Seven; Rückert songs (*Kindertotenlieder*); *Sieben Lieder aus letzter Zeit*. Song elements rigidly eliminated in symphonic creations, with emphasis on purely instrumental symphony. Peak of creative power and physical strength; dominant and domineering.

c. (1907) Eighth Symphony. Freedom from all limitations of the past. Reappearance of the spoken word, but devoid of early romantic inflections. Rise to hitherto unheard-of monumentalism. A final outburst of strength.

d. (1908–10) *Das Lied von der Erde*; Ninth Symphony; fragments of Tenth Symphony. New York activities. A fourth and final reversal of style; introduction of new style elements into a form until then considered purely lyrical or dramatic—the symphonic *Lieder* cycle. The heart is failing, the spirit of invention soaring, the gaze averted inward. The aspect of death becomes reality.

What position does Mahler occupy in historical retrospect: an end, a beginning, a milestone, a binding link, a summing up? In careful analysis he appears to be, in turn, all of these.

A definition of the "traditionalist" [2] composer, which Mahler also in part represents, may open a vista. Such a composer usually appears at a significant moment in history, when a specific style is about to reach its full bloom. Some of history's most illustrious names—Palestrina, Bach, Haydn—belong to this group. Their striving is not after novelty but for perfection. They do not seek new forms but are content to create gloriously within the established ones. Palestrina, within the prescribed field of the mass and the motet, attained supreme mastery of vocal polyphonic perfection. Bach's masterpieces of concerted polyphony were to lead to supreme perfection within the time-honored forms of the praeludium and fugue, the suite, the cantata, and the mass. Similarly, Haydn carried all of the tentative attempts at sonata and symphony to a peak of development within the Viennese classic style. So Mahler stands in the development of the symphonic style Haydn began—the peak, the ultimate elaboration, the farthest limit, the end. Such a position as the last, supreme exponent of a style is not always a happy one. The Roman school of Palestrina had to fight for survival. Bach became obsolete in his own time. Haydn's antiquated operatic style, overshadowed by Mozart's genius, receded into oblivion.

Mahler stood at the crossroads. Debussy challenged the terror of the tonic and the triad and emerged victoriously. Schönberg, Stravinsky, Bartok, and Scriabin were to challenge the old order, while Strauss, Rachmaninoff, and Sibelius continued to carry the musical banner of the nineteenth century into a new day. Thus Mahler became at once a beginning and an end: an end as the last flowering of symphonic tradition, begun in Vienna; a beginning because he was instrumental in musically inspiring others who were willing to accept his innovations while honoring him as a last standard-bearer of the classic tradition. Thus it was to a great extent

[2] The term "traditionalist" is not to be confused with "traditional." The "traditional" composer is but an epigone, an imitator who composes within an accepted style, e.g., à la Brahms, à la Debussy.

Mahler's influence, understanding, and inspiration which ushered in a new wave of musical giants in Vienna.

## DAS KLAGENDE LIED
*[The Song of Lament]*

The first of my work in which I found myself as "Mahler" is a fairy tale for chorus, soloists, and orchestra, *Das klagende Lied*. This work I designated as my opus 1.

> Mahler to music critic **Max Marschalk**, December 1896

Shuddering we duly pay our respects. . . . Compared with the collapse of the castle . . . the Twilight of the Gods [in Wagner's opera] is a purely local event.

> Max Kalbeck, Vienna, November 1901

As a composer, Herr Mahler enjoys an advantage given to few others: he has the power of entrusting his creation, [Das Klagende Lied] and his intention to one of the shrewdest conductors of all time—Gustav Mahler. These are helpful factors indeed, and under such auspices budding immortality does not fare too badly.

> *Reichswehr* review, Vienna, November 1901

*Composition begun in 1878, completed 1 November 1880, revised 1898.*[3]
*First performance, Vienna, 17 February 1901, Mahler conducting.*

In November 1880, two years after the idea for it was conceived, *Das klagende Lied,* which Mahler considered "a veritable child of woe," was finished.

While Mahler became a superb interpreter of Wagner, he adopted neither his musical style nor his form. All of his early attempts in the operatic field—*Die Argonauten, Rübezahl, Herzog Ernst von Schwaben*— were destroyed by the youthful composer, a process which also claimed an early *Nordic* Symphony. The only early creation remaining, the cantata *Das klagende Lied,* confirms the early romantic bond with the supernatural, brought to German consciousness so marvelously by Weber, to the French so thrillingly by Berlioz in his *Symphonie Fantastique.*

---

[3] Dates as to creation and revisions differ. Quoted above are Guido Adler's findings. According to Adler, Mahler eliminated the *Waldmärchen* part in 1888. Others offer the following dates. Heinrich Kralik: creation, 1880; first revision, 1888; second revision, 1896, in Hamburg. H. F. Redlich: first version (three-part), November, 1880; revised to two parts, 1888; second revision, 1896; rescored, 1898. Jack Diether: Date of the poem, 18 March 1878 (the year of Mahler's graduation from the Conservatory); completed, 1880; revised, 1888; second revision, 1896; published, 1899.

Although *Das klagende Lied* does not reflect the orchestral advances made by Mahler after years of conducting and experimentation, the future personality of Mahler nevertheless shines through. Romantic drama reaches its peak at the king's wedding feast when the murdered brother's voice is heard in flaming accusation, foreshadowing in its incredible range the vocal conceptions of Schönberg. The story is reminiscent of Heine's *Belsazar* and the medieval morality play *Jedermann,* as all who had come to partake of the feast flee in terror and the scene ends in destruction. Although Mahler followed Wagner's example to the point of writing his own libretto and although the work is steeped in arch-German romanticism à la Weber, this youthful work points the way to Mahler's musical future.

No reason was given as to why the opening thirty-minute *Waldmärchen* section had been deleted by the composer. After deciding on a two-part cantata, Mahler presented the *Waldmärchen* score to sister Justine, who handed it to her husband, Arnold Rosé. After Arnold's demise, his nephew Alfred Rosé inherited the score. Alfred prepared orchestral parts from the score and actually had it performed in Vienna and Brno in the 1930s. After the *Anschluss,* Alfred Rosé emigrated to Canada. When he suffered a heart attack he decided to let Henry L. Osborn, who had evinced interest in the score, purchase it. The score of *Waldmärchen* exists only in a copyist's version, but it contains comments and corrections in Mahler's hand and it is also prefaced with the cantata text (Mahler's own) in Mahler's handwriting. It is now in the Yale library's James M. and Mary Louise Osborn Collection, of which Henry Osborn is the curator. It is interesting that the *Waldmärchen* section was composed for four soloists (the remaining parts feature only three soloists). Osborn considers it "the most important unpublished known score by a non-living composer."[4]

Mahler's destruction of his earlier musical attempts—flawed according to Mahler's rigorous standards of perfection—is regrettable because it deprives us of an overview of Mahler's artistic growth. As the only surviving opus of Mahler's youthful days, *Das klagende Lied* is therefore invaluable in the study of a maturing genius. With this work, Mahler felt that

---

[4] The *Waldmärchen* score of *Das klagende Lied* is not the only Mahler manuscript which Osborn donated to the Yale library. The Osborns had acquired another "lost" Mahler manuscript after a similar odyssey: viz., the score of the *Blumine* movement of Mahler's First Symphony. Mahler had presented the manuscript of his First Symphony (the original five-movement version) in 1891 to his former pupil Jennie Feld, in whose house he had been a welcome guest for many years. Miss Feld, who married an American named Perrin, eventually handed the score to her son John. When the aging son wished to dispose of some items he sent the Mahler score to a London auction house, where Osborn acquired it. (He later presented it to Yale.) Mrs. Osborn, who had been a lifelong devotee of Mahler's music, was the proud owner of a fair copy of Mahler's Second Symphony, with the composer's marginal comments. It, too, was presented to the Yale library.

he had reached a certain acceptable level of composition and he therefore did not consign it to destruction.

Mahler's sense of the importance of *Das klagende Lied* was to prompt him to submit it in the Beethoven Prize competition, sponsored by the *Gesellschaft der Musikfreunde* in 1881, in high hopes of garnering the coveted prize and relieving financial drudgery. The conservative jury, however, defeated the hopes of the young admirer of Wagner and friend of Bruckner. The setback rankled Mahler for many years. As late as 1898, at the pinnacle of his achievement and fame, he bitterly spoke to Natalie Bauer-Lechner of that day.

Had the jury at the Konservatorium, which included Brahms, Goldmark, Hanslick, and Richter, given me the Beethoven Prize of 600 Austrian gulden at that time for *Das klagende Lied,* my entire life would have taken a different turn. . . . I would not have had to go to Laibach and would thus possibly have been spared my whole cursed operatic career. Instead, however, Herr Herzfeld got the first composition prize and Rott and I left empty-handed. . . . and I was (and shall always remain) condemned to the hell of theatrical life.

Natalie Bauer-Lechner, *Erinnerungen an Mahler,* 1923

One of the outstanding features of *Das klagende Lied* is Mahler's bending of poetry and story line to suit his romantic purposes, a process which we will observe many times in his subsequent works. As to the story's background: the basic story idea of "The Singing Bone" has its roots on three continents: Europe, Asia, and Africa. The singing bone usually represents a murder victim whose spirit is reincarnated in the musical instrument. In a variant, the hair of the murdered person is strung into a harp, which then sings of the evil deed. Another variant has a tree growing out of the burial site of the victim; an instrument fashioned from its wood reveals the murder tale. Fairy tales by both Ludwig Bechstein and the Brothers Grimm deal with the same basic theme, although titles and details differ. We cite both fairy tales below in abridged versions. Bechstein's version comes closest to Mahler's poem.

A king had died and was survived by the queen, a daughter, and a son. The children soon began to bicker as to who was to reign. The daughter was older: "I am the first born and I have precedence." But the brother would not hear of it: "I am a prince and as long as princes are about, princesses do not reign." Their mother, the queen, was grieved by her children's quarrel and sought a solution. "Children, look at this rare flower. Now go into the woods and whoever returns such a flower to me, will reign.

The children went forth and the princess soon found the flower. While holding it and waiting for her brother, she fell asleep. After a while the brother found her, still clutching the flower—whereas he had returned empty-handed. At that moment a sinister spirit appeared from the darkness of the forest and whispered: "Why should your sister reign? You must be king. Take the flower from her hand and see to it that her sleep becomes a sleep of death.

And the prince slew his innocent sister, dug a shallow grave, and covered it with earth and grass. Coming home, he told all that he had lost his sister in the forest and had thought that she had already returned.

Many years passed, but the old queen continued to mourn her lost daughter. After many years a shepherd came through the forest and while idly digging into the ground with his staff, dug up a snow-white bone. By making holes into it he fashioned a flute. When he put it to his lips there welled up the mourning sound of a child's voice.

Alas! Oh shepherd, dear shepherd
Thou playest upon my death bone.
My brother slew me in the grave
Took from my hand
The flower I'd found,
And then told it was his.
He slew me while I was asleep.
He dug my grave and buried me
My brother—in younger days.
Through you alone will they know the tale
Will God and man now mourn me.

And the forest fell silent and the shepherd cried. One day a wandering minstrel heard the shepherd's song, bought the flute from him, and brought it to the queen, who recognized her daughter's voice. Taking the flute from the minstrel, she planned revenge.

Every year the king, now mighty, had a singing contest at his castle to which many singers and guests were invited. His mourning mother had never attended, but, to his surprise, at the height of the festivities she appeared in mourning clothes, standing amid the guests like a marble statue. And then she began to play the snow-white flute. The king heard the voice, and a shudder of horror ran through him. And as the song of murder was heard to the horror of all, he stumbled from his throne, clutching his throat, and begged his mother to stop. But the song went on to its bitter end. While the guests and servants fled, the mourning mother held her dying son in her arms. Then she extinguished the candles in the hall and broke the flute. The mourning song had ended.

Bechstein, *Neues Deutsches Märchenbuch.* Fairy Tale No. 3:
*Das klagende Lied*

Grimm's fairy tale describes the same evil deed, but in a different milieu:

A wild boar did great damage throughout the land, killing man and beast so that no man dared to enter the forest where it roamed. One day the king let it be known that whosoever would kill the boar would receive the king's daughter for his wife. There were in the kingdom three bothers, the oldest one sly, the middle one of average intellect, and the third and youngest naive. They hoped to win the princess and wanted to find the wild boar and kill it.

The two older ones went together, but the youngest went alone. As he entered the forest, a little man approached him. He held a black lance in his hand and said: "Take this lance and with it attack the boar without fear and you will easily kill it." Thus it happened: when the lance hit the boar it fell dead to the ground. Thereupon he hung it over his shoulder and happily turned towards home. En route he came past a house wherein the two older brothers gaily enjoyed a drink of wine. When they saw him approach with the boar they called out to him. Thinking no evil, the naive one joined them, telling them of his good fortune and of how he killed the boar with the black lance. In the evening when they all went home, the two oldest brothers let him go ahead, and when they approached the bridge before the city, they slew him and buried him under the bridge. Then the oldest one took the boar before the king and pretended that he had killed it and received the princess for his wife.

This lasted for many years, but one day a shepherd walked across the bridge and saw a bone in the sand beneath him. Since it looked so clean and snowy white, he picked it up and fashioned the mouthpiece for his horn. When he wanted to put it to his lips to play the bone began to sing by itself and revealed the tale of murder.

> Brothers Grimm, *Gesammelte Märchen.*
> Fairy Tale No. 28: *Der singende Knochen*

Mahler's romantic vision had use neither for wild boars and village boors nor for a slain innocent maiden. His own version, fashioned in 1878 and closer to Bechstein than to Grimm was romanticism at its eeriest and most gruesome—the Biblical Cain and Abel story in romantic trappings. It is, however, surprising that Mahler did not avail himself of the tempting evil spirit, mentioned in the Bechstein version and so dear to German romanticism.

In this very first Mahler opus, we already observed his custom of giving explicit performance instructions: for example, that the offstage orchestra, consisting of wind instruments, timpani, additional percussion, and harp, should be placed far enough in the background so that it could play *fortissimo* but be heard only *pianissimo*. Progress on the work was halting, due to his demeaning summer occupations, and it took him two years to complete the first version.

Having completed what he considered a major artistic task, Mahler's concern and effort were directed toward securing a performance of his "child of woe." It did not occur to him in his youthful exuberance that this was an almost impossible goal for an unknown young composer, particularly one who was presenting a work which demanded a large orchestral ensemble, a chorus, and soloists and who had no financial resources or backing to make such a venture possible. Conservative Vienna, as might be expected, was deaf to any overture concerning a performance. Mahler was undismayed; he had realized that Vienna opinion would be difficult to overcome. Haydn had suffered total neglect in Vienna until he returned in triumph from London. Mozart had triumphed in Prague but had beaten his head in despair against a wall of Viennese indifference. Schubert, the most Viennese composer of them all, had hardly existed in Vienna's musical life; Bruckner had been harassed and reviled. But Beethoven had triumphed by perservance and genius; there was an example to emulate. Mahler was determined to do just that. Beethoven and Wagner, another stubborn genius who had persevered, remained his lifelong idols.

The work of the twenty-year-old Mahler had to wait another twenty years—until 17 February 1901—for a performance, in a more sophisticated version and at the hands of the composer himself, by then a conductor and composer of world renown. The updated, somewhat reorchestrated version, while sleeker in instrumentation, can hardly be considered an improvement over the primitive but authentically romantic expression of the aspiring composer. The overwhelming effect which might have been expected from a work employing the Vienna Philharmonic Orchestra as well as a mixed chorus and soloist was lacking. Mahler's efforts were not rewarded with praise or even appreciation. Vienna had hardly begun to musically digest Bruckner and was in no sense prepared for Mahler's torrential outburst.

Mahler originally entitled his poem for the cantata, *Ballade vom blonden und braunen Reitersmann,* but eventually adopted Bechstein's title *Das klagende Lied* [The song of lament]. For a fuller understanding of the course which Mahler's cantata took, we quote below an English translation of the original three parts.[5]

## THE SONG OF LAMENT

### I. Forest Legend

*(Waldmärchen)*

There was a proud and stately queen,
Of beauty without measure;
No knight within her favour stood,
All shared her great displeasure.
Ah woe, thou fair young lady bold!
To whom dost thou thy charms unfold?

Two brothers came into the wood,
The flower to discover,
The younger fair and of gentle mood,
But envy-blacken'd the other.
O knight, my evil-omen'd knight,
O turn away thy hateful spite!

[5] Translation courtesy of the Caramoor Festival, Katonah, N.Y.

When they had gone a little pace,
They ceas'd to walk together,
And now in search began to race
Through forest, field and heather.
My hasty knight, with darting eyes,
Who now will find the costly prize?

A flower lovely as the queen
Did grow in a forest shady;
The knight who could the flower find
Might win the royal lady.
Ah woe, thou proud and stately queen!
When will it break, thy haughty mien?

The younger search'd through wood and lea,
And had not long been seeking,
When saw he, by a willow tree,
Through grass the flower peeking.
He pluck'd and stuck it in his cap,
Then stretch'd he out to take a nap.

The other comb'd through crag and rill,
In vain through the heather peering,
And as the sun sank behind the hill,
He came to the grassy clearing.
Ah woe, whom there he sleeping scann'd,
The flow'r in his cap, in green-hu'd band!

Thou rapture-bringing nightingale,
And red-breast, thy long vigil keeping,
Methinks thy singing should prevail
To wake the poor knight sleeping.
Thou blossom red in sleeper's cap,
Thou shinest forth indeed like blood!

His eye doth gleam in frenzy wide,
To wilder mood replying;
A sword of steel hangs by his side,
To which his hand goes flying!
The elder laughs 'neath willow tree,
The younger dreameth blissfully.

Ye leaves there, why hang ye with dewdrops
    low?
Great tears ye might be shedding!
Ye winds there, why waft ye regretfully so,
Your rustle and whisper spreading?
"In woods, by a grassy pillow,
There grows a weeping willow."

## II. The Minstrel

*(Der Spielmann)*

By willow cool, in firry wood,
Where jackdaws and ravens hover,
There lies a knight both fair and good,
Whom the leaves and the blossoms
    o'ercover.
'Tis mild and fill'd with fragrance there,
And sounds like weeping fill the air!
    O sorrow, sorrow!

A minstrel's steps to the clearing did lead,
A glist'ning bone there did stay him;
He carv'd it out, as 'twere a reed,
A goodly flute to essay him.
Ah minstrel, wand'ring minstrel dear,
Strange is the music thou wilt hear!
    O sorrow, woe! O sorrow!

The minstrel put it to his mouth,
And set it loudly ringing.
What magic then did issue out,
What strange and doleful singing!
So sad it sounded, and yet so fair,
Who heard might die of sorrow there!
    O sorrow, sorrow!

"Ah minstrel, wand'ring minstrel dear,
Lament must I unto thee:
For a fine-colour'd flow'ret here
My brother rashly slew me.
My bleaching bones in forest hide,
My brother woos a fair young bride!
    O sorrow, Woe!" sorrow!

The minstrel took it far and near,
The doleful song essaying.
Ah woe, ah woe, ye people dear!
What think ye on my playing?
Away must I to the kingly hall,
Away to the beauteous queen of us all!
    O sorrow, woe! O sorrow!

## III. Wedding Piece

*(Hochzeitsstück)*

On rocky summit the castle gleams,
The trumpets resound from their stations;
With knightly followers bold it teems,
And ladies with gold decorations.

What tokens this gladdening, joyful
   recall?
What glitters and shines in kingly hall?
   O rapture, hey-ho! Rapture!

And know'st thou not, wherefore this rouse?
Ho, that can I truly say:
The queen exchangeth marriage vows
With yon youthful knight today.
See there, behold the stately queen!
Now will it break, her haughty mien!
   O rapture, hey-ho! Rapture!

"Ah minstrel, wand'ring minstrel dear,
Lament must I unto thee:
For a fine-colour'd flow'ret there
My brother rashly slew me.
My bleaching bones in forest hide,
My brother woos a fair young bride!"
   O sorrow! Woe, o sorrow!

The king leaps up from his royal chair
And strides through the wedding crowd;
Then takes the flute with a withering glare
And plays it clearly and loud.
O horror! What is now convey'd?
Hear'st thou the tidings undismay'd?

Why is the bridegroom so pale and cow'd?
Hears not the shouts of pleasure,
Sees not the guests, so rich and proud,
The queen in her stately measure.
Why is the bridegroom so cow'd and pale?
What casts upon his mind this veil?
A minstrel steps 'fore the portal wide!
What showeth he the guests inside?
   O sorrow, Woe! sorrow!

"Ah brother, dearest brother lost,
'Twas thou my life didst sever;
Now playest thou on my bone, that must
Lamenting sing forever.
Why hast thou my youth unfinish'd
To sombre death diminish'd?"
   O sorrow, woe! O sorrow!

The queen sinks down insensately,
The drums and the trumpets are humble;
In terror the knights and their ladies
   flee,

The ancient ramparts crumble.
The lights in the kingly hall have ceas'd!
What now remains of the wedding feast?
    Ah sorrow!

All this is being told in a medieval mode of expression, with almost every verse of the *Spielmann* and *Hochzeitsstück* ending with "O Leide, weh! o Leide!" [O sorrow, woe! O sorrow!] Mahler apparently felt that such language suited the tale and the times. Mahler's musical interpretation, however, is far from medieval. It is highly romantic but already displays the features that were to become his hallmarks: the occasional contrapuntal treatment, the march rhythms, all interwoven with the young man's romantic idols, Weber, Wagner, and Bruckner. The contrasts within the work are pronounced, as the drama ordains and as the twenty-year-old composer romantically felt them. Although concert performance was intended, the work smacks of stage drama throughout. The distant orchestra, usually in the wings, gives the work dimension and expanse.

As we have noted, no direct quotation from Mahler can be cited giving the reason for the deletion of the *Waldmärchen* section, but a number of fascinating hypotheses have been put forward as to why he wrote it. Jack Diether notes that there was a close relationship between Gustav Mahler and his brother Ernst: they were the closest in age, attachment, and interests. Gustav, in later years, described to Alma the shock, for him, of Ernst's death: "This was the first harrowing experience of my childhood." Somehow a gnawing feeling of guilt, which he subconsciously but unsuccessfully wished to extirpate, pursued Mahler. This feeling pervades not only the *Waldmärchen* section but other musical attempts of that period as well. We know that the title role of the libretto provided by his friend Josef Steiner bore the name *Ernst von Schwaben,* and while working on the music, Mahler wrote:

> I hear the greeting of Ernst von Schwaben. Now Ernst himself appears, holding out his arms to me; and as I gaze at him, I see it is my poor brother.

> Mahler to Steiner, June 1879

Dr. Theodore Reik, in his book *The Haunting Melody,* finds a further clue in Mahler's song cycle *Kindertotenlieder.* Friedrich Rückert wrote hundreds of poems, from which Mahler culled five, upon the death of his young son—Ernst. Perhaps this explanation is not farfetched in light of Mahler's urge to set those poems to music in the face of Alma's strong disapproval.

But it is Dr. Robert Still, in his paper "Gustav Mahler and Psychoanalysis" (1960), who finds a connection between the reasons for the composition and the elimination of the *Waldmärchen* section. Mahler felt a strong attraction for as well as sibling rivalry with respect to his younger brother. This may explain his having spent unending hours at his sick brother's bedside and yet still feeling guilt after his brother's death. Thus, Dr. Still feels, the use of brothers in the story of fratricide (rather than brother and sister, as in the Bechstein version, which was Mahler's primary source material), in the writing of *Das klagende Lied* in general and *Waldmärchen* in particular, was for Mahler a necessary confrontation in music. Having faced the problem, he had effectively exorcised it; the subject had lost its hold on Mahler and he was willing to consign it to oblivion by handing *Waldmärchen* to his sister.

Musically *Waldmärchen* is in the same vein as the other two parts of the cantata—exuberantly dramatic and youthful. We may therefore assume that lack of quality was *not* a reason for its exclusion. Length may have been one reason, as the prelude alone worked out to 120 bars, parallelling the equally long prelude to *Der Spielmann* and thus giving the impression of a double beginning as well as of musical and dramatic duplication, except for the inclusion of a fourth (bass) soloist who does not appear in the other two parts. Mahler must ultimately have felt that the tightening of the work into only two parts could only enhance its tension and drama. Indeed, the most logical explanation for the deletion may be the pragmatic consideration cited by Alfred Rosé in an interview with Robert Chestermann of the CBC:

> Mahler thought that the two movements in themselves were already very extravagant, and he thought he might not have a chance [at performance?] if he submitted the whole three parts: it was too long and it was too modern for that time.
>
> Jack Diether, *Mahler's Das Klagende Lied*

Romantic rustling of the forest over foreboding string basses, with ominous sounds and furious outcries, all foreshadowing danger, open the cantata, followed by a romantic call of the horns, in the prelude to the vocal recitation. The lovely melody of the *Spielmann* [minstrel], introduced in the strings, is heard, interspersed with bird calls in the woodwinds. Thereupon Mahler proceeds with the storytelling by the contralto, followed by the tenor and a duet by soprano and alto. With the entrance of the "Greek chorus" the air becomes ominous, and the story of fratricide unfolds in an aura of dark emotional suspense. Wild outcries in the orchestra accompany the evil deed. The *Spielmann* theme returns as the minstrel wanders about, and the song is heard as proclaimed by the tenor, answered by the concluding moans of the chorus.

Timpani, cymbals, triangle, and excited strings convey the festiveness and excited joy which fill the castle in the *Hochzeitsstück* [Wedding piece]. Suddenly a stunning silence foreshadows the catastrophe. There is a brief hint of the *Spielmann* theme in a minor key as the minstrel enters the festive hall. Slowly, the macabre scene unfolds in the contralto's recitation. The melody and text of the murder, already heard in the *Spiel-mann* section, are repeated before the king and his gathering, over the wailing of the chorus. The king's horror is mirrored in the chorus's excitement, as in the final stanza the *Spielmann* theme of murder now addresses itself directly and passionately to the king. The wailing of the chorus overwhelms all as the scene sinks into abysmal silence. The tenor then describes the finale of horror, death, and destruction. The end is one of desolation depicted in sound, ending in a final crash of destruction.

## LIEDER UND GESÄNGE AUS DER JUGENDZEIT
[*Songs and Chants from the Time of Youth*]

Alas for the music of Mahler! What a fuss about nothing! What a to-do about a few commonplace musical thoughts, hardly worthy of being called ideas. Never was poverty of invention more apparent than in these songs, in which triviality is the dominant quality.

L. A. Sloper, *Christian Science Monitor,* 20 January 1924, describing the body of Mahler's songs

The romanticism of the age and of Mahler's own nature and youth was bound to express itself in the Lied, its truest musical expression—so much so that Mahler often created his own poetic images to be set to music. In view of the obvious romantic spirit which permeates the poems, it is not surprising that the influence of Schumann should be discernible, particularly in the first group of songs, *Vierzehn Lieder und Gesänge aus der Jugendzeit,* composed between 1880 and 1892.

Just as *Das klagende Lied* seems somewhat crude and primitive when compared with *Das Lied von der Erde,* so the earliest songs of this first *Lieder* cycle would give way to others which combined the simplicity of romanticism with Mahler's painstaking sophistication and sense of perfection. It is as if Mahler wished to prove, in the leanness of his melodic line which often heightens the expressiveness, that "less is more." Dika Newlin cites as a perfect example of Mahler's musical intuition the ending of the song *Zu Strassburg auf der Schanz.* Instead of being resolved in the tonic, it ends on the subdominant, "as though the last complaints of the dying soldier were to remain forever unanswered." Surprisingly, despite a vogue in folk song, only Mahler and Brahms, in their own and wholly different ways, were able to truly and fully enter into its elusive spirit.

The time of composition of these fourteen songs spans twelve years, and, according to content and publication dates, they are divided into three phases or books—the first published in 1885, the other two in 1892. The first book draws on several sources for text: poems by Richard Leander, translations by Nikolaus von Lenau of Tirso de Molina's drama *Don Juan,* and a folk song text. Books two and three, on the other hand, use only poems from the anthology *Des Knaben Wunderhorn*. The contents of the three books are as follows:

Book I
    *Frühlingsmorgen* [Spring morning] (Leander)
    *Erinnerung* [Memories] (Leander)
    Serenade from *Don Juan* (Tirso de Molina)
    Fantasy from *Don Juan* (Tirso de Molina)
    *Hans und Grete* (originally entitled *Maitanz im Grünen*) (Mahler, after a folk song)

Book II
    *Um schlimme Kinder artig zu machen* [To make bad children behave]
    *Ich ging mit Lust* [I walked with joy]
    *Aus! Aus!* [Out! Out!]
    *Starke Einbildungskraft* [Strong imagination]

Book III
    *Zu Strassburg auf der Schanz* [At Strasburg's entrenchment]
    *Ablösung im Sommer* [Relief in summer]
    *Scheiden und Meiden* [To part and to shun]
    *Nicht Wiedersehen!* [Not to meet again]
    *Selbstgefühl* [Self-reliance]

The *Lieder und Gesänge* do not yet exhibit the full-blown maturity of feeling of the lyric Mahler of later Lieder cycles. Although his first song cycle is the only one scored for piano accompaniment, Mahler subconsciously was already reaching for orchestral effects, advising the accompanist to create illusions of woodwinds and percussion sounds ("like drums," "like a distant pealing of bells from a churchyard"), and urging him to play *"mit starkem Pedalgebrauch"* (with strong use of the pedal).

Although the *Jugendzeit* songs, their range of expression limited by the piano accompaniment, must be considered immature examples of a still budding genius which would flower in later song cycles, the variegation of moods exhibited in them is astounding. Especially appealing is the humor and charm of *Ablösung im Sommer* and *Selbstgefühl*. The martial overtones so dear to Mahler throughout his life already make their appearance in *Aus! Aus!,* and the gloom which was so often to pervade Mahler's inspirations appears in the soldier's sad tale of *Zu Strassburg auf der Schanz.* Unquestionably among the most delightful songs of this group is *Ich ging mit Lust durch den grünen Wald* [I walked with joy through the green forest]. In it, Mahler, with a sure hand, recreates the feeling of the forest so dear to German romantic minds since Weber.

It is important to realize that at this early point in Mahler's compositional life, the influence of the Arnim and Brentano collection of poems, *Des Knaben Wunderhorn,* was an all-pervading one. The appearance of nine *Wunderhorn* poems in books two and three of the *Jugendzeit* cycle has already been noted. Mahler was to embrace that influence fully in his own *Wunderhorn* cycle, in which he set twelve of the poems to music. Even in *Sieben Lieder aus letzter Zeit,* when already another poetic influence (Rückert's) had come to the fore, we still find two texts from *Wunderhorn. Wir geniessen die himmlischen Freuden* [We're enjoying the heavenly pleasures] was to make its appearance again in Mahler's Fourth Symphony. All in all, Mahler was to set twenty-four poems from the *Wunderhorn* anthology to music.

The piano accompaniment in the *Jugendzeit* cycle was bound to soon seem inadequate to the budding conductor and composer, particularly when he was constantly occupied with orchestral sounds and thus compelled to seek more descriptive sounds to express his ideas. The progression to orchestral accompaniment in the next song cycle was therefore a logical step.

## LIEDER EINES FAHRENDEN GESELLEN
[*Songs of a Wayfarer*]

The fact that we are discussing *Lieder eines fahrenden Gesellen* after the *Jugendzeit* songs should not be construed as implying that they were composed in that order. Actually there is an "interlapping" between the more than a decade in which the *Jugendzeit* songs were created (1880–92) and time of composition of the four-song cycle *Lieder eines fahrenden Gesellen,* on which work was begun in 1883.

It was inevitable that after the experience of the *Jugendzeit* songs Mahler should come out with another Lieder cycle, this time with symphonic orchestration rather than piano accompaniment. Yet closer scrutiny presents us with a baffling surprise. The earliest title, *Geschichte von einem fahrenden Gesellen* [Tale of a wayfarer] stems from about 1884. That version presents variances in keys as compared with the final version and appears with a *piano* accompaniment. Closer investigation actually reveals *four* different versions. The above-mentioned 1884 version differs from the published piano-score version, and it, in turn, differs from the published version with orchestral score. The date of orchestration of the *Lieder eines fahrenden Gesellen* is also uncertain. Natalie Bauer-Lechner recalls that Mahler orchestrated the songs for a concert of his music in Berlin under his direction, on 16 March 1896. Not surprisingly, the orchestral version is of greater sophistication than the younger-Mahler, 1884 version. And although the 1896 orchestral version can be assumed to be the final orchestration, it is not the only one; Donald Mitchell discovered a variant orchestral version in Amsterdam, bearing the date of 1895.

Discussion is continuing concerning the text of these songs. Bruno Walter, who had been closest to Mahler, maintained that Mahler did not know the poems of the anthology *Des Knaben Wunderhorn* at the time of his early Lieder cycles. His opinion is supported by H. F. Redlich, Heinrich Kralik, and Paul Stefan, Mahler's disciple and early biographer. However, Siegfried Günther, Paul Bekker, and lately Kurt Blaukopf are confident that Mahler was acquainted with them. Although it was not acknowledged by Mahler, there can be no question that Mahler's song *Wenn mein Schatz Hochzeit macht* [When my love marries] is identical with the *Wunderhorn* poem of the same name. This could be sheer coincidence, because Mahler might have known an isolated poem without being acquainted with the entire collection. However, Donald Mitchell adds fuel to the argument when quoting a conversation with the widow of the poet Richard Dehmel, who recalled Mahler's comment that the *Wunderhorn* collection had been "known and close to him since earliest youth," long before the age of twenty-four.

If we may trust Mahler's confiding to his friend, the archeologist Friedrich (Fritz) Löhr in Vienna, the *Gesellen* songs were the result of the unhappy ending of a torrid love affair with the actress Johanna Richter, who jilted Mahler while he was *Königlicher Musikdirektor* (Royal music director) in Kassel. The relationship between personal and musical experiences seems obvious, because the "wayfarer" also loses his love to somebody else, just as in reality Mahler lost Johanna's love.

With *Lieder eines fahrenden Gesellen* we observe the future pioneer, still steeped in German romanticism but already with a personality which differs greatly from its romantic past. Although Mahler had originally mentioned six songs, the cycle in its 1897 publication contained only four. The titles of the songs already express the continuity of story and emotion in music:

*Wenn mein Schatz Hochzeit macht* [When my love marries]
*Ging heut' morgen übers Feld* [I wandered over the fields this morn]
*Ich hab' ein glühend Messer* [I bear a burning knife]
*Die zwei blauen Augen von meinem Schatz* [My love's blue eyes].

The motif (and motivation) of Mahler's cycle parallels that of Schubert's *Winterreise*. The poet Bauernfeld, Schubert's friend, described for posterity the occasion when Schubert sang *Winterreise* to his friends:

In a voice filled with emotion he sang the entire *Winterreise*. We were dumbfounded by the gloomy atmosphere of the *Lieder*. Those who knew him realized how deeply his creations bit into him and in what anguish they were born.

Yet, while the emotional upheavals which prompted Schubert's and Mahler's songs emanated from similar emotional sources, the consequences were completely different. Mahler was at the beginning of his life; Schubert near the end of his. Mahler sublimated his feelings of loss in his music and found relief after having created his compositions, while Schubert's gloom persisted. Moreover, Mahler's Lieder, created at the beginning of his career, lingered on and reverberated in the vaster realms of his symphonies. *Ging heut' Morgen übers Feld* and *Die zwei blauen Augen,* for example, became part of his First Symphony (already in the planning state in Kassel), to be heard in the first and third movements, respectively.

The *Gesellen* songs have autobiographical meaning in more than one sense. First, of course because of the love interest; and secondly because the fields and nature in general were always important to Mahler. Whether it was the Danube and the Vienna woods, the Habichtswald and the Fulda near Kassel, or the lakes and mountains of southern Austria, nature was never far from his mind and music.

With the final 1896 version of *Lieder eines fahrenden Gesellen* Mahler entered into a new phase of his music. For one thing, Mahler no longer occupied himself with piano accompaniment but instead created an orchestral accompaniment—a logical outgrowth, as we have seen, of Mahler's preoccupation and experimentation with orchestral sound and color. Mahler also realized that the orchestra, by then already grown to gigantic size, had to be scaled down to chamber-music proportions in order not to overwhelm the delicacy of the vocal presentation. Here again Mahler's crossroads position is highlighted. If the twentieth century was to resent and reject overblown harmonies and return to the chamber-orchestra size of the Baroque and the early Viennese classics, it was Mahler who intuitively foresaw it. The resulting economy of musical means, as displayed in his songs, stands in marked contrast to the songs of Mahler's two contemporaries; consider the "fat" instrumentation of Brahms or the rich, lush sounds emanating from Strauss's pen. *Tonmalerei* (tone painting) in Mahler's Lieder is, with few exceptions, delicate, whether it depicts pleasure, passion, or sorrow.

No less significant is that Mahler was no longer bound to the orthodox tyranny of tonic and dominant. (In fact, the fourth was to become his favorite interval.) The resulting freedom of modulation, which disregards established progressions, gives his songs a strange expressiveness, often harking back to true folk song.

The opening song, *Wenn mein Schatz Hochzeit macht,* depicts the wayfarer's reaction to his former sweetheart's wedding day in an oddly undulating Slavic–Jewish theme. "Flowers, stop blooming, birds, stop singing, spring is gone and all is over."

*Ging heut' morgen übers Feld* opens with an oddly deceiving, spirited melody. The words speak of the beauties of nature, as the sun begins to shine and the birds and flowers greet him. But the ending of the song falls back into a morose mood: "No! No! My happiness can never bloom."

*Ich hab' ein glühend Messer* assails the listener with unexpected drama. This stormily romantic song rises to lamenting outcry, only to retreat into the wayfarer's painful rememberance of his sweetheart's blue eyes, blonde hair, and silvery laughter.

The fourth and final song, *Die zwei blauen Augen von meinem Schatz*, is the best known, because two of its melodies were incorporated into symphonies by Mahler. It is the wayfarer's farewell to his distant sweetheart, after he has said farewell to the place of happiness in the dark of night. But one place lingers on: the linden tree, under which he slept and dreamt and which had showered him with blossoms. His memory of it lingers as the song dies away, with the original phrase of "my love's blue eyes" echoing sadly.


## DIE DREI PINTOS
*(After sketches by Carl Maria von Weber)*

*First performance, Stadttheater, Leipzig, 20 January 1888. Dramatic parts by Carl Maria von Weber, musical parts by Mahler, conducted by Mahler, stage design by J. Kautsky of Vienna.*

In many commentaries on Mahler, the *Pintos* sketches are brushed aside with a mere mention. This is unfortunate because Mahler's work on the sketches to Weber's opera *Die drei Pintos* is significantly revealing of his artistic growth.

Despite his success in *Der Freischütz*, Weber had been stung by some adverse criticism, to the effect that he had selected an ill-chosen subject and could not rise above the style of a *Singspiel*.[6] ("Praise lifts me to dizzy heights," he wrote, "but I am shattered by the smallest, even most unjustified and ridiculous criticism.") Weber soon thereafter began work on the comic opera *Die drei Pintos*. The libretto had been prepared by Theodor Hell from the book *Der Brautkampf* by Carl Seidel. The scene was Spain, a milieu that was much in favor at that time and to which Weber was much attracted—as Wolf, another romantic composer, was to be in later years. At that time (November 1821), Weber received an inquiry from Domenico Barbaia, newly ensconced impresario at the prestigious *Kärnthnerthor Theater* in Vienna, for a new opera for the following season.

[6] A primitive German play, usually comic, interspersed with songs and dances.

Eager to prove his critics wrong, Weber agreed with alacrity. The result was *Euryanthe,* with a libretto by Wilhelmina von Chezy. Work on *Die drei Pintos* was set aside but never abandoned, because we know from many biographical references to Weber that as late as less than two years before his death Weber worked on the comic opera at the same time as he did on *Oberon. Pintos,* however, was destined not to be completed. Although rumors persisted that he had finished it, and Caroline Weber insisted that she had seen the complete score, only sketches have come down to us.

A number of men were interested in finishing the opera. Weber's successor in Dresden, Carl Reissiger, wished to attempt the work, but Caroline Weber reserved the right to decide who should complete her husband's unfinished task and decided on Meyerbeer. He kept the sketches for twenty (!) years, only to return them, with no work done, to Max Maria Weber, the composer's son. Upon Max's death in 1881 the manuscript sketches came into the hands of Captain Carl von Weber, the composer's grandson, in Leipzig. It was there that Mahler and manuscript met. When Mahler arrived in Leipzig to become second *Kapellmeister* at the opera under Nikisch in 1886, Staegemann, the opera director, introduced Mahler to Weber. Weber was impressed with the young romantic composer/conductor [7] and saw fit to hand his grandfather's sketches to him, with the request that he complete them into an opera. Mahler, in turn, was impressed with the charm of the extant parts and decided to create from them an opera in two musical acts and a third, spoken act. The idea turned out not to be feasible, however, and Mahler decided on a three-act opera in traditional style.

To accomplish his task Mahler not only orchestrated the existing sketches and composed the entr'acte music between acts I and II from them, but also searched through the remainder of Weber's music looking for suitable material. He eventually incorporated music Weber had composed for his brother Fridolin (the *Pastiche Der Freibrief,* after an opera by Haydn), for Friedrich Kindos's drama *Das Nachtlager von Granada,* and for a *Singspiel* by Anton Fischer (*Der travestirte Aeneas*), as well as music from such complete Weber compositions as his *Jubel Cantata* and the cantata *Den Sachsen-Sohn.* He also provided two alternate finales, one assembled from Act I themes, the other based on a theme from Act III.

In doing so Mahler trod a narrow path. By attempting to assemble into an entity *Pintos* and non-*Pintos* music, orchestrating all of it in the manner and spirit of Weber, he constantly had to be on guard not to let his own romantic feelings color the earlier composer's work. Nevertheless his own contribution was bound to be extensive. Besides, he thought the

---

[7] Mahler by then had composed *Das klagende Lied* and one Lieder cycle, with another cycle of songs and his First Symphony in the offing.

libretto supplied by Captain von Weber strayed from the composer's spirit and revised it to a great extent. His greatest task by far was to supply accompaniment, because all of the sketches, with the exception of one page, had been left unorchestrated. He was to the greatest extent successful in his task, and John Warrack calls the inspired entr'acte music a tour de force.

Controversy was bound to arise as to the merits of the Mahler adaptation. The correspondence between the young Richard Strauss and his mentor Bülow is characteristic of the strong feelings Mahler's work aroused in both camps. After Mahler had played the music of the first act to Strauss, the twenty-three-year-old Strauss wrote to Bülow a letter in which he burst forth about the charm and merits of Weber's "masterpiece."

> Most genuine, most likeable, and most gifted Weber! I believe you will be pleased with it too . . . with Weber's technical mastery, completely free of dilletantism.
>
> Strauss to Bülow, 29 October 1887

Bülow was not at all in accord with young Strauss's enthusiasm, however. Oddly enough, it was five months before he answered Strauss's enthusiastic approbation with a scathing critique, in which he characterized the work as

> a monstrosity of syntactical and orthographical impurity . . . odious, antiquated rubbish. I felt positively ill.
>
> Bülow to Strauss, 27 March 1888

Strauss, completely cowed by Bülow's expletives, let the dust settle for nearly three weeks before he replied, a chastened man.

> How salutary for me was your justifiable reproach. . . . It was terribly rash of me to recommend a work of which I knew only the first act. . . . Mahler has committed some frightful stupidities. . . . I now regret very much that you, most revered Master, should have been the innocent victim of my youthful impetuosity.
>
> Strauss to Bülow, 17 April 1888

Despite Mahler's integrity and caution—he subordinated his impulses in order to do justice to a romantic composer of another, earlier period—the opera became as much Mahler's as it was Weber's. It can only make one regret that Mahler had seen fit to consign his own early operatic attempts to the funeral pyre of compositional integrity.

The consensus after the Leipzig premiere and further performances in Dresden, Hamburg, and Vienna confirmed Bülow's impatient comment: "Wo Weberei, wo Mahlerei, einerlei"—a pun on Weber's and Mahler's names, meaning, freely translated, "Where does Weber, where does Mahler, begin or end—it's all the same!" A left-handed compliment, in a sense, to Mahler.

# SYMPHONY NO. 1 IN D MAJOR
(*Titan*)

> My work [the First Symphony] is finished! . . . people are likely to be surprised by many things! It grew to overwhelming—flowing out of me like a mountain torrent! . . . All the floodgates within me were thrown open at one sweep!
>
> Mahler to Dr. Friedrich Löhr, March 1888

> It is . . . the extraordinary technical abilities of Mahler . . . which hinder rather than assist him. . . . He frankly staggers with his virtuosity . . . which would be unthinkable without a thorough absorption of the scores of Berlioz and Wagner . . . he is easily led astray by this technical superiority into using harsh colors and exaggerations of expression. . . . This is especially true in the Finale. . . [which] deafens by its great array of instrumental forces, particularly its intensive use of timpani and cymbals.
>
> August Beer, *Pester Lloyd*, 21 November 1889

> Aside from the numerous musical beauties which are spread before us in Mahler's First Symphony, the fabulous art of its magnificent orchestration alone would recommend it to the study of the musician. The work is a compendium of modern orchestration. There is no effect that does not appear; every effect is carefully prepared [and] executed with the greatest expertise and not one misfired. . . .
>
> Max Kalbeck, *Neue Freie Presse*, 20 November 1901

*Composition begun in 1884 in Kassel, finished in 1888 in Leipzig. First performance, Budapest, 20 November 1889, Mahler conducting. Partially revised in 1892 and 1893 for Hamburg performance, 27 October 1893.*

*Scored for 2 piccolos, 4 flutes, 4 oboes, English horn, 4 clarinets, bass clarinet, 3 bassoons, contrabassoon, 7 horns, 5 trumpets, 4 trombones, tuba, kettle drums, bass drum, tam-tam, cymbals, triangle, harp and strings. (Ratz edition 1966)*

It should not surprise us that a novel approach to musical material is to be observed with Mahler as early as his first symphonic venture, at the comparatively young age of twenty-eight.[8] We are specifically referring to

---

[8] The musicologist Dr. Paul Stefan noted that: "Mengelberg felt that the Mahler First Symphony exhibited such perfection that it had not been a first. His conjecture was borne out when he discovered four youthful symphonies of Mahler in the archives of Baroness Weber, the wife of Carl Maria von Weber's grandson, in Dresden. After examination, Mengelberg and [composer] Max von Schilling actually played the scores on the piano, being so fascinated with them that they took all night and did not finish until six in the morning." Nothing further has been heard of these symphonies, and if they existed (and we have no reason to doubt Mengelberg's account) they presumably were destroyed by the British bombing attack on Dresden in 1945.

the introduction of originally vocal material into the symphony. Such inclusion was of course not novel per se. Schubert had reintroduced the themes of his own songs—and only his own songs—into his chamber music, (e.g., the Piano Quintet, opus 114 [*The Trout*] and the Quartet in D Minor [*Death and the Maiden*] and in his *Wanderer Fantasy*. Beethoven had made history of a different kind with the Choral Finale of his Ninth Symphony. But neither of these giants had advanced to Mahler's point—that of incorporating songs into the symphonic form and thus changing and again widening its format, as we observe in Mahler's First Symphony, by means of the orchestral use of songs from his cycle *Lieder eines fahrenden Gesellen*. It is at that point that we observe Mahler's departure from the classical or even early romantic concept of the symphony, which had its roots in Haydn and Mozart and which proceeds, with little innovation after Beethoven, through Mendelssohn, Schumann, and Brahms. It is Mahler's inclusion of the lyrical song element into the symphonic structure, along with the subsequent wedding of opposites— the lyric and the dramatic—in *Das Lied von der Erde* [The Song of the Earth], which constitutes one of Mahler's most important achievements.

Wherever we look in that first symphonic attempt we encounter novel treatment; the already mentioned use of his *Gesellen* songs, the setting of *Frère Jacques* in the third movement, the reference to Bohemian village musicians, reminiscent of Beethoven's *Pastorale* symphony. Thus, despite the uncertainties still observed in melodic and thematic treatment, and the looseness of and inconsistencies in form, development, and style, not unexpected in an opening work and never to be encountered again in Mahler's, his First remains an incredible, pioneering effort. The use of preconceived melodic lyricism is observed at every turn in this remarkable work, interspersed with moments of high drama such as the explosive *fff* chord which opens the final movement after the *ppp* finale of the funeral march. Such theatricalities, more integrated in subsequent compositions, indicate Mahler's love for the dramatic, nurtured by his experiences as operatic director and conductor.

At the premiere before an uncomprehending Budapest public at a time when Mahler headed the Budapest Opera, the work was referred to as a "Symphonic Poem in Two Parts." For the second and third performances (in Hamburg—1893—and Weimar—1894) Mahler went to the unusual step of supplying program notes à la Berlioz. These were subsequently eliminated [9] and the subtitle *Titan* applied to the work. Few people then knew that the subtitle did not refer to a mythological figure but rather to a novel by a favorite of Mahler, the romantic poet Jean Paul (Jean Paul Richter), and simply stood for a "vigorous, heroic man." Eventually the subtitle went out of favor with the composer, whose dislike for

---

[9] Mahler went so far as to admit to the critic Max Marschalk in March 1896 that he invented the program material *after* the actual composition.

realistic program music grew as he matured. He eventually preferred the symphony untitled, but for commercial reasons the subtitle *Titan* remained affixed. The symphony actually did not offer food for afterthought or elicit debate until the more conventional Andante of the third movement was replaced by the much-debated Funeral March.

Most commentators attach too much significance to Mahler's passing remark concerning Callot's painting *The Huntsman's Funeral* in relation to the third movement. Mahler's allusion to the picture was apparently as casual as Beethoven's with respect to the opening of his Fifth Symphony. When Schindler inquired of Beethoven concerning the meaning of the opening theme of that work, Beethoven, impatient with the superficial nature of the question, replied *"So pocht das Schiksal an die Pforte"* [Thus fate knocks at the portal], giving the theme a quasi-programmatic meaning. But Beethoven was also never comfortable with titled programs, as his hedging comment to his Sixth Symphony indicates. Bruckner, in his Fourth Symphony (the *Romantic*) made an equally unsuccessful attempt at programmatic interpretation. Although program music attained a place of respect in many quarters during the nineteenth century, Mahler was not convinced as to the merits of programmatic interpretation of his music, and his first symphony was a case in point. After attaching the subtitle he deleted it for the Berlin performance of 16 March 1896, considering it "quite inadequate" and misleading. He argued to the critic Max Marshalk:

> In the third movement [the funeral march] it is true that I got the immediate inspiration from the well-known children's picture [*The Huntsman's Funeral*]—but in this place it is irrelevant. . . . The only important thing is the mood which should be expressed and from which the fourth movement then suddenly springs forth, like lightning from a dark cloud. This is simply the cry of a deeply wounded heart, preceded by the ghostly, brooding oppressiveness of the funeral march.

Yet, only ten days later Mahler hedged on the statement.

> Just as I find it banal to invent music for a program, I find it unsatisfactory and unfruitful to attempt to provide a program to a piece of music—this in spite of the fact that the immediate cause of a musical conception is certainly an experience of the author, that is to say, a fact which is surely concrete enough to be described in words. . . . All the same, it is good when, during the first phase, when my style still seems strange and new, the listener gets some road maps and milestones on the journey or rather a map of the stars, that he may comprehend the night sky with its glowing world. But such an explanation cannot offer more.

In light of the above, no program expressed by Mahler should be taken literally except in the larger context of his overall cosmic philosophy. Therein lies the main difference between Mahler and Strauss. Mahler always looked askance at Strauss's realistic approach to a program, worlds apart from his own poetic/philosophic conception. Mahler's churning creativity refused to be forced into preconceived molds. To him each work demanded a fresh approach and was an entity unto itself—indeed, staked out a new world. Thus he declaimed, with reference to his First Symphony, "My symphony will be something of which the world has never heard the like before." It was, he wrote, "the greatest thing I've done yet—and so original in concept and form that it absolutely cannot be described."

The introduction to the First movement (*langsam*—slowly), is one of those *Naturlaute* (nature sounds) so dear to Mahler,

leading into the main theme, the orchestral version of Mahler's own *Gesellen* song *Ging heut' morgen übers Feld*:

Soon new sounds mingle, among them an initially inconspicuous phrase in the celli which gains in dimension and importance as the movement continues:

and shortly, thereafter, intermingled with bird calls, yet another theme appears in the horns in Mahler's favorite interval, fourths:

From these themes romanticism slowly builds inevitably into a climax, with all themes presented and interwoven, often in canonic treatment. Brucknerisms and Wagnerisms are glimpsed in the process, which ends in a delightfully abrupt timpani finale.

The brief second movement is, in its A–B–A construction, the one most steeped in classical traditionalism. With its tempo marking of *Kräftig bewegt* (powerfully moving), Mahler has moved the scherzo from its traditional position as the third movement of the symphony into the second movement. Using another song, *Hans und Grete,* as a *basso ostinato,* he lunges again into a nature-inspired atmosphere in the manner of Bruckner, who took delight in including entire Austrian peasant dances —*Ländler*—into the scherzi of his symphonies. The movement opens with a forceful, leaping interchange between the opening basses, the violins, and the woodwinds:

The traditional Trio (the "B" or middle section) is in Brucknerian *Ländler tempo,* with, however, an ever so slightly faster tempo, *Sehr zart aber ausdrucksvoll* (very tender but expressive), carrying it into the realm of the waltz:

The famous *Andante* Funeral March (*Feierlich gemessen,* solemn and measured) is a significant factor in the symphony. An oddly distorted *Frère Jacques* is given sinister canonic treatment over relentless timpani, building a quiet yet overpowering funeral mood.

A most amazing feature of the movement, in addition to the march, is the fervor, furor, and mockery which Mahler imparts to it after the march by the introduction of a tune whose melody and rhythm reveal it to be of Chassidic as well as Slavic origin:

Briefly a quotation from another Mahler song appears. It is the *Lindenbaum* motif from one of Mahler's most moving *Gesellen* songs, *Die zwei blauen Augen von meinem Schatz* [My Love's blue eyes]; but soon that oddly intoxicating Slavic–Jewish melody reappears, until the movement gently subsides. It is in these two middle movements that Mahler reveals himself, as early as his First Symphony, as an "Austrian" composer—as he presents in them themes and rhythms of such divergent origin as Austrian Alpine, Viennese, Jewish, and Slavic.

All of the preceding, however, seem only a preparation for the monumental Finale (*Stürmisch bewegt,* stormily agitated), which is almost as long as the preceding three movements. If the most general of programs is to be alluded to, then the "titanic" struggle of the last movement sees the hero victorious over all adversities.

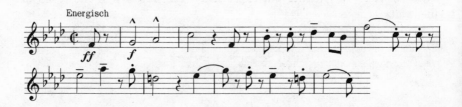

Soon Mahler thoughtfully, brilliantly, emphasizes the cyclic form of the work by injecting the delicate "dawn" (*Naturlaute*) theme of descending fourths in the oboes, intoning it in a variety of dynamics from *pp* to *fff,* in augmentation, intoned by seven horns, interspersed with the opening theme. Here again Mahler exhibits his penchant for theatricality. Exploring his expertise in modulation, employing the effective device of the *basso ostinato,* he builds toward a powerful finale, ranging across the full dynamic gamut in the span of thirteen bars. But again Mahler changes direction, as the celli and violins sing the *Cantilena* (*Sehr gesangvoll,* very songlike):

Only after that songful interlude does Mahler allow progress toward the triumphant finale. What had opened *"Wie ein Naturlaut"* (like a sound of nature) stands proudly in the finale:

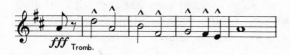

Thus a strong cyclic relationship between the two outer movements is expressed, but now the mysterious opening sounds are proudly, jubilantly transformed.

In majesty and splendor the final movement rivals another magnificent First Symphony, Brahms's C Minor. In another sense it is without peer in the history of first symphonies. If we are impressed with Brahm's achievement, we must not lose sight of the fact that he built on traditional ground, continuing in a familiar tradition. Mahler defied that tradition. Like Beethoven in his time, Mahler left the familiar behind to seek new musical frontiers.

If the two outer movements of the symphony have been compared to the covers of a book, the "pages" are no less significant, because in the inner movements Mahler's romantic eccentricity is given full rein in the previously quoted waltz-*Ländler* in the second-movement scherzo. And the ingenious treatment in the Andante of an innocent children's song in the somber garb of mourning, executed in medieval canon, is still a stunning tour de force.

Nine years were to pass between the symphony's initial performance and its eventual publication in Vienna, made possible through the help of Mahler's friend Guido Adler. Today, when Mahler's First Symphony is on the verge of becoming one of the most frequently performed concert-hall works (rivaling Brahms's First), it is difficult to realize that its performance in Vienna and Weimar prompted jeers and catcalls and garnered

such epithets as "sterile," "trivial" and "extravagant." The Weimar performance in 1894 had been important to Mahler (although the German
audience had reacted no more favorably than the Budapest audience before
it), because the city, under the benevolent eye of the Grand Duke and the
Grand Duke's chief conductor, Richard Strauss, had become a center of
musical culture of far more significance than the usual provincial capital.

Strauss, attending successfully to his own affairs right from the start,
had there performed his symphonic poem *Don Juan,* which had caused an
international sensation, as well as his opera *Guntram,* along with the
most famous children's opera ever composed, *Hänsel und Gretel* by Humperdinck. It was Strauss who had conducted Mahler's First Symphony. On
that occasion he and Mahler renewed their acquaintance, and Strauss
evinced interest in Mahler's Second Symphony and held out hopes for
a possible performance in Berlin. Although beset by doubts concerning
Strauss's promise (as will be seen later, Strauss half kept it), Mahler
secretly hoped for such an opportunity, because Strauss, although four
years younger than Mahler, had already attained a measure of fame and
notoriety.

Despite Strauss's performance, it is not difficult to imagine that the
Andante music must have had the same effect on Weimar (and Vienna)
at the end of the nineteenth century as Beethoven's *Eroica* funeral march
had had at the beginning of that same century.

A word, in passing, should be said about the "missing" *Blumine* (*Andante*) movement of the symphony. It must be remembered that at its first
performance in Budapest the First Symphony had been a *five*-movement
work. Only shortly before publication in 1898 was the *Blumine* movement eliminated by Mahler. Since the first independent performance of
the *Blumine* movement by Benjamin Britten on 18 June 1967 at the
Aldeburgh Festival, some interesting background material has come to
light.

In 1883, while in Kassel, Mahler composed the incidental music to
Scheffel's poem *Der Trompeter von Säkkingen.*[10] That work was among
those much disliked by Mahler at a later date. The manuscript disappeared; but what had apparently been the trumpet theme, as remembered
by a friend, was quoted by Paul Stefan in his biography of Mahler. It was
Donald Mitchell who discovered that the *Trompeter* theme as quoted by
Stefan and the opening trumpet theme of the *Blumine* movement were
identical (although in different keys). Mitchell goes so far as to suggest
that the entire *Blumine* movement may have been part of the *Trompeter*
suite.

---

[10] One year later (1884), Victor Nessler was to write an opera with the same title
on the same theme. Despite its tawdry music, the opera's fashionable "old-
German" style met with much acclaim in Germany.

Bruno Walter recalls:

Mahler was tireless in polishing and improving his works, and did not
spare himself in his work. Sometimes he destroyed whole piles of manuscripts. Once I was present at just such an auto-da-fé and rescued what I
could. In this way Mahler made me a a present of an unpublished fifth
movement of his First Symphony as a souvenir; it was a wonderful idyllic
piece with a trumpet theme, which he had found insufficiently symphonic.

*Der Tag,* 17 November 1935, quoted in *Personal Reminiscences*

## DES KNABEN WUNDERHORN
### [*The Boy's Magic Horn*]

No greater contrast could be imagined between Achim von Arnim (1781–
1831), the proper Prussian *Junker* aristocrat, and Clemens Brentano
(1778–1842), the roaming, guitar-strumming minstrel, but together
with Bettina von Arnim, Brentano's sister and Achim's wife, they made
an illustrious trio. Bettina had corresponded with Goethe and fallen in
love with Beethoven; it was through her that Beethoven and Goethe met.
Both Achim von Arnim and Clemens Brentano—particularly Brentano,
who had met Goethe, Herder, and Wieland during his student days in
Heildelberg—were literary lights of considerable influence in establishing
a German literary trend.

But it was Brentano's work in collaboration with Arnim which was
to earn them both undying fame, because Brentano, the roaming idealist,
and Arnim, the correct Prussian, pooled their interest in and love for the
ancient folk art of Germany and together began to collect hundreds of the
poems and songs which they had gathered in the course of their roaming—from oldsters who had heard them as children from *their* parents
and grandparents and now wished to pass them on to a new generation,
and from peasants, shepherds, and other wandering minstrels strolling
the countryside, wishing to entertain in return for a meal and a night's
rest.

Eventually that collection of hundreds of poems and songs was published in three volumes at the beginning of the nineteenth century under
the title *Des Knaben Wunderhorn,* with the first volume being dedicated
to Goethe. It was soon recognized as a veritable treasure trove of German
folk art and greatly influenced poets, such as Eichendorff and Heine who
stated: "We feel the heartbeat of the German people. . . . Here German
passion burns and German jesting makes merry; here German love blooms.
Here sparkle both truly German wine and truly German tears. The book
contains some of the loveliest flowering of the German spirit." Goethe,
enchanted with the anthology, recommended it to all intelligent people.

He particularly felt that the poems should inspire composers to set them to music.

It comes as a surprise, therefore, that for eighty years those inspiring, glowing, brooding romantic poems escaped the attention of such inspired Lieder composers as Schubert, Schumann, and Brahms; it was left to Mahler to discover them and practically make them his own. In enjoying Mahler's songs, however, one should realize that he was not beyond altering the poems to suit his romantic feelings, as will be seen in a later example. This, incidentally, had also been the case with Arnim and Brentano, who had no qualms about changing text and context on occasion to better express the romantic spirit as they understood it.

Mahler may have known the anthology even before he started his position in Leipzig. It is easily understandable that those songs and poems exerted an immediate influence on the conductor/composer's romantic mind. His *Lieder und Gesänge aus der Jugendzeit,* published in 1892, included nine *Wunderhorn* songs. Although at least three of the four songs of the next cycle, *Lieder eines fahrenden Gesellen,* were set to Mahler's own poems, the fascination persisted to such an extent that Mahler titled his next major song cycle *Des Knaben Wunderhorn.*[11]

A distinction should be made between the actual twelve-song *Lieder* cycle bearing the title *Des Knaben Wunderhorn* and the general designation of *Wunderhorn* songs referring generally to the poems from the Arnim–Brentano anthology. Poems from the anthology are actually set to music in three different Mahler cycles—*Gesänge aus der Jugendzeit, Des Knaben Wunderhorn,* and *Sieben Lieder aus Letzter Zeit*—and there also exists one independent song. Mahler's compositions of *Wunderhorn* songs thus took in a span of roughly twelve years and involve twenty-four poems, distributed as follows:[12]

| | |
|---|---|
| *Lieder und Gesänge aus der Jugendzeit* | 9 poems |
| *Des Knaben Wunderhorn* | 12 poems |
| *Sieben Lieder aus letzter Zeit* | 2 poems |
| *Wir geniessen die himmlischen Freuden* | 1 poem |

In the *Wunderhorn* cycle, Mahler—after a song hiatus of nearly ten years—emerges as the matured song composer. Some typical motifs are apparent: the military signal, the march in all its ramifications, the drum beat, the eerie scene—all are eloquently elevated from trite sounds to meaningful symbolism. So important did these songs become in Mahler's maturing as a person and in composition that *Urlicht* was to emerge

[11] Musicologists differ on the exact date of composition of the *Wunderhorn* songs. Ratz and Kralik place them at 1892–95, Redlich at 1888–90, and Blaukopf at 1891–97. Mitchell places the first four in 1892, the next three in 1893 and the last four between 1896 and 1898.

[12] The number could be increased to twenty-five if the *Gesellen* song *Wenn mein Schatz Hochzeit macht* is counted as a *Wunderhorn* song.

prominently as the fourth movement of his Second Symphony, as does another song from the cycle, the *Fischpredigt.*

Variation in approach to his subject matters is also interesting to observe in Mahler's *Lieder* progress. While in some of his cycles, like the *Gesellen,* he adds to the cohesion by consistency in mood, in the *Wunderhorn* songs he prefers complete diversity of mood and treatment. Such a determined change of mood from song to song adds to the charm of the complete cycle.

Thus, the first song, *Der Schildwache Nachtlied* [The sentry's night song] features an eerie midnight vigil in dialogue form utilizing a military theme. *Verlor'ne Müh* [Wasted effort], a delightful dialogue between a lad and his girl, has strong sensuous overtones, while *Trost im Unglück* [Consolation in sorrow] reflects a somewhat bitter, defiant negation of love between a hussar and his girl. *Wer hat das Liedel erdacht* [Who made up this song], in its lighthearted naiveté, harks back to Mahler's less sophisticated, younger years. No greater contrast could be imagined than that presented by the next song, *Das irdische Leben* [The earthly life], with its horrifying dialogue between a hungry child and its mother—in conception and spirit so akin to Schubert's *Der Erlkönig,* with its relentless rhythm driving toward an inexorable and bitter end. Again Mahler achieves contrast, this time reaching toward the lighter side with *Des Antonius von Padua Fischpredigt* [St. Anthony of Padua's sermon to the fishes]. Ranging from the comical to the sardonic, Mahler retells the famed story in music. St. Anthony, finding the church empty, goes to the river to preach to the fishes, who come in droves and enjoy his sermon immensely. But, with the sermon ended, the pikes remain thieves and the eels lovers, the lobsters still crawl backwards, the codfish remain stupid, and the carps eat voraciously. The cynicism of the parable is obvious; the sermon is forgotten and nothing has changed. In *Rheinlegendchen* [Legend of the Rhine] (its original title was *Tanzlegendchen*), cynicism and sarcasm are put aside in a song in three-quarter time filled with naive charm. Contrast is sustained in *Lied des Verfolgten im Turm* [Song of the pursued one in the tower], as Mahler again engages in defiant, impassioned philosophizing on the freedom of thought. *Lob des hohen Verstandes* [In praise of high intellect] again relates a tale of fine ironic humor in a song in which the cuckoo and the nightingale, engaged in a song contest, elect the ass to be the judge. Here already we find a foretaste of the polyphony which was to emerge five years later in Mahler's Fifth Symphony. The two songs which round out Mahler's *Wunderhorn* cycle, *Es sungen drei Engel* and *Urlicht,* will be discussed in subsequent sections in the symphonies in which they appear.

Although the song *Wo die schönen Trompeten blasen* [Where the beautiful trumpets blow] is not always located at or near the end of the cycle, we have put it at the end of our discussion because the song is a noteworthy example of how Mahler changed a text to make it completely his own. The lyrics of the song, orginally titled *Unbeschreibliche Freude* [Indescribable joy], was changed from a lovely midnight tryst into an eerie midnight rendezvous between a maid and the ghost of her dead soldier sweetheart. Mahler's hallmark, the trumpet motif underlining the macabre text, makes this song a miniature masterpiece. (The English translation presents only the Mahler version.)

## WO DIE SCHÖNEN TROMPETEN BLASEN

Wer ist da draussen and klopft an
Der mich so leise wecken kann?
Das ist der Herzallerliebste dein
Steh auf und lass mich zu dir ein.

} [original]

Was soll ich hier noch länger steh'n?
Ich seh' die Morgenröte aufgeh'n
Die Morgenröt, zwei helle Stern
Bei meinem Schatz da wär ich gern
Bei meinem Herzallerliebe.

} [added by Mahler]

Das Mädchen stand auf und liess ihn ein
Mit seinem schneeweissen Hemdelein
Mit seinem schneeweissen Beinen
Das Mädchen fing an zu weinen.

} [original eliminated by Mahler]

Das Mädchen stand auf und liess ihn ein
Sie heisst ihn auch willkommen sein.
Willkommen lieber Knabe mein
So lang hast du gestanden!

} [added by Mahler]

Sie reicht ihm auch die schneeweisse Hand
Von ferne sang die Nachtigall
Das Mädchen find zu weinen.

} [added by Mahler]

Ach weine nicht, du Liebste mein,
Aufs Jahr sollst du mein Eigen sein
Mein Eigen sollst du werden gewiss
Wie's keine sonst auf Erden ist!*
O Lieb auf grüner Erden.

} [original with one line (*) added by Mahler]

Ich wollt' dass alle Felder wären Papier
Und alle Studenten schrieben hier,
Sie schrieben ja hier die liebe lang Nacht
Sie schrieben us beiden die Liebe nicht ab.

} [original, eliminated by Mahler]

Ich zieh' in Krieg auf grüne Heid'
Die grüne Heid', die ist so weit.
Allwo die schönen Trompeten blasen
Das ist mein Haus, mein Haus von
    grünem Rasen.

} [added by Mahler]

### WHERE THE BEAUTIFUL TRUMPETS BLOW

Who stands out there, and knocks
Who can wake me so gently?
'Tis your heart's dearest love
Rise and let me in.

Why should I stand here longer?
I see the rosy dawn arise
The rosy dawn and two bright stars
By my sweetheart I long to be
By my dearest love.

The maiden rose and let him in;
She also bade him welcome.
Welcome dear lad of mine
So long you've stood out there.

She also gave him her snowwhite hand
From far off sang the nightingale;
The maiden began to weep.

O do not weep my dearest love
Within a year thou shalt be mine
My own thou shalt be for sure
Like no one else on earth can be!
O love of earth so green.

I go to war on the green heath
The green heath it is so far
Where the beautiful trumpets blow
There is my home, my home 'neath green sod.


## THE WUNDERHORN TRILOGY:
*Symphonies Nos. 2, 3, and 4*


An undeniable kinship, thematic as well as spiritual, is evident in Mahler's
first four symphonies. He seems to have aimed at integration and continuity by establishing philosophical and thematic connections between the
First and Second symphonies, the Second and Third, and the Third and
Fourth.

The Second, Third, and Fourth symphonies in particular must be
considered as constituting a symphonic cycle itself, going so far as to incorporate direct quotations from the Third Symphony in the Fourth. Of
course such a cyclic device (recurring material from one movement or

complete composition in a subsequent movement or composition), is not novel, having been encountered in Beethoven's Ninth Symphony, Berlioz's *Sinfonie Fantastique,* and Bruckner's Ninth Symphony and, even more deliberately, in Franck's D minor Symphony. Mahler's novelty of invention rests on his extension of such cyclic connections and quotations over a *cycle of symphonies,* with the *Wunderhorn* songs contributing the lion's share of connective musical and literary material. Thus Mahler went beyond the cyclic idea for the individual work, superimposing a vaster cyclic idea. Philosophically these three interrelated symphonies express Mahler's convictions at the time; melodically they are bound together by the use in each of them of songs from the composer's *Wunderhorn* cycle: in the Second Symphony, *Urlicht* (and Klopstock's *Aufersteh'n*); in the Third, *Es singen drei Engel einen süssen Gesang* (To dispel the gloom of Nietzsche's *O Mensch gib Acht*). In the Fourth Symphony, Mahler's *Wunderhorn* song *Das himmlische Leben* is heard. Moreover, Symphonies Two and Three are doubly bound together because they each contain another *Wunderhorn Lied,* now transformed into an instrumental symphonic offering. In the Second it is *St. Antonius von Padua Fischpredigt* and in the Third *Ablösung im Sommer,* from Mahler's *Jugendzeit* songs, also based on a *Wunderhorn* text.

Cognizance should be taken of the spirit which pervades these works, as marked by the selection of songs by the composer. Not yet has darkness and the spirit of gloom and struggle suffused Mahler's spirit and music; rather, the spirit of these song selections ranges from lighthearted and gay to a strong spiritual belief in triumph and redemption. The romanticism of Mahler's early years and of the *Wunderhorn* days permeates this cycle of symphonies, the skies are yet unclouded by the oppressive moods and the spirit of farewell and death expressed later. All three symphonies are also bound together by their programmatic content, initially elaborately devised by Mahler only to be, in typical Mahler fashion, promptly suppressed and abnegated. Such an attitude on the part of Mahler is understandable. Personally he disdained descriptive program notes; but in relationship with a public completely devoid of any comprehension of his intent, he felt the need for a program (on their behalf) "as a crutch for a cripple." In that connection **Arthur Seidl**'s significant comparison between the programs of Richard Strauss and Mahler is insightful. "Mahler's music arrives at a program as its last clarification," he remarks, "whereas in the case of Strauss, the program already exists as a given task." In other words, Strauss's programs, like those of Berlioz, are the extramusical foundation on which the music is built, whereas with Mahler the program is a clarification *after* the fact.

The importance of Seidl's statement cannot be overrated. The fullest and most visionary consequence of Mahler's use of "the word" and its fullest realization in a Mahlerian sense would have to wait until 1906 and

Mahler's Eighth. The full meaning of Mahler's search and philosophy reveals itself then as he scours the literature of the world to find a fitting text for his music.


## SYMPHONY NO. 2 IN C MINOR
(*Resurrection*)

This is to announce the auspicious birth of a strong, healthy last movement for the Second [Symphony]. Father and child are doing as well as can be expected; the latter is not yet out of danger.

It is to be baptized with the name *Lux lucet in tenebris* [The light shineth in the darkness]. Friends are asked for their silent sympathy; all flowers are gratefully refused. Other gifts, however, will be accepted.

Mahler to Dr. Friedrich Löhr, Steinbach am Attersee, 29 June 1894

This tragic symphonic dream of man's fate and confident faith was performed at Berlin Philharmonic Hall. The work, masterfully conducted by Mahler . . . had the effect of an elemental event. I shall never forget my deep emotion and the ecstasy of the audience as well as the performers.

Bruno Walter, 13 December 1895

*Composition begun in Leipzig 1888, completed in Steinbach in 1894. First, partial performance (orchestral movements only), Berlin, March 1895, in a Richard Strauss concert, with Mahler conducting the first three movements. First complete performance, 13 December 1895, Mahler conducting.*

*Scored for 4 flutes (interchangeable with 4 piccolos), 4 oboes (interchangeable with English horns), 5 clarinets (one interchangeable with bass clarinet), 10 horns, 8 trumpets, 4 trombones, tuba, timpani, bass drum, military drum, triangle, cymbals, high tam-tam, low tam-tam, rute, glockenspiel, 3 low cow bells of indeterminate pitch, 2 harps, organ, strings, soprano and alto solos and chorus.*

Program of the Second Symphony

We are standing beside the coffin of a man beloved. For the last time, his battles, his suffering, and his purpose pass before the mind's eye. And now, at this solemn and deeply stirring moment, when we are released from the paltry distractions of everyday life, our hearts are gripped by a voice of awe-inspiring solemnity, which we seldom or never hear above the deafening traffic of mundane affairs. What next? it says. What is life— and what is death?

Have we any continuing existence?

Is it all an empty dream, or has this life of ours, and our death, a meaning?

If we are to go on living, we must answer this question.

The next three movements are conceived as intermezzi.

Second Movement (Andante)

A blissful moment in his life and a mournful memory of youth and lost innocence.

Third Movement (Scherzo)

The spirit of unbelief and negation has taken possession of him. Looking into the turmoil of appearances, he loses together with the clear eyes of childhood the sure foothold which love alone gives. He despairs of himself and God. The world and life become a witches' brew; disgust of existence in every form strikes him with iron fist and drives him to an outburst of despair.

Fourth Movement: The Primal Dawn (Alto Solo)

The morning voice of ingenuous belief sounds in our ears.

"I am from God and will return to God! God will give me a candle to light me to the bliss of eternal life."

Fifth Movement

We are again confronted by terrifying questions.

A voice is heard crying aloud: "The end of all living beings is come— the Last Judgment is at hand and the horror of the day of days has broken forth."

The earth quakes, the graves burst open, and the dead arise and stream on in endless procession. The great and the little ones of the earth—kings and beggars, righteous and godless—all press on; the cry for mercy and forgiveness strikes fearfully on our ears. The wailing rises higher—our senses desert us; consciousness dies at the approach of the eternal spirit. The

"Last Trump"

is heard—the trumpets of the apocalypse ring out; in the eerie silence that follows, we can just catch the distant, barely audible song of the nightingale, a last tremulous echo of earthly life! A chorus of saints and heavenly beings softly breaks forth:

"Thou shalt arise, surely thou shalt arise." Then appears the glory of God! A wondrous, soft light penetrates us to the heart—all is holy calm!

And behold—it is no judgment. There are no sinners, no just. None is great, none is small. There is no punishment and no reward.

An overwhelming love lightens our being. We know and are.

Original program version of the Second Symphony, as related by Mahler to his wife Alma, 14 December 1901 [13]

When assessing such a program, Seidl's comparative comment on Strauss and Mahler becomes fully transparent. Donald Ferguson [14] speaks of romantic realists (Berlioz, Liszt) as compared with a different breed of romantic, whom he calls romantic idealists (Schumann, Mendelssohn, Chopin). While the romantic realist presets the program of his musical

[13] It is significant that other "authentic" program notes exist in Mahler's "own words." See Redlich, Bruckner and Mahler, pp. 186-7.

[14] Donald Ferguson, The History of Musical Thought, p. 425 et passim.

creation and composes music to conform to it, the romantic idealist creates romantic images reflecting the romantic feelings of the time, to the exclusion of extramusical thought in the form of a program. There can be no question but that Mahler exemplifies the latter type of romantic conception; although he provides a program, it always seems added as an afterthought. Here again, it is also promptly disavowed and repudiated.

> I drew up the program as a crutch for a cripple (you know whom I mean). It gives only a superficial indication, all that any program can do for a musical work—let alone this one, which is so much all of a piece that it can no more be explained than the world itself. I'm quite sure that if God were asked to draw up a program of the world he had created he could never do it. At best it would say as little about the nature of God and life as my analysis says about my C-Minor Symphony. In fact, as all religious doctrines do, it leads directly to misunderstanding, to a flattening and coarsening and in the long run so much to distortion that the work, and still more its creator, is utterly unrecognizable.
>
> Mahler to Alma, Dresden, 15 December 1901

We glean further insight from Mahler's comment to the critic Max Marshalk as to his attempt at continuity between the First and Second symphonies:

> I have called the first movement *Toten Feier* [Funeral pomp]. . . . it is the hero of my D-Major symphony whom I bear to his grave there and upon the clear reflection of whose life I gaze from a higher vantage point. Why hast thou lived? Why hast thou suffered? Is all this a ghastly joke?. . . . I give the answer in the last movement. . . . the second motive is a recollection . . . a sunny scene, calm and untroubled, from the life of the hero. It must have happened to you once—you had borne a dear friend to his grave and then . . . there suddenly appeared before you the image of a long-passed hour of happiness, which now enters into your soul like a sunbeam. . . . That is the second movement. Then when you awaken from this nostalgic dream and must return to life's confusion, it may easily occur that this perpetually moving, never ending, ever incomprehensible hustle and bustle of life becomes eerie to you, like movements of dancing figures in a brightly lit ballroom into which you gaze out of the dark night—from so far off that you do not hear the dance music anymore! . . . This is the third movement. . . . what follows is already clear to you!

Considering Mahler's aversion to any programmatic explanation, the above version can also not be considered as a point of departure for the novice listener, because Mahler strikes out on his own in his novel use of dramatic and lyrical themes, such as the woodwinds leading the portentous introduction to the weighty *Dies Irae*. The use of a solemn funeral march in both the first and second symphonies, each serving the same mournful purpose, clearly establishes Mahler's stated intention of spiritual continuity between the two works. Mahler had in his Second Symphony removed himself further from the Sonata allegro form which had dominated the classical and even early-romantic symphony; equally importantly, neither poetically nor musically is there a lack of continuity and cohesiveness, as could still be observed in the First Symphony. In order to maintain continuity and impact, Mahler was not averse to employing such theatrical devices as having the chorus remain seated while singing, only to rise abruptly at the bass passage *Mit Flügeln die ich mir errungen*—thus avoiding the customary and inevitable rustle and commotion at the rising of the chorus at the opening *ppp* chorus passage. Such a surprising novelty was doubtless the fruit of Mahler's operatic experience in Laibach and Kassel and especially in Budapest and Hamburg.

In connection with Mahler's scores, a word should be said concerning the marking of dynamics in general and Mahler's in particular. When looking back, for instance, at baroque scores, one is startled by the lack of dynamic direction. A composition might simply be labeled *andante* or *allegro;* beyond that even the barest dynamic indicators (such as *p* or *f*) were usually lacking, leaving interpretation entirely to the whims of temperament. Beethoven's time saw a remarkable change in that respect, owing to Maelzel's invention of the "metronome," whereby precise tempo indications, at least, could be provided. How different all this is from the situation at the end of the nineteenth century, when in Mahler's scores individual inflections are minutely indicated.

In the first movement (*Allegro Maestoso, Mit durchaus ernstem feierlichem Ausdruck*—with serious, solemn expression throughout), when Mahler speaks of death, of the funeral of the hero of his First Symphony, he does not make use of the musical imagery which Berlioz employed in his *March to the Scaffold*. Rather, Mahler speaks of funeral *rites*: his tone is not that of the morose lament or the wrenching sob, but that of the funeral march in the *Eroica* of his idol, Beethoven—i.e., one appropriate to the burial of his hero.

Despite the vague program he provided, Mahler, in his music, aspired to be acknowledged as a symphonist of absolute music. The emotional opening outburst of the movement gives simple expression to a theme of mourning:

As the theme is repeated in the basses, oboe and English horn are inton-ing a brief mournful melody, soon to be overcome by the song of the violins,

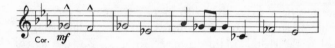

only to fall back into funereal somberness climaxing in a Mahler variation of that inexorable medieval melody of death, the *Dies Irae,* heard in chor-ale-like fashion in the horns, playing in sonorous solemnity.

But Mahler will not allow this mood to prevail, and the *Dies Irae* is promptly followed, for the first and only time in this movement, by the theme, announced by the trumpets, which will take on heightened impor-tance as the "resurrection" theme as the work progresses. Its import, even in abbreviated quotation, is tremendous in its excitement:

The forces of life and death, in their struggle, reach a tremendous climax, only to die away in subdued tragedy. The movement concludes with a horrifying and stentorian two-octave descent, ending in two ghostly, empty-sounding C's.

Then and there Mahler springs a theatrical as well as psychological surprise: "Here follows a pause of at least five minutes." In keeping with the program outlined by Mahler to Marschalk, the desire for a decisive break between the grave, somber mood of the opening movement and the "Schubertian" mood (Mahler's own term) of the second movement almost demanded a mental respite to let the echo of tragedy of the first movement fade from memory.

Yet it is really the second movement which interrupts the cohesiveness of the entire work and presents an interlude of sorts. Paul Bekker saw it as a novelty among symphonic interludes and called it an "idyll." While the first, third, fourth and fifth movements follow in logical sequence and constitute a thematic and spiritual entity, the second movement, mostly light, airy, and relaxed, is an entity unto itself. Mahler underlines the charm and lightness of the movement by easing the weight of the themes and enfolding them in a quasi-Rondo form. Thus, in startling contrast, the second movement (*Andante moderato*) features an Austrian alpine *Ländler*. Donald Ferguson facetiously calls it a Minuet, somewhat forgetful of the latter's aristocratic traditions.

Only the middle section breaks the idyll with more passionate expressions, which, in turn, are broken by a minor, sinister interlude whose importance is emphasized by the rising "Mahler fourth" interval. But the movement is balanced by the return to the original *Ländler*.

As if the ingenious virtuosity in the orchestration of the Andante did not suffice, it is promptly followed by another such exhibition, again in triple meter, with the timpani and bassoons propelling the motion. The occasion here is the orchestration of Mahler's own song of the *Fischpredigt*, from his *Wunderhorn* songs. The parable suggests the tone of the movement, from ironic to cynic to demonic.[15] The kinship to the First Symphony is again pronounced, with the inclusion of Mahler's own song. Like Schubert in his *Death and the Maiden* Quartet, Mahler does not begin with the melody but instead elevates the accompaniment to the song to thematic prominence before introducing the original song as well, again in innovative fashion—pitting the solo trumpet against the accompaniment of muted strings and harps.

However, all these innovations seem only preliminary to the introduction of the human voice in the final two movements of the symphony. Superficial reflection would deny any novelty here and aver that Mahler had simply followed a well-trodden path that was first traveled by Beethoven in his Ninth Symphony. An examination of Beethoven's purposes, therefore, merits consideration. Much has been written as to the reasons which

---

[15] To fully appreciate the ironic impact of the theme, the reader is referred to the text of the *Wunderhorn* song itself.

prompted Beethoven to bring the idea of a musical setting of Schiller's *Ode to Joy*—a project cherished from his youth—to fruition in the finale of his Ninth Symphony.

Wagner pointed to the reason why Beethoven chose that moment to do so. He maintains that Beethoven resorted to the expression of the human voice in solo and choral treatment because he had exhausted the instrumental possibilities of expressing his thoughts and emotions that were at his disposal at the time. A look at the score seems to reinforce this view. Actually the thematic material of the choral section had not been intended as a novelty, because part of it had already been introduced instrumentally. However, the vocal statements had been preceded by a welter of previously heard themes in near unruly profusion. The instrumental statement of the *Freude* theme proved incapable, however, of bringing order into this chaos. It is at that point that Beethoven introduces the human voice. He had faced one difficulty of expression because the sudden introduction of Schiller's ode would have been too abrupt, too unrelated a statement. Now he laboriously inserted a line of text of his own fabrication after numerous still-born attempts, one which clearly stated his intent:

> "*O Freunde, nicht diese Töne! Sondern lasst uns angenehmere anstimmen und freudenvollere.*"
> [O friends, no such tones! But let us sound more pleasant and more joyful ones.]

These twelve words indicate that the formlessness and confusion which preceded the voice was deliberate, inserted, so that the voice might bring order into chaos and be seen as the supreme form of musical and philosophical expression. With his philosophy declared and with a bridge established, Beethoven launches full-throatedly into that hymn to human values and virtues. A look at Mahler's letter to the conductor Seidl (see below, p. 275) will convince one that Mahler not only was aware of Beethoven's intentions and Wagner's opinion on the matter but fully endorsed it.

Despite the great advances evident since Mahler's previous symphony, however, the influence of Bruckner in the fourth—*Urlicht* or Primal Light—movement is obvious. Later Mahler may speak deprecatingly of Bruckner's music, but at this point the old master, steeped in his religio-musical faith, and the young, high-strung symphonist shake hands spiritually, as Mahler proceeds *Sehr feierlich aber schlicht; Choral-mässig* [Very solemn but simple. Hymnlike]. All innovations to come notwithstanding, Mahler testifies here to the continuity of the Vienna school and of tradition, as the alto and the solo violin speak of eternity.

| | |
|---|---|
| O Röschen rot! | O Rosebud red! |
| Der Mensch liegt in grösster Not, | Man lies in greatest need, |
| Der Mensch liegt in grösster Pein | Man lies in greatest pain. |
| Ja lieber möcht ich im Himmel sein. | I'd rather wished I were in heaven. |
| Da kam ich auf einen breiten Weg, | Then I came upon a broad road; |
| Da kam ein Englein und wollt' mich abweisen. | There came an angel who wanted to refuse me. |
| Ach nein? Ich liess mich nicht abweisen. | Ah no, I would not be refused. |
| Ich bin von Gott und will wieder zu Gott! | I am of God and wish to return to God! |
| Der liebe Gott wird mir ein Lichtlein geben, | The dear God will give me a light, |
| Wird leuchten mir in das ewig selig' Leben! | Will light my way into eternal blissful life! |

Redlich maintains that the alto solo of the *Urlicht* fulfills the same purpose as Beethoven's phrase, *"Oh Freunde, nicht diese Töne . . ."*—viz., it serves as a bridge to the climactic finale, the *Resurrection* movement for soprano, alto, and chorus. The comparison is, in our view, tenuous. The connective phrase in the Beethoven opus, clumsily hammered together by the composer, in no way does justice to the spirit in which it had been conceived, as a testimony to the emergence of the human voice as the ultimate expression of human emotion and spirit. Mahler's "connective" *Urlicht* movement, on the other hand, does rise to the occasion, and the statement *"Ich bin von Gott und will wieder zu Gott"* does lead spiritually into the *Resurrection* movement, while becoming a miniature masterpiece in itself in the process.

Furthermore, in terms of form, it should be noted that Beethoven wrapped the introductory baritone solo phrase and the choral outburst into one movement, while Mahler devotes an entire movement to "connective purposes" (if it can at all be considered as such), before arriving at the cataclysmic and transfiguring finale.

After the naive, almost childlike simplicity of the *Urlicht,* the drama of the Finale is doubly overwhelming. Again we suspect that this was intended to have a quasi-theatrical effect. After the "solemn but simple" admonition of the previous movement, we are confronted with an instruction demanding *Wild herausfordernd* (wildly charging) dynamics. Although the tempo title of the last movement reads *In Tempo des Scherzos–Kräftig–Langsam* (In Scherzo tempo–strong–slow), Mahler charges into a *fff* after the *ppp* ending of the previous movement.

Mahler leaves no doubt concerning the meaning of the finale: "The end of all living creatures . . . the Day of Judgment . . . terror unleashed. To the sound of the trumpets of the last judgment [Mahler directed that the four trumpets of the Apocalypse must blow from opposite directions], the shuddering earth opens its graves and releases the endless, ghostly stream of the pious and the tortured, the once rich and poor, all raising their voices begging for mercy." The sound reverberates in ghostly and ghastly dread, only to die away into awesome silence. Through and beyond that silence we hear the irrevocable, final sound, the sound of the nightingale in the piccolo: redemption is at hand.

In basic conception the opening of the movement has much in common with the finale of Beethoven's Ninth. "Wildly charging" references to previous themes are heard; the "Resurrection theme" and the climax of the Scherzo are interwoven with the brass and woodwind utterances, all converging on the march of the Last Judgment. There are repeated references to the *Dies Irae.* Eventually the horror subsides, and all that is heard is the eerie sound of the offstage horn,

intermingled with the bird calls.

Into that silence the choir intones *a capella "Aufersteh'n,"* and the blessing of a divine power is revealed, suggesting the majesty of Bach's music, which never failed to inspire Mahler, cleansing him from what he called "the dirt of the stage." [16]

"The moment" in the symphony has arrived. After the anticipatory

---

[16] Such a reference is doubly surprising from a man so deeply involved in stagecraft, which provided his livelihood and which was to reach its apex under his

opening, building to a climax, breaks off into ominous silence, an eerie dialogue leads into one of the greatest dramatic creations in symphonic literature, set to the verses of Klopstock's *"Aufersteh'n"*:

Auf - er - stehn, ja auf - er - steh'n wirst du, mein Staub, nach kur - zer Ruh!

As had been the case between movements three and four, so again between movements four and five there is no pause, as requested by the composer. The crowning moment unfolds like a mystery play in music. Fanfares are calling from far and near, we are shaken by "the last roll call," and to the sounds of the chorale we ascend to resurrection.

Sterben werd ich, um zu leben!          Die shall I, to live!
Aufersteh'n, ja aufersteh'n wirst du,    Rise, yes rise ye shall again,
Mein Herz                                My heart

The orchestra stage is magically transformed into the stage on which this mystery play of faith and redemption unfolds. Mahler was apparently himself overwhelmed and awed by the magnitude of his creation.

The soaring development and upward wave is here so immense, so unprecedented, that, afterwards, I did not know myself how I could have arrived at it.

Mahler to Natalie Bauer-Lechner, 1923

But the perfectionist in Mahler could permit the inclusion of the spoken word only if it fully conformed to his own idea. Thus what is generally assumed to be Klopstock's text soon became Klopstock–Mahler's ode in its final version. As the analysis that follows indicates, most of the Klopstock poem was retained unchanged, with only four lines omitted by Mahler. At that point Mahler became poet as well as composer, and the

---

guidance. It may be considered the retaliatory comment of a man whose innate personality as a symphonic composer was painfully emerging, challenging the giant of the conductorial and operatic worlds. In another sense this might be construed as biting the hand that fed him because much of Mahler's knowledge of the stage aided him in later incorporation of three-dimensional, theatrical, effects into his symphonies.

remainder of the text, more than twice as long as Klopstock's original, is Mahler's. Yet so perfect is Mahler's feeling for the subject, so sensitive his poetic ear to the Klopstock text, that the uninitiated would not suspect the verses to be the work of two authors. The conception of the *Resurrection* movement in general and the choral use of Klopstock's poetry in particular can only be described as stemming from a flash of genius.

> When I conceive a great musical idea, I always [17] come to the point where I must make "the word" the bearer of the idea. That is what must have happened to Beethoven in his Ninth—only that era could not yet furnish him with appropriate material. For basically Schiller's poem is not fitted for the expression of the unheard-of conception which was in Beethoven's mind.[18] Furthermore I recall that Wagner says this somewhere in quite uncompromising fashion. What happened to me with the last movement of the Second Symphony was simply this: . . . I had truly searched the entire world literature right to the Bible to find the redeeming word and was finally forced to express my feelings and thoughts in my own words. . . . For a long time I had in mind to include a chorus in the last movement, and only the concern that one might consider it a superficial imitation of Beethoven prompted me over and over again to postpone it. At that time Bülow died, and I attended his funeral here. The frame of mind in which I sat there and thought of the departed one was fully in the spirit of the work which then constantly occupied my mind. At that moment the choir . . . intoned the Klopstock ode *"Aufersteh'n."* [19] It struck me like lightning and everything stood clearly and vividly before my soul. It is such lightning the creator waits for that is the "Holy Annunciation." What I then experienced I had to create in tones. . . . Thus it goes with me always: only when I experience do I create in tones; only when I compose do I experience.
>
> Mahler to the conductor Arthur Seidl, Hamburg, 17 February 1897

### AUFERSTEH'N (RESURRECTION)

| | |
|---|---|
| Aufersteh'n, ja aufersteh'n wirst du | Thou shalt arise, yea, arise |
| Mein Staub, nach kurzer Ruh! | My dust, from brief repose! |
| Unsterblich Leben | Immortal life, |
| Wird, der dich rief, dir geben | Shall He, who called thee, give thee? |
| | |
| Wieder aufzublüh'n, wirst du gesät! | Again to blossom thou art sown! |
| Der Herr der Ernte geht | The Lord of the Harvest goes forth |
| Und sammelt Garben | Collecting sheaves, |
| Uns ein, die starben. | We who have died. |

[17] The word "always" was to prove an exaggeration because Mahler was to create symphonies numbers Five, Six, Seven, and Nine without availing himself of "the word."

[18] Beethoven had been aware of the exaggerations in the youthful Schiller poem and had excised the verses which he had considered overexuberant or inapplicable.

[19] It was never learned whose choral setting of the Klopstock text Mahler heard.

Tag des Dank's, der Freuden-
    tränen Tag!
Du meines Gottes Tag!
Wenn ich im Grabe genug
    geschlummert habe
Erweckst du mich.)

(Day of thanks, day of tears of joy!
Thou day of my God!
When I have slumbered in my
    grave enough Thou wakenst me.)

The last four lines were deleted by Mahler. The added verses emanate
from Mahler's pen.

O glaube, mein Herz, es geht dir
    nichts verloren.
Dein ist, ja dein, was du gesehnt
Dein, was du geliebt, was du
    gestritten!
O glaube: du warst nicht umsonst
    geboren
Hast nicht umsonst geliebt,
    gelitten.

Have faith, my heart, for naught
    is lost to thee.
Thine, yes, thine is all you yearned
    for
Thine what you loved and what
    you fought for
Believe: Thou wast not born in
    vain
Thou didst not live nor suffer in
    vain.

Was entstanden ist, das muss
    vergehen
Was vergangen, auferstehen!
Hör auf zu beben!
Bereite dich zu leben!

All that arose must perish

All that perished, rise again!
Cease thy trembling!
Prepare thyself to live!

O Schmerz, du Alldurch
    dringender
Dir bin ich entrungen!
O Tod, du Allbezwingender,
Nun bist Du bezwungen!

O Pain all-pervading

I have escaped thee!
O Death, thou all-subduer,
Thou art now subdued!

Mit Flügeln die ich mir errungen
In heissem Liebesstreben
Werd' ich entschweben zum Licht,
Zu dem kein Aug' gedrungen

With wings which I have won
In ardent love's endeavor
I shall soar to light
Never pierced by eyes.

Mit Flügeln die ich mir errungen,
Werde ich entschweben.
Sterben werd' ich, um zu leben!

With wings which I have won
I shall soar away.
Die I shall, to live again.

Aufersteh'n, ja aufersteh'n wirst
    du,
Mein Herz in einem Nu
Was du geschlagen
Zu Gott wird es dich tragen.

Thou shalt arise, yea arise,

My heart in an instant!
What you have conquered
To God it will carry you.

Mahler prepares the scene with utterances of the horns ("the greatest
possible number of horns"), three of them offstage, to depict the end of

the world in what is surely one of the most monumental of Mahler's creations, rivaling his Eighth Symphony. Relentlessly, inevitably, Mahler reaches a vertex of sound (*Mir grösster Kraftentfaltung*—with greatest display of power). Significantly, this becomes not only the end of the world, in proclamation, but also the end of the symphony proper and of the tradition of harmonic sound as inherited by Mahler. He realized and expressed this:

> It is really inadequate for me to call it a symphony, for in no respect does it retain the traditional form. But to write a symphony means to me to construct a world with all the tools of the available techniques: the ever-new and ever-changing content determines its own form.
>
> Mahler to Natalie Bauer-Lechner,<br>*Erinnerungen an Mahler*

Mahler's comment also sheds light on the text of the final movement, because it confirms Mahler's endless quest and struggle to evade and cheat death. The fear of death haunted him unendingly, but here it resulted in one of Mahler's most positive statements:

> O death, thou all-subduer,
> Thou art now subdued!

The triumphant magnificence of that spiritual statement brings to mind Brahms's *Requiem* outcry.

> Death, where is thy sting?
> Grave, where is thy triumph?

The seeker in Mahler has risen from subconscious depths. The quest for meaning, for truth, for a personal God, for immortality, would continue to occupy his mind and music from here on to the end.

## SYMPHONY NO. 3 IN D MINOR

> I have already told you that I am at work on a great composition. Can't you understand how that takes up all of a man? At such times I no longer belong to myself—labor pains of the creator of such a work are terrible.
>
> My symphony is going to be something the likes of which the world has not yet heard. All nature is voiced therein, and it tells of deeply mysterious matters. . . .
>
> I tell you, at certain passages I myself sometimes am overcome with an uncanny feeling, and can hardly believe that I could have written them.
>
> Mahler to Anna von Mildenburg, 18 August 1896

> It was magnificent. . . . At first they were a little puzzled, but with each movement they grew warmer, and when the contralto came on . . . the

whole hall was gripped and from then to the end there was the familiar rise in temperature. When the last note died away, the tumult of applause was almost frightening. Everyone said nothing like it could be remembered.

Mahler to Alma, 23 October 1904, after a performance in Amsterdam

*Composition begun summer 1893, finished 1896. First performance, Krefeld, June 1902, Mahler conducting.*

*Scored for 2 piccolos, 4 flutes, 4 oboes, English horn, 2 clarinets in E flat, 4 bassoons, contrabassoon, 8 horns, 4 trumpets, 4 trombones, tuba, kettledrums, bass drum, snare drum, tambourine, triangle, tam-tam, bells, cymbals, 2 harps and strings.*

It was in his Third Symphony that Mahler expanded and expounded his "programs," his cosmic ideas, for the first time. A measure of Mahler's preoccupation with the spiritual (aside from the musical) content of "the word" can be gleaned by reference to Mahler's numerous comments on this symphony; as Bekker observes,

> Mahler seems to have written and spoken about no composition with the readiness and explicitness that he did of the Third. . . . A remarkable abundant selection of revealing comments by Mahler has been preserved, while on many others scarcely a word has been reported.

Paul Bekker, *Gustav Mahler's Sinfonien*, 1921

Mahler's comments, however, were actually only an outward sign of the spiritual metamorphosis he underwent in the course of the conception and subsequent composition of the symphony. Mahler's primary intention in beginning a new work had been to obtain some relief from the emotional strain of his Second Symphony. With a new, "thoroughly humorous" (!) work he was to "win applause and money." In that early conception of his Third Symphony he suggested such subtitles as *Meine fröhliche Wissenschaft* [My joyous knowledge] and *Das glückliche Leben, ein Sommernachtstraum* [The happy life, a summer night's dream]. He was also bent on having the first movement sound joyous. As it happened, however, the first movement was to be composed last; if Mahler had been capable at all of writing humorous music, by the time he turned to the first movement, one year after starting on the symphony, the nature of his message precluded humor and the battle between the forces of winter and summer had grown to cosmic proportions. The original title of the movement, *Der Sommer marschiert ein* [Summer marches in], was no longer fully appropriate to Mahler's new vision of things. Pan's Dionysian influence had made itself felt during the sketching of the movement, and soon the definitive title, *Pan erwacht* [Pan awakens], suggested itself, and with it came full realization and revelation.

"It is the wildest thing I have ever written." So wrote Mahler to

Natalie Bauer-Lechner on 28 June 1896. While working on it he reached a point of exhaustion and intoxication. "It is frightening the way this [first] movement caused me to grow beyond everything I have ever composed." Gone were all thoughts of humor.

> I am so literally gripped with terror when I see where the path ordained for music leads that it has become my frightful responsibility to be the bearer of this gigantic work. . . . I have such a feeling about this movement and the prospect of what I will have to suffer because of it.
>
> Mahler to Natalie Bauer-Lechner, 28 June 1896

Just as labor pains and birth pangs are a terrifying joy which no mother would wish to miss, so Mahler suffered in joy and awe at the birth of his creation, which had attained gigantic proportions and assumed a life of its own, carrying the creator with it. In this connection Mahler's decision to subtly change the figure of Dionysos to that of Pan is significant. Although there is a measure of interchangeability between the two gods, the more spiritual lack of inhibition of Dionysos gives way to the realistic coarseness of Pan, and the shift is decisive—at least in terms of understanding Mahler's personality. Bekker observes:

> Here for the first time he had penetrated to the essence of his own nature and directed himself to it with the passionate intensity of the achieved consciousness of personality.
>
> Paul Bekker, *Gustav Mahler's Sinfonien*

The figure of Pan is markedly present in the first movement in his many guises: the god of music, the god of pastoral poets, the god of fertility, the god of the forest. Its prominence in the portion "Summer marches in" points up the importance of that season in Mahler's adult life; for summer was for him the time of creation, to which he longingly looked forward throughout the winter. So strong was the presence of the Pan figure and feeling in Mahler's life at that time that, according to Natalie Bauer-Lechner, he contemplated the title "Pan Symphonic Poems" for what was to become his Third Symphony.

Mahler was preoccupied with his Third Symphony throughout 1896; it made him irritable and unapproachable and filled his mind completely in waking and sleeping hours. He even related how a "dream voice" suggested a solution to a vexing problem in the horns. He threw himself into the task of composition with the strenuous concentration which had become his trademark; in the process he again drew inspiration from that already proven wellspring, the song cycle *Des Knaben Wunderhorn,* as well as from Nietzsche's *Also sprach Zarathustra.* Although Mahler selected only a tiny verse from Nietzsche's work, he drank deeper from the philosopher's well than the more superficially orientated Strauss, whose superficial treatment of philosophical thought was alien to Mahler. As for Nietzsche's philosophy, although Mahler in his early student years had been strongly influenced by it, he was later adversely inclined to Nietzsche's expressed idea of the "Superman," changing the meaning to "Man"—the universal being rather than the superior being—and making his "Man" the spiritual hub of the universe.

> "Summer marches in" will be the Prologue. Right away I need a regimental band. . . . Naturally, they don't get by without a battle with the opposing fòrce, winter, but he's soon thrown out of the ring, and summer, in his full strength and superiority, soon seizes undisputed leadership.
>
> Mahler to Natalie Bauer-Lechner

Mahler wrote to Lechner of seven movement titles, but eventually condensed them to six in the final work.

| | |
|---|---|
| Pan erwacht; Der Sommer marschiert ein | Pan awakens; Summer marches in |
| Was mir die Blumen in der Wiese erzählen | What the flowers in the meadow tell me |
| Was mir die Tiere im Walde erzählen | What the animals in the forest tell me |
| Was mir die Nacht erzählt | What the night tells me |
| Was mir die Morgenglocken erzählen | What the morning bells tell me |
| Was mir die Liebe erzählt | What love tells me |

Although the subtitles were officially dropped after the first performance, they seemingly developed a life of their own and are repeatedly referred to in program notes and books on the work. In any case, the symphony essentially falls into two parts: part one consists of the first movement (which was the last to be set down); part two comprises the balance. The symphony as a whole is among the longest ever written; its performance time is one and one-half hours.

The opening (Pan awakens, summer marches in), *kräftig, entschieden* (vigorous, decisive), is pure Mahler—eight massed horns, intoning in unison an Austrian march theme. Mahler called it *Weckruf* (reveille).

Against it and throughout much of the first movement we hear a piercing call by the trumpets.

From there on, to the relentless beating of the drums, the conflict between the inert, frozen earth and the excitement and bloom of summer, between major and minor modes, constitutes the basic theme of the movement, which ends in the triumph of light over darkness, in a philosophical conception akin to Beethoven's.

From the suspenseful rhythm of the big drum there arises a new melody, first in the oboe, then in the violin; unmistakably these are signs of awakening.

The surge of life is intensified in an urgent *fff* call by the horns,

and is carried further in an utterance by the trumpets.

The triumph of light over darkness, of summer over icy winter, is inevitable and irresistible. In a furious passage, the opening *Weckruf* is triumphantly heard against the strings. In a tumultuous whirlwind, with the *Weckruf* as its dominating theme, the gigantic movement comes to a sudden conclusion. According to Mahler, "Summer is victorious among the divergent forces of nature, and the jubilant intensity is characteristic . . . as Pan and Bacchus celebrate."

In the same letter to Natalie Bauer-Lechner (4 July 1891), Mahler reflects on the deeper meaning of the opening movement.

> This is really almost no longer music . . . just nature sounds. And it is frightening the way in which from out of soulless, inflexible matter . . . life gradually fights its way free.

In the second part (the balance of the symphony), Mahler the romantic prevails. In the second movement (What the flowers in the meadow tell me), *tempo di Menuetto,* Mahler, in a complete turnabout, reverts to a minuet tempo with a relaxed *Ländler* tune. He again makes certain that the intended spirit is achieved by indicating the tempo as *sehr mässig* (very moderately). The relaxed tune

is obviously harking back to another era. Only twice is its languid tempo interrupted, as the time signature changes from ¾ to ⅜ and a rippling new melody of Bohemian character is heard.

The second melody becomes quite agitated in its second statement, only to return for the third and last time to the original theme, now even more languidly and charmingly ornamented. .

The movement found an immediate acceptance with the public and

conductors, and Weingartner and Nikisch, began performing the movement independently from the main body of the symphony, much to Mahler's distress. He disapproved of the practice but felt helpless to stop it.

> That this little piece (more of an intermezzo in the entire thing) must
> create misunderstandings when detached from its connection with the
> complete work, my most significant and vastest creation, cannot keep me
> from letting it be performed alone. I have no choice; if I ever want to be
> heard, I cannot be too fussy, and so this modest little piece will doubtless
> . . . present me to the public as the "sensuous, perfumed singer of nature."
>
> Mahler to Dr. Richard Batka, 18 November 1896 [20]

The third movement (What the animals in the forest tell me),
*comodo, scherzando, ohne Hast* (without haste), points melodically to
Mahler's earliest *Lieder* cycle and one of its songs, *Ablösung im Sommer,*
the story of the cuckoo and the nightingale. Here *Tonmalerei* (tone
painting) is at its best. After we listen to the rustling and murmuring of
the forest, the themes of the cuckoo and the nightingale enter the scene.

The dialogue of the birds is disrupted by the first sign of a human sound,
the postillion's horn. It is an astounding melody, more Richard Straussian
than Mahlerian.

---

[20] This disapproving but resigned comment of Mahler points up a curious discrepancy between Mahler and his contemporary Richard Strauss. At the time of publication of his Third Symphony in 1898, Mahler was at the peak of his fame as
conductor and director of the Vienna Imperial Opera; yet, despite his fame,
Mahler could seldom receive a hearing for his compositions and had to be satisfied
with piecemeal excerpts such as the above. This stood in marked contrast to
Strauss, also famous as a conductor, whose compositions were in great demand
(after the initial controversy surrounding his early symphonic poems) and who
enjoyed innumerable performances. It was not until four years after the publication, in June 1902, that Mahler attained a performance of the complete Third
Symphony, at the Music Festival of the *Allgemeine Deutsche Musikverein* in
Krefeld. The impact of that performance seems to have been decisive in establishing Mahler as a composer.

With *Der Rosenkavalier* still some fourteen years away from creation, this delightful melody serves to again make a point—that Mahler is unquestionably an Austrian composer. Again Mahler is at great pains to give the approaching *Postkutsche* (stage coach) a three-dimensional (theatrical) effect. *"Wie aus weiter Ferne—wie aus der Ferne—sich etwas nähernd—sich entfernend"* (As if from a great distance—as if at a distance—approaching—receding) are the composer's instructions, as the postillion's horn, gracefully intermingling with the birds, is heard. The gracefulness of the bird theme is eventually shattered. *Grob* (coarse) demands Mahler, as the themes are flung out *ff* by six horns, accompanied equally forcefully by celli and string basses and reinforced by bassoons and contra bassoons. In a brief, more tender interlude, the horn call returns, soon to be abandoned. Restating bits and pieces of previous themes, Mahler, in recapitulation, again ends the movement *fff*.

In this symphony, Mahler again requested that the last three movements be played without pause. In the fourth movement (What the night tells me), *sehr langsam, misterioso* (very slowly, mysterious), which William J. McGrath calls "the intellectual center of the work," the human voice (in the alto solo) and the "Life motif" of the opening movement (in development) engage in dialogue, a dialogue between nature and eternity. If in the third movement Mahler had intimated the intrusion of the human element in the postillion's horn call, the fourth movement is totally given over to human and philosophical expression. Mahler turns to his early idol Friedrich Nietzsche for inspiration, as the alto intones the "Midnight Song" to the words of *Also sprach Zarathustra:*

| | |
|---|---|
| O Mensch! O Mensch! | O man! O man! |
| Gib Acht! Gib Acht! | Take heed! Take heed! |
| Was spricht die tiefe Mitternacht? | What says the midnight deep? |
| Ich schlief! Ich schlief! | I slept! I slept! |
| Aus tiefem Traum bin ich erwacht! | From deep dream I am awaken'd! |
| Die Welt ist tief! | The world is deep! |
| Und tiefer als der Tag gedacht! | And deeper than the day could read! |
| O Mensch! O Mensch! | O man! O man! |
| Tief! Tief! Tief ist ihr Weh! | Deep! Deep! Deep is its woe! |
| Tief ist ihr Weh! | Deep is its woe! |

| Lust, Lust tiefer noch als Herzeleid! | Joy, joy, deeper still than grief can be! |
|---|---|
| Weh spricht: Vergeh! Weh spricht: Vergeh! | Woe says: Pass on! Woe says: Pass on! |
| Doch alle Lust will Ewigkeit! | But all joy seeks eternity! |
| Will tiefe, tiefe Ewigkeit. | Seeks deep, deep eternity. |

The depth of thought and emotion being expressed is emphasized by Mahler's use of a "deep" pedal point throughout the somber song, echoing the repeated use of *"tief"*—"deep"—in the lyric. Only in the end does the song brighten into splendid lyricism as the alto intones "But all joy seeks eternity!"

In the fifth movement (What the morning bells tell me), *Lustig im Tempo und keck im Ausdruck* (merry in tempo and bold in expression), Mahler again reaches to one of the *Wunderhorn* poems, *Es sungen drei Engel* [Three angels sang a sweet song]. The melody is transcribed for alto solo and women's and boy's choirs, and we find in it an astounding contrast and paradox, as a delightful, almost naive melody is accompanied by a sophisticated orchestral body containing four flutes, four oboes, four bells, three horns, four clarinets, a bass clarinet, a glockenspiel, two harps, three bassoons, and the lower strings (with the violins silent), while a boy's choir joins in with a typically German imitation of the chiming of bells. Again the perfectionist Mahler is explicit as to performance: "The tone is to imitate the pealing of a bell; the vowel is to be attacked sharply, and the tone is to be sustained by humming the consonant 'm,' so as to render the bell effect more natural-sounding: bimmmm, bammmm. While the boy's choir sings the chiming of the bells, the women's choir raises the listener from the darkness and depth of the previous song to the splendor of Elysian fields."

| Es sungen drei Engel einen süssen Gesang; | Three angels were singing a song so bright |
|---|---|
| Mit Freuden es selig in dem Himmel klang. | It set the Heavens ringing with joy and delight. |

The sixth and final movement (What love tell me), *Langsam, ruhevoll, empfunden* (slow, calm, with feeling), reveals again that genius is found not so much in the thunder and lightning of orchestral ecstasies and explosions but in the lyrical quiet of an Andante or Adagio movement. The placement of this quiet *adagio* ending brings to mind Tchaikovsky's *Pathétique* Symphony, which antedates Mahler's work by three years. But there the similarity ends. In Tchaikovsky's work the *adagio lamentoso* is a subconscious farewell; in it a man turns his gaze beyond his world, his thoughts leaving us behind, to be remembered only as a long, last, lingering sound. The symbolism of Mahler's Third Symphony operates on a totally different level. "I could almost call [this movement] "What God tells me"; in a sense God can be conceived only as love" (Mahler to Dr. Fritz Löhr).[21]

The spirit of the final movement, whose essence can only be defined as reverent, evokes the image of Wagner's *Parsifal,* of Bruckner at his most devout, of the late Beethoven. The opening and most important theme of the movement sets the tone in the violins.

In an almost motionless musical sea, the theme progresses tightly to the final, affirmative apotheosis of the work. In the process Mahler again achieves total cyclical unity by requoting the themes of previous movements, particularly the opening, affirmative motifs.

Unquestionably we encounter here an echo of the man who wrote some of the most inspired and moving Adagios in the symphonic literature—Bruckner. Despite the sonority of his massive, organlike movements, Bruckner's devotion was most deeply documented in those gentle manifestations, whose significance he fully realized. If Mahler claimed a kinship with the classics in previous moments, that kinship is abandoned here in favor of the romantic. "So I end my Third contrary to custom," wrote Mahler, "although at the time, I myself was not conscious of the reason for it—with Adagios, as with a higher form in contrast to a lower." If for reasons of their own—form, contrast, balance, applause—the classical masters chose a lively finale, be it a graceful rondo or a rollicking *Kehraus* (the last, fast dance of a ball), the romantic chose the "higher form," the Adagio.

Mahler apparently originally intended a final movement, to be entitled "What God tells me" and to bear this motto, quoted by him in a letter to Anna von Mildenburg:

> Father, look thou upon my wounds
> Let none of thy creatures be lost!

Yet his eventual decision to omit this seventh movement bespeaks a certain logic, because when Mahler speaks of nature, he is, in his own mind, speaking of God. Mahler had not yet reached the philosophical eloquence of personal prayer that he was to attain later. But in the spirit of St. Bernard—"God is never sought in vain, even when we do not find him"—

---

[21] Closer in spirit to Tchaikovsky's last *Pathétique* movement is the finale of Mahler's *Das Lied von der Erde,* when the alto sings a farewell of fading sounds, repeating the word *ewig* (eternal) over and over.

he had made giant strides on his spiritual and compositional path in this most significant creation, giving humanity in the process some of the most profound and moving pages in musical history.

> That nature hides within everything that is ghastly, magnificent, and also lovable, of that naturally no one hears anything. I think it strange how most people, in speaking of nature, only think of flowers, birds, the forest, etc. No one seems to know anything of Dionysos, the great god Pan. There you already have a sort of program, an example of how I make music: it is always and all over only the voice of nature. . . . I recognize no other kind of program than "nature"— at least not for my work. . . . It is the world itself, nature as a whole, which, so to speak, is awakened to tones out of an unfathomable silence.
>
> Mahler to Dr. Richard Batka, 18 November 1896

## THE RÜCKERT SONGS: *Kindertotenlieder*
## [*Songs of Dead Children*]; Sieben Lieder aus letzter Zeit
## [*Seven Songs of Latter Days*]

Mahler returned to the song cycle in 1899 with *Sieben Lieder aus letzter Zeit* and the *Kindertotenlieder* cycle. The creation of the *Lieder* after Rückert poems coincided with the composition of the Sixth Symphony. Five of the poems make up the *Kindertotenlieder:*

> *Nun will die Sonn' so hell aufgeh'n*
> *Nun seh' ich wohl warum so dunkle Flammen*
> *Wenn dein Mütterlein tritt zur Tür herein*
> *Oft denk' ich, sie sind nur ausgegangen!*
> *In diesem Wetter, in diesem Braus.*

and another five are to be found in *Sieben Lieder aus letzter Zeit:*

> *Blicke mir nicht in die Lieder*
> *Ich atmet einen linden Duft*
> *Ich bin der Welt abhanden gekommen*
> *Um Mitternacht*
> *Liebst du um Schönheit*

along with two *Wunderhorn* songs:

> *Revelge*
> *Der Tamboursg'sell*

It should be kept in mind that the two cycles were composed simultaneously (the first three songs of each cycle were composed within two weeks during the summer of 1901), and our separate discussion of them is undertaken only for the sake of clarity.

The songs themselves show a matured Mahler, intense and lean, far removed from the pseudomedieval romanticism of the *Wunderhorn* songs of earlier days. The only exceptions are *Revelge* and *Tamboursg'sell,* whose eerie settings fascinated Mahler. Otherwise, both cycles reflect a more gentle and more intimate mood and approach and are characterized by what was, for Mahler, an unusual delicacy of orchestration altogether foreshadowing the depth of feelings of *Das Lied von der Erde.* Among the loveliest songs is *Liebst du um Schönheit,* dedicated to his wife Alma; among the most unusual is *Um Mitternacht,* a nocturnal vision backed by the unique instrumentation of winds, harp, timpani, and *oboe d'amore.*

One stands in awe before the man who, in the midst of his strenuous conductorial and directorial duties and while composing his most mournfully enigmatic work, the Sixth Symphony, would find the time and energy to compose two song cycles expressing every imaginable emotion.

To **Friedrich Rückert,** who wrote over four hundred poems in which he bemoaned the loss of his son Ernst, death was an overwhelming emotional upheaval. To Gustav Mahler, on the other hand, the first three *Kindertotenlieder* were only an artistic experience without emotional overtones, because at the time of their composition in 1901 he was unmarried and childless. When he composed the last two songs, however, he was already married and a father. Alma writes:

> I found this incomprehensible. I could understand setting such frightful words to music if one had no children, or had lost those one had. . . . Rückert did not write these harrowing elegies solely out of his imagination; they were dictated by the cruelest loss of his whole life. What I could not understand was bewailing the deaths of children who were in the best of health and spirits . . . hardly one hour after having kissed and fondled them. I exclaimed at the time: "For Heaven's sake, don't tempt Providence!"
>
> Alma Mahler, *Erinnerungen und Briefe,* 1946

Alma's and Gustav's view on the *Kindertotenlieder* reflect their different psychological relationship to the songs. The mother in Alma could not understand how a man whose two children were happily romping outside his door could set to music poems bemoaning a father's loss of his child; Mahler saw no such connection or connotation. The setting of the poems was to him an artistic challenge to be dealt with on artistic terms. Alma felt that Mahler was tempting fate (and saw in the death of their oldest daughter, two years later, fate's vengeance); Mahler, on the other hand, had constantly struggled with death in his music, and in life had witnessed the deaths of his brothers and sisters and friends. Thus he was to some extent steeled against death and fortified against the horror with which Alma viewed the songs. (On the other hand, if the name of the dead Rückert child—Ernst—presented a psychological challenge to

Mahler with respect to his own dead brother Ernst [see *Das klagende Lied*], then we may assume that Mahler acted out of compulsion in comparing the songs.)

Compared with the apparatus Mahler employed in his symphonies, the much-reduced instrumentation of the *Kindertotenlieder* impresses one as sparse. Thus in a musical and spiritual sense Mahler had returned to Schubert's late conception of the song cycle, inasmuch as all five songs deal with the same subject. Sorrow pervades the entire brief cycle, beginning with *Nun will die Sonn' so hell aufgeh'n* [Once more the sun will dawn so bright]. The wound of sorrow is open: "One tiny lamp went out; my soul's delight." Tenderness infuses the second song, *Nun seh' ich wohl warum so dunkle Flammen* [Now I know why oft I saw you gazing]: "We'd gladly stay with thee, not grieve thee! Alas, 'tis Fate's decree that we must leave thee. Look at us now, for soon from here we're going! What now are eyes to you these days, in future nights stars will be, shining for you." Tears fill the poet's eyes in *Wenn dein Mütterlein* [When thy mother]. "When thy mother enters her gaze does not go to me but to the spot where your face should be . . . thou quickly extinguished ray of joy!" The fourth song retreats from grim reality into wistful thinking and forlorn hope. It begins with the title line: "Oft do I think they have just stepped outside and soon I shall see them returning home. . . . They've gone ahead of us. We will find them on the sunlit heights." Reproach, despair, resignation, and belief in God fill the last song, *In diesem Wetter, in diesem Braus* [In such weather, in such tumult]. "I should not have let them go outside. . . . now they have been carried from the house . . . despite these storms they slumber as safely as in their mother's arms, protected by God's hand."

*Revelge* [Reveille], employing a *Wunderhorn* text, is one of Mahler's most terrifying creations. The story of a drummer hit in battle, dying among his fleeing comrades, and rising in death to lead them on employs Mahler's favorite instrument, the drum, and his favorite rhythm, the march. *Tamboursg'sell* [Drummer boy] is the only other song of the *Sieben Lieder* cycle to employ a *Wunderhorn* text. Here, again to a relentless drumbeat, terror gives way to gloom and melancholy as the drummer boy, on his way to the gallows, says good-bye to life and friends. With *Blicke mir nicht in die Lieder!* [Do not look at my songs], Rückert's lyricism dominates. *Ich atmet einen linden Duft* [I breathed a gentle fragrance] is among Mahler's most lyrical song inspirations. And it is easily discernible what immense attraction *Ich bin der Welt abhanden gekommen* [I am lost to the world] must have had for Mahler:

I am dead to the world's turmoil
I dwell in a realm of peace
I live alone in my own heaven
In my love, in my song.

It thus comes as no surprise that this song becomes the climax of the cycle for the man who, through long winter months, yearned for the quiet and solitude of his composer's hut in the mountains. (The melody appears again in the Adagietto of his Fifth Symphony.) *Um Mitternacht* [At midnight] is sheer perfection in its lugubrious solemnity; a midnight reverie backed by wind instruments, harp, and timpani, with the exquisite *oboe d'amore* representing the infinity of nature in the sound of the nightbird. *Liebst Du um Schönheit* [Lov'st thou but beauty] ends the cycle on a note of graceful simplicity.

The lyricism of the *Sieben Lieder* cycle contrasts sharply with the sorrow reflected in the *Kindertotenlieder* texts. Within the *Sieben Lieder* cycle, the darkness of the two *Wunderhorn* songs contrasts starkly with the gentle lyricism and grace of the songs set to Rückert texts. Finally, the tenderness and grace of these last Rückert songs are worlds apart from the symphonic creations of the same period—the middle symphonies, which represent a time of great upheaval in Mahler's creative life.

## SYMPHONY NO. 4 IN G MAJOR

> What touches us most in Mahler's symphony is the feeling which emanates from the work. The longing for simplicity—"Unless you become children you will not enter God's realm." Mahler's G Major symphony is a work for children and those who will become children.
>
> Max Kalbeck, Vienna, 16 January 1902

> The drooling and emasculated simplicity of Gustav Mahler! It is not fair to the readers . . . to take up their time with a detailed description of that musical monstrosity which masquerades under the title of Mahler's Fourth Symphony. There is nothing in the design, content, or execution of the work to impress the musician, except its grotesquerie. . . . To the writer of the present review . . . it was an hour or more of the most painful torture to which he has been compelled to submit.
>
> *Musical Courier*, New York, November 1904

*Composition begun in Maiernigg (Carynthia) during the summers of 1899 and 1900. The soprano solo of the last movement was composed in 1892 and thus antedates the rest. Revisions between 1903 and 1910. First performance, Munich, 25 November 1901, Mahler conducting.*

Upon his return from the near-disastrous Paris excursion with the Vienna Philharmonic, Mahler all but fled back to Carynthia and his composer's cottage. It was there that his Fourth Symphony took shape. Like Beethoven, who deliberately interspersed works of lighter spirit between his dramatic Third, Fifth, Seventh, and Ninth Symphonies, so Mahler relaxed in his Fourth Symphony and created a work relatively less charged with drama, emotion, and philosophical peregrinations. Thus his Fourth Symphony represents a respite before his renewed onslaught toward loftier aims and accomplishments. If Mahler had been accused on previous occasions of having pursued novelty for its own sake, he now takes great care to end in the same key in which he began, another sign of his deliberate attempt at kinship with the classics in an age—of romanticism and post-romanticism—of which Mahler was destined to be the final representative.

Despite luckless performances in Vienna and elsewhere, the Fourth Symphony always remained close to Mahler. He felt (as always) that it was his finest symphonic effort up to that period. It was characteristic of Mahler's involvement and enthusiasm that the work he was working on at the moment, be it a new symphony or a new operatic production, was always the best thing he had ever done. But if the Fourth has become one of the more frequently performed symphonies of Mahler, it is for reasons having little to do with his enthusiasm. Although it is overshadowed by the Fifth and other symphonies, the Fourth Symphony enjoys great acceptance among audiences and conductors alike because it is of less "unwieldy" length (approximately forty-five minutes). It is charming, and it is hence more easily digestible than other Mahler creations. Furthermore, such factors as the symphony's small orchestra and the absence of a chorus make the symphony less expensive to perform and thus financially more palatable to conductors and orchestra managers.

Generally speaking, the symphony surprises in its straightforward themes and tonality. The orchestration is deceptively light, with trombones, tuba, and percussion conspicuously absent; it seems to hark back to Haydn and Mozart. By asking to have the violin tuned a whole tone higher in the Scherzo, and advising that it should sound like *"eine Fiedel"* (fiddle)—thus striking a primitive, medieval tone in this macabre scene rather than the more refined tone of a modern violin—Mahler further surprises an audience which had expected explosions but received deceptive charm instead.

One is easily lulled into a false sense of serenity by the fact that the first three movements adhere more closely to the symphonic past (with the exception of the finale of the third) than is generally expected of Mahler; only in the last (song) movement does he depart from the "classical norm" (a term to be employed with care when dealing with Mahler). Yet such considerations should not distract the attention from the often fantastic, even demonic character of the work, which all but explodes in the third movement.

There are indications, as Redlich points out, that the Fourth Symphony grew out of the originally planned seventh movement of the Third

Symphony, variously titled *Das himmlische Leben, Was mir das Kind erzählt,* or *Was mir Gott erzählt.* One would thus assume that the last movement of the Third Symphony would simply become the first movement of the Fourth Symphony. But Mahler had different ideas, and the first line of the soprano solo, *Wir geniessen die himmlischen Freuden* [We enjoy the heavenly pleasures], becomes the opening of the final movement instead. The melody also reminds us again of the interrelationship of Symphonies Two, Three, and Four, because we meet again with a *Wunderhorn* song. Yet despite these ties, the Fourth somehow seems to stand alone. There is a polyphonic logic about the Fourth Symphony which separates it from previous symphonic endeavors but does not yet tie it to the contrapuntal upheaval which was to permeate Mahler's Fifth Symphony.

The opening movement reverts to the time-honored sonata form. The second movement, with its *scordatura* notation for the solo violin, sounds eerie and unreal, an effect intended by Mahler. In a reversal of the classical order, the Adagio follows the Scherzo. The final movement clearly establishes the continuity which, consciously or subconsciously, was never far from Mahler's mind.

Perhaps it was a conjurer's trick, this lulling of the senses with the naiveté of the themes, the "correctness" of the architecture, the house appearing classical while what went on inside resembled Haydn and Mozart gone mad or being satirized. Prokofieff's *Classical Symphony,* if heard at the turn of the century, might have suffered a critical fate similar to that of Mahler's Fourth. The work was particularly enervating to the critics because it was presented in the spirit of absolute music, with no programmatic explanation. Mahler had actually anticipated the critics' resultant insecurity. "I know the most wonderful names for the movements, but I will not betray them to the rabble of critics and listeners so they can subject them to banal misunderstandings and distortions."

The symphony had its premiere in Munich, and the hostile reception it received must have surprised all except Mahler. There was something puzzling in Mahler's having produced so charming a work, after the stormy symphonies which had preceded it, which caused the negative response. Mahler was supposed to be monumental, not charming. Having expected another outburst from the Mahler volcano, critics and public alike were first thrown off balance, then taken aback, and finally infuriated. They felt short-changed by the composer. Every innovation—the sound of tiny bells, the gentle *Biedermeier* themes, the retuned violin in the Scherzo—dismayed them.[22]

[22] Not all listened to the symphony in disgruntled displeasure. Upon hearing it at its premiere in Vienna, young Alban Berg was so overwhelmed by the experience that he appropriated Mahler's baton and kept it as a cherished memento.

The hissing which followed the Scherzo was so loud that even Mahler's ardent young admirers, who filled the parquet standing room in a stifling throng, could not drown it out with all their clapping.

Natalie Bauer-Lechner, diary entry, 25 November 1901

Mahler, who was initially infuriated by the negative reception, was to comment later, laughingly: "They didn't know how to swallow it, forwards or backwards." In the meantime the critics harshly likened the work to a practical joke on the audience, "a composer's trick," a "black Mass," "a stylish monstrosity," "not a single authentic feeling . . . nothing but calculation and falsehood," "nothing but an unpleasantry."

Yet nobody, not even Schubert, could have written a movement of greater Viennese charm or with more songlike flow than the opening movement (*bedächtig, nicht eilen*—deliberate, unhurried) of the symphony. There is hardly any introduction, only three bars of sound; and then, to the steady beat of the basses (reminiscent of the *allegretto scherzando* of Beethoven's Eighth Symphony), Mahler leads into the main theme of the movement, itself consisting of three components (indicated as a,b,c), opening with the violins, answering with an ascending line in the basses and concluding with the horns.

Mahler barely gives the listener an opportunity to revel in the brief variations on this theme before he presents his next theme in the clarinets.

Practically on the heels of this theme Mahler presents us with a new and beguiling one, this time in the celli,

followed by yet another one in the celli,

and then by interplay among the various themes. Throughout the movement the opening theme attempts, not always successfully, to remain the
dominant melody; sometimes it is overwhelmed amidst the other themes,
before the movement wafts away in dreamy languor.

The Scherzo is marked *in gemächlicher Bewegung, ohne Hast* (in
easy motion, without haste). Its theme

> is the gruesome dance of Death, led by a figure of popular demonology,
> *Freund Hein* [death]. It is the mistuned fiddle of the skeletal figure of
> death which is heard at the opening of the movement. . . . It is a grisly,
> sudden feeling which comes over us, just as one is often panic-stricken in
> broad daylight in a sunlit forest. The Scherzo is so mysterious, confused,
> and supernatural that your hair will stand on end when you hear it. But
> in the Adagio to follow, where all this passes off, you will immediately
> see that it was not meant so seriously.
>
> Mahler to Natalie Bauer-Lechner

If Saint-Saëns treats death with Gallic humor in his *Danse macabre,*
Mahler attempts something even more droll and grotesque, a dance of
death in *Ländler* time. The opening of the mistuned fiddle sets the grotesque tone of the Scherzo.[23]

A brief romantic intrusion into classical form occurs when the *Ländler*
melody makes its appearance in *two* middle sections (Trios) of the
Scherzo in distinct contrast to the eerie mood of the opening and closing
parts of the movement.

---

[23] This provides something of a hardship for the solo violinist because he is obliged
to have two instruments ready, one in the usual tuning and one in the higher
tuning, as indicated by Mahler.

Mahler was especially pleased with the Adagio movement (*Ruhevoll* —restful). Bruno Walter recalls Mahler's comment that the quiet and clear beauty of the Adagio "was caused by his vision of one of the church sepulchres showing a recumbent stone image of the deceased with his arms crossed in eternal sleep." But Dika Newlin's interpretation of the movement (in *Bruckner, Mahler, and Schönberg*) as conveying a picture of Mahler's mother is persuasive:

> the gentle Jewish girl . . . who limped a little and so was considered only too lucky to be able to marry the stubborn, hard-headed Bernard Mahler, when she really loved someone else . . . who suffered poverty, ill health, and neglect, yet whose loving, forgiving nature remained unaltered through it all.

The double-variation form of the Adagio foregoes all but one climax to maintain the gentle, undramatic mood of the work and the movement. The celli open the movement with a heart-rending melody.

Mahler then proceeds into a set of free variations, calmly, melodiously measured. Only near the end does the orchestra rear up in tragic outcry before the movement ends, softly and gently.

With regard to the song finale—*sehr behaglich* (very comfortably)— Walter writes: "The words of the poem in the last movement depict the atmosphere out of which the music of the Fourth grew." The finale was, indeed, composed first. This still leaves open the question whether the song was composed with its place as part of a symphony in mind or whether the symphony of 1900 was an afterthought to the song composed eight years earlier.

The song finale's lightness and charm, after the elegiac peace of the previous movement, offer a carefully planned contrast. Its spirit is one of naive, joyous delight; as expressed by the soprano:

| | |
|---|---|
| Wir geniessen die himmlischen Freuden | We enjoy the pleasures of heaven |
| d'rum tun wir das irdische meiden | and so we avoid earthly ones |
| Kein weltlich Getümmel | No earthly turmoil |
| hört man im Himmel! | in heaven is heard |
| Lebt alles in sanftester Ruh! | All lives in gentlest peace |

Mahler fashioned his song from the original *Wunderhorn* poem *Der Himmel hängt voller Geigen* [Heaven is hung with violins], a saying especially *heavenly dinn* (handwritten note in left margin)

popular in Vienna. In that "very comfortable" tempo Mahler speaks of celestial joys, tenderly, charmingly, and amusingly. And the tune matches the spirit perfectly.

Wir ge-nies-sen die himm - - - - - lisch - en Freuden

## THE MIDDLE SYMPHONIES (NOS. 5, 6, AND 7)

Although the three "middle" symphonies must be treated as individual creations, even cursory comparison of these three works brings to light strong similarities between Symphonies Five and Seven, which in themselves point up even more strongly the uniqueness of the Sixth Symphony.

Both the Fifth and Seventh Symphonies utilize Mahler's favorite introductory device—the funeral march. In both symphonies Mahler decided to end the work with a movement in the form of a rondo with variations. The expected Andante movement, with its contrasting gentle charm, is replaced in both compositions by a sort of romantic serenade harking back to Mahler's earlier days. Further contrast is achieved through phantasmagoric Scherzi which, in turn, provide contrast with respect to the vaster final movement; and the endings of both symphonies, jubilantly bursting with majesty and joy, stand in stark contrast to the solemn finale of the Sixth. Similarities do not end there. Echoes of the *Wunderhorn* march melodies are in evidence in both symphonies. Most important, the emotional gradation in both is carefully planned; Beethoven's *per aspera ad astra* (through night to light) becomes evident. Both works begin in funeral gloom and end in solemnly glowing jubilation.

There is, however, a significant characteristic common to all three "middle" symphonies: to wit, "the word" has been left behind. Mahler had found the inspirational strength to express himself in instrumental terms only, and not until the Eighth Symphony would he again avail himself of the spoken word and the human voice. Bare of program or even of an extended song melody to fall back on, these symphonies are abstract, absolute music.[24]

Mahler's creative output of that period would undoubtedly have been prodigious had he been able to address himself solely to composition. If one realizes that superimposed upon colossal creativity—the Fifth Sym-

[24] Although some musicologists feel that most Mahler symphonies are "programmatic" regardless of whether or not an explicit program is provided.

phony in 1902, the Sixth in 1904, and the Seventh in 1905—were the tortuous duties of director and premier conductor of the world's foremost opera house, one stands in awe before the capacity of the man and the magnitude of his accomplishments.

## SYMPHONY NO. 5 IN C–SHARP MINOR

It is a matter of extreme difficulty to detect tangible themes in the second movement of Mahler's Fifth Symphony, and it is an almost impossible task to follow them through the tortuous maze of their formal and contrapuntal development. One has to cling by one's teeth, so to speak, to a shred of theme here and there, which appears for an occasional instant above the heavy masses of tone, only to be jumped upon immediately by the whole angry herd of instruments and stamped down into the very thick of the orchestral fray. The fighting grows so furious toward the finish that one is compelled to unclose one's teeth on the morsel of theme, and lo and behold! It is seized upon, hurled through the screaming and frenzied ranks of the combatants, and that is the last seen or heard of the poor little rag of a theme.

*Musical Courier,* 21, February 1906

### A MODERN SYMPHONY

One Saturday at evening
The critic's work was done,
He sat within the Music Hall,
The concert had begun.
And by his side there might be seen
His little grandchild Wilhelmine.

Young Peterkin was also there
With program book in hand
And asked the critic to explain
What ailed the music band.
What was the work that they had found
That was so big and full of sound.

The critic gazed upon the boy
That stood expectant by.
He knit his brow, he scratched his head,
He heaved a natural sigh.
'Tis some poor fellow's score, said he,
That wrote a monster symphonie.

With chords of ninths, elevenths, and worse
And discords in all keys

He turns the music inside out
With unknown harmonies.
But things like that, you know, must be
In every modern symphonie.

Great praise the big brass tubas won,
And kettle-drums, I ween.
Why, 'twas an ugly thing,
Said little Wilhelmine.
Nay, that you must not say, quoth he,
It is a famous symphonie.

Louis Elson, *Boston Daily Advertiser*,
28 February 1914 (after hearing Mahler's
Fifth Symphony)

*Composition 1902, First performance in Cologne, 1904, Mahler conducting.*

*Scored for 4 flutes (3 interchangeable with piccolos), 3 oboes, English horn, 3 clarinets (1 interchangeable with bass clarinet), 2 bassoons, contrabassoon, 6 horns (including solo obbligato horn) 4 trumpets, 3 trombones, bass tuba, kettle drums, bass drum, snare drum, cymbals, triangle, glockenspiel, gong, harp and strings.*

The year was 1902. It was still five years before Mahler's departure from Vienna—nine years to Mahler's death and twelve years to World War One. By a peculiar musicopsychological change beyond explanation, Mahler had turned to a new means of expression in his Fifth Symphony. "I cannot understand how I could have at that time written so much like a beginner. Clearly the routine I had acquired in the first four symphonies deserted me altogether, as if a totally new message demanded a new technique. . . . It is the sum of all the suffering I have been compelled to endure at the hands of life."

In making his radical departure in his Fifth Symphony, Mahler never lost sight of the past. Just as Beethoven cannot be considered a romantic without keeping in mind that he also represented the height of classicism, so Mahler's decisive ventures into the twentieth century are also part of that romantic trend which extends, in glittering variegation, from Beethoven to Mahler. Yet, within that vast mass of often futile symphonic attempts during the nineteenth century, Mahler brought about a radical transformation. No longer is the main trend of the work deposited in the first movement; on the contrary, all movements are designed to lead up to the summation of the finale. The public's response to Mahler's Fifth Symphony was deplorable but understandable; they had barely come to accept his first four symphonies when a new thunderclap descended upon them. And there was no return to be expected with Mahler. Just as Beethoven could not have returned to the style of his earlier symphonies after the *Eroica,* so Mahler could not turn back after his Fifth.

What actually did happen in Mahler's Fifth Symphony was the superimposition of Bach's genius upon Mahler's creation; specifically, the superlative use of polyphony, which never deserted him from then on. It was that polyphony which was to become Mahler's greatest contribution in the growth of twentieth-century music.

During a walk with friends through a country fair, Mahler once attempted to explain to Walter his new type of polyphony. Pointing to the intermingling and overlapping sounds of barrel organs, the laughing, shouting, and singing of the milling people, the crackling noises of the shooting galleries, and the blaring sounds of a military band, he shouted: "Do you hear that? That's polyphony—and that's where I get it from . . . that is how—from a lot of different sources—the themes must come, and like this they must be entirely different from each other in rhythm and melody—and anything else is only part writing and disguised homophony. What the artist has to do is to organize them into an intelligible entity."

But Mahler went even further. To achieve his musical aims he revolutionized orchestral sound and introduced what he termed a "ruthless contrapuntal technique." Until then composers had confined themselves to the ordinary range of each instrument. Mahler was among the first to create new timbres and textures by using instruments *beyond* their accustomed ranges, creating sounds of screeching and rasping or of ghostly whispering, intimating the grotesque and bizarre—creating, in a word, new worlds of musical experience, destined to lead into Schönberg's polytonality and tone-row concept. Thus his Fifth Symphony led the way to the new world of twentieth-century music in timbre and texture, just as the reduced orchestra of his Seventh Symphony anticipated Schönberg's chamber-music style.

As the master of these innovations, Mahler felt, rightly or wrongly, that the time had passed when interpretation could be left solely in the hands of the conductor. No longer could a composer afford to write music and leave dynamics and tempi to players and conductor, as had been the case in the Baroque era and even into the Classical period. Instead, Mahler increasingly felt that minute instructions were needed to guide ensemble and leader through these new worlds of sound and to the meaning that he wished to impart. Thus Mahler's scores teem with minute marginal markings.

Blaukopf points out another significant development beginning with the Fifth Symphony; *viz.,* Mahler worked with orchestral conception from the outset of the work, doing away with the piano, on which he had previously worked out initial conceptions (a habit which most composers maintain to this day). Mahler advised even Marschalk not to compose "from the piano." This remark is fascinating because another composer— in another field and practically another world, although he was a contemporary of Mahler—had expressed the same thought. Johann Strauss, who shared with Brahms the habit of composing at a stand-up desk, shared with Mahler a disinclination to compose at the piano. ("I never compose at the piano. The piano has the habit of making you do what *it* wants you to do.") Mahler's emancipation from the piano changed twentieth-century orchestration habits, because musical imagery no longer had to be transposed from the keyboard into the orchestra. Now the symphonic form could be invested with an even richer tapestry, a more three-dimensional sound, as Mahler, not unlike Richard Strauss, added glockenspiel, bells, celesta, and hammer. (Strauss even added a wind machine in *Don Quixote*.) All this tended to widen the emotional and tonal impact, though without imitating Debussy, whose *Prélude à l'après-midi d'un faune* eight years earlier had opened the door to twentieth-century musical sound. For while Debussy consciously, contemptuously strayed from the symphony, Mahler recreated it in his Fifth, in new, twentieth-century garb. He failed to realize, however, that he was to be the last one to uphold the glory that was the symphony. The form had, through him, reached its vastest possible tonal, harmonic and structural expansion.

But to return to 1902, which was a busy year for Mahler. He had met, wooed, bedded, and married Alma Maria Schindler and was to become a father in November of the same year, and completed his Fifth Symphony. Musically as well as personally his life had taken a completely new turn. The summer was spent in Maiernigg, where Mahler could retire into his *Komponierhäuschen* in the woods for musical solitude (except for the singing of the birds, which occasionally spoiled his concentration— they sang in the wrong key). The symphony that emerged from that forest solitude was to be a revelation, even to Mahler.

Mahler grouped the symphony's five movements into three parts.

Part I   1. *Trauermusik* (Funeral music), C-sharp minor
         2. *Stürmisch bewegt* (stormily agitated), A minor
Part II  3. Scherzo, D major
Part III 4. Adagietto, F major
         5. Rondo Finale, D major

Contrasts pervade this Mahler opus. Funeral darkness turns to struggle, strife, and turmoil. The mood then becomes energetic, lively, and hectic, to be succeeded by rapt, expressive quiet (which makes the brief Adagietto for strings and harp one of Mahler's most beloved creations, often performed as an independent concert piece) and then by a *Hochgesang* (apotheosis) of tremendous vitality, ending in a Brucknerian chorale.

The opening *Trauermusik* (*in gemessenem Schritt, Streng, Wie ein
Konduit*—Funeral music; in measured step, stern, like a funeral cortege)
is purest Mahler, a funereal four-trumpet fanfare, soon to be followed by
more brass harmony in the horns and then in the trombones.

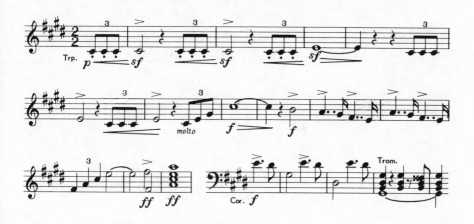

Nor are spirits raised by the lugubrious melody, still in march tempo, now
spun out by the violins.

The dark, forlorn mood, darkened even more in modulation, persists in
the woodwinds and celli, and eventually returns to the ominous rhythm
of the funeral fanfare. The picture of solemn gloom is suddenly shattered
by an intruding passage of vehement, passionate grief and despair. Against
the bassoons and basses, the trumpet shrieks in grief and pain as the
strings wail. This passage is among the most exciting in Mahler's music;
its mood of despair is so piercing that it dwarfs even the most hysterical
outbursts of Tchaikovsky into insignificance. The climax is shattering, but
it subsides as the opening fanfare asserts itself against the dying orchestral tumult.

It is difficult to realize that such a remarkable opening movement
should be considered only as the introduction to the next movement (*mit
grösster Vehemenz*—with greatest vehemence). The opening utterance,
more a phrase than a theme, sets the mood,

to be answered by a succession of searing trumpet calls and, shortly there-after, by another despairing scream in the woodwinds.

The recurrence of the funeral march injects a slower tempo, and against it the celli intone a somber yet warm melody.

Returning abruptly, almost rudely, to the stormy opening theme and the elemental ejaculations to follow, the movement runs the gamut from *Klagend* (grieving) to wildly agitated expression, constantly rising in emotion in the process. But Mahler does not give himself freely to his climaxes. Several times, when sentiments and expectations surge toward an emotional and orchestral height, he reins up short, until he allows the proceedings to burst into a chorale in a build-up so carefully constructed and extended that Mahler feels obliged to mark its climax with the word *Höhepunkt* (climax).

Only then does he allow the movement to resolve itself and descend into a misty, mysterious haze at the end.

The scene changes abruptly with the Scherzo

The Scherzo is the very devil of a movement. I see it is in for a peck of troubles! Conductors for the next fifty years will take it too fast and make nonsense of it, and the public—Oh, heavens, what are they to make of this chaos, of which new worlds are forever being begotten, only to crumble in ruin the next moment? What are they to say to this primeval music, this foaming, roaring, raging sea of sound, to these dancing stars, to these breathtaking irridescent and flashing breakers? What has a flock of sheep to say but "baa" to the *Brüdersphären Wettgesang* (singing contest of the brotherly spheres)? Oh that I might give my symphony its first performance fifty years after my death!

> Mahler to Alma, Cologne, 16 October 1904,
> after the first rehearsal of the Scherzo

Mahler ordained a long pause after the second movement, if for no other reason than to indicate that the two opening movements actually constituted the first part of the symphony, to be separated from the remaining three movements (in two parts). The Scherzo (*kräftig aber nicht zu schnell*—forceful, but not too fast) is a far cry from the scherzo of Beethoven, its inventor. It is, first of all, enormous (over 800 bars), and despite the employment of delightful Austrian Alpine dance forms, it does not offer the humor that its title would lead one to expect. Instead it offers unsurpassed orchestral virtuosity in instrumentation. The movement also furnished further proof (if proof was needed) that Mahler was truly what he had always considered himself to be, an Austrian composer. The powerful opening phrase

leads to a delightful flow of melody in which ideas jostle each other, to be borne on the sounds of flutes, violins, and glockenspiel. The dances of the Austrian Alps and of Vienna are interspersed in undulant counterpoint, until the Scherzo ends with a sonorous repetition of its first theme.

Set against the exuberant mood of the mammoth Scherzo, the Adagietto to follow—*sehr langsam* (very slow)—appears restrained and refined in its gentle sounds. Beginning with its romantic, almost introspective opening theme (*seelenvoll*—soulfully),

the movement allows us a glimpse of the wistful, withdrawn side of Mahler, surpassing in its entrancing dreaminess even the trios of the preceding Scherzo.

The Rondo Finale begins without a break, clearly indicating that the Adagietto was intended as an introduction to the Finale, the two movements thus constituting the final portion (Part III) of the work. Mahler first imparts into that typical finale of the classical symphony, the Rondo, that touch of classicism which one really did not expect from Mahler, along with an occasional dash of unexpected humor. But the incredible feat of the final movement is the superimposition of a vibrant polyphony, leading with joyous abandon into a Bach-like fugue. Mahler's supreme mastery of such polyphony is an unexpected surprise, because it previously had had no place in his work.

If the listener now expects to be led into a final chorale to the strains of a stentorian march, he will have to bide his time. Mahler again toys with an Adagietto theme, but inevitably all the shining rivulets of themes lead into the broad stream of the chorale. There, in final polyphonic exclamation, the fugue, now played in unison by the strings and woodwinds, is intoned in counterpoint against the chorale, heard in all its splendor in the trumpets and trombones.

Much has been made of the chorale ending. Alma Mahler objected to it when Mahler played it to her for the first time in a piano version. It was considered an outward musical sign of a schizophrenic Mahler tendency (Alma called it "a rift in his personality")—he was philosophically and religiously independent, yet strongly attracted to the mysticism of the Catholic church. Alma felt that in the context of Bruckner's unquestioning faith a church chorale had its proper place, but not with Mahler. The latter, however, found the chorale meaningful as a symbol of majesty and triumph, proclaiming a moral universe—meaningful to him, in other words, beyond musical values and considerations. And when the chorale sounded in the monumental splendor of his orchestration, then Mahler may have experienced one of those rare moments when his mind was at rest, above and beyond the battles with the demons of his questing mind.

## SYMPHONY NO. 6 IN A MINOR

A man without genius had better stay away [from composition], and a man with genius has nothing to fear. It seems to me that all this hair-splitting on the subject is like a man who begets a child and afterwards begins to worry . . . whether it was begotten with the right intentions and so forth. The point is: he loved—and he had the vigor. *Basta!* [Enough!] And if he does not love and has no vigor, then there will be no child!

Again, *basta!* And according to what one is and the vigor one has, the child will turn out! Yet again, *basta!*

My Sixth is finished. I think I had the vigor! A thousand times *basta!*

Mahler to Bruno Walter, Summer 1906

The only Sixth, despite Beethoven's *Pastorale.*

Alban Berg to Anton Webern, May 1906

Wastefulness of instrumental means in inverse ratio to the power of inventiveness . . . making conception and execution of an orderly plan illusory. . . . Instead of reviewing his musical ideas capable of review . . . he refines his mastery of the art of the instrumental and attempts through it to surpass other rivals, but failing to recognize that the limit of the possible has long been reached and left behind.

Max Kalbeck, *Neues Wiener Tagblatt,* 1907 (?)

*Composed during the summers of 1903 and 1904 in Maiernigg. First performance at the* Tonkünstlerfest *of the* Allgemeine Deutsche Musikverein, *27 May 1906, Mahler conducting.*

*Piccolo, 4 flutes, (3 and 4 interchangeable with piccolos), 4 oboes (3 and 4 interchangeable with English horn), English horn, clarinet in D and E flat, 3 clarinets in A and B flat, bass clarinet, 4 bassoons, contrabassoon, 8 horns, 6 trumpets, 3 trombones, bass trombone, bass tuba, kettledrum, glockenspiel, cowbells, lowpitched bells, whip, hammer, xylophone, 2 harps, celesta and strings.*

The demons which bestrode Mahler could be shaken off temporarily only by two activities: vigorous physical activity, such as walking or swimming, and playing with his infant children. The summers of 1903 and 1904 found Mahler fully at rest playing with his small daughter and (in 1904) with his new infant daughter. He would talk to them, tell them stories, dance with them. It was at that time that he began his Sixth Symphony. More than ever Mahler felt in a romantic mood, and his musical portrayal of Alma in the first movement of the symphony attests to that brief but happy moment in his life. It is fascinating, therefore, that this time period should have produced the otherwise brooding Sixth Symphony and the *Kindertotenlieder.*

Such a near-schizophrenic frame of mind is not unusual with composers. While composing his Fourth Symphony, in which "he laughed for the last time," Beethoven was much beset by family problems; yet when he was in love and in high spirits he wrote the dramatic Fifth Symphony. It was while Mozart was too wretched and too poor to buy wood to heat his apartment that he was nonetheless capable of creating his inspired last three symphonies. The comparisons are apt, because a time of discontent in Mahler's life produced the delightful Fourth Symphony, while

the happiest time of his life, spent with his children, produced the Sixth
Symphony, with its sense of impending tragedy, from which only the
Adagio movement manages to escape.

Despite the flattering portrait of her, Alma was disturbed by the spirit
of the symphony. She pronounced the Scherzo "ghastly" and resented
Mahler's playing with his children one moment and speaking of the death
of children in the next (in the symphony as well as in the *Kindertotenlieder*). Yet in spite of her reservations pertaining to that sense of tragic
foreboding, Alma Mahler could not deny the genuineness of the work:

> After he had drafted the first movement, he came down from the
> forest to tell me he had tried to express me in a theme. "Whether I've
> succeeded, I don't know; but you'll have to put up with it."
>
> This is the great, soaring theme of the first movement of the Sixth
> Symphony. In the third movement,[25] he represented the unrhythmic
> games of the two children, tottering in zigzags over the sand. Ominously
> the childish voices became more and more tragic, and at the end died out
> in a whimper. In the last movement he described himself and his down-
> fall; or, as he later said: "It is the hero, on whom fall three blows of fate,
> the last of which fells him as a tree is felled. . . .
>
> None of his works came as directly from his innermost heart as this
> one. . . . The music and what it foretold touched us so deeply.
>
> Alma Mahler, *Memories and Letters*

Again, analogies with Tchaikovsky come to mind. Tchaikovsky was
described as hale and in the best of spirits after the premiere of his
*Pathétique*. But the subconsciously expressed spirit of farewell, of death,
of the final movement, was to become reality ten days later, when
Tchaikovsky died of typhoid fever after drinking unboiled water. So it
was with Mahler. The three blows of fate of the final movement [26] fore-
told the three blows that were to fall on him only a year later; his resignation from the Vienna Opera in the spring, the death of his older daughter
in the summer, and his realization of his heart disease, the last, fatal blow.
Yet the Tchaikovsky finale is one of pity and lament, which earned the
work the fitting title of *Pathétique;* it is the Mahler work which descends
into the bottomless pit of utter tragedy and human disaster, which often
prompted the appending of the title *Tragic* to the work.

There is a clarity of thematic material about this exceptional work
which lifts it beyond the profusion of themes of the Fifth Symphony.
Owing to its dark, "tragic" pessimism, the Sixth is among the least per-

[25] The symphony was first published with the Scherzo second and the slow movement third, but Mahler switched them around for a second publication. Shortly
before his death Mahler reverted to the original order, and that is the order in
the version which was published as "final" by the International Mahler Society of
Vienna in 1963. Depending on what edition is used in performance, the Scherzo
may appear as the second movement (as Cooke, Kralik, and Blaukopf indicate)
or it may be third (as suggested by Redlich and Engel). Our discussion presents
the Scherzo as the second movement.

[26] The three hammer blows were reduced to two in the final version.

formed of Mahler's works. Yet that very sense of tragedy, coupled with
its boldness of harmonic treatment, seems to have exerted a strong influence on the next wave of Austrian composers, Schönberg, Berg, and
Webern. Mahler was, in any case, aware of the symphony's dark features
and mentioned to the music critic and musicologist Richard Specht that
only those who had absorbed his first five symphonies would be able to
comprehend the "riddles" which the Sixth propounded. He was himself
deeply moved and emotionally torn by his creation; Alma Mahler described
him after the Essen premiere as pacing the room, sobbing, wringing his
hands, unable to control himself.

While the similarities between the Fifth and Sixth symphonies are
not as numerous as those between the Fifth and the Seventh, some definite likenesses can be noticed: the huge outer movements; the mammoth
orchestra, with its emphasis on brass and percussion; the presence of
march themes.

The first movement—*allegro energico ma non troppo*—opens with
an enormous outburst, a march of symphonic breadth,

to be followed by a contrasting, dominant theme of "grim relentless
power" (Engel).

Soon after the movement has reached a mighty climax, the "tragic" theme
of the work is introduced, its symbolic major-minor change (a brilliant
A-major chord in the trumpets descending into a *pp* A-minor chord in
the oboes) underlining the tragic character of the work.

But the opening of the movement does not long remain in the minor key, as the next major theme, the "Alma" theme, is passionately introduced.

In a somewhat macabre scene to follow, in which Mahler uses the xylophone for the only time in his music, the march rhythm returns, only to be led by the violins unto Alpine heights peacefully resplendent with the sound of *Herdenglocken* [cow bells] "echoing from the valley below." The march rhythm returns, now more joyfully, leading into the final portion of the first movement. There is a constant modulation from major to minor until, rising from a *pp* whisper to a towering climax ("furious with anger"), we arrive at a final, joyful affirmation and majestic restatement of the "Alma" theme.

The Scherzo (*Wuchtig*—heavy), "a sinister, Hoffmannesque puppet show" (Redlich), features an eerie dance with themes often derived from the opening movement. "Lurking demons . . . with gargoyle leers" (Engel) flit by in this movement, which begins with a furious stomping dance.

Mahler's annotation for the Trio part of the Scherzo—"*altväterisch*" (old-fashioned)—does little to dispel a different kind of spookishness, whose essence provides a distinct and deliberate contrast between the old-fashioned themes and the eerie rendition. Here one finds the "unrhythmic games of children" mentioned by Alma Mahler.

The ending of the movement poignantly recalls Alma's foreboding words: "Ominously the childish voices became more and more tragic, and at the end died out in a whimper."

The third movement (*andante moderato*), gentle and intimate, presents a welcome interlude amidst the surging, frenzied flow before and after it. The cow bells are heard here again but in an almost melancholy manner, providing a sense of continuity. Peace pervades this movement in the serene singing of the violins,

leading into a second theme, a haunting English horn melody.

Mahler makes no mention here of either the tragic or the "fate" themes, nor does the jubilant "Alma" theme disturb the serenity, thus making the Andante movement an entity unto itself within the work.

We thus witness a militant, triumphant mood in the first movement, becoming grim, tense, and eerie in the Scherzo as disaster looms. After an interlude of world-removed gentleness in the third movement, the gargantuan final movement (*allegro moderato*), almost a symphony within a symphony, opens when the violin theme is flung out.

The leaping octave of the opening theme is also incorporated in the next theme, but emerges there as a mournful statement in the tuba.

As if to counteract the tuba's doleful theme, the cowbells are heard again. Then, after we pass through a misty free-form passage, strongly anticipating the sounds of future twentieth-century masters, a chorale-like theme sounds darkly in the woodwinds. The dark spirit is roused and peaks again in the fate theme before two more incisive themes are introduced: first, *pp* in the lower woodwinds

and then what might again be considered a theme in the spirit of fate, this time *f* and intoned by six horns.

Despite tremendous climaxes the minor key prevails, and the drama is intensified by the powerful presentation of these themes, be they march or chorale, in sharply chiseled outline. From these themes grow three waves of development, each reaching its own climax only to be crushed under cruel hammer blows. Mahler provides specific instructions as to the sound of the hammer—"short, powerful, but dull in sound . . . not of metallic character." The hammer blows assumed immense importance for Mahler in the scheme of the movement: they became symbol and signal, heralding changes and highlights. They tend to heighten tension in their decreasing strength, ending the first wave *fff* and becoming weaker with the second blow, in doing so clearly bespeaking doom and death.

Significantly, this is not one of Mahler's blazing finales but a dirge solemnly intoned by the trombones. Only at the very end is there one plangent outcry by the brass before the finale descends into darkness.

It is typical of the differences in musical conception between Mahler and Strauss that the theatrical realist Strauss was completely oblivious to the basic theme of the finale movement and the sinister meaning of the hammer blows. He could not conceive why Mahler had the hammer sounded with diminishing force and thus deprived himself of "a wonderful effect." That in this symphony, even more than in the Fifth, a new Mahler had emerged, a polyphonic master far removed from the romantic fervor

of his first four symphonies, was apparently beyond Straus
sion or interest.


## SYMPHONY NO. 7 IN E MINOR

*Composed during the summers of 1904 and 1905 in Maiernigg. First performance, Prague, 17 September 1908, Gustav Mahler conducting.*

The Seventh Symphony is a curious work. Though impressive when considered by itself, by comparison it signals a temporary regression of genius, although even in regression Mahler remains fascinating. Comparative listening will reveal that the outer movements correspond to those of the Fifth Symphony. The opening horn solo parallels the trombone opening of the Third Symphony. Rhythmically the main theme of the first movement is nearly identical to that of the Sixth, and *Nachtmusik 1* (the first part of the three "inner movements" of the symphony) echoes the workmanship of Mahler's early symphonic years. Only *Nachtmusik 2* (the third inner movement) introduces a novel element, aided by the gossamer sounds of mandolin and guitar. The Rondo Finale again closely resembles the identical movement of the Fifth Symphony, but its execution, though impressive, is less convincing. The contrasting section compares poorly with light Viennese operetta music at its best. Although that genre was always enjoyed by Mahler, who loved Johann Strauss's lilt, it was decidedly not a field in which Mahler felt at home.

In assessing the symphony, consideration must be given to changes, both positive and negative, in Mahler's environment at the time. Beginning with his Fifth Symphony, Mahler had undergone a complete change in symphonic conception. His leadership at the Vienna Opera had been terminated in 1907, and his first year of activity with the Metropolitan Opera Company in New York had begun. The death of his beloved older daughter from diphtheria was a terrible blow. Alma's memoirs tell of the horrifying atmosphere at Maiernigg under which the Seventh Symphony was created.

Mahler confided to a friend that the *Nachtmusik* movements had been composed first, in 1904, promptly after he finished the Sixth Symphony, and preceding the balance of the symphony by one year. After a frustratingly hesitant start in 1905, inspiration began to flow, and the remaining first, third, and fifth movements were completed within four weeks.

Prague was to be the testing ground for the new work. Once before, Prague had provided a haven and a happy proving ground for a composer from Vienna: Mozart had been feted there as his *Marriage of Figaro* and *Don Giovanni* along with his Symphony in D (K. 504) reaped the laurels which Vienna was determined to withhold from him. Mahler had every ᴖason to hope for a similar reception. While his themes could not be whistled in the streets as Mozart's had been, Prague's respect for him was high. Mahler was not happy with the noisy city itself, which added a sense of uncertainty to the preparation and innumerable alteration of the score. To escape conventional activities such as social events and courtesy calls, he spent much time in bed, resting, working on the score, and writing to Alma, who had remained in Vienna. Slowly friends and disciples drifted in and assisted Mahler in his editing efforts (though many errors still remained). Mahler's spirits were also lifted by a superb performance in Prague of his Fourth Symphony.

Despite a competent orchestra, the presence of many friends, and a generally receptive and anticipatory audience, the work received only a reservedly polite reception, tempered by stupefaction. The simultaneous use of major and minor modes must have contributed to the perplexity of the premiere audience. Entire orchestra sections, such as flutes and trumpets, are set against each other in contrasting dynamics. The horns engage in dialogues, one statement being answered in distant antiphonal response. Cowbells evoke memories of the Sixth Symphony. Perhaps conservative Prague, which had barely digested Mahler's bright Fourth Symphony, had expected a similar experience. The fact that the Seventh Symphony was considerably longer than the recently heard Fourth contributed as much as the spirit of the work, so different from that of the Fourth, to bring about its no more than half-hearted acceptance.

By then Mahler had regained his full powers of compositional genius; his Eighth Symphony was completed and *Das Lied von der Erde* sketched. Thus the lukewarm Prague reception made him doubly dissatisfied with his Seventh, and he embarked on radical revisions without even waiting for further performances. Nevertheless, this symphony, which represents the last of the spiritual trilogy of "Middle Symphonies," remains one of the least often performed.

The drama begins *adagio* with a horn call sounded in B flat by a tenor horn,[27] an instrument found nowhere else in Mahler literature. The opening theme

---

[27] An instrument known in English as a baritone horn. Jack Diether comments: "Here Mahler calls for an instrument which is not found . . . in the standard symphonic literature. . . . This is believed to be the same instrument known in English-speaking countries as the baritone horn, in the same key."

leads immediately into a rising passage in the oboes

and a sharply chiseled passage in the trumpets and winds,

only to return to the opening tenor horn theme, now heard against the strings.

The tempo quickens in a manner—the march—dear to Mahler, until we hear in the trombones and then in the trumpets a seemingly new theme which is actually a derivation of the opening horn theme.

The remainder of the opening movement, in fiercely martial (*allegro con fuoco*) and majestically solemn (*Feierlich*) moments, is dotted and dominated by brass announcements, often recalling the magnificent opening themes, often reveling in sumptuous Straussian harmonic splendor, sometimes presaging Stravinsky and Schönberg. The movement ends by recalling the opening themes in breathtaking fashion, though its jubilation is surprisingly contained and controlled.

The inner movements, *Nachtmusik 1* and *Nachtmusik 2*, interconnected by and contrasted with the Scherzo, are the most interesting feature of this Mahler opus. They reveal a cohesiveness within themselves which almost marks them as an entity apart from the larger framework of the symphony into which they were incorporated by the composer.

The *Nachtmusik 1* movement, equal in length to the opening movement, begins *allegro moderato* with an evocative horn motif,

with its echoes imitated soon by oboe, clarinet, and English horn, in a twittering dialogue reminiscent of nightbirds. From this interlude Mahler leads again into his favorite domain, the march, as the main theme of the movement is intoned by the horns.

This theme, in various variations and guises and intermingled with material from the opening movement, dominates *Nachtmusik 1*. The violins soon take over the horn theme, first shadowy, later with great verve and old-fashioned grace. Eventually the oboes, in thirds, enter with a theme which Mahler wanted to be played *"sehr ausdrucksvoll und hervortretend"* (with much feeling and pronounced).

But accents of sadness soon distort the theme, and Mahler again returns to the previously employed form of dialogue, this time between trumpets and oboes. From there the movement runs the gamut of moods—from grotesque marches to gossamer quotations of previous themes, receding into quiet and darkness as the eerie nocturnal procession passes.

It is difficult to find adjectives to describe the Scherzo (*schattenhaft, fliessend, aber nicht zu schnell*—shadowy, flowing, but not too fast) which separates the two *Nachtmusiken*. "Shadowy," "sinister," "ghostly," and "grotesque" come to mind. Bruno Walter speaks of the movement as "a spooklike, nocturnal piece." Solo instruments briefly take the spotlight in phantasmagoric succession, only to disappear in an eerie dance. Alma Mahler recalls the monster drum especially demanded by and constructed for Mahler, who considered the standard bass drum not loud enough. It gave off hardly a thud and eventually had to be replaced by the original bass drum. At one point Mahler demanded that the celli and basses attack their *fffff* in such a violent manner that the strings should rebound against the wood. This foretokens the timbre changes of the twentieth century, of which Mahler was to be one of the first and foremost innovators.

The movement begins with a timpani heartbeat which is joined in succession by the horns and woodwinds. Thereupon the whirling dance of the movement begins in the muted violins.

The dance becomes wilder in whirling motion, but subsides into a lamenting song of the flutes and oboes.

Soon the eerie dance is resumed in wildly disjunct leaps in the violins. But Mahler is always intent on contrast, even in this grotesque movement, and a melody reminiscent of the postillion's theme of his Third Symphony is heard in the oboes

leading into another, no less charming oboe theme of considerable length. A resolute dance melody is heard in the celli

until Mahler reverts to the opening rhythm. Now the demonic rhythm and tempo of this *danse macabre* grows in furious intensity. "Wild," demands Mahler. Shrill sounds emanate from the violins, while the brass brays in unbridled dissonance. Suddenly there is a descending run in the basses, a pause, and a timpani beat, and without warning, the dance is ended.

The tempo heading of *Nachtmusik 2—andante amoroso*—gives the clue to the fourth movement of the symphony: it is a serenade *à la* Mahler. Mahler intensifies the mood by adding two new instruments, for centuries identified with the "amorous" serenade: the guitar and the mandolin. The adding of the harp makes for a string trio of incomparable charm and grace. The opening of the solo violin *Mit Aufschwung* (with verve) sets the mood.

Against this the playful clarinet and bassoon present a rhythm which will permeate the entire movement.

Soon Mahler introduces two warm nocturnal themes, the first one in the horn,

the second in the oboe.

In the finespun instrumentation of this movement the violins enter with a delicate theme against which the horn repeats its previous statement, now somewhat extended. But the violin is not to be denied, and *graciosissimo*, supported by the guitar, its *pp* theme sings out.

Here Mahler indulges his full mastery of instrumentation and technique, employing inversion of themes, with the mandolin and bassoon supplying exquisite, near-Oriental harmony. While sustaining a carefully controlled nocturnal mood he conjures up a marvel of Schumannesque [28] *Schwärmerei* (fancifulness). The mood is deepened by the final song of the violin.

Slowly the mood changes, becoming more agitated until Mahler returns to *tempo primo subito*. The opening mood and motif of the serenade return as the movement gently retreats into shimmering darkness.

Although only the second and fourth movements bear the title *Nachtmusik*, a nocturnal spirit binds all three middle movements together. Night vanishes with the opening timpani solo (*con bravura*) of the Rondo Finale, followed immediately by the *ff* of the strings.

[28] Mahler had admired Schumann. Wrote he in 1910 to Natalie Bauer-Lechner: "Schumann is one of the greatest song composers, worthy of being named in the same breath with Schubert. No one is a more consummate master of the rounded song form, complete in itself, then he; his conception never exceeds the bounds of lyricism, and he does not demand anything beyond its realm. Suppressed emotion, true lyricism, and deep melancholy fill his song."

From that pulsating opening grows the main theme of the movement, blazing forth in the trumpets and horns.

In this final movement, as he did in the last movement of his Fifth Symphony, Mahler reverts to the time-honored form so dear to the Viennese Classics, the Rondo Finale. Although Mahler's Rondo is worlds apart from Haydn's, Mozart's or even Beethoven's, his awareness of tradition is obvious, in tonality and spirit.

Having established the brilliant theme, so brimming with life and bright vigor, Mahler elaborates on it in the balance of the movement in eight episodes (*Rundgesänge*), in the Rondo fashion indicated in the heading of the movement. In each restatement the main theme is also accompanied by a side theme; the most prominent of these is intoned in the violins and grows in importance until it actually becomes a counter-theme to the main theme.

Near the end of the movement Mahler again executes a masterstroke: he reintroduces the *allegro* theme of the opening movement of the symphony, interwoven with the Rondo theme.

He does that not once but five times, each repetition differing from the previous one in tonality and timbre. There is no turning back now: the woodwinds and strings race *accelerando* and trumpets and horns lead the proud procession *"feierlich, prachtvoll"* (solemnly, with splendor) as the trombones lend it majesty. Here the inventive power of Mahler is irresistible as, tonally, Ossa is piled on Pelion in a climax that represents one of the most affirmative statements in Mahler's life, far removed from the darkness and despair of his previous symphony.

## SYMPHONY NO. 8 IN E–FLAT MAJOR

I have just now completed my Eighth . . . [it] will be something the world has never heard the likes of before. All nature is endowed with a voice in it. . . . it is the biggest thing I have done so far. . . . Imagine the universe beginning to ring and resound. It is no longer human voices. It is planets and suns revolving in their orbits. . . . All my other symphonies are but preludes to this one.

Mahler to Willem Mengelberg, 18 August 1906

At the end of the first part of Mahler's Eighth Symphony, the *Veni Creator Spiritus,* I strolled about the lobby, absolutely disheartened and disillusioned. That these lovely old Latin iambics, filled with the breath of the Holy Spirit, should be wrenched in rhythms, square and round, and yelled and shouted by hundreds of vociferous ladies and gentlemen, ponderously piled in superiorcumbent tiers, with a howling orchestra with additional instruments galore—seemed gross and irreverent. Dry Teutonic intricacies of melody and harmony seemed to instill a furor, with the accent on the roar.

Charles Peabody, *Boston Daily Advertiser,* 12 April 1916

If you are perverse enough to endure over an hour of masochistic aural flaggelation, here's your chance! This grandiose Mahler "Symphony of a Thousand," with all its elephantine forces, fatuous mysticism, and screaming hysteria, adds up to a sublimely ridiculous minus-zero.

R. D. Darrell, *Down Beat,* Chicago, 4 June 1952

*Composed during the summer of 1906; orchestrated in 1907. First performance, 12 September 1910 in Munich, Mahler conducting.*

*Piccolo, 4 flutes, 4 oboes, English horn, 5 clarinets, bass clarinet, 4 bassoons, contrabassoon, 8 horns, 10 trumpets, 7 trombones, bass tuba, a large battery of percussion, organ, harmonium, harps, mandolins, augmented strings, 3 sopranos ("Magna Peccatrix," "Una Poenitentium," "Mater Gloriosa"), contralto, mezzo-soprano ("Mulier Samaritana," "Maria Aegyptiaca"), tenor ("Doctor Marianus"), baritone ("Pater Ecstaticus"), bass ("Pater Profundus"), boys choir and large chorus.*

Despite his strenuous New York activities during the 1909–10 season, Mahler's work and thoughts were predominantly directed toward the world premiere of his Eighth Symphony, to take place in Munich. As a matter of fact, we may assume that at that point the Eighth had assumed an all-consuming importance in Mahler's life. As early as 1906, Mahler had described some aspects of the newly completed symphony to Mengelberg in glowing terms. Now the date was drawing near when his dream would come to realization at the *Neue Musikfesthalle* in Munich, especially built to coincide with the premiere of the symphony.

The composition, which the impresario in charge, Emil Gutmann of Vienna, had dubbed the "Symphony of a Thousand," was truly a colossal undertaking. The assembling itself of the masses of vocalists and instrumentalists required was an arduous task, and Mahler was determined that no facet of it remain unattended. The array was staggering. The enlarged orchestra of the Munich Concert Society alone consisted of 84 strings, 2 harps, 22 woodwinds, and 17 brass, plus 4 trumpets and 3 trombones set apart from the main body of the orchestra. They had to be reinforced until the orchestra body reached a total of 171 instrumentalists. The vocal contingent of 858 singers was composed of 250 members of the *Singverein* of the *Gesellschaft der Musikfreunde* (Vienna); 250 members of the *Riedel Verein* (Leipzig); 350 children from the *Zentral Singschule* (Munich); and 8 soloists (from Berlin, Frankfurt, Hamburg, Munich, Vienna, and Wiesbaden). Although Mahler had jocularly called the undertaking a "Barnum and Bailey show," foremost on his mind was his concern for artistic dignity and his fear that the concert would disintegrate into a gigantic musical circus.

As early as January 1910 he had begun preparations for the performance. The various participating choirs had, of course, to be rehearsed in their respective home towns, but Mahler made sure that annotated meanings and accents clearly indicated his intentions. According to impresario Gutmann, "nearly every instrument is adjoined by an indication of the quality required . . . a model of detailed work." Special and specialized attention was needed to guide the eight soloists; disciple Bruno Walter was entrusted with the task of their proper selection and rehearsal.

There was no end to Mahler's care. The program was prepared under his supervision; he inspected the choir in Leipzig; and he discussed with another co-worker, Alfred Roller, the grouping of these masses of singers so as to ensure their maximum effectiveness, especially within the specific acoustical entity that was the new hall, and their balance with respect to each other, the orchestral mass, and the soloists. He sought a total atmosphere conducive to the visual, musical, emotional, and mental experiencing of the work; in order to create it he departed from the custom of having the concert hall fully lit during the performance and instead plunged the *Festhalle* into near-darkness. When he noticed that in quiet passages during the rehearsal the clanging of Munich street car bells intruded, he saw to it that during the time of the performance they would pass quietly.

With the fear of death in his mind and in his heart, Mahler had changed. The fierce, unyielding, forcefulness of his Vienna days had given way to a mellower mood, open to compromises. Yet the Munich premiere, so late in the evening of his short life, was a triumph of uncompromising mastery, the last burst of flame in his creative life, the culmination and realization of any creative man's dream. From the opening incantation of

| | |
|---|---|
| Veni, Creator Spiritus | Come thou, Infinite Creator |
| Mentes tuorum visita | Let Thy Spirit visit us |
| . . . . . . . . . . . . . . | |
| Accende lumen sensibus | Inflame our senses with Thy light |
| Infunde amorem cordibus | With Thy love fill our hearts |

Mahler gave the world, for the last time in person, the testimony of his beliefs and the power of his spirit.

As rehearsal progressed and the day neared, Mahler's closest friends and disciples began to assemble: Arnold Schönberg; conductors Otto Klemperer, Oskar Fried, and Leopold Stokowski; Georges Clemenceau; composers Siegfried Wagner, Alfred Casella, and Anton Webern; writers Stefan Zweig and Thomas Mann; and the rising genius of the theater, Max Reinhardt.

Stokowski, who was to introduce the Eighth Symphony in America (in Philadelphia, in 1916), compared the experience of hearing it to "the [impression that the] sight of Niagara Falls must have [made upon] the first white man." Alma, in *Memories and Letters,* also illuminated the historic event:

> The dress rehearsal provoked rapturous enthusiasm, but it was nothing compared to the performance itself. The entire audience rose to their feet as soon as Mahler took his place at the conductor's desk; and the breathless silence which followed was the most impressive homage an artist could be paid. . . . And then, Mahler, god or demon, turned those tremendous volumes of sound into fountains of light. The experience was indescribable. Incredible, too, was the demonstration that followed. The whole audience [of 3,000] surged towards the platform [and gave Mahler a 30 minute ovation].

Walter, in *Theme and Variations,* describes the end of the concert.

> When the last note of the performance had died away and the waves of enthusiastic applause reached him, Mahler ascended the steps of the platform, at the top of which the children's choir was posted. The little ones hailed him with shouts of jubilation, and walking down the line, he pressed every one of the little hands that were extended towards him.

The loving greeting of the young generation filled him with hope for the future of his work and gave him sincere pleasure.

Why Gutmann chose Munich for the premiere of the Eighth Symphony is not clear, particularly since that German city was not then known as one of the great music centers of Europe, and the thousand musicians and singers needed for the performance could not be found within its walls. The *Singverein,* one of Vienna's finest choral organizations, had to be rehearsed there, while Walter trained the soloists. The children's chorus was rehearsing in Munich and a third chorus in Leipzig. Furthermore, the concertmaster was soon found not adequate to the task, and the Munich preparations for the performance began with a *faux pas* attributable to Mahler, as usual innocently oblivious to anything but his music. Mahler wanted Rosé as concertmaster and requested that the orchestra manager make the appropriate announcement, but the latter was unwilling to do so. Thereupon Mahler, without further inquiry or announcement, brought Rosé to Munich. As Rosé was about to seat himself in the concertmaster's chair, the entire orchestra, stung by Mahler's affront, rose and began to leave the stage. Rosé promptly withdrew and seated himself in the auditorium, thus saving the situation by his tact.

Gutmann was also the cause of many misunderstandings that were compounded by distance, because Mahler was occupied with artistic matters in New York. He hastily and prematurely announced, for example, that the scores were ready and rehearsals had begun when not even the piano reduction had been readied. He also wanted to substitute a Leipzig chorus for the Vienna *Singverein,* whose participation Mahler had requested, and he even attempted to eliminate one of the three rehearsals on which Mahler insisted. Mahler finally became so annoyed with Gutmann's machinations that he threatened to resign from the contract unless prearranged conditions were met; whereupon things began to fall into their proper place.

Emotionally as well as creatively, the night of 12 September 1910 constituted the highpoint of Mahler's life. By then he had outgrown the early image of the famous conductor who also composed symphonies that were uncomfortable to listen to. His fame was worldwide and secure. The audience rose in silent awe whenever Mahler appeared before the assembled musical forces.

While Klemperer exclaimed that "I confess that for the first time I understood the music of Mahler well enough to tell myself: here is a great composer," the judgment of history on this work has not been decided to this day. Redlich places it "somewhere near the bottom of the ladder," while Bekker considers it "a summit, from which an overview [of Mahler's work] can be gained." But regardless of how kind or cruel history's judgment will be, Mahler's Eighth Symphony unquestionably

represents the end of one development which began with Beethoven's
*Eroica*—with respect to the enlargement of sonorities and form—and of
another which began with Beethoven's Ninth—with respect to inclusion
of the human voice into the symphonic structure.

Actually the antiphonal juxtaposition of tonal masses can be traced
much further back, to the Venetian Renaissance of the sixteenth century.
There Adrian Willaert, the first prominent non-Venetian to attain the
position of choirmaster at the Cathedral of San Marco, discovered instrumental antiphony through the use of the two organs in the cathedral. The
men to follow him, Giovanni and Andrea Gabrieli, greatly enlarged antiphony and polyphony and started a development in musical history that
was to reach its apotheosis in Mahler's Eighth. The supreme masters of
that early period—the Gabrielis, Palestrina, Lassus, Vittoria—could build
multitiered choral edifices with a surprising number of choruses, proceeding in multilayered, polyphonic splendor. Their contemporary
epigones, however, could duplicate only the arithmetic progression but
not the spirit of the masters, because they had largely forgotten that
music must be heard and appreciated by the public and that admiration
by their peers did not suffice. The musical end product of what had looked
good on paper was thus an indistinguishable sound serving no purpose,
musical or otherwise. Predictably, the public not only turned away but
inevitably raised the cry, "Enough of this nonmusical noise in the land of
music; let us return to the beauty of the single voice." In Florence in
1600, opera was born.[28]

Few, if any, on 12 September 1910, realized the significance of the
occasion in terms of historical development. Less than a century and a
half had passed since Haydn had experimented at Esterhaza castle with
the symphonic form, employing an orchestra of twenty-eight players. From
that point of departure, symphonic development was relentless and irresistible. Already during Haydn's London concerts, the number of strings
alone surpassed the size of his entire early orchestra. Divergent reasons
prompted the composers of the romantic age to yearn for an enlarged
orchestra. To Beethoven the orchestra was the means of expressing long-
suppressed, by now explosive emotion. Berlioz enlarged it to virtuoso size.
With Tchaikovsky, enlargement of the orchestra filled a subconscious
need: to wit, a yearning for strength and brutality. Hysteria was thus
channeled into symphonic form. Liszt needed a large orchestra, to conceal
the shallowness of his thoughts and the emptiness of his sentiments. Strauss
demanded it because of the infinite variety of sensuous sound it yielded.

With Mahler the orchestra grew as his metaphysical search became

---

[28] Aside from these musical considerations, another, often overlooked factor brought
on the demise of polyphony in sixteenth-century Italy: *viz.*, political jealousy. It
eventually became unbearable to the Italians that a Northern (Netherlands) invention should maintain such a strong hold on Italian music.

deeper and more intense. The man who spoke of his symphonies in terms of "the universe resounding" could not deal with such images in terms of a chamber orchestra or string quartet; only a mammoth orchestra, with its inherent ability to express vastness and eternity, would do. And the more intense the search, the more furious the groping, the greater the need for expression through the vastest possible of orchestral bodies in the desperate hope of expressing the inexpressible.

Yet that hope persisted. Who but Mahler could have envisioned a symphony of the vastness of the Eighth? Even he, however, could go no further, and therefore all his creations after the Eighth represent a retreat from such massed sonorities. Whatever Mahler's need for and justification of the giant orchestra may have been, he was dealing with a form which had outlived its usefulness and whose initial meaning and purpose no longer applied. Yet it was no such realization which prompted Mahler to retreat from such peaks of sonorities, but rather the blows of fate, which changed the man and turned his gaze inward. Schönberg, still composing in the image of Mahler, would once more employ an even more gigantic apparatus in his *Gurrelieder*. But it was also Schönberg who led the revolt against giantism and already in *Verklärte Nacht* reverted to a chamber orchestra of Bachian proportions.

The vast audience at the premiere, however, was undoubtedly more awed by, than understanding of, the composer and the meaning of the music and the moment. Only in historical retrospect do we realize that the term "symphony" had outlived its meaning and usefulness and that the piling of sonorities could serve no further purpose. Just as sixteenth-century polyphony, run amok and dry, had spawned homophony, so the symphony had reached a point of no return. The time was ripe for another evolution, which was to come about while Mahler was still alive.

Although Mahler returns in his Eighth Symphony to the spoken word, it must be understood that this is no longer the Mahler of the *Wunderhorn* songs but a man at his mentally and musically most mature. The only resemblance the Eighth still bears to earlier "song symphonies" is in the chorale finale. The symphony had originally been planned with two vocal and two orchestral movements, but the idea of orchestral movements was abandoned. Consequently we find ourselves presented with a curious kind of symphony: one that is, for all intents and purposes, sung from beginning to end, yet which observes classical traditions—such as an involved sonata form in the *Veni, Creator*—and reaches even further back to the baroque by placing a double fugue at the high point of the development section, along with an abridged recapitulation.

As early as 21 June 1906, Mahler had asked his friend Dr. Friedrich Löhr for specific translations with accents of the medieval Latin text *Veni, Creator Spiritus,* by **Hrabanus Magnentius Maurus.** The text originally was an invocation devised for the feast of the descent of the Holy Spirit, the Pentecost. Mahler's manner of setting it to music surprises. One would expect a predominance of Gregorian chant or early harsh *organum* in connection with such a text, yet Mahler combines two opposites, the medieval text with an extended sonata form, while doing justice to every inflection of the Latin text and meaning in this shorter first part, lasting twenty-four minutes.

Interestingly enough, when he was first setting the *Veni, Creator* to music Mahler was mystified to find that the music somehow did not fit the words. The thought occurred to him that he might not have remembered the word sequences correctly. Impatiently he wired Vienna and requested that the complete original text be wired back to him promptly. When it arrived Mahler's suspicions were confirmed: he had not remembered correctly. The correct text fitted the already composed music perfectly.

In the second, larger part, lasting nearly an hour and set to the final scene from the second part of *Faust,* Mahler, according to musicologist Deryck Cooke, "mirrors the more rhapsodic language of Goethe." Thus the essence of two divergent spiritual conceptions is served fully by the composer. Still, as Mahler expressed it succinctly to his wife: "Insofar as a soul needs a body, an artist is bound to derive the means of creation from the rational world. But the chief thing is still the artistic conception, which no mere words can explain." Overall, the first part of the Eighth is strongly analogous to the religious music of the past, particularly its greatest form, which reigned supreme for six centuries—the Mass.

It seems as if Mahler, in his Eighth Symphony, was driven by forces beyond his control in his feverish surge of composition. The result of such compulsive effort was astounding in all respects. No composer before Mahler, not even Bach in his B-Minor Mass or Berlioz in his Requiem, had mastered such a huge ensemble of participants or such a complexity of parts, or had faced such problems as rehearsals in far-flung cities and placement for best acoustical effects. And Mahler's touch was sure: in contrast to almost any previous work, there was a minimum of corrections in his Eighth.

The discrepancy between the first and second parts of the Eighth Symphony is so pronounced—in text, philosophy, and style—that one almost wishes that the two parts had been conceived as two separate entities. One wonders whether the German text by Mahler's idol Goethe may have subconsciously prompted the composer to revert to the stylistic concept of another one of his German idols, Wagner. Again, there can be no question of an epigonic effort on the part of Mahler, but rather there is a veering, in Part II, into the romantic style of bygone days, now developed with Mahler virtuosity. Thus it is astounding, even shocking (a shock Mahler may have intended) to suddenly find oneself confronted with a presentation in concert opera style after the stark contrapuntal treatment of Part I.

The Latin hymn which constitutes Part I of the Eighth Symphony is in three parts. The opening one, *Veni, Creator Spiritus,* comprises eight lines: it is an invocation of and address to the heavenly creator. The second part, beginning with *Infirma nostri corporis, Virtute firmans perpeti* [Our body's weakness strengthen by Thy miraculous power], is the longest of the three and addresses itself to a prayer for strength, enlightenment, peace, grace, and acknowledgment of the Trinity. The third part, of the same length, concludes with an entreaty for heavenly grace. It opens with *Da gratiarum munera* [Give us your saving grace]; and the entire hymn ends with the words of praise *In saeculorum saecula* [From eternity to eternity].

Mahler's construction of Part I follows closely the tripartite division of the Latin text—only what he envisions musically is surely worlds removed from the medieval conception of Hrabanus Maurus. And Mahler loses no time in setting forth, in march rhythm, his thematic vision. Immediately after the opening *ff* burst by the organ and string basses, the choir, *allegro impetuoso,* hurls forth its entreaty.

The harmonies are surprisingly tonal, because it is with rhythm and power that Mahler decides to express himself. The opening *Veni* theme and those to follow are ecstatically hurled back and forth between soloists and chorus. Only in the *Imple superna gratia* [And fill with Thy heavenly grace], the second theme (performed *dolce espressivo*), does warmth and quiet descend upon the scene.

The quiet prevails as the solo soprano intones *Et spiritalis* [And soul's anointing from on high].

Et spi - ri - ta - - lis   et spi - ri - ta - - - - lis   spi -

But soon, inevitably, ecstasy returns, as the choir, in mighty voice, intones *superna gratia,*

Su - per - na, su - per - na su - per - na gra - ti - a

after which we return to the *Veni* again in the horns and trombones. The mood changes with the intonation of the *Infirma nostri,* the prayer for strength, the opening theme of the middle part. After a shadowy orchestral interlude, the solo bass again intones the *Infirma* theme.

In - fir - ma, in - fir - ma,   nos - tri cor - por - is

It continues *leidenschaftlich* (passionately) but ends in a deeply felt entreaty, *Accende lumen sensibus* [Fire our senses with Thy light]. What starts as a prayer, intoned *espressivo,* suddenly explodes with overpowering force. *Plötzlich sehr breit und leidenschaftlich* (suddenly very broad and with passionate expression), demands Mahler; *mit plötzlichem Aufschwung* (with sudden sweep). In the double chorus, the children's chorus, and all of the soloists, an ecstatic shout rends the air.

Ac - cen - de   ac - cen - de   lu - men   sen - si - bus

It is one of the mightiest incantations in the history of music; perhaps only Haydn's *"Und es war Licht"* (from *The Creation*), Brahms's *"Tod wo ist dein Stachel"* (from his *German Requiem*), and Verdi's *Dies Irae* (from his *Requiem*) can compare in emotional impact. From there on the intertwining orchestra, chorus, and soloists reach one peak after another: *Infunde amorem cordibus* [Expand our hearts with your love], *ff; Hostem repellas* [Repel the enemy], *ff; Pacemque dones* [And give us peace], *ff;* with the mighty *Veni* theme interjected in the process. The music sinks to a surprising *p* when Mahler, in the *Praevio*, speaks of overcoming temptation.

But soon, welling up with the towering splendor of Mahler's vision, the children's chorus intones, with moving magnificence, the finale's opening *Gloria.*

From there on Mahler builds with the virtuosity of inspired, fired genius. A timpani roll leads into horns and strings, and suddenly, the solo sopranos, above the mighty ensemble, repeat the theme in slight variation. The vision of the Trinity is conjured up by the double chorus, orchestra, and soloists plus, *isoliert, postiert* (isolated, placed offstage), the four trumpets and three trombones, as, above them all, the children's chorus intones the *Gloria* text to a variation of the *Accende* theme, and the movement ecstatically comes to a close.

To repeat the fervor of Part I in Part II would not have been possible or advisable, because it would have weakened both parts; yet the remarkable thing about the entire work is that despite the complete change of style, the two parts of the Eighth Symphony remain distinctly Mahler. But where drama was the dominant element in Part I, lyrical serenity is the main emphasis in Part II.

Goethe describes the opening scene as depicting "Mountain gorges, forests, rocks, solitude." Musically celli and string basses open, followed promptly by a theme in the flutes and clarinets.

These two themes dominate the opening, which is in the manner of an overture and is the longest orchestral section of the entire work. The woodwinds theme in particular, heard next *ppp* as a chorale and as a closing phrase in the flutes, is pervasive. But that is not the end of it. Celli and horns, *appasionato,* carry it again in surging motion

against strongly disjunct melodies, until it reappears *ppp* in a passage for four flutes and, finally, is heard in the tuba beneath woodwinds and horns

eventually fading from *f* to *pp*. The overture is ended; the drama begins.

The opening chorus parallels Goethe's description of a gloomy landscape.

The picture is abruptly dispelled by Mahler's command *"sehr leidenschaft-lich"* (very passionately).

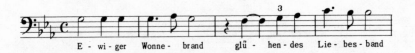

E - wi - ger Wonne - brand glü - hen - des Lie - bes - band

The spirit is straight out of *Meistersinger,* yet the music is inimitably Mahler. Continuing, Peter Ecstaticus (baritone) exclaims equally passionately, *mit mächtigem Ton* (with mighty voice).

Wie Fel-sen-ab-grund mir zu Füs-sen auf tie-fem Ab-grund lastend ruht

The jubilantly disjunct melody swells into a *ff* chorus of the angels, intoning *Gerettet* [Saved] in polyphonic interchange with the woodwinds and bringing female voices into Part II for the first time.

Ge - ret - tet ist das ed - le Glied der Geis - ter-welt von Bö - sen

The children's chorus to follow is no less inspiring,

Hän - de ver - schlin-get euch freu - dig zum Ring-ver - ein

particularly in its jubilant finale, *Jauchzet auf! Es ist gelungen* [Rejoice! It is achieved], before the orchestra dominates.

Jauchzet auf! Jauchzet auf! Es ist ge - lun - gen

The chorus of the "older angels" leads into an alto solo, followed by a sparkling chorus of the "younger angels." Mahler marks the tempi *frisch* (brisk) and *flott* (gay).

The tempi and intensity become *allmählich stärker* (gradually stronger) until Doctor Marianus (tenor) bursts forth *mit voller Stimme* (with full voice).

He repeats his theme in variation and then prepares the listener for his vision.

*Adagissimo,* to the *pp* voice of the solo violin, the vision appears. Again Mahler's admiration for Schumann is evident.

The chorus enters again, slowly raising its voice in intensity, only to fall back as the Magna Peccatrix (soprano) intones her plea for sinners.

Mulier Samaritana (alto) enters with plaintive voice, as does Maria Aegyptiaca (alto), and the three female voices are joined in canonic treatment, beginning *p* and ending their entwining polyphony in a pleading but strong finale.

Slowly the mood brightens in the orchestra until the boy's choir enters strongly. The initially light orchestration becomes more triumphant, and the voice of Una Poenitentium (soprano) is heard. Slowly the ensemble sinks into *pp*. We are still in the antechamber of the final revelation. Mater Gloriosa (soprano) intones *dolcissimo,* and very slowly, as the choir whispers *"Komm"* [Appear]; Doctor Marianus (tenor) begins "in hymnal fashion" *Blicket auf* [Look up]. His adoration becomes more intense as he ends jubilantly: "Virgin, Mother, Queen, Goddess, remain merciful."

The theme continues, carried aloft in a tremendous orchestral wave. The heavens open. *Blicket auf* appears in the horns and woodwinds and *Gloria* is intoned *fff* in the trombones and harps until the vision passes, to the gently diminishing sounds of harps, celesta, harmonium, and flutes.

Then, *wie ein Hauch* [like a breath], Goethe's philosophy rises from the depths: *Alles Vergängliche ist nur ein Gleichnis* [All things transitory are but a parable]. Once more, for the last time, the chorus rises to full voice,

supported by and carrying with it the mighty organ, followed by the orchestra in full force. Again, *isoliert, postiert,* the trumpets and trombones intone the mighty *Veni, Creator.* The orchestra responds with a solemn, magnificent *Gloria*, as the work ends with Mahler's baroque vision of the heavens.

In essence, Mahler's Eighth is not only an end to symphonic development per se but also the climax of a specific phase of Mahler's creative development. The triumphant mood, expressed for the last time in this symphony, gives way, in *Das Lied von der Erde* and the Ninth Symphony, to a spirit of resignation and farewell. Actually, with Mahler's Eighth a dream which, musicologists feel, had been a goal in Beethoven's mind— the total choral symphony—had come to fruition. Despite the vastness of the work, it is a structural marvel, surprisingly compact and integrated. Aspects of three pronounced musical periods are evident: the structure of the Vienna classics; the color and glow of the romantic age; and at the high point of symphonic drama Mahler reaches back to Bruckner and even further back to the splendor and spirit of the baroque. It is the interplay among these diverse influences that makes Mahler's Eighth Symphony a milestone of its time and a highlight of his creative life. Most significant is the use of diverse texts, held together through Mahler's genius. The difficulty of fusion cannot be overestimated because of the extreme diversity involved: a mystical medieval prayer followed by an equally mystical text of transfiguration; Latin followed by German; the spirit of the church in contrast to the world of the German stage. All are integrated in one musical masterpiece and heightened in intensity by Mahler's grandiose vision.


## THE TRILOGY OF FAREWELL:
*Das Lied von der Erde* [The Song of the Earth]; *Symphony No. 9 in D Major*; *Symphony No. 10 in F-sharp Major*

Although Mahler worked on *Das Lied von der Erde* and his Ninth and Tenth symphonies during the last three years of his life, he was not to hear them in his lifetime. The fateful year 1907 binds the three works: Mahler's severance from the Vienna Opera, the death of his child, his discovery of his diseased heart, and the promise of a new future in America changed the man, changed his mode of life and his outlook on life, and inevitably changed his music.

> I have been going through so many experiences (for the last year and a half) that I can hardly discuss them. How should I attempt to describe such a colossal crisis? I see everything in such a new light and I am in such continuous fluctuation. . . . I am thirstier than ever for life and I find the "habit of living" sweeter than ever.
>
> Mahler to Bruno Walter, 1909

Thus Mahler's burning desire for life was colliding with his fear of impending death. Both impulses were destined to receive moving and meaningful expression in the final song of *Das Lied von der Erde, Abschied* [Farewell]:

> I shall no longer seek the far horizon
> My heart is still and waits for its deliverance

Although the lines were taken from a Chinese poem, Mahler seems to have adopted them as his motto at his life's ending. His new gentler life-style sought only the aims of today and tomorrow. Financial security for his family became a primary consideration. His burning perfectionism gave way, in some cases, to less stringent artistic demands. While the ut-most attention was still lavished by him on all details of performance of his own work, such as at the premiere of his Eighth Symphony, he ap-plied a less exacting yardstick to his work at the Metropolitan Opera, where he even acceded to cuts in Wagner operas, a practice he peremp-torily forbade in Vienna.

The Ninth Symphony also exudes a spirit of farewell, with its first movement carrying the notation "Oh vanished days, oh scattered love" and the final movement (*adagio*) fading out in a phrase marked by Mahler *"ersterbend"* (dying away). The spirit which pervades the work was recognized by Alban Berg, Schönberg's disciple and a Mahler ad-mirer, who wrote, after study of the symphony in 1910:

> Once again I have played through the score of Mahler's Ninth Symphony, The first movement is the most heavenly thing Mahler ever wrote; it is the expression of an exceptional fondness for this earth, the longing to live in peace on it, to enjoy nature in its depths—before death comes.
>
> For he comes irresistibly. The entire movement is permeated by premonitions of death . . . most potently, of course, in the colossal pas-sage where this premonition becomes certainty, where in the midst of greatest strength (*höchste Kraft*), of almost painful joy of life, Death it-self is announced with greatest force (*höchster Gewalt*).

As was the case with practically every one of his works, Mahler felt that *Das Lied von der Erde* and his Ninth Symphony were his greatest crea-tions; but he also remarked in a letter of 1908 to Bruno Walter: "*Das Lied* is the most personal thing I have created until now."

It was at that point in his creative life that Mahler attempted to "cheat fate," as Alma Mahler puts it. It is not by accident that *Das Lied* and the Ninth Symphony were not performed in the lifetime of the man who had so avidly sought performances of his previous works. Just as Schönberg, after Mahler, was to be virtually possessed by the number 13 and Alban Berg was to attribute special meaning to the number 23, so Mahler feared the number 9. He left the work after his Eighth Sym-phony unnumbered and called it *Das Lied von der Erde: A Symphony of*

*Songs;* and when he had finished his Ninth Symphony (actually his Tenth), he deliberately avoided mention of a number. His superstition was based on the fact that the number 9 represented the last symphonic ventures of Beethoven, Schubert, Bruckner, and Dvořak. But fate and Mahler's heart were oblivious to his fears and futile machinations. The symphony which he finally had to number as his Ninth was to be his last completed one. In the end the tables were turned. It was the creator who was cheated out of hearing his creations.

So ingrained were Mahler's fears that during the last summer of his life he refused to make corrections on *Das Lied von der Erde* or the Ninth Symphony. He felt that to bring these works to the perfection which had been his lifelong pursuit would be to bring his life to completion along with the music. As long as they were uncorrected, however, he could construe that they were unfinished. Indeed, some musicologists go so far as to suggest that the completion of the Tenth Symphony would have been an impossible task for Mahler even if he had lived. Many signs point to a death struggle already taking shape in Mahler's mind on the existing pages of that symphony, a struggle that reminds us of the fine line that separates genius from insanity.

The three works followed each other in rapid succession in the three summers of 1908, 1909, and 1910, in the splendid Alpine environment of Tyrol and Carynthia. *Das Lied* was actually originally sketched during the summer of 1908 and was ready, fully scored, in 1909. The Ninth Symphony was completed in New York in March 1910; the sketching of the Tenth was begun in Toblach in the summer of 1910. Mahler was literally striving for life in the presence of death: his frantic work on the Tenth Symphony and his race against death and mental and physical disintegration proceeded side by side with his preparations for the most momentous event in his life, the premiere of his Eighth Symphony, his last great personal testament to life, which he loved so dearly.

All later performances had to wait until death had overwhelmed Mahler's valiant struggle for life. Six months after Mahler's death, *Das Lied von der Erde* had its first performance in Munich on 20 November 1911, under the baton of Bruno Walter. Walter also conducted the premiere of the Ninth Symphony in Vienna in 1912. The first performance of the two completed movements of the Tenth Symphony had to wait until 1924, when Franz Schalk performed them at a Mahler memorial concert with the Vienna Philharmonic.

Public response to and demands for performances of the late Mahler symphonies has varied. While performances of the monumental Eighth Symphony always arouse great interest, the artistic and financial resources involved in securing the choral and instrumental forces required discourage frequent performance. There can, however, be no question as to the wide public acclaim which *Das Lied von der Erde* has received, beginning with its first performance.


## DAS LIED VON DER ERDE
### [The Song of the Earth]


*Composition—first sketches during the summer of 1908, full scoring in 1909. First performance posthumously on 20 November 1911, Bruno Walter conducting, in Munich.*

Surprises never ceased to emanate from Mahler's inventive mind. In the shadow of death he descended from the heights of concert music drama to the gentler plain of the song symphony. Superficially viewed, this would not seem to reflect novelty so far as Mahler's musical achievements were concerned. Yet differences are apparent on several levels. Previous song cycles, although presented with orchestral accompaniment, did not reflect the spiritual and emotional integration with which *Das Lied von der Erde* is imbued. Even the interrelated songs of the *Kindertotenlieder* do not approach the spiritual cohesiveness of *Das Lied*. There can be no question but that Mahler's tortuously acquired maturity had contributed to the inspired fusion of material and feeling involved.

The six poems which constitute the literary basis of *Das Lied von der Erde* are not from the quill of one poet but rather were selected from several Chinese poems, introduced in German translation by Hans Bethge in *Die Chinesische Flöte* in 1908. Through a friend, Court Councillor Dr. Theobald Pollak, Mahler had become acquainted with this anthology of Chinese poems. The poems struck a responsive chord in him and he selected seven as the text for *Das Lied,* combining two poems into one (*Der Abschied*) and altering some of the poems in the process.

Neither a song cycle nor a symphonic endeavor was on Mahler's mind as he began to compose individual songs to the texts. In the course of composition, however, he began to realize that there existed a cohesiveness of mood throughout the songs, and his work subsequently proceeded to take shape as a symphonic song entity. The songs exhibit a wide variety of moods; despite this, and despite authorship by several poets, we find here greater textual and spiritual unity than in previous symphonies with text, because in his Second Symphony Mahler had used such disparate texts as the *Wunderhorn* poems and text by Klopstock; in the Third, more *Wunderhorn* texts along with excerpts from Nietzsche; and in the Eighth, a Latin hymnal prayer plus Goethe's *Faust*.

We may assume that, as usual, Mahler deliberately sought text to fit the spirit of his music and the resultant hour-long song symphony reflects a triumph of music over text. Neither Schubert nor Schumann had been able in their song cycles to achieve so total an integration of spirit. Mah-

ler accomplished this by means of a unifying spiritual motif which permeates every phase of the work.

Because from the beginning the cycle speaks mostly of sadness, darkness, farewell, and death, the songs demand the utmost of sensitivity,
tenderness and understanding. The six parts of the work are further held
together by instrumental interludes, very much in the spirit of the poems
and binding rather than dividing them.

When Mahler handed Walter the orchestral score of *Das Lied,* it was
the first time that he had not actually played a work for his friend and
disciple. So much of Mahler's subconscious feelings had been imparted
to the work that he did not trust his emotions. He wanted his friend to
experience the resignation and farewell without the composer's comments.
Fate did not grant him the privilege of hearing either it or his Ninth
Symphony; but it was fitting that the first performance of *Das Lied von
der Erde,* six months after Mahler's death, should have been at the hands
of this greatest of Mahler apostles, Bruno Walter. Surprisingly, Walter
selected two American artists to sing the solo parts: the contralto Madame Charles Cahier (born Sarah Jane Layton-Walker) and the tenor
William Miller. The premiere took place in Munich, which was appropriate because it was there that the echoes of Mahler's last personal triumph
still reverberated. Vienna heard the work in 1912. Actually Mahler had
not been definite as to whether the alto part should not be sung by a baritone. Walter experimented once by entrusting the part to the baritone
Friedrich Weidemann of the Vienna Opera, who had always been a strong
Mahler supporter as well as a sensitive artist; afterwards Walter felt that
the alto range was better suited and provided better contrast, and he
never again used two male voices.

*Das Lied von der Erde* opens with *Das Trinklied vom Jammer der
Erde* [The drinking song of earth's woe] (tenor; by the poet Li-Tai-Po,
702–63), one of the most striking and original inspirations ever to flow
from Mahler's pen. In the spirit of the work Mahler subtly shifts textures
to convey a delicate, Oriental atmosphere, emphasized by the repeated
use of the pentatonic scale, and particularly noticeable in his treatment
of woodwinds, percussion, and harp. The opening song runs the gamut
of emotions from frenzied abandon to defiance to darkness and death. A
driving, blazing theme opens the "Drinking Song" with four horns, followed, equally impetuously, by the woodwinds and violins,

followed promptly by the tenor *"mit voller Kraft"* (with full force),

but the singer cautions: "Do not drink yet; first let me sing you a song! The song of grief. . . ."

And then the inevitable refrain: *"Dunkel ist das Leben, ist der Tod"* [Dark is life, is death].

Thus the song runs the gamut from jubilation to sorrow, from a toast to death. A muted trumpet speaks of grief, answered by the English horn. "The firmament is eternally blue . . . but you, Man, how long do you live?"

A toast is offered in a false sense of morbid jubilation.

Jetzt nehmt den Wein! Jetzt ist es Zeit.

"Comrades! Empty your golden cups to the bottom!" But the sound heard is belied by the final theme, *"Dunkel ist . . .,"* resounding again for the third and final time. A brief coda and a jarring *ff* orchestral blow end the song.

The second song, *Der Einsame im Herbst* [The lonely one in autumn] (contralto; by Tschang-Tsi, c. 800) reflects a sublimely sensitive contrast. Over an undulating accompaniment of muted violins, the oboe sings its song of loneliness *molto espressivo*.

The opening by the contralto does nothing to dispel the mood of loneliness and sadness.

Herbst- ne - bel wal - len bläu - lich überm See

Thoughts of a cold wind bending scentless flowers, of faded lotus blossoms, fill the air. The voice is sad, for "my heart is weary."

Mein Herz ist müde

"My little lamp went out," says the singer. "Give me rest. . . . I need refreshing. . . . I cry much in my loneliness. The autumn in my heart lasts too long." "*Mit grossem Aufschwung*" (with a great upward sweep) demands Mahler, as we hear a final desperate outcry. "Sun of love, will you shine for me no more, to . . . dry my bitter tears?"

Sonne   der   Lie - - be,   willst du nicht mehr scheinen

The vehement outcry is of short duration, and the last words, in tonal continuity and lack of expression, repeat the notes of "*Mein Herz is müde*" in hopeless repetition. *Molto espressivo,* the lamenting voice of the oboe is heard again.

A delicate gaiety fills the third song, *Von der Jugend* [Of youth] (tenor; by Li-Tai-Po) which offers a subtle yet decisive contrast with respect to the gloom of the two previous songs. "*Behaglich und heiter*" (with ease and serenity) is Mahler's dynamics instruction, and the opening flute and oboe, followed by the clarinet, spin out a gossamer line.

Soon the tenor enters, with a dainty description of the picture: "In the middle of the small pond stands a pavilion of green and white porcelain."

Mit - ten   in   dem   kleinen   Teiche   steht ein Pa - vil - lon aus grünem

und   aus   weis-sem   Por - zel - lan

A subtle pseudo-Chinese texture pervades the song suggesting a romanticism which is emphasized by a delicate melodic line. Despite the artificiality of texture we gladly succumb to it, because its romanticism seems perfectly appropriate to the thoughts expressed. The description continues —of a jade bridge, of the pavilion, of friends passing the time.

In   dem   Häuschen sitzen Freunde   schön ge-klei-det,   trin - ken,   plau - dern

Sinking to a quiet *pp* whisper, the poet/painter and poet/composer describe the reflection of *"Freunde, schön gekleidet, trinken, plaudern"* [friends, beautifully dressed, drinking, chatting] in the lake with a bridge near the pavilion, closing with the same melody with which he described the opening.

Auf des kleinen kleinen Teiches     stiller     stiller     Wasser - fläche

"Everything's standing on its head," observes the singer, looking at the water's reflection of the scene.

Al - les auf dem     Kopfe     stehend

*Von der Schönheit* [Of beauty] (contralto; by Li-Tai-Po) presents an even brighter musical panorama of youth and beauty: a sunlit landscape with maidens gathering flowers and youths on prancing horseback. The instrumental opening, *comodo, dolcissimo,* introduces flutes, violins, and horns in delicate interplay.

The contralto first presents the maidens, interwoven with woodwinds,

Jun - ge     Mädchen pflücken     Blu - men,     pflücken

their slender limbs gleaming in the sun.

Sonne     spiegelt ih - re     schlanken Glie - der

The graceful scene suddenly changes to a strongly pronounced rhythm, emphasized by trumpets and timpani. The male element appears, with a strongly accented march rhythm and near-passionate excitement.

O    sieh, was tum-meln sich für    schö - ne Kna - ben

In the description of their bodies, Mahler returns to a motif strongly related to the description of the girls.

Gold'ne    Sonne    webt um  die Ge - stalten

"And the most beautiful of the maidens sends long looks of longing, her proud bearing but a disguise. . . ."

Und die schön ste von den Jungfrau'n sendet    lange    Blicke ihm der Sehn -    sucht    nach

The dreamlike beauty of the scene does not linger. In a shimmering postlude, the vision of youth and beauty fades away.

*Der Trunkene im Frühling* [The drunkard in spring] (tenor; by Li-Tai-Po) is a drinking song of another sort. After only three bars of introduction in the horns, oboes, and clarinets, joined by the flute, the "Drinking One" is heard *"keck"* (saucy).

Wenn nur ein Traum das Leben    ist

Before he is able to finish his first sentence, the sparkling "drinking theme" is heard in the flutes and oboes.

It will be heard in several variants throughout the song, but first the drinker must finish his sentence.

Wa - rum denn Müh' und Plag?

He continues his drinking bout throughout the entire day,

Ich trin - ke bis ich nicht mehr kann    den gan - zen lie - ben Tag

and when he can drink no longer he "sleeps wonderfully." When he awakens, the bird sings in the tree: "Hark!" Above the tenor, the oboe, as the bird, sings its song before it is transformed into the delicate voice of the violin.

Ein vo - gel singt im Baum

The drunkard asks the bird if spring has arrived, and the bird answers, "Yes! Yes! Spring is here; it has come overnight."

Der Lenz ist da, sei kommen über Nacht

In deep emotion the drunk one listens as the bird laughs and sings; then he fills his beaker anew and empties it,

Ich fül - le mir den Becher neu und leer' ihn bis zum Grund

and he sings all day until the moon glitters on the dark firmament—

"What do I care about the spring? Let me be drunk!"

The final song—*Der Abschied* [The farewell] (contralto; by Mong-Kao-Jen and Wang Wei, c. Eighth Century)—is, not surprisingly, the longest and most significant of *Das Lied von der Erde,* indicating by its vastness alone the significance Mahler accorded it. It is not yet a finale; it is more the gesture of a man ceremonially robing himself for the stately ritual of death. The lower registers of emotion are exquisitely and grandly explored. The farewell of two friends thus takes on a larger significance. Whether consciously or unconsciously, the near-funeral mood evokes a farewell in the vaster context of death. Words have become symbols of moods and thoughts, of change and eternity.

"*Schwer*" (heavy) is Mahler's annotation at the opening of the song, as he brings the low registers of the orchestra—contrabassoon, low horns, and string basses—into play. Above them is heard a contrasting, shepherd-like melody. The opening of the vocal part inevitably brings to mind, in spirit and in melodic line, the opening of the *"Abendstern"* aria of *Tannhäuser: "Wie Todesahnung Dämm'rung deckt die Lande"* [Like death's foreboding dusk covers the land]. As the contralto begins her story of the *Abschied,* Mahler remarks: *"In erzählendem, Ton, ohne Ausdruck"* (in narrating tone, without expression)

describing the mood and the setting as two friends meet for the last time. Over harps and clarinets the oboe sings of life, of peace, and of beauty, of nature and the soul. "Tired humans go homeward to learn anew in sleep of forgotten fortunes and of youth. . . . The world's asleep. . . . I stand here waiting for my friend . . . for a last farewell."

Ich stehe hier   und harre meines Freundes   Ich harre   sein zum letzen Le-be- wohl

The violin sings *"mit innigster Empfindung"* (with most ardent feeling), reminiscing of the beauties of earth and sky.

Waiting for the friend, the contralto gives her sentiments full rein

Ich   seh - ne mich     o  Freund, an   deiner   Sei - te

ending rhapsodically: "O Beauty! O eternal love's, life's, elated world." But in an orchestral interlude, the jubilant outburst of life gives way to the pitiless vision of death.

The appearance of the friend nearly repeats the opening phrase.

Er stieg vom  Pferd und reichte  ihm den  Trunk   des Abschieds dar

The friend's tale is veiled, sad, resigned—

Du,   mein  Freund,     mir  war  auf die - ser Welt  das

Glück nicht  hold!

"I wander to my home, my place. I will no longer roam to the far places. Still is my heart and it awaits its hour."

At the very doorstep to the beyond, there is a final looking back. Once more the "eternally blue firmament" and the beauties of earth and of spring are beheld.

Die lie - be Er - de all - ü - ber - all blüht auf im Lenz und grünt aufs neu!

In this last triumphant fling, life rises once more beyond and above grief, despair, and death, before *"gänzlich ersterbend"* (totally dying out) to the repetition, nine times, of the word *"ewig"* (eternal).

## SYMPHONY NO. 9 IN D MAJOR

*Composition begun in 1909 in Toblach, completed in March 1910 in New York. Premiere, posthumously, in the spring of 1912 at the Music Festival in Vienna, Bruno Walter conducting.*

*Piccolo, 4 flutes, 4 oboes, English horn, E-flat clarinet, 3 clarinets in A and B flat, bass clarinet, 4 bassoons, contrabassoon, 4 horns, 3 trumpets, 3 trombones, bass tuba, timpani, bass drum, glockenspiel, triangle, cymbals, harp and strings.*

> Alma Mahler handed the score to me for final revision before printing. In November 1911, six months after [Mahler's] death, I conducted the first performance of *Das Lied* in Munich, and early in 1912, the Ninth in Vienna. It was a heavy responsibility to take my great friend's place and introduce his work to the world. Here was the fulfillment of the sense of dedication which, when I first had been shaken by his First Symphony, had made me see my future as one of service to his work.
>
> Bruno Walter, *Gustav Mahler*

Thoughts of farewell, of death and transfiguration, pervade the Ninth Symphony. It is natural, therefore, that the two slow movements, the opening Andante comodo and the final Adagio, exude the main spirit of the work. It is not solely a mood of resignation which fills the first, meandering movements; life is not to be surrendered without a struggle. Mahler indicates *"mit Wut"* (with fury), and a monumental struggle ensues, to be resolved only by the inevitable (with Mahler) funeral march. The lucidity of the development of this movement, from a simple melody through the terror of battle to the finality of dissolution, marks it as one of Mahler's most outstanding creations. It is an utterance magnificent in its subdued spiritual splendor.

After a dark opening of premonition the main theme dawns in the second violins in counter melody with the horn.

The first violins continue the basic idea, but the *pp* of their delicate melodic line suddenly wells up in furious motion.

The theme races on, reaching the high A, and is followed by the horns. Soon thereafter the trumpets take over with a solemn chant, soon to be taken up by the violins in ecstatic fashion.

There are moments of relaxation which recall previous themes, but these are not of long duration. The violins and horns passionately swing into new rhythms and new heights until a new *fff* theme appears:

Struggle reaches inevitably into all sections but dies away to the ominous rumble of timpani and basses. But the end of the struggle is not in sight. Over the *espressivo* of the violins and horns, muted trombones *ff* restate the opening theme. A previously briefly heard dance melody reappears in this near-idyllic scene, marred only by the ominous timpani.

Suddenly, without forewarning, the thunderbolt appears. "With fury" demands Mahler.

With passionate intensity all sections of the orchestra race into battle,

reaching a climax, *molto appassionato,* in the strings,

and at the same time a point of rest, as the horns, with *"höchster Kraft"* (greatest strength), roar into the opening theme, leading the ensemble into quieter waters.

*"Morendo"* and *"schattenhaft"* (shadowy) now advises Mahler. Out of the shadows appear two horns, in thirds, with the violins in contrasting voices, *"sehr zart aber ausdrucksvoll"* (very tender but expressively).

The idyll is not to last. With sweeping power the spirit of struggle returns, racing to a final, utmost climax. *"Mit grösster Gewalt"* (with greatest power) demands Mahler, and he advises the brasses *"schalltrichter auf"* (bells up) as trombones, above the orchestra, proclaim the climax.

The funeral march sounds above the relentless timpani beat.

To the sound of bells, woodwinds, and the violins the lament of death swells to a wail.

The end is unexpectedly sudden. Tempo and passion lessen into *misterioso;* the voices become gentle. Longingly the clarinet is heard above the quieted horns.

*Zögernd* (hesitantly), *schwebend* (floating), *dolcissimo,* the movement, and the struggle, come to an end.

In the *Ländler* Scherzo the composer reminisces. Mahler seems to imitate Mahler as the themes recall themes in corresponding movements in Symphonies five, six, and seven. But although Mahler appears imitiative within his own creative cycle, the workmanship of this movement is superior to that of the corresponding movements in the other symphonies. Here, for instance, Mahler ingeniously intersperses a later dance, the waltz (a Mahlerian waltz, to be sure), and an earlier one, a sort of Minuet, with the lilting *Ländler.*

Mahler's opening instruction *"Etwas täppisch und sehr derb, im tempo des gemächlichen Ländlers"* (somewhat clumsy and very coarse, in the tempo of a relaxed *Ländler*) is deceiving. The opening, however, is fully in accord with Mahler's definition.

This rumbling theme in the bassoons and violas is answered by the clarinets in later repetitions. In the entire opening section Mahler continues in the same vein. *"Schwerfällig, wie Fiedeln"* (clumsily, like fiddles) is the dynamic instruction, and the violins clumsily hammer out the rhythm, answered *"keck"* (saucily) by the horns.

Slowly, imperceptibly, what had begun as clumsy and coarse becomes distorted and grotesque. As the scene becomes more driving, a new, strongly rhythmic element makes its appearance.

Trombones enter and the tempo of the dance, driven by the timpani, increases, leading into a theme of wildly powerful jubilation intoned by three trombones and the tuba.

Section by section the entire orchestra is drawn into the maelstrom of this bacchanalian dance. As it abates, the *Ländler* theme surfaces *ganz langsam* (quite slowly).

A previous waltz tempo appears, faster, wilder than before, leading into a coarse waltz rhythm in the violins and woodwinds, whipped into stomping and demonic whirling.

Only gradually does this Witches' Sabbath Scherzo slow its mad whirl. Muted brass quiets the scene in descending chromatic line; bits of themes float by. Finally the ghostly sound of contrabassoon and piccolo, echoing the opening theme in utter contrast, ends this incredible movement.

There is a harsh beauty about the Rondo Burlesque movement. The violins and whirling woodwinds, the braying brass, all punctuated by hammering timpani, contribute to a vision of demonic splendor, a last, defiant shaking of the fist before going down to the grave.

The mood is set with the first dynamic comment, *"Allegro assai. Sehr trotzig"* (very defiant). Again the opening theme is destined to be of great significance as the trumpets and strings, followed by the horns, intone

Horns and trombones continue the defiant statement,

and the rhythmic elan reaches up to the violins.

A sudden retreat into *p* is not of long duration. The sound swells as the horns pronounce the opening theme. They soon enter into a new theme only to yield to the strings and woodwinds, which present the opening chords in new elaboration, *sempre ff*, each note emphasized with heavy, marchlike articulation and intensity.

They are joined by the trombones and woodwinds, and soon the trumpets hammer the theme with renewed intensity. Suddenly there is a change of mood: *"leggiero"* requests Mahler. In a total change of direction the violins now broadly spin out their theme.

Soon, however, the first theme rises again, now more darkly, more wildly than before. The horns, *ff*, intone in unison a strong positive theme.

Strength gives way to idyllic beauty, to charm, to humor in the horns.

But the driving, near-sinister force of the movement cannot be contained. Below the horns the string basses stormily bring back the opening theme, eventually broadening into a hymnal outpouring as the violins take over.

As the storm and the elation abate, we witness the great, elegiac moments of the movement, first in the trumpets, then, *"mit grosser Empfindung"* (with great feeling), in the violins.

The restless, demonic, agitated powers cannot be held in check any longer. Trombones and horns, muted, portend ominously over the timpani. Themes are distorted grotesquely as Mahler launches into the ultimate *danse macabre* in the finale of the movement. Unleashed, unfettered, the movement races, rages *piu stretto* into a wild *presto*. An attempted moment of respite, a remembrance of beauties past, is deluged as the storm of scorn, of defiance, of despair is whipped up beyond all restraints and the trumpets and trombones blare out the triumph of defeat.

*"Sehr langsam und noch zurückhaltend"* (very slow and still restrained) is Mahler's dynamics instruction at the opening of the final Adagio, as the violins intone a theme of sorrowful quiet

which further unfolds in *espressivo* splendor. Although the theme is still in *adagio,* it is in no way hesitant. *"Stets grosser Ton"* (big tone throughout) demands the composer.

There is neither lament nor pain, as Mahler averts his gaze from earthly sights. The violas repeat the opening theme, and then the solo bassoon *langsam* (slowly) unfolds this theme.

The violins and contrabassoon again engage in a restatement *f* of the opening theme, which is continued *ff* and *stark hervortretend* (strongly pronounced) in the horn.

The brief emotional wave recedes again into a typically Mahlerian interplay of great contrast. "Slowly and hesitantly," the violins lead into their song against the previous bassoon theme, now heard against the violins *pp und ohne Empfindung* (without feeling) in the celli, string basses, and contrabassoon.

As their voices intertwine, the horn repeats the main theme in slight variation before the middle section of the movement ascends from repose to heights of jubilation. Over the excitement of timpani and bass drum, trombones and trumpets solemnly unveil their vision.

Once more, for the last time, Mahler's spirit rises in *fff* splendor. The violins attain brilliant heights of the utmost intensity.

In tumultuous splendor the massed voice of trombones and tuba mingles with the horns, woodwinds, and strings. Life once more appears in noble majesty; once more the summit has been reached and from it Mahler looks ahead to transfiguration. Now the descent begins: earthly pleasures and splendors are left behind, as previous themes appear briefly and remain unfinished, unfulfilled. The final violin melody is heard *ppp* and *mit inniger Empfindung* (with ardent feeling), *ersterbend* (dying away) in beauty, without regret.

The last descending sound is heard *pppp* in the violins, violas, and celli.

The Adagio, the final statement of Mahler's last complete work, is more of an epilogue to the work than a part of the work itself. Beneath the song of the upper strings, the shadow of death looms in the elegiac opening. A fervent outpouring is tinged with the shadow of farewell in an emotional musical experience seldom equaled. In the end, we have an artist's vision of "dust to dust": scattered phrases, seemingly trailing away into nowhere. It is a comment of man on his fate, touching as it fades into dusk, darkness, and death, and leaving us oddly, sadly unfulfilled, yet in stunned wonder, having beheld one of the great moments of farewell in music.

The fact that Mahler's Ninth Symphony recalls themes from a number of his works and particularly the mood and spirit of *Das Lied von der Erde* has often given rise to the assumption that it is to be considered a continuation of that work. The fact that both works were created by Mahler at about the same time (within one year from each other, to be exact) reinforces such an assumption. Many feel that quotations from *Das Lied* are intentional, meant to indicate such continuity. In other ways also the Ninth is reminiscent. After such innovative creations as the Fifth, Sixth, and Eighth Symphonies and *Das Lied,* the Ninth is oddly nineteenth-century in many details. Wagnerian and Straussian sounds appear at surprising points, and the *Ländler* of the second movement harks back to early Mahler and to Bruckner. But in contrast to these earlier creations, the Ninth speaks of farewell.

## SYMPHONY NO. 10 IN F-SHARP MAJOR

Mr. Cooke's brilliant detective work leaves us in little doubt that Mahler's premature death deprived us of yet another of this remarkable composer's searching explorations of a new world of sound and feeling.

Donald Mitchell, *London Daily Telegraph,* 20 December 1960

It seems idle to me to raise the question whether [Deryck Cooke's] re-construction is artistically justified. The facsimile edition has provided the means of realizing the sketches of the Tenth Symphony, and now the actual performance of this last work of Gustav Mahler has, at the very last, acquainted us with a creation of unexpected greatness.

Dr. Egon Wellesz, *Austrian Musical News,*
*Osterreichische Musikzeitschrift,* April 1961

A few years ago Deryck Cooke undertook the attempt to weld the existing sketches . . . through added composition "in the sense of Mahler" into a complete symphony. We consider this an unnecessary and unsuccessful attempt.

Heinrich Kralik, *Gustav Mahler,* 1968

*Sketches of the symphony composed in 1910 in Toblach. Two movements, in* Ernst Křenek's *orchestral adaptation* (Adagio *and* Purgatorio) *performed on 14 October 1924 in Vienna, Franz Schalk conducting. First publication of the sketches in facsimile in 1924. First complete performance of Deryck Cooke's performance version on 13 August 1964, Berthold Goldschmidt conducting the London Symphony Orchestra.*

On 19 December 1960 the British Broadcasting Company, during an anniversary broadcast celebrating the one hundredth anniversary of Mahler's birth, performed Deryck Cooke's performance version of two movements of Mahler's Tenth Symphony. Five days later a letter from Mrs. Alma Mahler was received, demanding withdrawal of the performance. Although further performances had already been publicized, the BBC withdrew the tapes.

Subsequently Cooke was asked by *Chord and Discord* to write an article on Mahler's Tenth Symphony. He began with an analysis of the original unfinished manuscript, which had been published in facsimile in 1924 by the Paul Zsolnay Verlag in Vienna. The article was written without musical quotations in order to avoid conflicts with Mrs. Mahler as well as with the copyright owners.

The matter of performance of the Tenth Symphony had been a subject of intense discussion as early as shortly after Mahler's death. The eminent musicologist Richard Specht, after an initial negative statement which he subsequently withdrew, recommended further work on it and branded Alma's refusal "false piety." Her refusal had been based, according to Specht, on Mahler's supposed request to have the original sketches burned after his death. While Alma could not bring herself to accede to the request, she was said to have attempted a middle road by withholding from publication any version that went beyond the original sketches.

Eventually the composer Ernst Křenek, then the husband of Alma's daughter Anna, was approached and agreed to work on the sketch. He restricted his work to the two most complete movements, the Adagio and

Purgatorio. They, in turn, were examined for mistakes by such *cognoscenti* as Alban Berg and Franz Schalk, and were eventually performed by Schalk and Zemlinsky. Křenek's initial effort was not crowned with lasting success, however, because the ascendancy of Hitler in 1933 made performances of Mahler's music a crime, first in Germany and, after the *Anschluss,* in Austria as well. The Tenth lay dormant, only partially brought to life and with even those parts barely performed, even before Hitler's edict against all non-Aryan music and art.

In time, Křenek's adaptation acquired a great number of accretions at the hand of Schalk (who had done the same disservice to Bruckner scores) as well as Zemlinsky, with one copy actually reading in German: "arranged by A. Zemlinsky." When Křenek and Mahler expert Jack Diether eventually visited American Music Publishers (AMP), the present copyright owners, in New York, they found an additional footnote further confusing the matter: *viz.,* a notation by AMP editor Otto Jokl reading "Marks in parenthesis are not Mahler's." Jokl did not realize that this would tend to add to the confusion by implying that all other marks were Mahler's; he did not know of the previous notations by Křenek, Schalk, and Zemlinsky. The issue was further obfuscated by AMP's giving the work the title of Mahler's Symphony No. 10, when actually only two touched-up movements had been published.

Meanwhile a number of avenues were explored toward accomplishing the goal of competent orchestration of the sketches. In 1942 Diether approached Dimitri Shostakovich. The great Russian replied:

> Despite my love for this composer I cannot take upon myself this huge task. This calls for deep penetration into the spiritual world of the composer as well as his creative and individual style. For me this would be impossible.
>
> D. Cooke, *The History of Mahler's Tenth Symphony*
> [manuscript]

Schönberg was approached, first by Specht, in 1949 by Alma Mahler, and later by Diether. Too busy wrestling with the demons he had conjured up in his own music, he never rose to the challenge. In retrospect his refusal may have been a blessing in disguise, for the Tenth might otherwise have emerged as a Mahler–Schönberg opus, just as *Die drei Pintos* had become, sixty years earlier, a Weber–Mahler opera.

A number of independent attempts at orchestration were made by, among others, the British composer Joe Wheeler in 1954, the American Clinton Carpenter, and the German Hans Wollschläger. None was destined, however, to have the emotional and musical impact of Deryck Cooke's work. Indeed, logic almost dictated that a musicologist undertake the Mahler task and not a composer too deeply immersed in his own style and work to become involved in another's "spiritual world."

Cooke's work began with the festival brochure issued on the occasion of Mahler's one hundredth birthday anniversary in 1960. It had not been until 1959 that Cooke had seriously begun to study the facsimile edition of the symphony in preparation for writing the brochure. It was then that the need to know more about the Tenth Symphony sketch began to fully occupy Cooke's mind, because he realized the impossibility of grasping anything meaningful about the entire work from the two orchestrated movements alone. Only after he had copied the entire facsimile sketch by hand did Mahler's comment "fully prepared in sketch" begin to emerge in its full weight. Yet anything approaching even an attempt at completion seemed a remote if not impossible task. Encouraged by the BBC, which had commissioned the brochure, Cooke prepared a musically illustrated radio talk, in the process fleshing out the sketch in the orchestral style of Mahler, which was, of course, well known to Cooke. Slowly the sketch yielded its secrets to the dedicated musicological researcher and his friend, Mahler expert and conductor Berthold Goldschmidt, who acted as catalyst and adviser. Thus it came about, owing to Cooke's diligence and dedication, that the broadcast on 19 December 1960, by the Philharmonia Orchestra under Goldschmidt's direction, proved much more than an illustrated talk. Interestingly, the final movement, which was presented in full orchestration, made a deep impression, while the middle movements, presented in excerpts, evoked less interest. This spurred Cooke to enter into the completion of his task, the preparation of a complete concert performance of the work.

> The musicologist Richard Specht had noted that the fully-prepared sketches comprise five movements. Two of them have reached the stage of performable full scores. . . . The other three seem to be written out from beginning to end in the sketch; but they obviously need to be filled out with orchestration, and with counterthemes and inner parts, by some musician of high standing who is devoted to Mahler and intimate with his style, and who, by comparing the sketches and completed scores of his earlier works, would surely find the right way to the goal.[29]

In clear-cut contrast to Viennese Mahler scholars, Cooke felt that the Mahler sketch of the Tenth was not sacrosanct, but rather was a record of live, vibrant music and not a museum piece. Here Cooke openly clashes with Schönberg, who declared in a lecture on 12 October, 1912:

> Concerning the Tenth Symphony, for which, as in the case of Beethoven, sketches exist, we shall know as little about what it would have said as

---

[29] Specht, at that time, had ventured one step further.

"Such a musician is, above all others, Arnold Schönberg, whose whole heart belongs to the master, who is at home with his style, and who may lay claim to the mastery and modesty appropriate to such a task."

Schönberg, of course, declined, whereas, Deryck Cooke's inspired determination succeeded.

we know about Beethoven's. . . . It seems that the Ninth is the limit. He who wants to go beyond it must pass away. It seems as if something might be imparted to us in the Tenth for which we are not yet ready. Those who have written a Ninth have stood too near to the hereafter. Perhaps the riddles of the world could be solved, if one of those who knew them were to write the Tenth. And that is probably not to take place.

Cooke calls this viewpoint "mythical" and "superstitious," and to prove his point he refers to Mozart's and Haydn's massive symphonic output. But here Cooke leaves himself open to argument on two fronts. First of all, Schönberg *believed* in numerology. To him it was *"Glaube nicht Aberglaube"* (belief, not superstition), and he expresses that belief in the phrase "He who wants to go beyond it [the Ninth] must pass away." To Schönberg the number 13 was personally of deadly significance; it even prompted him to number the measures of his composition 12, 12a, 14. Secondly, a world of difference separates Haydn and Mozart from Beethoven. The most glaring difference is that after Beethoven's nine symphonies in general and his *Eroica* in particular, not even a Haydn or Mozart would have dared to engage in the mass composition of 104 or 41 symphonies, respectively. Beethoven's nine established a new plateau in spirit, conception, and length which made them landmarks and could neither be ignored nor circumvented by the composers that followed him. The fact that some composers, such as Miaskovsky, continued to engage in wholesale symphonic composition only serves to prove the point. Thus the "Mystic Nine" became an ominous and fearfully visible horizon on the symphonic firmament.

In the course of his research Cooke exposed a number of entrenched misconceptions:

*Item:* Mahler did not request of Alma that his manuscript of the Tenth Symphony be destroyed. Specht, who had quoted such a statement in his book, later retracted it.

*Item:* Schönberg was not familiar enough with the Tenth Symphony score and sketch to consider it "unknowable."

*Item:* In discussing the body of the symphony, the word "sketch" is applicable only in the sense that the orchestration is mostly absent. Otherwise, to use the word "sketch" or "fragment" is misleading, because Mahler's manuscript continues on numbered pages in a progression fully indicated by the composer. This holds true also with respect to the individual movements, which Mahler himself had described as prepared with complete melodic continuity.

It was, as we have seen, Cooke's mastery of the vast final movement which drew most of the critics' comments and convinced him to complete the task even if, in rare instances, he would have to call on his own intuition to complete the work. What finally emerged from Cooke's inspired labors, however, by no means garnered the applause of all.

> Sometimes the conjectural, basic solution was audibly too primitive: the simple Johann Strauss accompaniment to the waltz trio of the fourth movement, for example. [In the finale] . . . this melody grew until the coda; how much more it would have grown if Mahler had tended it to its final blossoming.
>
> William Mann, *London Times,* 20 December 1960

A *Sunday Times* critic wrote:

> It is hard to believe that the composer would have made many structural changes in this deeply moving finale, even though he would doubtless have enriched its texture and added to its contrapuntal interest.
>
> Desmond Shaw-Taylor, *London Sunday Times,*
> 25 December 1960

Generally Deryck Cooke's performance version of the entire Tenth Symphony won enthusiastic acclaim; "in time," *Time* magazine was to say later (7 September 1962), "it could conceivably become the accepted version."

Then came the thunderclap: Alma Mahler forbade any further performance of the Cooke version, a decision made without even bothering to listen to either performance or tape. Alma simply felt that she was acting in the spirit of Mahler. Cooke, fired to his task, continued undeterred, working on the completion of the score despite the looming wall of Alma's intransigence.

Meanwhile Jack Diether argued with Alma in favor of realization of the sketch and its performance, while Bruno Walter and Dr. Erwin Ratz spoke out for tradition and nonperformance, as did Schönberg. Their arguments did not lack eloquence.

> Even with his finished works, Mahler did retouching in the instrumentation after a few performances; you cannot say that *Das Lied von der Erde* and the Ninth have the same character they might have had if Mahler himself had lived to perform them.
>
> Dr. Erwin Ratz, President of the International Mahler Society in Vienna

Eventually it was conductor Harold Byrns, a Mahler expert and friend of Alma Mahler, who, on the strength of his knowledge, gained Alma's ear. He convinced her of the merits of Cooke's work and argued for her listening to the tapes. In consequence Deryck Cooke received a letter from Alma Mahler, dated New York, 8 May 1963.

> Dear Mr. Cooke:
> Mr. Harold Byrns visited me here in New York. Today he read me your excellent articles on Mahler's Tenth Symphony and [showed me] your

equally authoritative score. Afterwards I expressed my desire to finally listen to the London BBC tape.

I was so moved by this performance that I immediately asked Mr. Byrns to play the work a second time. I then realized that the time had come when I must reconsider my previous decision not to permit the performance of this work.

I have now decided once and for all to give you full permission to go ahead with performances in any part of the world. I enclose a copy of my letter of even date to the BBC.

Sincerely yours,
Alma Maria Mahler

After Alma Mahler's death, her daughter Anna had Baron Henri Louis de la Grange, the eminent Mahler scholar, supply Cooke with the forty-four pages missing in the original facsimile edition. The same information was also furnished Dr. Erwin Ratz, who then proceeded to include the complete facsimile in the edition of Mahler's works published in 1967.

Cooke modestly assessed the significance of his inspired effort, whose reverberations are felt to this day in the musical world.

> After more than half a century, Mahler's draft for his Tenth Symphony has at last been restored to life as a totality. . . . The present score is in no sense intended as a completion or reconstruction of the work. First of all, no completion has been necessary, in the usual sense. . . . But far more important, it is utterly impossible to "complete" the work, in the true sense. . . . Obviously [Mahler] alone could have done this. . . . On the other hand, it would be wrong to say that the present score cannot claim to represent Mahler's Tenth Symphony in any sense whatsoever. It does, quite simply, represent the stage the work had reached when Mahler died, in a practical performing version.

Although the key signature in the first movement (Adagio) is F-sharp Major, the movement opens in the keys of B Minor and D Minor with a wistful, lonely melody in the unaccompanied violas. Only when the violins intone the main Adagio theme does the key of F-sharp Minor appear. The melody is spun out in vibrant passionate arches as, in many transformations, it mingles with the initial viola theme, employing Mahler's favorite major–minor–major transformations in the process. The accumulating tension eventually explodes in an outburst, expected yet still overwhelming in its tragic overtones. It is as if the entire orchestra had suddenly been transformed into a gigantic organ of solemn, majestic pronouncements, culminating *ff* in a dissonant outburst by the full orchestra, in turn surmounted by a piercing trumpet. The descent from that summit of sound does not return to the valley of the opening melodies but proceeds into a lengthy coda, barely touching on the opening themes which, until the climax, had dominated the scene. The movement ends in touching gentleness, wistful and resigned.

The annotation by Mahler of "Scherzo Finale" (Allegro) in the second movement leads Cooke to believe that Mahler had initially intended a symphony in two movements, and he consequently further conjectures that the Adagio and Scherzo together make up Part I of the symphony, while the Purgatorio, Scherzo, and Finale constitute the second part of the work. The fact that the Adagio and Scherzo, although contrasting in mood, are in the same key strengthens this assumption. The Scherzo consists of a main section (A) and two Trio sections (B and C). Boisterous music opens the movement (A), in bold interchange between strings and brass. A basic rhythm motif ♩♩ ♩, also observed in the Adagio, sets the mood as the movement raises to a brash, crashing climax, only to descend into a gentler offering of the original material. In the first Trio (B), the tempo remains the same but the mood is gentler. The first and second Trio sections are separated by the reappearance of the vigorous material of the opening section, although without the same fierceness. In the second Trio (C), the mood changes from boisterous strength to the gently undulating ¾ time of waltz and *Ländler*. From there on Mahler ingeniously uses the stated materials in combinations and variations. First we find a coupling of the main Scherzo section with the first Trio (A and B), a combination of the fierce opening theme and the quieter material of the first Trio. This is followed by a combination on and variation of the themes of the two Trios (B and C), after which there is a more lyrical treatment of the materials of the opening movement and the second Trio (A and C), in a radiant, relaxed episode which leads into a surprisingly impetuous climax but ends abruptly. The combination of Trios B and C serves as a coda. The prevailing mood of strength, vitality, and confidence is maintained as the movement, in restatement, brilliantly goes from climax to climax, triumphantly presenting the first Trio theme in martial rendition and the *Ländler* in augmentation. It is all boisterous affirmation, with a sudden, unexpected ending.

The middle movement, Purgatorio (*allegretto moderato*), is in its briefness totally out of proportion to the two movements that precede and follow it. Its overall construction of A–B–A is deceptive, because Mahler's varied thematic treatment belies such simplicity. The main feature of the movement is its delicate "perpetual motion" theme, nonintrusive but ever-present. Against it the themes are presented in flowing succession (*"etwas fliessend"*), at one point descending into the darkness of the bassoons and string basses. The central section presents the expected contrast fiercely, almost violently, rising to an emotional outburst and then dying away, leading back into the opening section in shortened restatement. With the orchestra receding into the distance, one is lulled into an erroneous expectation of a delicate ending in the woodwinds but is rudely pulled up short by a deliberately coarse ending of considerable volume. This brief movement, the core of the symphony, can be considered "the motivic and emotional source of the two large-scale movements to follow," according to Cooke.

The fourth movement, although untitled and without tempo markings, is nevertheless generally also considered a Scherzo, a logical assumption which lends balance of construction to the work. Again we find a main section, two Trio sections, and a coda. The movement opens with an orchestral outcry of electrifying power. This is Mahler at his most demonic, wild and fierce, foreshadowing and leading into the struggle between negative and positive forces, clearly indicated by minor and major keys, with the forces of darkness eventually winning the struggle. No greater contrast could be envisioned than that between the violently crashing theme of the opening and the graceful waltz tune which follows after a brief transition. But again the charm is not of long duration as the theme of storm and stress gains the upper hand again and, in a passage of "fierce lament," reaches its climax. The first Trio section retains the mesmerizing atmosphere of a sentimental waltz melody, eventually, toward the end of the Trio, leading into a new theme of dashing vitality. Before the second Trio is reached, however, the excitement of the opening is recalled, interlaced with waltz quotations from the first Trio and reminding the listener of the opening movement of *Das Lied von der Erde*. In ingenious manner, the second Trio is nearly a continuation of the first Trio section, whose final, dashing theme the second Trio employs as its opening statement. The music is joyful but oddly driven, reaching a climax of great jubilation; in the process there is constant quotation from themes in the opening Scherzo movement and the first Trio section. The expected climax is sadly, fatally negative. Slowly, joy and vitality diminish, receding into shadowy, ghostly themes which flit by only to disintegrate. Finally only the percussive skeleton of the once joyous waltz remains. The movement ends in the toneless *ff* of a muffled bass drum.

The Finale (*lento, non troppo; allegro moderato*) immediately establishes continuity with the preceding movement by hammering out *ff* the ominous drum beat which ended the preceding movement and which is now heard six times at the opening of the movement and five times at the end of its slow introduction. The negative minor also prevails in this movement, at least for the time being, as do the themes of the *Purgatorio*. The procession is slow, morbid, almost lumbering. As the flute enters, singing its serene, consoling song over tranquil harmonies, the mood changes and is continued *ppp* in the violins. The flute returns as the music rises in a soaring arch. It is at that point that the muffled drum interjects itself abruptly, almost brutally, bringing with it the threatening themes of the *Purgatorio*. The first attempt to escape the darkness of minor harmonies and reach through to the happier mood of major modes is doomed, and the struggle begins anew, in the *allegro moderato,* the main body of the final movement.

It opens with driving, agitated themes, mainly quotations from the Purgatorio movement, rising *ff* to a feverish climax yet still imprisoned in the D Minor key. The mood varies from there on, sinking to a *p*, rising with great romantic feeling to brief ferocity, then returning to the romantic mood, still in the key of D but with a significant change from minor to major.

Suddenly we are confronted with a surprising, unexpected expression running the gamut from forceful lamentation to *ff* joy. Struggle resumes anew between serene themes and their sardonic counterparts. After agitated interplay calm prevails and pervades the central section of the movement, in a major key. The serenity is shattered by a pronouncement of high drama; it subsides only to rise again in a quotation from the first-movement theme. A *ff* high point is reached again. Here the genius of Mahler conjures up a moment of magic as the trumpet, reaching a piercing A, holds the note, persistently, seemingly endlessly, triumphantly, against constantly shifting melodies. As the trumpet descends from its high perch so does the mood, as the minor key again appears. Modulation leads into the final section of the movement, which proceeds to the positive key of F-sharp Major, announced in the first movement. Serenity, triumph, and transfiguration wait in the wings as the violins lead the way. The major key can no longer be denied, and surprisingly it makes its final and permanent appearance not after a violent struggle, unsuccessfully attempted before, nor in passionate or strident utterance, but amidst an aura of nobility and calm. With the major key now firmly established, the orchestra soars to tonal splendor and majesty. Already in the sketch Mahler had marked at this point "all violins, *ff*, big tone." The music surges, declamatory, passionate, assertive. The climax over, the music descends, now firmly major in key and mood, reaching a new plateau in the Coda. Cooke expresses the ending succinctly: "The symphony ends in a mood of transfigured serenity quite different from the bitter-sweet resignation of the ending of *Das Lied von der Erde* or the Ninth Symphony." The music reaches an unearthly, otherworldly calm, only to leap up once more, *ff*, before descending to its final rest. "The effect is of a great sigh of contentment at finding peace at last."

## EPILOGUE

> [Mahler] seems to me to embody the most serious and sacred artistic purpose of our age.
>
> Thomas Mann, Munich, 13 September 1910

> Mahler emanates from the Austrian group of symphonists. [His] style combines feeling with intellect . . . is spiritually akin to Beethoven . . . but partaking of its time. Thus Mahler's work does not belong to a past from which we turn but a future to which we aspire. As the last

and highest product of the romantic world view, Mahler's symphonic creations are at the same time art and basis for a new idealism. . . . [Today's] generation recognizes its creator as the highest musical cultural apparition since Beethoven.

Paul Bekker, von Beethoven bis Mahler, 21 May 1918

The symphonies of Gustav Mahler have never received genuine recognition [in America]. . . . He was a profound musician and one of the best conductors of Europe, and it is possible that . . . he occupied himself so intensely and constantly in analyzing and interpreting the works of the great masters that he lost the power to develop himself as a composer along original lines. . . . Moments of real beauty are too rare, and the listener has to wade through pages of dreary emptiness which no artificial connection with philosophic ideals can fill with real importance. [His] feverish restlessness . . . reflects itself in his music which is fragmentary . . . and lacks continuity of thought and development. He could write cleverly in the style of Haydn or Berlioz or Wagner, and without forgetting Beethoven, but he was never able to write in the style of Mahler.

Walter Damrosch, My Musical Life, 1923

The supreme value of Mahler's creative work does not lie in the newness which is so movingly revealed in the essential elements of a . . . daring, adventurous and bizarre character, but in the fact that this newness with its added . . . beauty, inspiration, and soulfulness, has become music, and that the lasting values of artistic power and eminent humanity are at the bottom of these creations. This is why they have preserved their full vitality to this day . . . and will maintain it in the future.

Bruno Walter, Gustav Mahler, 1924

Mahler . . . admittedly, is long-winded, trite, bombastic, lacks taste, and sometimes plagiarizes unblushingly, filching his material from Schubert, Mozart, Bruckner. . . . But when all is said, there remains something extra-ordinarily touching about the man's work. . . . All his nine symphonies are suffused with personality. . . . The irascible Scherzos, the heaven-storming calls in the brass, the special quality of communing with nature . . . the gargantuan *Ländler,* the pages of incredible loneliness—all these, combined with [his] histrionics, an inner warmth, and the will to evoke the largest forms and the grandest musical thoughts, add up to one of the most fascinating composer–personalities of modern times. . . . Mahler would be an important figure even if his music were not so engrossing [and] years in advance of its time.

Aaron Copland, The New Music, 1967

His music is . . . the utterance of a genius, an authentic original. No amount of carping about how derivative the music is of Mozart, Schubert, Wagner and the lot, can possibly erase the shining fact that it comes out always sounding like Mahler, with the extraordinary individual personality constantly uppermost. Nobody else could have written it, nobody, ever. It is a treasure-trove of originality.

Leonard Bernstein, Carnegie Hall Speech, 1960

# Biographical Sketches

ADLER, GUIDO, 1855–1941. Austrian musicologist. First active at the University of Prague. In 1898 he succeeded Hanslick at the Vienna University, a position which was considerably broadened and modernized under his aegis. He was a student of Bruckner and a close friend of Mahler, and editor-in-chief of *Denkmäler der Tonkunst in Oesterreich* [monuments of tonal art in Austria]. His main achievement was the monumental standard work, *Handbuch der Musikgeschichte* [Manual of the history of music]. Among his students were Anton Webern, Egon Wellesz, Hans Gal, Karl Geiringer, Paul Pisk, and Josef Weigl.

ADLER, VIKTOR, 1852–1918. Austrian journalist and statesman, founder and leader of the Austrian Social Democratic Party. At the collapse of the Austrian empire he became foreign secretary. He died one day before Austria was proclaimed a republic. In his youth he had been a member of the Pernerstorfer Circle. He remained a lifelong friend of Mahler.

BAUER-LECHNER, NATALIE, 1859–1923, prominent violinist and chamber-music performer. Arranged the first performance of the Wolf String Quartet in her home. She was a close friend of the Mahler family and especially of Gustav. Her correspondence with Mahler is most informative.

BILLROTH, THEODOR, 1829–1894. Viennese surgeon of Swedish origin. Lectured at the Vienna University beginning 1876. First specialized in throat surgery, later became a surgeon of world renown in gastrointestinal care. His interest in music was proverbial in Vienna. He was a close friend of Hanslick and Brahms, whose chamber music was often premiered in Billroth's home.

BLECH, LEO, 1871–1958. German conductor and composer. Studied with Humperdinck; conductor in Aachen, Prague, Berlin, and Vienna; one of the foremost conductors of his day. During Hitler's time Blech went to Riga, from where he fled to Sweden. He returned to Berlin in 1949. Mahler performed his opera *Das war Ich* [This was I], with a libretto by Batka. Blech's main prominence was as a conductor.

BRÜLL, IGNAZ, 1846–1907. Austrian pianist and composer. Studied in Vienna under Epstein and Dessoff. Prominent concert pianist before turning to opera composition. His outstanding success was the opera *Das Goldene Kreuz* [The golden cross]. Belonged to the intimate Brahms circle. Played Brahms music by sight at Brahms gatherings.

BÜLOW, HANS VON, 1830–1894. German pianist and conductor. Premiered the first version of Tchaikovsky's Piano Concerto in B-flat Minor in 1875, in Boston. Became a proponent of the neo-German school of Wagner and Liszt. Married Liszt's daughter Cosima, who later left him to become the mistress and wife of Wagner. Bülow transformed the orchestra of the Duchy of Meiningen into one of the foremost ensembles in Europe. He later became the supreme interpreter of the music of Brahms and an admirer of Mahler as a conductor.

BUSONI, FERRUCCIO, 1886–1924. Widely traveled pianist of Italo–German parentage. Met Delius and Sibelius. First American tour in 1891–94; later in residence in Berlin. Flamboyant style in the tradition of Liszt. Later expanded his activities into conducting and composition. Devoted friend of Mahler, who performed Busoni's music.

D'ALBERT, EUGÈNE, 1864–1932. German composer and pianist, despite the French name; born in Britain. At age thirteen he appeared in major concerts in London, and later in Vienna as pianist at Richter's insistence. Composed numerous operas, of which only *Tiefland* [Lowlands] survives. Mahler produced his opera *Die Abreise* [The departure]. One of the most prominent musicians of his day.

DAMROSCH, WALTER, 1862–1950. Son of famed violinist, composer, and conductor Leopold (1832–85). Became assistant conductor at the Metropolitan in New York under his father, later under Anton Seidl. Prominent conductor of American musical societies. Founder of the Damrosch Opera Company and Symphony Orchestra. Conductor of the German repertoire at the Met, and also Philharmonic conductor. Later prominent in musical radio broadcasts, including the first concert relayed from the Pacific coast across America to the Atlantic.

DECSEY, ERNST, 1879–1941. Austrian musicographer, biographer, and critic. Pupil of Bruckner. Among his writings are biographies of Bruckner, Wolf, Lehar, and Johann Strauss. Active and prominent in the Vienna musical life of his time.

DESSOFF, OTTO FELIX, 1835–1892. German conductor who found his most rewarding sphere of musical activity in Vienna during 1860–1875.

Became conductor of the Imperial Opera, conductor of the Philharmonic, and professor at the Vienna Conservatory. After leaving Vienna he was active in Karlsruhe and Frankfurt am Main. His daughter founded the famed Dessoff Choir in New York.

DUSTMANN, LUISE, 1831–1899. German soprano. After engagements in Germany she settled in Vienna and became a prominent member of the Vienna Opera and teacher at the Conservatory. Prominent in Wagnerian roles. She was a close friend of Brahms, on whom she prevailed to settle in Vienna.

ECKERT, CARL, 1820–1879. German conductor, composer, and instrumentalist. Student of Mendelssohn. Successful early performances of his music in the opera and oratorio field. In 1852 he became conductor of the Italian repertoire at the Paris opera. Appointed director of the Imperial Opera in Vienna in 1853. Later appointments to Stuttgart and Berlin. Better known as a conductor than as a composer.

EPSTEIN, JULIUS, 1832–1926. Prominent Vienna piano teacher at the Conservatory. Mahler was one of his most important pupils and gave lessons to Epstein's son. Epstein supervised Mahler's piano transcription of Bruckner's Third Symphony.

FRIEDJUNG, HEINRICH, 1851–1920. Austrian historian and political journalist. Member of the Pernerstorfer Circle. Strong pro-German spokesman until anti-Semitism ended his political ambitions, although he had put German liberal nationalistic feelings before religious considerations. He was a friend of Viktor Adler.

FUCHS, ROBERT, 1847–1927. Teacher of harmony at the Vienna Conservatory. Wolf and Mahler were his pupils. Friend of Johann Strauss. Composer of music for small ensembles. His brother Johann Nepomuk Fuchs was conductor at the Vienna Opera and attempted to prevent Mahler's appointment there.

GRÜNFELD, ALFRED, 1852–1924. Born in Prague, but Vienna became his focus of pianistic activity. Close friend of Johann Strauss, whose waltzes he interpreted with flamboyant grace. Mahler had been housed with his family in early youth. Brother Heinrich Grünfeld was a prominent cellist.

GOLDMARK, KARL, 1830–1915. Austro-Hungarian composer. Early musical talent. Entered the Vienna Conservatory at age 14. First favorable notice as a composer in 1857. Permanent residence in Vienna in 1860. The composition that established his fame was the symphony *Ländliche Hochzeit* [Rustic wedding]. After ten years of work, his opera *Die Königin von Saba* [The Queen of Sheba] brought him enduring fame in Europe and the United States. Close friend of Brahms and a friend of Mahler. His violin concerto and *Sakuntala* overture are also still heard in concert performance.

GRAF, MAX, 1873–1958. Austrian musicologist and historian and music critic for leading Vienna newspapers. Professor at the Conservatory and the Austrian State Academy of Music and Dramatic Arts. Author of books on musical history and the music of Vienna. Student of Bruckner, teacher of Egon Gartenberg. Emigrated to the United States in 1938; continued his writing career and musicology lectures.

HANSLICK, EDUARD, 1825–1904. Austrian musicologist and critic, of Czech birth. Studied in Prague; fame as international music critic established in Vienna while writing musical criticism for the *Wiener Zeitung* (1844–64) and the influential *Neue Freie Presse.* An early Wagner admirer, he turned into the most literate and articulate anti-Wagner proponent of his time. His most enduring musicological contribution is his book on musical aesthetics, *Vom musikalisch Schönen* [The beautiful in music], published in 1854 (nine editions) and translated into four languages.

HEUBERGER, RICHARD, 1850–1914. Critic, conductor, composer. As music critic of the *Neue Freie Presse,* he was critical of Mahler's music. Later he fell victim to criticism himself for composing the successful operetta *The Opera Ball* (1898) in Vienna. Had the operetta been a failure it would have received a respectful burial and obituary; a successful operetta by a "serious" music critic was unforgivable.

HRABANUS MAURUS MAGNENTIUS, 780–856. German scholar and theologian, and man of encyclopedic knowledge. As abbot of Fulda, he made the abbey school and library an intellectual source of renown. Later became Bishop of Mainz. His fame extended throughout the German-speaking regions.

HUMPERDINCK, ENGELBERT, 1854–1921. German composer. Assisted Wagner in 1880 in Bayreuth with *Parsifal* production. Beginning in 1881, received important appointments in Germany and Spain. His foremost opera, *Hänsel und Gretel,* was premiered in Weimar in 1893. Wagner's influence was promptly noted. It nevertheless became an immediate and lasting success, not to be repeated with Humperdinck's later operas. Mahler admirer.

HÜTTENBRENNER, ANSELM, 1794–1868. Austrian composer. Friend of Antonio Salieri, the teacher of Schubert; also befriended Beethoven and particularly Schubert. He had held the Schubert manuscript of Symphony No. 8 in B Minor (Unfinished) for many years until it was discovered by the Viennese conductor Johann Herbeck.

JOACHIM, JOSEF, 1831–1907. Austro-Hungarian violinist, conductor, and composer and leader of the Joachim Quartet. Performed in his first violin concert at age 7. Studied in Vienna under Hellmesberger, later with David in Leipzig, under Mendelssohn's guidance. Concertmaster, together with David, of the Leipzig Gewandhaus orchestra at age 19. Later headed the music department of the Berlin Royal Academy of Arts. Unsurpassed violinist of his time, a close friend of Brahms, strongly anti-Wagnerian.

KALBECK, MAX, 1850–1921. Vienna music critic. Close friend of Brahms, whose first biography he authored. As the conservative music critic of the *Neues Wiener Tagblatt*, he shared Brahms's unrelenting hostility toward Bruckner. His appraisals of Mahler's music were eminently fair.

KLEMPERER, OTTO, 1885–1973. German conductor. Scharwenka and Pfitzner were his early teachers. Recommended by Mahler, he held important conducting positions in Hamburg, Prague, and Berlin. Known for significant performances of contemporary music—Janaček, Schönberg, Stravinsky, and Hindemith. Despite his friendship with Mahler, his appreciation of Mahler's music came late.

KLIMT, GUSTAV, 1862–1918. Austrian painter. Cofounder of Vienna's dissident "Sezession" art movement. Vienna's foremost exponent of *art nouveau* in highly stylized symbolism. Greatest fame in murals, portraits, and landscape paintings, often with sensuous overtones. Friend of Gustav and Alma Mahler.

KLINGER, MAX, 1857–1920. German sculptor and painter. Until 1886 creative in etchings; later turned to painting on a monumental scale. From 1894 to his death, became famous as a sculptor. His statue of Beethoven and bust of Nietzsche are considered among his best work. Much of his work was done in Vienna among the artists of the "Sezession" whom he befriended.

KLOPSTOCK, FRIEDRICH GOTTLIEB, 1724–1803. Important German lyric poet who influenced Goethe and the *Sturm und Drang* (Storm and Stress) period. His important poetic contributions are the epic *Messias* [Messiah], a drama trilogy extolling the German hero *Hermann* [Arminius], and his rhapsodic odes and sacred poems, which inspired C. P. E. Bach, Beethoven, Gluck, Mahler, and Schubert.

KOKOSCHKA, OSKAR, 1886–    Austrian expressionist painter. In 1937 all of his creations were ordered removed from German galleries and museums. He established a summer school in Salzburg, Austria. He soon outgrew the early influence of Klimt to develop a restless style of portraiture with psychological overtones. Among Austria's and the world's foremost expressionist painters. Companion of Alma Mahler.

KRALIK, HEINRICH, 1887–1965. Viennese music critic and musicologist. Chronicler of the history of the Vienna Opera and the Vienna Philharmonic orchestra. From his earliest youth a proponent of the music of Mahler, which he introduced to the public at large in a series of radio broadcasts.

KŘENEK, ERNST, 1900–     Austrian composer and musicologist. His greatest successes were the jazz opera *Jonny spielt auf* [Johnny strikes up] (1927) and the opera *Karl V* [Charles V] (1933). Prominent also as a writer on musical topics. Together with Bruno Walter, he wrote a treatise on Mahler (1941). He also partially orchestrated Mahler's unfinished Tenth Symphony. Was married to Mahler's daughter Anna from 1922 to 1927.

KRENN, FRANZ, 1818–1897. Austrian composer and theorist at the Vienna Conservatory. Hugo Wolf and Mahler were among his students.

KRUMPHOLZ, WENZEL, 1750–1817. Prominent violinist at the Vienna Court orchestra. Czerny introduced him to Beethoven, who gave him piano lessons while Krumpholz gave Beethoven violin pointers. Became an enthusiastic Beethoven supporter. Beethoven also enjoyed Krumpholz's virtuosity on the mandolin and composed three brief compositions on that instrument for him. Krumpholz's death affected Beethoven deeply and he composed *Gesang der Mönche* [Song of the monks] in his friend's memory.

KRZYZANOWSKI, RUDOLF, 1859–1911. Austrian conductor and friend of Mahler during their student days in Vienna. Collaborated with Mahler on the piano transcription of Bruckner's Third Symphony. Later court conductor in Weimar.

LACHNER, FRANZ, 1803–1890. Bavarian by birth but strongly identified with Austrian music. Studied with Sechter, became a close friend of Schubert; also befriended Beethoven. His orchestral music was much favored in his day. Known for his dislike of Wagner's music.

LEVI, HERMANN, 1839–1900. German conductor. Became a friend of both Brahms and Wagner. Wagner so appreciated Levi's interpretations of his operas that he overcame his anti-Semitism and asked him to conduct *Parsifal*. Levi was also a friend of Bruckner, whose music he performed successfully, as well as one of the great Mozart interpreters of his day.

LIPINER, SIEGFRIED, 1856–1911. Writer and philosopher whose writings impressed Wagner and Nietzsche, despite the author's youth. He was a late joiner of the Pernerstorfer's Circle, in whose debates he figured prominently. His play *Adam* deeply influenced the young Mahler. Alma Mahler disliked and distrusted him. Although his *Prometheus Unbound,* created in his teens, stamped him as a writer of great promise, his prominence ebbed quickly during his lifetime. At his death in 1911 he was all but forgotten.

Loos, Adolf, 1870–1933. Austrian architect. Was strongly influenced by his residence in the United States (1893–96). Emphasis on functional, unornamented architecture in office buildings as well as private residences. Together with Otto Wagner, he changed the face of baroque Vienna. His best-known building is the office building on Michaeler square in Vienna. Loos's emphasis on pure form infuriated the Viennese and revolutionized architecture in Vienna.

Löwe, Ferdinand, 1865–1925. Austrian conductor. Together with the brothers Schalk, one of the foremost disciples of Bruckner and performers of Bruckner's music. Premiered Bruckner's Fifth Symphony in 1903. Often arrogated unto himself "improvements" in Bruckner's orchestration.

Makart, Hans, 1840–84. Austrian painter of Vienna portraits and of strongly erotic, monumental canvasses. His artistic success was phenomenal but short-lived. He became Vienna's foremost painter of his day, and to have been painted by him was a mark of rank in society. Emperor Franz Joseph provided him with a studio where he painted in overabundant splendor. He was called upon to arrange the entire festive procession for the twenty-fifth anniversary of Franz Joseph's reign, which he designed in all its details.

Marschalk, Max, 1863–1940. Music critic of the *Vossiche Zeitung* and also a minor composer. Brother-in-law of famed German dramatist Gerhart Hauptmann. Interesting correspondence with Mahler, giving insight into the composer's interpretative thinking.

Mildenburg, Anna Bahr-, 1872–1947. Austrian dramatic soprano and student of Rosa Papier in Vienna. Close personal and musical friend of Mahler, who guided her operatic destinies in Hamburg and later called her to the Vienna Opera, then under his directorship. She remained there as a prominent member long after Mahler's departure and death. In 1909 she married the prominent Austrian playwright Hermann Bahr.

Mottl, Felix, 1856–1911. Austrian conductor. Educated at the Imperial Court Chapel in Vienna and the Vienna Conservatory under Hellmesberger. Stage conductor in Bayreuth in 1876. Later was hailed as the "perfect" Wagner conductor in Bayreuth. Held important conducting positions in London, Berlin, New York, and Munich; also composed operas, which were overshadowed by his successes as a conductor.

MUCK, KARL, 1859–1940. German conductor. Early success as a pianist. Conducted throughout the Austrian empire. Appeared in Berlin and London, where he became Royal Music Director. Conducted famous Bayreuth performances. Conductor of the Boston Symphony Orchestra in 1906; during World War I, anti-German feeling drove him from the post. He continued to conduct in Munich, Hamburg, and Amsterdam.

NICOLAI, OTTO, 1810–1849. German conductor and composer. After studies in Germany and Rome, conducted at the Vienna Opera. Although most of his operas were composed and performed in Italy, his most enduring success, *The Merry Wives of Windsor* (1849), was premiered in Berlin. During his Vienna tenure, his desire to give perfect performances of Beethoven's symphonies prompted him to found the Vienna Philharmonic. Vienna's yearly performance of Beethoven's Ninth Symphony commemorates his name as the "Nicolai Konzert."

NIKISCH, ARTHUR, 1855–1922. Austrian conductor. Studied with Hellmesberger and Dessoff at the Vienna Conservatory. At age 19 he became a member of the Vienna Court orchestra, playing under Herbeck, Liszt, Brahms, and Wagner. Began conducting in Leipzig in 1877, featuring Wagner, Schumann, and Liszt. Conducted the Boston Symphony in 1889. Later held important appointments in Leipzig and Berlin. One of the foremost conductors of his time.

NOTTEBOHM, MARTIN GUSTAV, 1817–1910. Teacher and musicologist. Friend of Mendelssohn and Schumann. Later settled in Vienna; studied counterpoint with Sechter and became a close friend of Brahms. Best known for his research of Beethoven's music sketch books. Collaborated on editions of Bach, Handel, Beethoven, Mendelssohn, and Mozart.

PERNERSTORFER, ENGELBERT, 1815–1918. The leader of the circle named after him. Anti-Habsburg in his strong stand for unification with Germany on socialist principles. Many young men of the circle were destined for prominence; the historian Friedjung, the future socialist leader Adler, the writer Lipiner, as well as Hugo Wolf and Mahler. Pernerstorfer eventually became the socialist leader in the Austrian Reichstag, the lower house of Parliament.

REDLICH, HANS FERDINAND, 1903–        Austrian musicologist, naturalized British subject. Specialist on Monteverdi. Active musical experience in the Berlin and Mainz opera houses. Disenchantment with German nationalism prompted him to emigrate to England, where he has been active in institutions of higher learning. His treatises on Monteverdi and Mahler have become standard works.

REINHARDT, MAX (Max Goldman), 1873–1943. Austrian actor and director. First became known as actor in famous elderly roles. Beginning in 1902 he began to manage his own theaters with great success, introducing a neo-romantic style in contrast to prevailing naturalistic tendencies. Produced nearly all the plays of Shakespeare, Goethe, Ibsen, Strindberg, Molière, Shaw, and Wedekind, sometimes on a gigantic scale. Became most famous for staging Shakespeare's *Midsummer Night's Dream* in Germany and in an American movie version, and the medieval play *Everyman,* staged yearly in front of the Salzburg cathedral. Became a U.S. citizen in 1940.

Rosé, Arnold, 1863–1946. Violinist. Founder of the famed string quartet that bore his name, concertmaster of the Vienna Philharmonic at age 18; he remained in that position for 55 years (1881–1936). Brother-in-law of Mahler, whose sister Justine he married. In 1938 he emigrated to England; his son Alfred Rosé went to the United States.

Rott, Hans, 1859–1881. Vienna composer, student of Bruckner. Became a close friend of Mahler. Rumor has it that the harsh judgment of Rott's music by Brahms drove the sensitive young composer into insanity.

Rückert, Friedrich, 1788–1866. German poet and professor specializing in Oriental languages. His lyric poetry was set to music by Schumann and Mahler. Of Rückert's more than 400 poems bemoaning the death of his son Ernst, Mahler selected five which he set to music in his *Kindertotenlieder.*

Salten, Felix, 1869–1945. Austrian writer, journalist, and critic whose animal stories for children won him world renown. His best-known stories are "Bambi" (1923), filmed by Disney, and "Florian, The Emperor's Stallion" (1933), filmed in 1940. Died in Switzerland, where he had fled during World War II.

Schalk, Franz, 1863–1931. A student and disciple of Bruckner. On the urging of Mahler, he joined the Vienna Opera as a conductor in 1900. After World War I he was called upon to head the Vienna Opera as artistic director, a position he shared with Richard Strauss until 1924. Despite strained relations with Mahler he continued to champion his music as well as that of Bruckner and Wolf.

Schiele, Egon, 1890–1918. Austrian painter and draftsman. Was early on influenced by French impressionists, later by Klimt. Eventually developed a terse, lean style which was as powerful as it was psychologically exciting and expressionistic. With Kokoschka, he was in the forefront of Austrian expressionists until his untimely death at age 28.

Schmidt, Franz, 1874–1939. Austrian cellist, organist, pianist, and composer; for fourteen years cellist with the Vienna Opera orchestra. In 1910 he became professor of piano at the Vienna Academy for Music. He eventually headed the institution as director and retired from it in 1937. His rich and colorful orchestral style was in the tradition of Schubert and Bruckner. Teacher of Egon Gartenberg.

SECHTER, SIMON, 1788–1867. Austrian organist and musical theorist of renown. Court organist and professor in Vienna. Schubert, Bruckner, Richter, Thalberg, and Lachner were his pupils. Bruckner in particular cherished Sechter's theoretical principles. Schubert took only one lesson before his death. Sechter was known to have written a fugue each day. However, he remained historically important primarily as a theorist.

SEIDL, ANTON, 1850–1898. Austrian conductor educated in Leipzig. Highly regarded by Wagner, whose music he conducted with spectacular success despite his indulgence in truncated versions. Important posts in Leipzig, Holland, England, Italy, and Prague where he originated his brand of Wagner performances. Conductor at the Met in 1885. Later succeeded Theodore Thomas as conductor of the New York Philharmonic. Held both posts with distinction. Tremendous success in New York. Premiered Dvořák's *New World* symphony in America.

SEIDL, ARTHUR, 1863–1928. German music critic, educator, and prominent writer on music aesthetics. His correspondence with Mahler, Richard Strauss, and Pfitzner contributed to understanding of those composers in their time.

SPECHT, RICHARD, 1870–1932. Viennese music critic, musicologist, and biographer of Johann Strauss, Richard Strauss, Brahms, Mahler, and Puccini. Wrote a thematic analysis of Mahler's music which gained importance because of Specht having had the opportunity to discuss the music with the composer.

SPIERING, THEODORE, 1871–1925. Concertmaster with the New York Philharmonic; appointed by Mahler. Studied with Joachim. Held playing and teaching positions in Berlin and Chicago. After Mahler's death he returned to Berlin, but in 1914 he again returned to the United States.

TIRSO DE MOLINA (Gabriel Tellex), 1571–1648. Although a priest in the Order of Mercy, he was a prodigious writer of dramas. He was the first dramatist to present *Don Juan* on stage. His popularity in Spain was second only to Lope de Vega and Calderon.

THALBERG, SIGISMUND, 1812–1871. Studied piano with Hummel and Kalkbrenner, theory with Sechter. He became the piano virtuoso idol of Europe and the western hemisphere and a great rival of Franz Liszt.

WAGNER, OTTO, 1841–1918. Austrian architect. Together with Adolph Loos, revolutionized Vienna's architectural face. His standard work,

*Moderne Architektur,* was greatly influential in changing building and architecture in Vienna. His most prominent creations are the Vienna Postal Savings building and the "Steinhof" church.

WEINGARTNER, FELIX, 1863–1942. Austrian conductor, composer, and writer. Studied with Liszt. Court Opera conductor in Berlin until 1898. In 1908 succeeded Mahler as director of the Vienna Opera; he later retired from the post but continued as conductor of the Vienna Philharmonic, thereby gaining an international reputation. After World War I he became director of the Vienna *Volksoper.* Despite his worldwide activities, Vienna always remained his foremost city of musical activities.

WOLF-FERRARI, ERMANNO, 1876–1948. Italian composer. Despite parental resistance he followed a musical career, stirred by Wagner's music. Enjoyed greater early success in Germany than in Italy. His meticulous workmanship combined the melodies and harmonic effects of his day with the spirit of Mozart. His most important operas were *Le Donne Curiose* [The curious women] (1903), *Il Segreto di Susanna* [The secret of Susanna] (1909), and *The Jewels of the Madonna* (1911).

ZEMLINSKY, ALEXANDER, 1872–1942. Austrian composer and conductor and a musical personality of renown in Mahler's Vienna. He was Schönberg's only teacher, and Schönberg later married his sister, Mathilde Zemlinsky. Held in high esteem by Mahler, Berg, and Schönberg; Mahler performed his music in Vienna. Held important conducting positions in Vienna, Prague, and Berlin. In 1938 he emigrated to the United States.

ZICHY, COUNT GÉZA VON, 1849–1924. One-armed Hungarian aristocrat, pianist, and amateur composer, who learned to play the piano with the left hand alone. A pupil of Liszt. Influential in Hungarian music circles, mixing music with politics. His ambitions made it impossible for Mahler to continue his successful tenure at the Budapest Opera. In 1892 Zichy became president of the Hungarian Musical Academy in Budapest, a post he held until 1918.

# Bibliography

## GENERAL REFERENCE WORKS

ADLER, GUIDO. *Handbuch der Musikgeschichte.* Berlin, 1930

AUSTIN, WILLIAM W. *Music in the Twentieth Century.* New York, W. W. Norton, 1966

BÜCKEN, ERNST. *Handbuch der Musikwissenschaft.* Potsdam, Akademische Verlagsgesellschaft Athenaion, 1929

*Encyclopaedia Judaica.* New York, The Macmillan Co., 1971

FERGUSON, DONALD M. *A History of Musical Thought.* New York, Appleton-Century-Crofts, 1959

GROVE'S *Dictionary of Music and Musicians.* New York, St. Martin's Press, 1966

LANG, PAUL HENRY. *Music in Western Civilization.* New York, W. W. Norton, 1941

RIEMANN, HUGO. Musiklexikon. Leipzig, 1929

SALAZAR, ADOLFO. *Music in our Time.* New York, W. W. Norton, 1946

SLONIMSKY, NICHOLAS. *Lexicon of Musical Invective.* New York, Coleman Ross Co., 1965

STEIN, WERNER. *Kulturfahrplan.* Berlin–Grünewald, Verlag Herbig, 1946

STUCKENSCHMIDT, H. H. *Musik des 20. Jahrhunderts.* Kindler's Universitäts Bibliotheks Verlag, 1969

VETTER, HANS JOACHIM. *Die Musik unseres Jahrhunderts.* Mainz, B. Schott's Söhne, 1968

## BIOGRAPHY

ADLER, GUIDO. *Gustav Mahler.* Vienna, Universal Edition, 1916

BAUER-LECHNER, NATALIE. *Erinnerungen an Mahler.* Leipzig, E. P. Tal, 1923

BLAUKOPF, KURT. *Mahler, der Zeitgenosse der Zukunft.* Vienna, Moldau Verlag, 1965

——. *Gustav Mahler.* New York, Praeger Publishers, 1973

ENGEL, GABRIEL. *Gustav Mahler, Song Symphonist.* New York, Bruckner Society, 1932

KARPATH, LUDWIG. *Begegnung mit dem Genius.* Vienna, Fiba Verlag, 1934

KLEMPERER, OTTO. *Erinnerungen an Gustav Mahler.* Zurich, Atlantic Verlag, 1960

LA GRANGE, HENRI-LOUIS DE. *Mahler,* vol. I. Gollancz, 1974

KRALIK, HEINRICH. *Gustav Mahler.* Vienna, Verlag Elisabeth Lafitte, 1968

KŘENEK, ERNST. *Gustav Mahler.* New York, Greystone Press, 1941

MAHLER, ALMA WERFEL. *And the Bridge is Love.* New York, Harcourt, Brace & Co., 1958

——. *Erinnerungen an Gustav Mahler.* Edited by Donald Mitchell. Frankfurt am Main, Propylaen Verlag, 1971

——. *Gustav Mahler. Briefe, 1879–1911.* Vienna, 1924

——. *Gustav Mahler. Memories and Letters.* New York, The Viking Press, 1946

——. *Mein Leben.* Frankfurt am Main, S. Fischer, 1960

REDLICH, H. F. *Bruckner and Mahler.* London, J. M. Dent & Sons, 1963

SPECHT, RICHARD. *Gustav Mahler.* Berlin, Schuster & Loeffler, 1913

STEFAN, PAUL. *Gustav Mahler: Eine Studie über Persönlichkeit und Werk.* München, Piepe, 1912

WALTER, BRUNO. *Gustav Mahler.* Greystone Press, 1941

## THE MUSIC OF MAHLER

BEKKER, PAUL. *Gustav Mahler's Sinfonien.* Berlin, Schuster & Loeffler, 1921

——. *Die Symphonie von Beethoven bis Mahler.* Berlin, Schuster & Loeffler, 1918

BLAUKOPF, KURT. *Gustav Mahler.* New York. Praeger Publishers, 1973

CARDUS, NEVILLE. *Gustav Mahler: His Mind and His Music.* London, Gollancz, 1965

KŘENEK, ERNST. *Gustav Mahler.* New York, Greystone Press, 1941

MITCHELL, DONALD. *Gustav Mahler: The Early Years.* London, Rockliff, 1958

——. *Gustav Mahler, The Wunderhorn Years.* London, Faber & Faber, 1976

NEWLIN, DIKA. *Bruckner, Mahler, Schönberg.* New York, Kings Crown Press, 1947

REDLICH, H. F. *Bruckner and Mahler.* London, J. M. Dent & Sons, 1958

SPECHT, RICHARD. *Gustav Mahler's Sinfonien: Thematische Analysen.* Vienna, Universal Edition

WALTER, BRUNO. *Gustav Mahler.* New York, Greystone Press, 1941

WELLESZ, EGON. *The Symphonies of Gustav Mahler.* 1940

## MUSIC: RELATED TOPICS

ARMSTRONG, T. H. *Strauss Tone Poems.* London, Oxford University Press, 1931

BARZUN, JACQUES. *Berlioz and the Romantic Century.* 2 vols. Boston, Little, Brown & Co., 1950

COLLAER, PAUL. *La musique moderne, 1905–55.* Paris, Elsevier, 1955

COPLAND, AARON. *The New Music.* New York, W. W. Norton, 1968

DAMROSCH, WALTER. *My Musical Life.* New York, Charles Scribner & Sons, 1923

DECSEY, ERNST. *Bruckner, Versuch eines Lebens.* Berlin, Schuster & Loeffler, 1920

———. *Hugo Wolf.* Berlin, Schuster & Loeffler, 1928

EINSTEIN, ALFRED. *Music in the Romantic Era.* New York, W. W. Norton, 1947

ENGEL, GABRIEL. *The Life of Bruckner.* New York, Roerich Museum, 1931

GAL, HANS, ed. *The Musician's World.* New York, Arco Publishing Co., 1965

GARTENBERG, EGON. *Vienna: Its Musical Heritage.* University Park, Pa., Pennsylvania State University Press, 1968

———. *Johann Strauss: The End of an Era.* University Park, Pa., Pennsylvania State University Press, 1974

GEIRINGER, KARL. *Brahms: His Life and Work.* Boston, Houghton-Mifflin Co., 1936

GRADENWITZ, PETER. *The Music of Israel.* New York, W. W. Norton, 1949

GRAF, MAX. *From Beethoven to Shostakovich.* New York, Philosophical Library, 1947

———. *Modern Music.* New York, Philosophical Library, 1946

GROVE, GEORGE. *Beethoven and His Nine Symphonies.* London, Novello & Co., 1886

HAAS, ROBERT MARIA. *Anton Bruckner.* Potsdam, Akademische Verlagsgesellschaft, 1934

HAMMELMANN, HANNS, and OSERS, EWALD (eds.) *A Working Friendship: The Correspondence Between Richard Strauss and Hugo von Hofmannthal.* New York, Random House, 1961

HERZFELD, FRIEDRICH. *Musica Nova.* Berlin, Verlag Ullstein, 1954

IDELSOHN, A. Z. *Jewish Music.* New York, Tudor Publishing Co., 1944

KALBECK, MAX. *Johannes Brahms.* Berlin, Deutsche Brahmsgesellschaft, 1908

KOLODIN, IRVING, ed. *Composers as Listeners*. New York, Horizon Press, 1958

——. *The Metropolitan Opera*. New York, Alfred A. Knopf, 1967

LANG, OSKAR. *Anton Bruckner: Wesen und Bedeutung*. Munich, Beiderstein, 1947

LEIBOWITZ, RENÉ. *Schönberg and His School*. New York, Philosophical Library, 1949

MAREK, GEORGE R. *Richard Strauss: The Life of a Non-Hero*. New York, Simon & Schuster, 1967

NETTL, PAUL, ed. *The Book of Musical Documents*. New York, Philosophical Library, 1968

NEWLIN, DIKA. *Bruckner, Mahler, Schönberg*. New York, Kings Crown Press, 1947

NEWMAN, ERNST. *The Life of Richard Wagner*. 4 vols. New York, Alfred A. Knopf, 1949

NIEMANN, WALTER. *Brahms*. New York, Alfred A. Knopf, 1929

REDLICH, H. F. *Bruckner and Mahler*. London, J. M. Dent & Sons, 1963

REICH, WILLI. *Alban Berg*. Vienna, H. Reichner, 1937

SCHICKEL, RICHARD. *The World of Carnegie Hall*. New York, Julius Messner, 1960

SCHÖNBERG, ARNOLD. *Style and Idea*. New York, Philosophical Library, 1950

SHANET, HOWARD. *Philharmonic: A History of New York's Orchestra*. New York, Doubleday & Co., 1975

SPECHT, RICHARD. *Richard Strauss und sein Werk*. Leipzig, E. P. Tal, 1921

STEFAN, PAUL. *Arnold Schönberg*. Vienna, Zeitkunst Verlag, 1924

——. *Bruno Walter*. Vienna, H. Reichner, 1936

TEUSCHERT, RICHARD. *Richard Strauss und Wien*. Vienna, Verlag Brüder Hollinek, 1949

WALTER, BRUNO. *Theme and Variations*. New York, Alfred A. Knopf, 1946

WARRACK, JOHN. *Carl Maria von Weber*. New York, Macmillan, 1968

WORNER, KARL H. *Neue Musik in der Entscheidung*. Mainz, B. Schott's Söhne, 1954

## THE VIENNA OPERA AND THE VIENNA PHILHARMONIC

BEETZ, DR. WILHELM. *Das Wiener Opernhaus, 1869–1945*. Vienna, Panorama Verlag, 1949

BOESE H., and ROTTENSTEINER, A. F. *Botschaft der Musik: Die Wiener Philharmoniker*, Vienna Österreichischer Bundesverlag, 1967

DIEMAN, RUDOLPH. *Die Wiener Staatsoper*. Vienna, Verlag Elisabeth Lafitte

GRAF, MAX. *Die Wiener Oper*. Vienna, Humboldt Verlag, 1955

KRALIK, HEINRICH. *Das Grosse Orchester*. Vienna, W. Frick, 1952

———. *Wiener Staatsoper.* Vienna, Bundestheaterverwaltung, 1955

MITTAG, ERWIN. *Aus der Geschichte der Wiener Philharmoniker.* Vienna, Gerlach & Wiedling, 1950

PETSCHULL, DR. JOHANNES. *Wiener Philharmoniker, 1842–1942.* Vienna, Universal Edition, 1942

PRAWY, MARCEL. *The Vienna Opera.* New York, Praeger Publishers, 1970

PIRCHAU, E., Witeschnik, A., and Fritz, O. *300 Jahre Wiener Operntheater.* Vienna, Fortuna Verlag, 1953

SCHÖNFELDT, CHRISTL. *Die Wiener Philharmoniker.* Vienna, Bergland Verlag, 1956

SPECHT, RICHARD. *Das Wiener Operntheater.* Vienna, P. Knepler, 1911

STAUBER, PAUL. *Vom Kriegsschauplatz der Wiener Hofoper: Das wahre Erbe Mahler's.* Vienna, Huber & Lahme, 1909

UNTERER, VERENA. *Die Oper in Wien.* Vienna, Bergland Verlag, 1970

WEIGEL, HANS. *Das Buch der Wiener Philharmoniker.* Vienna, Bundesgemeinschaft Donauland, 1967

WELTNER, ALBERT JOSEF. *Das K. K. Hof-Operntheater in Wien, 1869–94.* Vienna, Verlag Adolph W. Kienast, 1894

WICKENBURG, ERIK G. *Burgtheater und Oper.* Vienna, Kunstverlag Wolfrum, 1960

WITESCHNIK, ALEX. *Wiener Opernkunst.* Vienna, Verlag, Kremayer & Scheriau, 1959

## VIENNA: RELATED TOPICS

BAREA, ILSA. *Vienna.* New York, Alfred A. Knopf, 1966

BAUER, ANTON. *150 Jahre Theater an der Wien.* Vienna, Amalthea Verlag, 1952

———. *Oper und Operetten in Wien.* Graz, Hermann Bohlaus Nachfolger, 1955

GARTENBERG, EGON. *Vienna: Its Musical Heritage.* University Park, Pa., Pennsylvania State University Press, 1968

———. *Johann Strauss: The End of an Era.* University Park, Pa., Pennsylvania State University Press, 1974

GRAF, MAX. *Legend of a Musical City: The Story of Vienna.* New York, Philosophical Library, 1945

GRÜNWALD, MAX. *The Jews of Vienna.* Philadelphia, Jewish Publication Society, 1936

GUTMANN, ALBERT. *Aus dem Wiener Konzertleben.* Vienna, Hofmusikalien A. G. Gutmann, 1914

HADAMOVSKY F., and OTTO, H. *Die Wiener Operette.* Vienna, Bellaria Verlag, 1947

HANSLICK, EDUARD. *Aus dem Concertsaal.* Vienna, Wilhelm Braumüller, 1870
——. *Aus meinem Leben.* Berlin, Allgemeiner Verein für deutsche Literatur, 1894
——. *Geschichte des Wiener Concertwesens.* Vienna, Wilhelm Braumüller, 1868
JOHNSTON, WILLIAM M. *The Austrian Mind.* Berkeley, The University of California Press, 1972
KOBALD, KARL. *Alt-Wiener Musikstätten.* Vienna, Amalthea Verlag, 1929
LHOTSKY, ALPHONS. *Geschichte Österreichs.* Graz, Hermann Bohlaus Nachf
OREL, ALFRED. *Musikstadt Wien.* Vienna, Eduard Waucura Verlag, 1953
PLEASANTS, HENRY, ed. *Vienna's Golden Years of Music.* New York: Simon & Schuster, 1950
REDLICH, JOSEPH. *Emperor Franz Joseph of Austria.* New York, Macmillan, 1929
SCHUERICH, D & A. *Geschichte der Musik in Wien.* Vienna, A. Haase, 1921
SRBIK, HEINRICH, and LORENZ, REINHOLD. *Die geschichtliche Stellung Wiens.* Verein für Geschichte der Stadt Wien, 1962
ZEMAN, Z. A. B. *Twilight of the Habsburgs.* New York, American Heritage Press, 1971
ZWEIG, STEFAN. *The World of Yesterday.* Lincoln, University of Nebraska Press, 1964

# RELATED GENERAL TOPICS

BECHSTEIN, LUDWIG. *Neues deutsches Märchenbuch.* Vienna, Verlag A. Hartleben, 1909
FEUCHTMÜLLER, RUPERT, and MRAZEK, WILHELM. *Kunst in Österreich, 1860–1918.* Vienna, Forum Verlag, 1964
FISCHER, ERNST. *Von Grillparzer zu Kafka: Sechs Essays.* Vienna, Globus Verlag, 1962
HOFFMANN, EDITH. *Kokoschka: Life and Work.* London, Faber & Faber, 1947
JONES, DR. ERNEST. *Sigmund Freud: Life and Work.* London, 1955
McGRATH, WM. J. *Dionysian Art and Populist Politics in Austria.* New Haven, Yale University Press, 1974
PANZER, FRIEDRICH, ed. *Die Kinder—und Hausmärchen der Brüder Grimm-Vollständige Ausgabe in der Urfassung.* Wiesbaden, Emil Vollmer Verlag, no date
UHL, OTTOKAR. *Moderne Architekten in Wien: Von Otto Wagner bis heute.* Vienna, Schroll Verlag, 1966
ZOHN, HARRY. *Wiener Juden in der deutschen Literatur.* Tel Aviv, Olamenu, 1964

## PERIODICALS, NEWSPAPERS, ETC.

BERGES, RUTH. "Mahler and the Great God Pan." *Musical Courier,* January 1960

BEYES, RUTH. "The Tragic Star of Hugo Wolf." *Musical Courier,* March 1960

BROD, MAX. "Gustav Mahler: Beispiel einer deutsch-jüdischen Symbiosis." *Ner-Tamid Verlag,* Frankfurt am Main, 1961

COOKE, DERYCK. "The Facts Concerning Mahler's Tenth Symphony," in *Chord and Discord*

———. "The History of Mahler's Tenth Symphony" (in manuscript). London, 1975

COOKE, DERYCK; Colin Matthews; and David Matthews. "Introduction to the Ms. and Performing Version" (in manuscript). 1975

DAVIS, PETER G. "Faces in the Mahler Crowd." *New York Times,* 1974

DIETHER, JACK. "Mahler's *Klagendes Lied*: Genesis and Evolution." *Music Review,* 1968

ERICSON, RAYMOND. "A Mahler Score is Resurrected." *New York Times,* 6 April 1964

GOLDBERG, ALBERT. "Bruno Walter: Poet of Conductors." *New York Times,* 9 August 1964

GRAF, MAX. "Mahler als Operndirigent." *Almanach der deutschen Musikbücherei,* 1926

HENAHAN, DONALD. "Mahler Madness at Fever Pitch." *New York Times,* 2 August 1970

———. "The Last, Great Romantic." *New York Times,* 15 January 1970

HEYWORTH, PETER. "Catching up with Mahler." London, *The Observer Review,* 21 April 1974

HOFFMANN, EVA. "Mahler for Moderns." *Commentary,* June 1975

KLEIN, HOWARD. "Just How Important was Mahler?" *New York Times,* 7 January 1968

MITCHELL, DONALD. "Mahler under the Microscope." *Times Literary Supplement,* 29 November 1974

NEWLIN, DIKA. "Alienation and Gustav Mahler." *The Reconstructionist,* 15 May 1959

PLEASANTS, HENRY. "Alban Berg's Retrospect in Vienna." *New York Times,* 20 June 1954

RATZ, DR. ERWIN. "Gustav Mahler." Rede an der Akademie für Musik und darstellende Kunst, Vienna, 15 November 1954. Internationale Gesellschaft für neue Musik.

REILLY, EDWARD R. "Mahler and Guido Adler." *Musical Quarterly,* July 1972

SCHÖNBERG, ARNOLD. "My Evolution." *Musical Quarterly,* October 1952

SCHONBERG, HAROLD C. "Mahler's Sufferings: Do They Explain His Music?" *New York Times,* 18 March 1973

———. "Would Mahler Have Raised the Roof?" *New York Times,* 16 September 1973

SELDEN, GOTH, C. "Schönberg's Life: A Struggle in Letters." *Musical Courier,* April 1960

"The Man Who Speaks to a High-Strung Generation." *Time,* 23 June 1967

TRAMER, HANS. *"Umgenannte und umgetaufte: Gustav Mahler und seine Zeit.* Tel Aviv, *Leo Beck Institute,* 1960

"Unfinished Symphony?" *Time,* 7 September 1962

WELLESZ, EGON. "Anton Bruckner and the Process of Musical Creation." *Musical Quarterly,* July 1938

# Index

# Index